Original Story By

Original Story By

A MEMOIR OF BROADWAY AND HOLLYWOOD

Arthur Laurents

ALFRED A. KNOPF  NEW YORK 2000

THIS IS A BORZOI BOOK
PUBLISHED BY ALFRED A. KNOPF

www.aaknopf.com

Knopf, Borzoi Books, and the colophon are registered
trademarks of Random House, Inc.

Grateful acknowledgment is made to Marian Reiner for permission to reprint
an excerpt from "The Coward" by Eve Merriam in *Family Circle*. Originally
published as part of the Yale Series of Younger Poets. Copyright © 1946
by Yale University Press. Copyright renewed 1974 by Eve Merriam.
Used by permission of Marian Reiner.

Library of Congress Cataloging-in-Publication Data
Laurents, Arthur.
Original story by : a memoir of Broadway and Hollywood /
by Arthur Laurents.
    p.   cm.
Includes index.
ISBN 0-375-40055-9
1. Laurents, Arthur.   2. Dramatists, American—20th century Biography.
3. Broadway (New York, N.Y.)—Social life and customs.
4. Hollywood (Los Angeles, Calif.)—Social life and customs.
5. Motion picture producers and directors—United States Biography.
6. Theatrical producers and directors—United States Biography.
7. Screenwriters—United States Biography.   I. Title.
PS9629.A6277460   2000
812'.52—dc21
    [B]   99-40733
            CIP

Manufactured in the United States of America
First Edition

Composed by North Market Street Graphics, Lancaster, Pennsylvania
Printed and bound by Quebecor Printing, Fairfield, Pennsylvania
Designed by Barbara Balch

For Tom, of course

Contents

Acknowledgment

The morning after I spoke at a memorial for Stella Adler, Victoria Wilson called to ask if I had thought of writing my memoirs. The suggestion had been made before but this time, I took it seriously. She was Stella's stepdaughter; she was also an editor at Knopf with a distinguished reputation. She became my editor for this memoir and from our first meeting I knew her reputation was completely justified. I am very grateful for her strong views and gentle guidance, in equal proportions.

Original Story By

CHAPTER ONE

Beginnings
Home of the Brave

IT'S THE STUFF OF DREAMS. The audience is on its feet calling "Author! Author!" my mother is calling "Arthur! Arthur!" my father's eyes are wet and a handsome young actor has flown in from the Coast to share the night with me. My father wouldn't want me to see the tears any more than I'd want him to see the actor.

The producer, all smiles, is Humpty-Dumpty in a brown suit. By now, I know it's his good suit. He motions me forward to the stage. My feet tell me I am walking down the aisle; I feel a fireman boost me up on the stage. I can see the actors behind me applauding but can't hear them. I'm unsure whether the moon is out or not but I know it has to be. I turn from the actors and look out front. I don't see anyone. Not my father, not my mother, not my actor. I hear no cheering, I see no audience, just a big black hole of silence. I turn to the wings and say to the stage manager, "Bring in the curtain, Jimmy."

It was Jimmy Gelb who told me about the moon the day of our first preview and he was a Marxist like the producer, the director and half the cast. Stop worrying whether my play was good enough to be a hit, he commanded. Success in the theatre had little to do with merit; what it really depended on was the moon. If the moon was out, we were in; if it wasn't, we weren't.

That was December 1945. It was the first play I'd ever written, it had gotten produced and there it and I were on Broadway. More specifically, east of Broadway on Forty-fourth Street in a theatre with a marquee and lights and boards that creaked when someone walked down the aisle. The theatre was the

3

Belasco, the lights said the play was *Home of the Brave,* and I was twenty-eight years old.

A decade later, I had another play at the Belasco, *A Clearing in the Woods,* and the boards still creaked. That play starred Kim Stanley whose brilliant acting talent was almost matched by her talent for self-extinction. She spent the first matinee of *Clearing* sleeping off a massive hangover in her dressing room. I was devoted to her anyway. She was capable of other things, maddening things that reduced me to tears but I never lost that affection for her. Her heart was as big and full as her laugh; she just had to be reminded.

Kim was the Goddess of the Actors Studio where, under Lee Strasberg, neurotics and alcoholics were mistaken for geniuses. From its inception, the Studio lacked a sense of humor. At one of Lee's scene classes for professional actors, I drew attention to that by pointing out that Arthur Kennedy had complimented Ben Piazza by saying, "I thought Ben made great progress. I could understand 50 percent of what he said. And," I added, "no one laughed."

Then Lee spoke. When he spoke and only when he spoke, a recording machine was turned on. When he finished, it was turned off. Moses, he was, and he looked at me with disdain from his Mount. "A sensitive playwright," he said to his worshippers, "and all he can do is accuse us like everyone else of mumbling." They did indeed mumble, so I couldn't back down. Well, I could have but I wouldn't and in fact, went further and faulted them for their lack of respect for the word, for their misconception that reality came from paraphrasing and inserting *uh*s and *you know*s until Strasberg turned on the machine, struck back, and we went at it while the acolytes wailed: Anne Bancroft, Madeleine Sherwood and Jane Fonda in real tears.

Ironically, Kim, the Goddess herself, had immaculate diction and an ear so perfect, she could do any accent. She identified heavily with her role in *A Clearing in the Woods*—a psychologically crippled woman who finds and accepts herself. The central character of *Home of the Brave* becomes psychologically crippled because of bigotry, then finds and accepts himself. When I read the play again the other day, there was no identification; the character was a stranger to me. Where was I in him? The theme of discovery and acceptance, that was familiar; it informs much of my work, but so do prejudice and betrayal. Anti-Semitism crops up now and then but peripherally; it's central to *Home of the Brave,* but how central was it to me when I was writing the play? My concentration appears to have been more on the dramaturgy: how to use anti-Semitism as a dramatic element to propel the story and to justify the conflict in the central character, a Jewish GI trapped in a South Pacific jungle in World War II.

Nineteen forty-four was the year I wrote that play. I was a sergeant in the

Army but I found a producer who had to find the money. By 1945, I was still waiting for the producer to find the money and I was still in the Army. I'd been in the Army since 1941 but had never been out of the country; five years in uniform but never overseas, never even near the South Pacific I wrote about. If I should have felt guilty, I didn't. I had new, apparently healthy young friends like Jerome Robbins, Harold Lang, Montgomery Clift and Oliver Smith who weren't in uniform. I didn't ask why they weren't—I supposed it was their sexuality—and I didn't wonder if they felt guilty.

Not that I was a gung ho patriot. I didn't want to be inducted—I was drafted before we were at war—but it was unthinkable for me to admit my sexuality to anyone except a friend in the same leaky boat and I didn't have such a friend until after I was in the Army. My first year and a half in uniform, I went protectively numb. Then I was put on detached service in New York and went hurling out into orbit.

The city was unhinged in wartime. I wallowed and whirled like a Born-Again Hedonist, drinking my head off, fucking my brains out, looking for romance, hoping to find where I belonged. What kept me together was being a writer with a writer's discipline that came automatically with the yellow legal tablets and the Blackwing pencils. In the center of homemade chaos, in the eye of my hurricane, week in, week out for most weeks in more than three years, I wrote an original radio propaganda play for the Army of the United States of America until I hit a bad bottom with a wallop and had to get psychiatric help.

Hedonism was booming when I sublet a series of apartments, the first from Katrina Wallingford, a grain elevator heiress from Kansas City who lived on Sutton Place. She was going overseas to play the squeeze box, as she called it, for the USO. A piece of her life turns up in *The Way We Were* interwoven with pieces of mine. Fiction can mingle genders with impunity. The apartment in the movie bore no relationship to Katrina's; hers was in a small, squat building on the wrong side of that fancy street just off the East River. It had no view of the river, the rooms were small but unbelievably, this enlisted soldier, this GI born and bred in Brooklyn, was living on Sutton Place.

The journey to Manhattan is easier from Texas than from Brooklyn. Lots easier than from Flatbush and middle-middle class in a middle-class house with a bedroom for my parents, one for me and another for the maid until my sister came. Then she and the maid shared the third bedroom and secrets from me, or so I suspected.

The house had a yard that was exceptionally deep in back and very wide on one side. There was a rabbit hutch for me against the back fence, and a fertile vegetable-and-herb garden; outside the kitchen door, a cool grape arbor under which we often had meals in warm weather; and along the side, my mother's rose garden. Flowers were hardly enough for her, though.

My parents were popular, the attractive leaders of their group. My father, courteous and witty, was a lawyer in private practice in the City—meaning across the river in far-off Manhattan. His office was near Times Square, not far from the theatres. Until Hitler, he went to Germany regularly for some of his clients, doing what, I don't know. The only cases he ever discussed involved the husband of one of my mother's sisters in Florida: my Uncle Henry who was chronically crooked. He had been a silent movie actor, an airplane pilot, the inventor-manufacturer of a urinal disinfectant that someone else had invented (my father to the rescue), a bootlegger (my father to the rescue several times), and now a Citrus King of Florida (my father to the rescue constantly). No one in Miami had a Southern accent like Uncle Henry's except his wife and children. They were family and he had to be kept out of the clink. Even though he was in love with law, my father obliged. He once took me to Washington to see the Supreme Court and introduced me to Justice Brandeis whom he revered but didn't know. He didn't pretend to know Brandeis, he simply wanted me to know that justice existed in a man as real and as necessary as the building he worked in.

And my mother? Energy and guile, an emancipated woman too early. At fourteen she got a Saturday job as a saleslady at the A&S department store in downtown Brooklyn, a job she didn't need because her father owned a prosperous shirt factory. A pretty strawberry blonde with very good legs, she brought a wooden box with her to stand on behind her counter much the way J. Edgar Hoover stood on one behind his desk. Her parents, Jewish by Hitler's standards, were Socialist atheists. My father's parents were Orthodox Jews; his mother didn't approve of my mother and the marriage. My mother was determined: she kept a kosher house for my father but it took a year before his mother would come to dinner. When she did, she asked for a boiled egg in a glass. Mother threw the dishes out the window. Grandma wouldn't come to my Bar Mitzvah, either. Why should she? It was in a Reformed temple, my Hebrew was learned phonetically, and it was held on a Saturday, a day that had to have been chosen by my mother because she knew Grandma wouldn't drive on a Saturday. Before the ceremony, we went to pay our respects. Grandma gave me the customary gold watch and then asked why my mother hadn't taken me to communion. I threw the watch back on the table. My mother was shaking with rage, blinded by tears but silent, for once. I took her arm and escorted her out.

The meaningless Bar Mitzvah—Grandma was right about that—was the end of my religious training and the beginning of my turning against religion, most emphatically against any and all fundamentalist religions. I was still proudly a Jew, but it wasn't Judaism of any kind that made me a Jew or the kind of Jew I was.

Although my father was born of fundamentalist Jewish parents, he left Orthodoxy for Reformed Judaism which outwardly consisted of going to temple on Yom Kippur. I suspected more was going on inwardly but he would never force his beliefs on anyone. A humanitarian above all, he was the most tolerant man I ever knew. My mother, on the other hand, was intolerant. Born of atheists, she paradoxically became a Jew with a vengeance against all gentiles. Her temple attendance was marked by truancy, her Yom Kippur fasting was broken at noon by a splitting headache that necessitated a little orange juice and since she'd had the orange juice, why not a sandwich and from there it was one step to serious cooking which she was a very good at. But her watchcry was "Every one of them hates every one of us!" When Tom Hatcher came into my life and we lived together openly, it was far more difficult for her to accept that he was gentile than that we were gay.

From left to right: my parents and maternal grandparents, circa 1916.
My father seems the least intimidated by the camera.

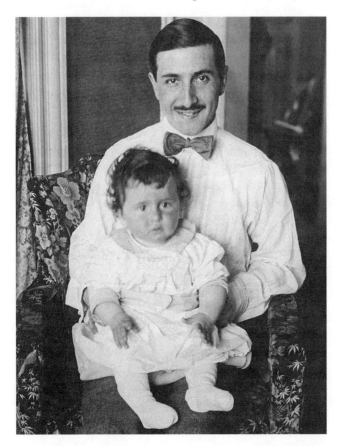

1917. My twenty-seven-year-old father is still camera friendly; I'm not.

The son of both my parents, I was intolerant of anything I considered bigotry. I believed most Americans were prejudiced against homosexuals, Negroes and Jews, in that order. I still do. It's somewhat less overt now because it's somewhat less sanctioned, but bigotry is still alive and killing in the U.S.A.

Before she was married, my mother was a schoolteacher. The moment my sister was old enough to be left with the maid, back my mother went to teaching—part-time because she also played bridge and mah-jongg and gave luncheons where the food was all dyed one color. She also set her eye on the Eastern Star. I helped her rehearse the speeches my father had written for her until it dawned on me that she wasn't stumbling, she was rewriting. Rewriting my father? Sacrilege! Yes, he's very intelligent, she said, that's all well and good, but unlike him (and me), she knew what her audience wanted, she knew the measure of the ladies who were going to elect her Matron. Which they did, so she must have.

During the Depression, we moved to a two-family house, a reflection of my father's caution and my mother's lack of interest in running a house or pruning roses. We still had a maid, which left her free to open a knitting shop. In six months, she opened another and then had to close both. What had made her a success were her sparkle and energy. Her knitting ladies were as mad about her as her Eastern Star ladies were, as all her friends were. But in each shop, her clients wanted her all to themselves; even she couldn't get them to accept less than all of her.

When she was in her eighties and my father was dead, she became very friendly with two widows in her Miami Beach apartment building. Both were younger than she and both, according to a rumor she repeated, were lesbians. Because both were now vying for her affections (I'm sure she flirted), she supposed there were rumors that she, too, was a lesbian. She laughed when she reported this—she enjoyed rumors about herself—but I looked away so she couldn't see my eyes. I had remembered a rumor she didn't enjoy. I was seven or eight at the time and I didn't enjoy it, either.

I could hear the anger from my side of the wall between my parents' bedroom and mine. I got out of bed and went into the dark hall where eavesdropping was easier because the door to their room was thinner than the wall. My father's voice was shaking as he repeated a rumor linking my mother and the husband of her best friend. Indignant and insulted, she dragged out a suitcase: she wasn't going to put up with this, she was going to pack and leave. He dragged a suitcase and started to pack: he wasn't going to put up with it, either; if anyone was going to leave, it was he.

Listening in the hall, barefoot in my pajamas, I understood it was funny. Of course both of them couldn't leave, one of them had to look after my sister and me. But which? How could anything have happened between my mother and the husband? When and where? She had flirted with him, I knew that. I'd seen her at it one day when they took me to the beach in Coney Island. She looked pretty and trim in a bathing suit; he had a belly. I could tell she enjoyed flirting and I somehow understood she needed to flirt. But I knew that was all, I knew the flirting was all. Still, either my mother or my father was going to leave and I was afraid it was going to be my wonderful father. Wasn't it he who had been betrayed?

Neither of them did leave then. Later my mother took my sister to visit her sister, the crook's wife, in Miami. Most of her family lived there. Every one of them was more than a little nutty which made all of them a lot of fun.

Being alone with my father and the maid of the moment was also fun. Then one Thursday, while he was at the office and the maid was off, I went

With my mother and my sister Edith who was
a sickly child.

into my mother's closet with a pair of scissors and cut the fringe off an evening
dress. (In *A Clearing in the Woods,* a little girl cuts up her father's tie.) That
night, I had stomach pains which frightened more than they hurt. My father
kept me home from school; I vomited most of that day and night. In the
morning, I had elephantiasis of one leg and a fever of 104. While the doctor
debated whether it was typhoid fever or rheumatic fever (it was the latter;
luckily, my heart survived undamaged), my father telephoned my mother. As
she traveled back North, the fever broke, of course. The episode brought them
back together but it split my sister and me. For years, she thought that our
parents preferred me, I thought my mother preferred her. We were both
wrong. My father did prefer me; for my mother, preference didn't come into
play. Edith needed her and I didn't.

As a child, Edith suffered from chorea, Saint Vitus' dance. The doctors
tried to burn it out of her by inducing volcanic fevers. She survived, I think,
because of a silent, inner rage and emerged a fragile auburn beauty with a

My sister and I in our teens. She had become an auburn-haired beauty,
which made her popular, which made her happy.

stubborn determination that was awesome. My father and I retreated, my
mother gave support. When Edith died in her midforties of pneumonia, leaving three children, my mother was more devastated than the kids or their
father. She and my father were living in Florida by then because he was
severely crippled with chronic rheumatoid arthritis that prevented him from
coming North for the funeral which was in New Jersey, my brother-in-law's
home state. Probably because of him, my one firm prejudice was against people from New Jersey. I thought their dream was to die in Westchester. Anyway,
they were notoriously lousy drivers. There were exceptions, but to the dream-
ers, not the drivers.

My mother arrived at the Jersey synagogue, unexpectedly composed. She
had divided her life into taking care of my father and taking care of my sister
and her children, even long-distance. She couldn't take care of me—I wouldn't
let her, which she resented. But she avoided a confrontation; she always
avoided a confrontation she couldn't win. During the ceremony, the rabbi,

chosen by my brother-in-law, patronized my dead sister because she hadn't been a member of his corseted congregation. My mother tightened at his snide remarks but didn't shake her head as she ordinarily would have. And when we walked together from the car to the grave site in the cemetery, her hand was quiet on my arm, she remained quiet and composed. She held on to her dignity until the moment of lowering the casket into the grave. As it came sliding out on mechanized beams, she began to tremble. I put my arm around her and held her tight to me—she was shaking terribly—but she gasped "Not a machine!" and began to cry and cry, not as though her heart was breaking, for it had broken. She just let go.

By the time I graduated Cornell University, we'd moved from that two-family house to a larger, airier apartment in a new building in the neighborhood. The Depression was on and Roosevelt was our hero. Then he instituted the draft. I drew a low number and my mother denounced him as a warmonger. My father would not renounce FDR but did suggest I try for a civilian job with the war effort before the draft caught up with me. I had begun writing for radio. Why not try for the OWI?

I had one possible string to pull: Bill Robson, a CBS director-producer, a big, generous man with a big laugh and a big moustache, handsomer than the facsimile who turns up in *The Way We Were* in Bill's familiar trench coat. He chain-smoked, took his girls to the Stork Club and El Morocco and swept into rooms that were never as big as he hoped. For one semester, he had taught a special evening class in radio writing at NYU that I had taken—not to learn anything (I knew everything), but to gain entrée to the networks. Robson sent substitutes for the first two or three sessions, then turned up and asked for an adaptation of a short story. Well, that couldn't be sold to anyone, so I was set to ask for my thirty dollars back when he asked for an original play. I wrote one and the fat lady began to sing. Quite undramatically, my career had begun.

He read my play to the class and I reacted somewhat as Robert Redford does in *The Way We Were*: embarrassed, pleased, I examined the ceiling, the floor and—unlike Redford—fought the giggles. But it got through to me that Robson really liked *Now Playing Tomorrow*. The play was a comedic fantasy about the danger of being clairvoyant. Robson got CBS to buy it for a prestigious experimental series broadcast on Sunday nights. The network paid one hundred dollars for a script; I was paid thirty, my tuition fee. I had to hold back from sounding off, not because of the money, the money didn't matter, it never has. Even after college, when I was selling towels in Bloomingdale's, I had lunch at Longchamps. What mattered was the unfairness. It always has.

Robson assembled a starry cast: Shirley Booth played two roles, a cynical heroine and a succulent Louella Parsons. Despite Shirley's distinctive nasal quaver—she, too, was from Brooklyn—the listener was unaware the same actress played both parts. That's how good she was. The most brilliant comedienne I have ever worked with, she was both incredibly skilled and infallibly intuitive but her essence as an actress came from the loneliness of her life: that was what made her comedy more than just funny, it made it touching.

The last play of mine she appeared in was *The Time of the Cuckoo,* which her good friend, Katharine Hepburn, shoplifted from her for the movie version called *Summertime.* The difference in performance was epitomized by the difference in the name of the character for what was ostensibly the same role. For Shirley in the play, it was Leona Samish; for Hepburn in the travelogue, it was Jane Hudson. Shirley was infinitely better.

CBS paid the full one hundred dollars for the next radio play I wrote, and thanks to Bill Robson, I was launched. Offers came amazingly fast from weekly dramatic radio shows like *Lux Radio Theater.* Commercial pulp, all of it. There I was, at the outset, faced with the art vs. commerce dilemma. Except it wasn't a dilemma. I was too flattered that I was wanted, too thrilled at being paid for being happy. Writing plays was happiness.

I said Yes too easily, with too much confidence that I could come up with an original story whenever one was wanted. I couldn't, of course, but I invented a method for devising plots. It was so wondrously simple that it made me laugh but it worked. What I did was list the twists and turns in successful mainstream movies and number them from 1 to 15. For a new play, I would choose at random Plot Devices 3, 7, and 13, for example. The necessity to link them together gave me a sense of the story line needed to support the twists and turns and, more important, of the nature of the characters who could do the twisting and turning. Then I would twist at least one or two of the turns. It was fun and I learned.

First, a basic insight into plot: A good plot depends on character. Then economy, which is best learned on radio because radio time, unlike stage or screen time, is not flexible. There is a precise number of minutes to be filled on a program; there cannot be more or less, it can't be too short or too long. What must be said has to be said in that precise amount of time which never seems enough but is enough. On the other hand, there is almost nothing on stage, screen or the printed page that isn't too long, largely because of the notion that length equals importance.

From being limited to one of the six senses, hearing, I learned how to establish character through words and how to propel action through dialogue. The more I wrote, the more exciting the whole process was, and most exciting of all was the day my father took me to open a bank account. I had justified his faith in me: I was a professional writer!

And then I was drafted.

We were not at war, there was no patriotic fervor, no attention was being paid. My passionate politics, my fervent belief that we had to support England and Russia to stop Germany slid out the window. Unlike my mother, I didn't turn against Roosevelt but I came close. He wanted an army and that army was going to end my career before it really began.

But it didn't. Amazingly, unexpectedly, it started me on my career as a playwright, the career I had been headed for since I was a kid and wrote a short story entirely in dialogue. Published in the grade school magazine, it was about Sleeping Beauty and what happened after the Prince kissed her awake. Since she'd been asleep for a hundred years, she was out of touch and bored the Prince who sent her off to Reno. Where did a ten-year-old learn that cynicism? I don't know. What I do know is that dialogue came easily: plays seemed the natural form for me.

Ironically, what I learned writing radio plays for an Army I thought was going to end my writing career, I used in writing *Home of the Brave,* a play set in a South Pacific jungle I never saw in a war I never fought. I could never have written that play had I not been in the Army. I would have lacked the technical knowledge, I wouldn't have understood soldiers, I wouldn't even have thought of writing a war play. But a war play was my beginning as a writer for the theatre.

Going to the theatre was a good way to learn about theatre. My introduction began with Saturday matinees at a stock company in Brooklyn. I tagged along with two quasi cousins, the daughters of my mother's best friend and that husband with the belly. The dazzle of the parasols twirling in *No, No, Nanette* and the real rain falling in *Rain* epitomized theatre to me. I was only eight; that was long before helicopters and chandeliers epitomized theatre. It was *Rain,* however, Somerset Maugham's wrestling match between Sadie Thompson's earthy sexuality and Reverend Davidson's Bible-bound hypocrisy, that ended my attendance at those Saturday matinees. My mother pulled the plug and I couldn't figure out why.

I went over every element of the play, every situation, every line I could remember. The best I came up with was a curtain line for one scene: "Did you ever notice that the foothills of Nebraska resemble a woman's breast?" "Breast"! That must have made the play unfit for me! I was flummoxed again when my parents and some friends cut short a discussion of Noël Coward's *The Vortex* when I walked into the living room. I ran to the dictionary to look up *vortex*. "Whirlpool." Whirlpool? Vortex? They must have said Kotex.

When I was nine or ten, my father's secretary, Miss S. (her last name was unpronounceable), took me to Broadway matinees and the opera. My mother liked operetta: she accompanied herself on the piano as she sang Victor Herbert, Sigmund Romberg, Friml; "New Moon" was a favorite for her light soprano. Miss S. dutifully took me to hear Lily Pons trill away in *Lucia* but we both preferred Irene Bordoni burbling in *Paris*. I fell in love with musicals early on.

Miss S. was a short, unfortunately fat young woman who always wore black and adored my father. Once, on her birthday, I heard him call her Pearl, and she burst into tears. In my early teens, I said farewell to Miss S.; off I went to the theatre on my own. Tickets were bought cut-rate in the basement below Gray's Drugstore in Times Square. The prices, posted behind the counter on a board that changed like stock market quotations, were odd: $1.21, $3.17, etc.

People in the audience around me often glared with disapproval and voiced it loudly: "Disgraceful! A child! Where are the parents?" They wanted me to hear and I did but that didn't bother me. What did was their enthusiastic response to a play like *Grand Hotel*, which I knew was kitsch without knowing the word itself any more than I knew why the play was kitsch. But somehow I knew; and it may have begun out of stubbornness but I realized then it was not a question of whose opinion was right. What was important was that I had an opinion. That realization made it easier for me to sit among my enemies, read my book, and wait for the Philip Barry or the Eugene O'Neill or the Rodgers and Hart to begin. I was happy being in a theatre, any theatre with a surprise waiting behind the curtain. Today, giants like Barry and O'Neill and plays like theirs are as rare on Broadway as curtains. And as kids in the audience at plays. And as serious audiences for plays. But plays continue to be written because that's what playwrights do.

I began reading plays while I was at Cornell; in fact, that's almost all I did one whole year. If you had a certain average, the university allowed you to invent a course not covered in the curriculum, provided an assistant professor or better would agree to teach it. The course I invented was in the socially conscious drama since 1848. The assistant professor who agreed to "teach" the course and I had two common causes: the theatre and prejudice. He didn't love the theatre quite as much as I did, though, and his anger at prejudice was less than mine. But then, his anger came from having been the only Protestant in a Catholic school. I was grateful he had experienced that much. The course we took together—I read the plays and reviewed them for him—was one of the pathetically few I took at Cornell that I enjoyed or from which I learned anything. We both learned it was much easier to be a critic than a playwright. Or a teacher.

I took a playwriting course from the noted Prof. A. M. Drummond, a huge man on crutches who right off the bat delivered a ukase never to begin a play with the telephone ringing. I immediately wrote a one-act play that began with a telephone ringing. If it hadn't, there wouldn't have been a play. It wasn't just rebelliousness that prompted that play; Drummond was a casually overt

On the beautiful Gothic campus at Cornell where I immediately
learned to smoke, drink and gamble (unsuccessfully).

anti-Semite. He had no compunction about beginning a sentence with "You Jews"—there were two others in the class—and I was declaring war. I didn't win, not while I was at Cornell anyway. He advised me to give up playwriting.

It wasn't until I was writing professionally for radio that I did happen on a good teacher: Ned Warren, who was Bill Robson's story editor. Also best friend and maker of Prairie Oysters for hangovers. Bald and rosy-cheeked, Ned looked as though he got his clothes in London (he wore ascots). He sat me down one day to discuss the scripts I had been writing. He was so wry and sardonic that I was completely unprepared when he told me I had talent. Just that, in those words: I had talent. No one had ever said that before and he was definite. I wanted to run out of the room before he continued because I knew there had to be a caveat. As indeed there was. My problem was that I was too facile. Too often, I made transitions in a scene through words, not as they should be made, through emotions. Emotions precede thought, emotions determine thought; plays are emotion. The single best lesson I have ever been given.

Along with Ned's wife Virginia, Bill and Ned adopted me. I adored Virginia. She had a deep voice with laughter underneath. She wore sweater sets, pearls, and a headband. She read constantly, anything, box tops, flyers, Trollope in paperback; she sat in corners from which she tossed out off-the-wall comments; she chuckled at everybody's jokes. We all drank millions of very-dry-Beefeater-martinis-straight-up and smoked Chesterfields and Camels around the red-checkered tablecloths at the old Billy's Steakhouse on First Avenue. Sunday brunch was at Willy's—Bill became Willy when you became his friend—where he made huevos rancheros with Bloody Marys before and during, and Irish coffee after. I had never been so happy as I was as a member of their wedding. I was twenty-two.

Sometimes I brought Eve Merriam, who wrote the poem I quoted in *Home of the Brave.* Small, birdlike, and given to shawls and Mexican silver, she looked more like a casting director's idea of the poet she was rapidly becoming than the date she was pretending to be. Her intelligence was not intimidating and she was quirkily funny. She hardly drank but she deftly concealed that and so she was trusted. We had been classmates at Cornell, where her wit and what she says in that poem brought us together:

> *Let our howling encircle the world's end.*
> *Frightened, you are my only friend.*
> *Someone must take a stand,*
> *Coward, take my coward's hand.*

Outsiders longing to be allowed in recognize one another easily, Eve and I were smart, but not campus smart. Our peers knew when to wear saddle shoes, we didn't; they knew what to do in the backseat of a roadster, we didn't. She didn't know that I was learning what to do in a deserted fraternity dormitory with an athletic classmate who was very accomplished at doing what he pretended we weren't doing; I didn't know if she was picking any fruit in that garden but I wondered. What we both knew, surprising each other, was how to dance. We belonged on the dance floor; we submitted to the music, letting it tell us to swirl, to dip, to turn, me to be tall, Eve to be beautiful. Our dancing fooled a lot of our classmates and for a sweet moment here and there fooled us. We enjoyed a verbal shorthand and a *Through the Looking-Glass* humor that joined us and kept us close, even to the last of her life.

Bill and the Warrens delighted in our humor. Politics, Eve and I instinctively avoided with them; the barricades were put in storage. Bill and Virginia were liberal and we divined Ned was Republican. I was not in the Party (I was never invited to join). I never asked whether or not Eve was, nor did she ever ask whether I was. As indiscreet and as giddy as we both seemed, we knew when it mattered to keep our mouths shut. Unfortunately, we also thought it mattered to keep silent about sexuality.

Four or five years after those martini nights at Billy's, near the end of the war, at five o'clock one morning, the bell rang at the West Fifty-fifth Street apartment I was subletting. I opened the door to an Eve in a tight black satin dress, a huge circular black hat and a defiant red mouth. She pushed by me and sashayed her black satin into the bedroom where Nora Kaye, the ballerina, lay astonished among the sheets. Eve launched into a scathing stream-of-conscious monologue, lifted a pack of cigarettes along with Nora's lighter, and sashayed her way out. We thought she was drunk; she was having a nervous breakdown. The pathetically farcical scene was predicated on a false assumption: that because I had been in bed with Nora, I was a cocksman who had been holding out on Eve. I wasn't above making a false assumption of that order myself:

During the period when I was stationed at Fort Monmouth in New Jersey, I would stay with Ned and Virginia Warren whenever I could get to New York on a pass. The last time, I arrived just as Ned was taking Virginia to the hospital for the birth of their first baby. Even in the taxi, she was Virginia-in-the-corner, laughing at idiot jokes only she could find funny. Ned had a shaker of martinis which he and I worked on in the waiting room. Virginia wasn't in labor long—that was a given, she would never inconvenience anyone. The baby was the boy Ned wanted and she, of course, gave him.

Exhilarated and boozy, we kissed Virginia good-bye and went home to their apartment on the top floor of what had been a mansion. I closed the gate of the tiny elevator and flopped back against the wall as the elevator groaned and started shaking us up to the top. Ned's eyes were closed, his lips pressed tightly shut. Then he opened his eyes, grabbed me, and tried to shove his tongue down my throat.

I gagged and shoved him away. I was startled, shocked, appalled, angry—a hundred things for a hundred reasons that ran into and over each other. Anger dominated: angry he assumed I was homosexual; angry that he betrayed Virginia; angry that he was an ugly, bald-headed man with too many teeth; angry he assumed I would respond; angry I couldn't be compassionate; angry that he had effectively finished off the friendship. And then—really angry that I had assumed Ned wasn't homosexual. Hadn't I known?

Of course I had. Just as Eve knew I was. Doesn't everyone always know, if only at the subconscious level? I knew my own thought process: Ned was married, Ned was now a father, Ned therefore wasn't queer. But I knew now he had married to have a wife and Virginia was a wife who was too glad to have a husband. It was all too clear too late, clear as well that his hypocrisy had shattered the family. The four of us—Willy had to be included—might somehow stay friends but we wouldn't be the same. And of course we weren't. There was no dramatic breakup; the friendship just dribbled away like a watercolor left out in the rain. They took off for sunny California and disappeared.

When I was drafted, it was into the Broomstick Army, so called because there weren't enough guns to go around. When a snafu yanked me out of my draftee Signal Corps company in New Jersey and flung me into a regular army Photographic company in Georgia that was getting ready to be shipped overseas, I was sure it was Joke Over, The End. But then—pure corn, soap opera, a twist on one of those turns I used to write, a 5 and a 12 and a twist on a 3: at the last possible minute, something happened, something so totally unforeseen that I didn't have a hint it was coming but it did come and it changed my life. Not just my life in the Army, the rest of my life as well. *Lux Radio Theater,* too extravagantly purple but fortunately for me, true.

My army career started with a snafu, this one at the induction center at Camp Upton on Long Island. I was supposed to stay three days; I wandered around for five weeks, doing nothing but smoke—I even saluted a lieutenant with a cigarette in my hand to his visible disgust—and wash the one uniform I had to wear. Next: Fort Monmouth for basic training in the Signal Corps. What corps didn't matter: Monmouth was in New Jersey, happily close to home. I learned nothing, not even something I wanted to learn: touch-typing. That was taught by a regular army tech sergeant with a glittering Elvis pompadour and fingernails longer than Barbra Streisand's. I speculated silently—

At Fort Monmouth in
the Broomstick Army in
fall 1941 before Pearl Harbor.

also on how he could type with those nails—but nobody else said anything. I
went in typing only with my index fingers and that's how I came out. Eighty
words a minute, though.

They weren't prepared for draftees at Monmouth, they didn't know what
to do with us. Most of the day, I did nothing, just as at Upton, except that
when I saluted an officer at Monmouth I shifted the cigarette to my nonsalut-
ing hand. I marched along lethargically, safely inside an invisible glass cage I
made for myself, talking to almost no one. There was a big tree with deep
shadows half hidden behind a building where I sat and smoked and dreamt.
An MP came by, scaring me. He sat down and asked for a light, scaring me
even more. He was very attractive, chatted easily, brought his leg against mine.
I trembled. He rubbed his crotch; that terrified me. He was too attractive, and
an MP. Entrapment? I fled—alas.

There's no shadow, no echo of that in *Home of the Brave,* but there is of
another unexpected, frightening moment at Monmouth. Preparing us for barracks inspection, our regular army sergeant complained how badly the "kikes
cleaned up." Two seconds later, he was flat on the floor, decked, though not by

me. Isn't there an echo of that in *Home of the Brave*? When it's not the Jewish soldier but his buddy who punches the bigot? In the barracks at Monmouth, it wasn't a buddy, it was a new friend, another recruit: Bob Hopkins, son of Harry Hopkins, the President's closest adviser.

What a lovely irony that anti-Semitic slur was! In truth, the happy turn in my army life began with being called a kike. I don't know if Bob Hopkins was at all aware how much my life changed then and later because of what he did. I don't know what happened to him or where he is now or if he is here now, but should he read this: Thank you, Bob.

A more affecting snafu got me shipped out of Monmouth months ahead of anyone else in my company. That one was a mistake in my classification number, which landed me in Fort Benning, in a Photographic company where, since I couldn't take a snapshot with a Brownie, I was demoted to truck driver.

Benning was in Columbus, Georgia, which had a park with a large sign at the entrance: NO DOGS, NEGROES OR SOLDIERS ALLOWED. Southern accents were so thick, I was never sure I heard what I heard. At roll call the first morning, the sergeant checking in his disheveled troops called out: "Wallace."

No answer. Louder: "Wallace!" Nothing. Angry now: "Where the fuck is Wallace?"

A very Southern growl from a nearby barracks window: "Hold your water, Mary!"

No reaction from anyone but me: I blushed. "Get your fuckin' ass outa here," said the sergeant and went on with his roll call. This was the Army, Miss Jones.

Freddie Wallace was an apparition: an extremely tall, extremely thin Cajun ghost from Louisiana. I had never really seen a screaming queen but I knew he was the real thing. He camped incessantly; apparently he couldn't talk or walk any other way and saw no reason to. He was so flagrantly flamboyant, not a soldier on that post could believe for a moment he could be a "homo." Not Freddie Wallace. Freddie was a wildman, Freddie was funny, crazy, fearless, definitely not a fruit. Didn't he bring whiskey into the barracks? Didn't he leave it out in the open for anyone to see at inspection? Liquor was the yardstick that measured a man. Freddie was a man. I avoided him like the plague.

Much later, after I left Benning, I ran into Freddie at the One Two Three, a chic New York nightclub with thick carpets and deep chairs where every man and woman pretended to be heterosexual and maybe two of each were. Freddie hooted and hollered: Oh, if he had known, well, he suspected, somebody with my eyes had to be One Of Us, but I was so drag-ass angry, I coulda been butch and weren't all these fancy New York folk red-ass buttholes!

Freddie had his rules, number one being Never have anything resembling sex with anyone who knew anyone in the company. He knew who he was and how he was regarded and didn't give a shit in a Dixie cup. He also knew he could spread his gaudy peacock feathers wide open without a care because he had an ace in his hole: he was a brilliant photographer and the Army knew it. Take him as he was or heave him out. They took him and he took photographs for them at Yalta.

Freddie Wallace was the first homosexual I met who had no guilt. He liked himself, who he was and what he was. To me at that time, he was an outrageous queen and that defined him. I didn't have the sense to envy his pride.

The week before we were to go overseas, most of the company was given weekend leave. I was not. I was put on KP. I was a truck driver who still had never driven a truck; a tech sergeant lectured about repairing a crankcase but I wasn't sure where the crankcase was; and I had had absolutely zero training to prepare me for overseas combat. It wasn't any of the above that yanked me out of my limbo of lethargy and propelled me into the orderly room to protest angrily. What sent me berserk was the unfairness of singling me out and putting me on KP. Injustice, as usual, fueled my tank.

The corporal on duty in the orderly room was just as angry, and at me for some undefined reason. So were the few soldiers left on company duty. They all glared as though I were Hitler, wouldn't say why, wouldn't even speak to me. Had they just discovered I was a Jew or a homosexual or both? I spent the miserable weekend in Coventry.

Monday morning, I was informed with contempt and not entirely concealed envy that the company was going overseas to God-knows-where while I was being transferred to another company. My first job after college was selling towels in Bloomingdale's; I hated it but when I was fired I wanted to cry. I felt somewhat like that about leaving Benning. The transfer was to Astoria, Queens, New York City. Why and to do what, they didn't say. They didn't know, but I found out. Astoria was an old movie studio the Army had taken over to make training films. I was transferred there because of Bob Hopkins and a soldier from the Bronx named Harry.

The three of us had developed a friendship like the friendships that develop during production of a play: a quick intense intimacy for the duration of the work, then promises and pledges that are meant but don't materialize. Bob and Harry and I didn't meet on a play, we met on garbage detail at Monmouth. Harry was sincere to the bone: he believed in total devotion to serving his country and disbelieved there was such a thing as a snafu in his country's Army. His soft spot was his love for stars, even radio stars. He knew every name and took it for granted that since I had been in radio, I knew the stars intimately. I didn't disabuse him. I embellished, I invented, I lied, and I made Harry happy. Which was accidentally smart of me because Harry earned his stripes in the Classification Center.

From Benning, I had written Bob Hopkins that I'd been mistakenly classified as a photographer instead of a writer. Bob, true son of his troubleshooting father, bypassed channels and went straight to a higher-up: Harry from the Bronx. Harry, indignant at this breakdown in the accuracy of His System, moved fast. In the nick of time, my father was driving all the way from Brooklyn to Georgia. He didn't care how far it was, he was coming to pick up his son and bring him home. Never demonstrative in public, when he got to Benning, he got out of the car and hugged me hard. The weather collaborated: it was perfect for the two days we spent rolling along the back roads to Astoria. The trip brought back the trips to Washington when I was little. He was so much my wonderful father that I was sure he would understand anything and know what to do about everything: I could confess my homosexuality. But I looked at his face and he was too happy.

A decade later, I learned how I had underestimated his love. Tom Hatcher had come to New York to live with me. One night, we took my parents to dinner and the theatre (the musical *She Loves Me!*); our relationship was unmentioned: it was simply there, without explanation, without risk. If they wanted to look, they would see. At the end of the evening, just before he stepped into the taxi we had gotten them, my dad put an arm around Tom and said: "I feel as though I have another son." Tears spilled into my eyes.

Astoria was located down the rabbit hole. Whatever had been up in Hollywood—point of origin for everyone except me—was now down, top was bottom, in was out, and revenge was the watchcry. Anyone with talent or craft—writers, directors, animators, editors—was an enlisted man; B producers, unit managers, prop boys were the officers. A Capt. Julian Blaustein, producer of remnants, ordered privates like Irwin Shaw and John Cheever to flatten their backs against the wall when he passed, goddammit. Like alcohol, little gold bars on epaulets produced the grandiosity that issued such orders. There were always one or two kiss-ass weasels who obeyed—war or no war, it was the movie business—but there was also George Cukor.

Cukor, overage and only a private, was nevertheless directing an OWI short with Ingrid Bergman on one of the small soundstages in Astoria's basement. Half the personnel thundered like elephants down to the set, crowded into every bit of space behind the lights and wires to see Ingrid Bergman, to watch her work, to fall in love. In command as "producer" was a Capt. George Baker who preened and strutted, and to show it was his parade, yelled: "Clear the set!"

Private Cukor, quietly: "It's OK with Miss Bergman and me. The boys can stay."

Capt. Baker, turning purple: "I'm in charge here, Private Cukor! I want them out and they're going! Now!"

Cukor, sharply: "Listen, you little pipsqueak: you were a prop boy at Metro before the war, you'll be a prop boy at Metro after the war. The boys can stay!"

We stayed, Baker fled. Privates Shaw and Cheever didn't blink as they ignored Capt. Blaustein and continued on to their offices to resume work on short stories for *The New Yorker.* They were the nucleus of a group, along with William Saroyan and Gottfried Reinhardt, son of the great Max, that met regularly for luncheon at Manny Wolf's Chop House on Third and Forty-ninth in Manhattan. Irwin's grandiosity might have signaled his future alcoholism had anyone known anything about alcoholism then, but he was always affable and very generous—he and Gottfried passed big cigars around.

Irwin was relentlessly macho, as were most of the Manny Wolf luncheoneers. They talked American: the verb "fucking," as in "fucking women," was used figuratively as well as literally. Even the fey Cheever tried to join in. He smiled as he moved dreamily through a protective haze of alcohol, never so drunk that he couldn't manage to be witty and funny. You hoped he wouldn't be funny about you, however, because his tongue was tart. The disclosure years later of John's homosexuality came as no surprise; what did surprise greatly was the revelation that this New England gentleman born and bred was a self-invented persona. The character he played was as good as any he wrote in his novels.

Is persona-invention a writer's disease? Lillian Hellman, Tennessee Williams, and Truman Capote, among others, have been infected, though not as felicitously as Cheever. The character of Lillian in her "Julia" and *Scoundrel Time* (fiction passed off as memoir) is not comparable to Regina of *The Little Foxes* or Fanny of *Watch on the Rhine.* Character is the core of drama: Lillian's own may have been mean and mendacious, but the characters she created for her plays—Regina and Oscar and Leo and Birdie, and Fannie and Bodo—are permanent portraits in the theatre's gallery.

Saroyan was working on a persona to get him out of the Army. The air around him was heavy with the kind of unhappiness that comes to the writer who believes the praise heaped on him by the critics for his first play and then is enraged when they dismiss the plays that follow. His later plays put Saroyan near the head of the line of wearers of the Emperor's New Clothes, a line that gets longer every year. Still, he was an original and he didn't belong in the Army.

Saroyan enjoyed Manny Wolf's even less than I did. He resented his peers working successfully at their civilian careers. Even Gottfried Reinhardt was collaborating on the book of *Rosalinda,* a musical based on one of his father's old hits, *The Merry Widow.* Saroyan set to work bucking for a 4-F discharge as a psychoneurotic: he read a newspaper at formations. This, he thought, would prove conclusively that he was a nut. In the Cookie Jar of Astoria? Pathetic, futile, the rest of us thought, but as always, we underestimated the Army. Our commanding officers were insulted by Saroyan's obvious fakery: he had to be put in his place and shown they were not fooled for a moment. So they transferred him to London where he had a lovely war.

My first Astoria assignment was to write a short training film, *Resistance and Ohm's Law.* All the writers laughed. I didn't have a clue who Ohm was or what his law dealt with—electricity, as it turned out. I had failed algebra, I knew nothing about physics, but I figured if I could explain that law, whatever it was, so that I could understand it, any idiot could understand it. That meant doing it simply—no special effects or animation, just putting a drafted ignoramus like me in a classroom with a regular army instructor. To provide some conflict, I gave the private a sense of humor and made his sergeant-teacher humorless but incapable of giving up on anyone. Each wins out: the private finally understands Ohm and the sergeant finally gets a joke. The conflict and the humor kept the piece alive and made it a little jazzy.

Private Cukor was assigned to direct. He looked up from the script when I walked into his cubicle and said, "I don't believe it."

"Did you believe *Her Cardboard Lover?*" I asked. This was a snotty reference to a turkey with Norma Shearer and Robert Taylor that Cukor had directed just before he was shanghaied into the Army.

"You're pretty fresh," he snapped. And so began our friendship which was helped by the fact that we didn't actually work together: he didn't change the script and I stayed away from the set. *Resistance and Ohm's Law* was cited as an example of what a training film should be but by that time, Cukor was long gone, our friendship suspended until I went to work in Hollywood after the war.

My second assignment sent me to a dreary hellhole of sand-pocked ground and stunted trees in Maryland called Fort Aberdeen. The training film was to be called *How to Carve a Side of Beef.* In seven reels. Obviously, we were going to lose the war. If confirmation was needed, it came from a poster tacked to a scraggly pine: TONIGHT AT THE SERVICE CLUB! AN ALL-MALE ALL-SOLDIER CAST IN JOHN-FREDERICS HATS IN CLARE BOOTHE'S "THE WOMEN"!

The play had been a hit on Broadway. It called for a dozen sets; a battalion of actresses; racks of dresses, gowns, bras, panties and, of course, those John-Frederics hats. The Aberdeen production answered every call and the All-Male All-Soldier Cast played the play absolutely straight. Mary, the deceived wife, was seriously distraught in a series of tasteful gowns gliding over tasteful, if immovable, breasts. Her loving, pubescent little daughter had correspondingly little "bumps" on her chest and short, enormous legs like Ozymandias. Crystal, the hussy husband-thief, had a dicey moment at the end of her bubble-bath scene: when she stood up to get out the tub, the curtains jammed and we all saw that Crystal wore a jockstrap.

There are no men in *The Women* and there didn't appear to me to be any on the stage of the Service Club. They weren't drag queens or transvestites or Hasty Puddings or anything I had ever seen or heard of. They were girls, women, ladies who happened to have hair and muscles in masculine places. The sole exception was Sylvia, the bitchy, troublemaking gossip. She wore the John-Frederics hats and got a hand on every entrance. She screeched, she hooted, she camped enough to make up for the straightforward feminine demeanor of the rest of the cast. The audience—officers, enlisted men, wives, and girlfriends—was mesmerized. They adored her, they cheered her, they howled at her every leer, her every lash, her every what-can-only-be-called moue. There must be a correlation between this country's homophobia and its hysterical delight in drag, any drag, even a husband in a tablecloth-dress and a lampshade-hat.

The triumph of the evening was the appearance at the thunderous curtain call of the author herself, Clare Boothe, in person. Our future ambassador to Italy made a brief, gracious speech thanking all the "ladies" and complimenting Crystal for "having the most beautiful back of anyone who has played the role."

I didn't know what to make of any of it. Why this soap opera had been a critical success, why its author was regarded as an aphoristic wit—these were questions not in my mind at that moment. What I wanted desperately to know was, What were those people on the stage? Sylvia had to be a queen, he made Freddie Wallace look butch. But he was a soldier, they were all soldiers, the audience was soldiers; the Army would not have permitted the performance if anything were out of GI line. If I'd had any sense, lonely as I was, I would have made a beeline for the stage door. I had no notion of how to tell who was or wasn't an ordinary homosexual—there is no way—but I couldn't even tell when eyes locked that it was in mutual anticipation. I wasn't sure what queer was, I was too afraid of being caught and I didn't lose my inhibitions and throw my sexual hat over the dam until some months later.

Not that I was either virgin or innocent. I hadn't been either since I was fourteen, when I was gone down on by a kid my age who went from house to house like the Avon lady, blowing everyone available and acquiescent on the block. Age of consent was no obstacle and daytime was safe because nobody thought sex occurred in daylight. He grew up to be a respected professor at home and at the Sorbonne. Until recently, he taught in both places and was still on his knees, though less frequently.

His blow jobs continued to be given sporadically until we went away to different colleges. Our relationship was both distant and intimate: no mutual friends except a girl who lived next door to him who had a crush on me I wished she hadn't, no mutual interests except the movies and blow jobs. Even though we were aware we each read a great deal, we never discussed a book. We never mentioned blow jobs either, but the title of a movie we saw as teenagers at Loew's Kings on Flatbush Avenue supplied a verbal signal we used to announce readiness for The Act. Why that title, how there could be such a prescient coincidence—this was in the early Thirties—I don't know, but the movie was called *Let Us Be Gay.*

The future professor also took me to my first gay bar, Little America. (The name delighted me so, I sent some of my characters there in *The Enclave.*) Located in the East Fifties, it was done up as an igloo, with papier mâché icicles over the bar. The professor met a hustler and left me alone at the bar, nursing the dregs of my drink. An older man—at least twenty-seven; I was twenty and just out of college—who looked like Cary Grant came over and said: "At last. The most attractive person in the room alone." He was close to all my romantic and sexual fantasies, he even had a good job. I wouldn't go home with him, I wanted to make a date for another night. He pleaded: his mother lived with him, she was away for the night, he didn't know when he would have the apartment to himself again—no luck, I wouldn't. I have been to bed with a few hundred men, some of them more than once. I don't remember their names, I don't even think about them. That man's name, I remember because I didn't go to bed with him and regretted it.

Why didn't I? Not because I was afraid of venereal infection. No, it was because I wanted to have an affair and if I went to bed with him the first night, in my Flatbush mind, that would be that. Was I behaving like the girls of that day? Probably.

Certainly homosexual boys were more romantic and less promiscuous in the Thirties. During the war, we went wild but who of what sex didn't? Even when I was having and enjoying sex with those unremembered hundreds, more often than not I had one eye open for romance which, more often than not, is born of sex. That, too, I learned in the Army.

On my way back to Astoria after carving the cows of Aberdeen in seven reels, I had a stopover in Washington, D.C., that allowed time to see a real movie. During the war, it was almost impossible to tell one movie from another because they were almost all war movies with variations on one plot. *The Purple Heart* would have been just another war picture but it introduced

Farley Granger. Instant infatuation. Not only because he was beautiful, which he was, but because he had the attraction necessary and fatal for me: he was pure in heart. How did I know? Just by looking at him on the screen. Only a few years later, in a house in Laurel Canyon in Hollywood where Farley and I were living, he pounded the floor, protesting, "I'm only pure in your crazy head!" I didn't believe him. Then.

Back in Astoria, the Army maintained its high dementia level. Since production was expanding, space was needed; the writers were shifted to an office building in the Thirties on the atypical logical assumption that we could write anyplace if we could write at all. To remind us we were still troops, we had formations and drilled in the streets, where we were ticketed by the police for obstructing traffic. The drilling was shifted to the Sixty-ninth Regiment Armory on Lexington Avenue, but I was exempted: a telegram, an ordinary Western Union telegram arrived at the office ordering me to report to Rockefeller Center, period. Precisely where, when, and why were mine to work out. I wasn't a mystery buff for nothing. A glance at the newspaper listings and I reported to the radio studio broadcasting *Armed Service Force Presents.* What was presented was an original play each week, dramatizing the work of a different branch of our armed forces. The lieutenant who had been writing the program hadn't pleased Washington. He was leaving for Burma and I was his replacement.

I flirted with using the pick-three-numbers-and-get-a-plot-to-twist-and-turn method, but reality was needed here; the craft I had learned from writing radio plays, even soap operas, came into service. The stories themselves had to be invented from incidents I dug out of official combat reports. To help me technically, I was slammed through crash courses from time to time—in tanks, on firing ranges, in dive-bombers (I threw up in my cap in a dive over Matagorda, Texas). The characters were based in part on soldiers I had met at Monmouth and Benning, in the crash courses, in bed. But soldiers in drama so often seem limited to an accent and a regional hometown that I used what is always there to be used: people I knew or people I imagined. As a result, sometimes the soldiers I wrote were people; often enough, anyway, so that Burma never threatened.

When whoever in Washington made such decisions decided we might possibly win this war, a special unit was created to produce a weekly series called *Assignment Home:* propaganda in the guise of drama to prepare the home front for the men returning home. The unit consisted of a colonel to direct the show, a captain to research the material, and a sergeant to write it. I was the sergeant. The colonel and the captain in their new tailor-made uniforms announced they were going overseas to observe combat firsthand, and of course I was coming along. Except that I couldn't because I was an enlisted man and no enlisted man was permitted to go overseas in that small a unit. And because I wasn't permitted to go, the captain and the colonel couldn't go either. They were very angry with me and resentful. Obviously, even the Army knew I was the one doing the work. If I had been an officer, we all could have gone. But I was prevented from going to OCS (officer candidate school), I couldn't even be appointed a warrant officer, because of a casual remark made by Russel Crouse over a drink with the army head of radio in Washington. I was suspected of being a Communist.

Russel Crouse and his partner Howard Lindsay wrote plays like *Life with Father* and musicals like *The Sound of Music,* bringing fame to red hair and fathers with one and to dirndls and nuns with the other. At a meeting of the Radio Writers Guild, Crouse heard me agitate passionately as usual for the Soldier Vote, a position called leftist by Republicans of the right, i.e., Lindsay and Crouse. How far is it from leftist to Communist? Over a drink, not very. Howard Lindsay and Russel Crouse were not McCarthyites later on, however. They hired a director (Mike Gordon, who had directed *Home of the Brave*) whom they knew was blacklisted in Hollywood because he had taken the Fifth Amendment before the House Un-American Activities Committee (HUAC). There was no blacklist in the theatre.

But Russel Crouse's casual remark got me hauled down to Washington to account for my political views. It was a mild conversation, no grilling, I wasn't nervous. I was too ignorant to be nervous, unaware that imprisonment in Leavenworth was a possibility if I put a foot wrong. Although my inquisitors cleared me, from then on my scripts had to be vetted in Washington, a restriction that inadvertently brought vindication and more. A play of mine called *The Knife* was canceled by Washington. It was about Negroes in the Army and it was honest about discrimination in the Army. But it was 1945 now; the war was coming to an end and the brass were under no illusion about the Negro's place after the war: Back to the back of the bus, boy.

The script had aroused a good deal of excited enthusiasm, however, and in one of those fuck-you-let's-go-for-it moments in a bar, it was decided to fight for *The Knife.* A copy was sneaked to Henry Stimson, who was secretary of war. Stimson insisted that the play be aired, he ordered it to be aired; then he further stuck it to the Army by giving us a citation. I don't much respect prizes, but that citation I was proud of. Along with the unexpected publication of my *Assignment Home* scripts like *The Face* and *The Last Day of the War* in Best Play collections.

. . .

I was being noticed, I was getting a reputation; the best actors in radio were juggling schedules to work for scale on *Assignment Home* because they liked the parts and what the scripts were saying. I was making friends, good friends who suggested I get an agent. They didn't know I already had one: the Army. Without the standard ten percent commission, the Army arranged for me to work for CBS as a writer on its commercial program, *The Man Behind the Gun,* for $350 a script (add a zero for what that amount of money would be today). The format of the show called for a narrator, usually third person. I tried first person: effective but too limiting. I tried second person: it brought the listener directly into the experience, it lifted the story into immediacy. The device became so popular it was eventually the basis of a series called *You Are There.*

Whoever investigated my politics must not have been around, for I was still in uniform when I was asked to write the first program of a new series, *This Is Your FBI.* Trust was total: when I went down to FBI headquarters in Washington for research and to get acquainted with their "guidelines," I was left alone in a room with all the files on people investigated. I located the "L" cabinet, I had a drawer halfway open—then one of those men in gray walked in. I opened and closed several drawers loudly: sound effects, I explained, I was checking sound effects. He believed me; in fact, he must have gotten quite a favorable impression because after that pilot program was aired, a letter arrived from J. Edgar Hoover that began, "I wanted you to know how happy I was with the program last evening," then continued more personally farther down with "I regretted so much that I was not in my office on the occasion of your recent visit to the bureau for I would like to have said hello to you." Would it only have been hello or would Clyde have been jealous? Oh, the missed moments!

From the beginning, the radio propaganda shows took precedence and made me unavailable to write training films. Consequently, Astoria put me on detached service and gave me a per diem: I could live where I wanted and how I wanted. Out of the barracks was out of the cage and I went wild sexually. I had guilts—I was a nice Jewish boy, I was politically to the left, I wrote socially conscious dramas—but much of the time, I had the visceral good sense to just enjoy myself. I took comfort that I had an internal governor to stop me before I did myself in. Or so I thought.

In New York during the Second World War, everything was rationed except the two things everyone wanted most: sex and booze. The city reeked of sex. Everybody inhaled and enjoyed: it was so available, as much as you wanted and who didn't want? Water was a liquid that formed ice cubes to put in drinks that inevitably led to sex. I whirled in a blender of sex and booze.

If I'd been looking, signs of drinking too much were apparent in 1939, when I was twenty-one. The origin was a nightclub act of "bright young satirists," six of us in a small, original musical revue. We did individual thirty-second blackouts of Husbands and Mothers; we had group numbers where each of us was one of the five boroughs (#6 played the piano); we performed musical sequels to scandals. I wrote much of the material, but to be paid, I had to perform. The act was called—this is not easy to admit—the Nitewits. Our brief moment was at Leon and Eddie's on Fifty-second Street (the model for the nightclub in my play *The Bird Cage*), where our success resulted in Eddie Davis, our boss and the Star, turning off our microphones. The people ringside flipped pats of butter at us with their butter knives. Eddie Davis set out to kill his hired hands in his own club. Resentment is suicidal.

I was too self-conscious to get myself out onstage in front of anybody unless I was embalmed, so I started on brandy at 3 in the afternoon when I woke up, switched to scotch at 7:30 p.m. when we had to check in at Leon and Eddie's, and stayed with it until 4:30 a.m. when we were released. I drifted around the club, onstage and off, in a pleasant haze and hangover free. Then romance struck, my first romance: the haze became blissful, the drift got a bounce and the only thing wrong was that I was too liquored to hold on to every single thrilling moment.

Eddie had a very handsome pianist, a Black Irish Texan named Addison Bailey who lived in black tie as though he'd been born in it. He casually invited me back to his apartment one night. I didn't hesitate for a second, for half a second. It was new, it was exciting, it and he were hot and glamorous, this was what life was for. Performing onstage became easier because Addy was watching from the bar. I didn't cut back on the booze, though; he and I drank more than we did anything else. Over a weekend, we would often kill one of the huge bottles of Ballantine's scotch then on display in the windows of "21." It must have been late one morning—it was always night in his apartment because the curtains were always closed—that he nudged me awake and asked me to get his doctor's number from his phone book. An ambulance took him away.

When I went to the hospital, blocking the door to his room was Herbert Fields, co-librettist of Cole Porter's current show, *Dubarry Was a Lady.* Addy, it seemed, was Cole Porter's boyfriend of the moment; I was the other—what?

He came close to dying of acute alcoholism, close enough to scare me onto the wagon. When he got out of the hospital, he gave up drinking permanently. I was told that; he never spoke to me again. I was bewildered, thrown, in pain.

Knowing he would be there, I went to a matinee of *Dubarry*. He was with Herbert Fields and cut me dead—which bewildered me more and hurt more. All I remember about the show is that Cole Porter wrote it, Ethel Merman and Bert Lahr were in it, and I hated it. A few years later, I walked into whatever the room for drinks and piano music at the Drake Hotel was called and there was Addy with a glass of water on his piano. We exchanged half smiles; I wasn't sure he remembered. There was no quickening of the heart, Leon and Eddie's was a blur: a disappointing coda to my first affair.

My serious drinking resumed with Bill Holden. We met in the Army: sunbathing and reading on the roof at Astoria. To see a movie star reading "Gerontion" was intriguing enough to start a conversation. When I discovered he was unaware the poem was anti-Semitic, as was its author, I wondered whether Holden himself was anti-Semitic or just not very knowledgeable. I was glad to find it was the latter, not because he was so good-looking (I thought his good looks antiseptic) but because he was completely unaffected and eager to learn. Poor guy. Teacher was ready with a passionate attack on Eliot for being obscure and opaque in too much of his work but viciously clear in his bigotry and racism. Those who defended him as a great artist and a genius, I dismissed. That was no excuse and anyway I wasn't too sure he was either.

Holden just listened. When I finished, he took a deep breath and said, "Why don't we have a drink?" Which we did later, when we were off duty. That began our bonding—not T. S. Eliot, very dry gin martinis. We both loved them and began a competition to see who could drink the most. I won the last bout we had before we both left Astoria: fifteen dry gin martinis straight up. How did I do it? War makes the boy into a man.

The loser had to buy dinner. That last time, Bill chose the Bistro on Third Avenue under the El. As we walked in, I smelled mussels and said, "The floor is going to hit me in the face." It didn't, then or ever, but it did hit Bill.

It isn't the amount consumed, it's not crossing the lines: first the dangerous line from social drinker to serious drinker, then the lethal line from heavy hitter to alcoholic. I never crossed that final line. Bill Holden died too early, an alcoholic.

My drinking actually decreased with my sexual explosion. A lot of drinking goes with a lot of talking but a lot of fucking doesn't leave you free to hold a glass. On-the-prowl drinking led me first to the Bird Circuit: gay bars with bird names like the Blue Parrot (it looked like the Black Parrot). Brighter and better was the Astor Bar in Times Square, wall to wall with GI Joes and our allies, a sort of gay Stage Door Canteen. Socially higher but pissier was the Oak Bar at the Plaza; best was the old Savoy-Plaza Hotel on East Fifty-eighth Street: it was New York and you knew it the moment you walked in. The bar, at the end of a room that had music and a dance floor, was generous with drinks and attractive officers and enlisted men ready for action. For me, it also had a memory:

On a weekend vacation from college, I heard Helena Horne, as Lena Horne was then known, sing so sweet in that room. I had despaired of getting in, then suddenly, magically, there she was, floating toward me in flame-colored chiffon. I told her I had driven all the way from Ithaca just to hear her sing. She was so beautiful, I believed my own lie. I didn't tell her the truth about that first encounter until the early Fifties, when we sailed on the *Ile de France* for Paris. By then, there were other lies and we were launched into a friendship that became unique before it ended badly in the liberated Sixties.

Bathhouses, which flourished then, were never for me. Straight bars, mixed, bisexual, dubious bars, I went to for a while when they were comfortable, relaxing—like Bradley's in the Village for jazz, the front room of the Blue Angel for show tunes on a piano, the old Tony's down the street from "21" for singers like Mabel Mercer. Gay bars didn't relax me, they made me uncomfortable; in the Army, I soon eliminated them. How then did I meet a few hundred bedmates? Referrals.

A fond example: One Sunday evening I was more than ready for sleep in my Sutton Place bed. I'd had ten different partners over the weekend. By different, I also mean no two from the same branch of our armed forces or from the same rank; thus there was an English captain and a lance corporal from Down Under. Anyone who would draw up rules like that and follow them was on his way around the bend, but I reveled in checking off the branches on a chart I'd drawn up. I was alert to no warning bell, only the knock on the door or the sound of the telephone which that night rang one last time: a civilian friend connected with the Philharmonic. He had struck out with a young sailor up from Virginia who, he insisted, was perfect for me. Carlos (despite the name, honeysuckle Southern) got a kinky pleasure out of matchmaking.

"No, Carlos, I've had ten since Friday night."

"Baby, what's one more? And this one definitely is more, wait til you see him! Just let him come over, talk to him—all right, I will make my confession. He heard about you through Pete and came up all the way from Norfolk just hoping he would have the good fortune to meet you."

He came over. We had a short affair and his name I do remember. That example may be extreme but it wasn't atypical. Where the energy and stamina came from was no concern: when I needed them, they were there. During all my sexual shenanigans, I met deadlines for those original radio plays which kept improving, gaining me more and more recognition. How and why? I was disciplined, yes; I enjoyed writing, yes; but the point, the pertinent point was that when I was writing, I knew where I belonged. When I was on the prowl, I didn't; so I kept looking for where I could belong.

My family's world was not mine, but while I blamed the Army for the infrequency of my visits, when I did see them, I loved them and brought home the inevitable guilts. So for my sister's birthday, I took her to the Stork Club; I got the colonel who directed *Assignment Home* to make the reservation. My sister and I got as far as the velvet rope at the entrance when we were barred: I was an enlisted man. My usual anger at injustice was nothing compared to the anger I felt at that moment because my sister read Winchell regularly and had spent the day getting dressed for the night. And thought I was a small god. A scene based on that moment is in *The Way We Were,* not for revenge but in her memory.

Oddly, the snub didn't upset her. She was upset that I was upset, she wanted me to be in a good mood. She always did, so it didn't occur to me she had a special reason. Which club we went to instead of the Stork is a blank; what happened after we sat down is engraved. I order drinks, lighting our cigarettes. The drinks arrive, we drink to her birthday. She leans forward and I hear what she asks. For my advice. About virginity. Specifically, her virginity. More specifically, when it was all right for her to lose it. Then it's as though I blacked out.

A picture flashes across the years: my little sister running desperately across the grass to me at summer camp ten years earlier. I was one of the brothers who dutifully but resentfully marched over from the other side of the lake. Edith hurled herself at me, grabbed me around the waist, in tears because I hadn't shown up the week before. She hated summer camp on her side of the lake but I loved it on mine.

Sitting in that nightclub I can't place, I knew the advice my mother would have wanted me to give Edith. I knew a sister was to be protected. I also knew she was not to be cheated. I kissed her; I took a lot of time lighting another cigarette for her; I weighed both sides, all sides; then finally I said that if she loved him—there obviously was a particular him—it was all right to do it. I didn't get into what love was, I wasn't crazy. Over and over, I would get in trouble for saying what I thought but if ever there was a time to say what I thought, that was it. And thank God I said it because my dear little sister had already lost her virginity. To her particular him. On the back stairs leading to the apartment in Brooklyn. Evidently we shared sexual genes.

She didn't mention love, only that he was eager to marry her. She should have grabbed him, he was a catch in every way. But he was strong and what my sister wanted was someone she could push around, someone she could boss. Our mother's daughter? My mother respected my father, my sister married a boy who grew up to look like Queen Victoria. My parents and I never liked him. We didn't understand it, but she loved him, he loved her, they had three kids and a nice house paid for by my mother and me without my father knowing.

My maternal grandfather used to say fifty percent of the secret of happiness was knowing what you wanted. Not all that easy when you get down to the specifics, but Edith knew what she wanted and got what she wanted. Not what I or my father wanted for her, not even what my mother wanted for her, but what she wanted, and that was what was important. That's what had to be accepted and I did accept it. It didn't have to be liked and I never did like it. But I could see it was a good marriage.

I compartmentalized my lives and my friends. There were the Carloses who were bright and fun but with whom the main connection was the same sexual wavelength. There were the liberals, progressives, left-wingers I met through

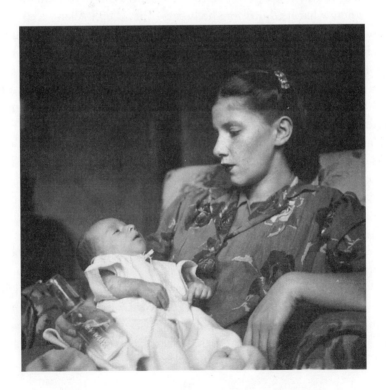

Edith with my nephew Andy, the first of her three children.

radio whom I really wanted as friends. Ever since I collected tinfoil for Republican Spain as a teenager, I had gravitated to people on the left. They were more intelligent, more informed; they were caring, they bled; they didn't just talk about injustice, they fought it; they were compassionate and friends to the outsider. A Jew and a homosexual, I was, of course, an outsider, if not a pariah, no matter what my achievements. But there was a problem.

Much as I wanted these leftist friends—and since many of them were in or nearly in the theatre—I was uncomfortable with them because I had to be deceitful; I had to be deceitful because the Communist Party didn't sanction homosexuality. Whether the friends were actually card-carriers or not, I didn't know. It didn't matter: the left didn't approve of homosexuality either. How could I call them compassionate? Easily. Justification was no problem: no one in his right mind would approve of homosexuality. The solution? I pretended to be straight and made the problem mine, not theirs.

Peaceful Allen approved of any sexuality, was neither left nor right, and had never bothered to vote. He was a chubby, always cheerful, always hungover person in uniform, attached to Astoria for what reason no one knew. Nor did anyone know what he did before he became Pfc. Ralph Allen except that he was the chum of people who dwelt in high places like the Algonquin and Sands Point and had given him the nickname, and that he was both funny and witty. Little Powerhouse, he called me, after a candy bar; he admired my energy. Hoping he might absorb it by osmosis, he took me under his wing and introduced me to various women he squired around town, beginning with Dorothy Parker.

When we picked her up at the old Murray Hill Hotel to take her out for drinks and dinner, Mrs. Parker had already started the evening. Ever so daintily, she picked her way across the marble lobby, accompanied by one of those repellent little dogs that come with ladies who like liquor. The dog stopped to take a long pee. The clerk behind the desk glared. Mrs. Parker glared back, snatched up her dog and said: "I did it!"

Alas. I had too recently read a book by her friend Alexander Woollcott, who attributed the exact same remark to Mrs. Patrick Campbell, also a lover of liquor and disgruntled little dogs. My first meeting with a celebrity in the flesh was a major disappointment but I learned: Don't expect. After that first meeting, I took whatever Mrs. Parker offered. Aggressively saccharine when sober, when drunk—which, fortunately, she usually was—she was hilariously mean.

. . .

Then Peaceful introduced me to an ex–Ziegfeld showgirl named Peggy Fears, a celebrity in her own odd world where she was the unofficial leader of a group of women who were all beautiful, all rich, all lesbians. They were all also divorced and called Mrs. Harkness, Tiffany Saportas, DeLamar, Whitehouse—very good pedigrees, they had. They were Republicans but unlike their male counterparts who, like other minorities, thought being Republican made them belong, Peggy's women didn't give a hoot in hell about belonging to anything but their coven. They were Republican because their money came from rich men and their rich men were Republican; they behaved as they wanted right in the faces of their men. Unlike other women, they rarely went to the powder room in pairs; they went alone, to cruise. The best cruising places for women, Peggy confided, were the powder rooms at chic clubs or four-star restaurants.

Although Peggy was rich—she had married a man with millions and took several with her when she divorced him—she worked sporadically as a Dietrich-inspired chanteuse at the Savoy-Plaza, cruising simultaneously. Strolling around the floor, she croaked out a song about her "six-foot-two blue-eyed blond baby," handing out red roses to the rich men seated ringside as she winked at their pretty girls. After the show, the coven met in her suite. There was always a buffet table, but the plates remained untouched until the ladies got smashed. Being incestuous as most lesbians are, their smoldering jealousy flared up then and the crockery began flying. Any man present just ducked.

If someone had accused them of being amoral or decadent, they would honestly have been bewildered. One delicate blonde was puzzled when it was explained to her that her fifteen-year-old daughter might have run away because she opened a closet to find fragile Mummy inside doing it with a noted English actress. Whose autograph her daughter had. Life was a well-earned bowl of cherries for these women. Because they remained emotionally uninvolved with men, they made good courtesans; they had worked hard in a variety of beds and felt entitled to enjoy the material results. They were very comfortable with themselves as what they were. Not the least of the reasons I enjoyed them was that with them, I was comfortable with what I was sexually. That wasn't enough, however; eventually my curiosity waned and I moved on. I wasn't missed. They liked their young men to empty their ashtrays and I was never one for that.

Beatrice Farrar was very different: she was disappointed my parents were alive because she wanted to adopt me. At eighty, Beatrice was embalmed in gin. Never hatless in public, teal blue eyes heavily outlined in kohl, ramrod posture making her small frame seem tall, she came from Boston and Brahmins. Early

in the century, she would drive each morning in her carriage to the Boston
railroad station. Day after day, she watched the trains pull out and disappear
over the horizon until one day she went aboard and kept traveling until she
was in Paris. There she became the mistress of Marcel Duchamp and lived on
absinthe and potatoes. When she was retired, she came home and married a
man almost as jolly as Peaceful and twice as gay. His name was Tommy Farrar,
"of the Virginia Farrars"; he was dying, he had run through all his money and
Beatrice was his last friend on Fire Island. He shared her house at Cherry
Grove where, as Beatrice observed, "each year, the boys get gayer and the girls
get grimmer."

The Grove was a mixture of gay, straight, and impartial. In what she called
her upstairs drawing room, Beatrice sat in her cocktail corner drinking Crystal
Chandeliers—gin and vodka on ice—and discussed all things French with
Janet Flanner. Janet was Citizen Genêt, *The New Yorker's* man in Paris: dry,
witty, endlessly informed, she spoke English as rapidly as though it were
French. Her lover, Natalia Danesi Murray, a married Italian beauty and a

Helping berth a flying
water-taxi from the main-
land at Cherry Grove,
Fire Island.

shrewd literary agent, was the perfect other half. Juicy, full of laughter, Natalia gave room to all the fools Janet wouldn't suffer.

There was no food at Beatrice's (I never saw her eat). For meals, we went to drink at Duffy's, the only hotel at the Grove; it was a mom-and-pop operation constantly petitioning Albany to allow the boys to dance together—the girls didn't need official sanction. Rainy days weren't dreary as at most beach resorts; they brought out the madness that was more characteristic of that Cherry Grove than the gayness. A shower, even a drizzle, could summon a Town Crier who ran up and down the boardwalk, banging on a tray from Duffy's, calling out: "Madame Butterfly Day! Madame Butterfly Day!" Within an hour, the walkways were filled with queens in kimonos carried in makeshift rickshaws by lesbian naval officers. For Cherry Grove, war with Japan did not mean war with Puccini.

Through another of Peaceful's women, I got a front-seat look at Money. A White Russian Princess, Alexandra Loris-Melikov, introduced me to a family so rich no one had heard of them. Sandra herself didn't have a ruble; she worked two day jobs simultaneously: she was a pearl wearer and a reader. Because her skin contained the natural oil essential for real pearls to keep their luster, she sat in bank vaults wearing priceless necklaces while she read scripts for MGM. "Amusing," she termed it.

She took me for "amusing weekend" at the Davisons' summer estate in an unmapped county of money on the North Shore of Long Island. Three Rolls-Royces were the transport between the main house and the three houses in the vast park for each of the three children. I was given my own valet to press and lay out my uniform for dinner while I lay in the bath he had drawn.

When we went swimming, it was off the division's own beach. The white sand looked as though it had been sifted through a strainer. A sliver of not-quite-so-white beach was separated from theirs by barbed wire. German submarines had been sighted off Long Island's south shore, but this wasn't the south shore.

"What's the barbed wire for?" I asked Sandra.

"To keep servants out," she said. "Amusing, no?"

The Herbert Bayard Swopes were not as rich but much more complicated. He ran the *Herald-Tribune* and was a devout Republican and an Episcopalian who had misplaced his memory of having been born a Jew. His wife Maggie had wiped out her memory of having been born the daughter of a Long Island potato farmer. He railed against FDR, she dismissed the poor.

"Give 'em coal to heat their houses, they'll just store it in the bathtub," she said. "They're poor because they want to be poor."

"Can I quote you?" I asked.

She shot me a look, began calling me Sgt. Stalin, but invited me back and seated me on her right. "You're a prick but I like your lip," she said. The compliment pleased the woman who had brought me there: Maggie's best chum and a chum of Peaceful's was Evelyn Weil Richardson DeMeir Arostige—and after I met her, Backer.

The model for the chic, sparkling heroines her friend S. N. Behrman wrote for Ina Claire to play in his high comedies *Biography* and *End of Summer,* Evie was to be adored; I joined the long line. She called me "Sargiedarling" (one word). High comedy wears a shimmering mask of wit; it turns on an emotional dime from laughter to heartbreak. So did Evie.

Born a Weil, related to the Kuhns and Loebs of Chicago and the Strauses of Macy's, she had to be told she was a Jew. Rich and German Jews often do, and I, of course, told her. My motive was suspect: Sam Behrman had finally gotten around to writing a play with a Jew in it but he was only one-eighth a Jew. Evie saw nothing shameful in that; she adored the play, she adored Sam and I was jealous. She took my news that she was eight-eighths very well. Two o'clock one morning, she phoned from her duplex on Gracie Square with the solution to the Jewish problem. We would place an ad on the back page of *The New York Times:*

"Take the J out of Jew—it spells You."

It was the beginning of her breaking ranks, of her pride in being one of the chosen people. Which was fortunate, for she soon fell in love with George Backer who was very much chosen. Without love, Evie was an incomplete woman. She had been without since her husband was shot down over Dunkirk. She had a child she loved, she had become a successful interior decorator; she glittered, she charmed, she amused as though all that was enough. It wasn't: she needed to be in love.

George Backer was handsome, charming, and important—which was good; a political intellectual and the liberal editor of the then liberal *New York Post*—which was not good. Anathema, in fact, in Evie's world and George knew it. Like most men, he was attracted by the Ina Claire in Evie but he was a serious man, a very serious advocate of a Jewish state in Palestine. It was only when he discovered that Evie was truly a *Jewish* Ina Claire that he became serious about her.

Peaceful wasn't invited to the wedding and neither was I. A classic Jewish joke is to ask about anything: Is it good for the Jews? Homosexuals don't have that joke; homosexuals don't have to ask. Not being invited was bad for homosexuals, par for the course.

The last time I saw Evie while I was still "Sargiedarling" was the opening night of Jerome Robbins's *Fancy Free.* We were there by accident. Evie had expected to see Ballet Theatre's *Swan Lake,* I had to persuade her to stay in her seat. A few months earlier, I had never seen a ballet; a few months earlier, I had not passed through backstage doors into a world whose attitudes toward art and homosexuality shook mine; a few months earlier, I hadn't met two dancers who seesawed importantly in my life for a long time, and a third with whom I had a sporadic, wonderfully sexual affair.

Across Seventh Avenue from the elegantly seedy old Metropolitan Opera House where Ballet Theatre was playing was the lovely Empire Theatre. Looking across at its marquee, I didn't even dream that, several years later, the last play performed there before it was torn down to make way for another office building would be my *The Time of the Cuckoo.* At its final performance, crammed in among the standees, I hugged the rail at the rear of the orchestra, pleased that our successful run had delayed demolition of that jewel box, if only for a few months. A very small place in theatre history, and only the history of theatre buildings, but I was happy to be part of it.

That double closing night was awash with the sentiment that doesn't embarrass theatre people. Shirley Booth—in her third and most triumphant appearance in a play of mine—was more nervous than on opening night but gave a far better performance. The audience of her peers went wild at the curtain calls; the audience of her fans went even wilder. Ornately framed pictures were yanked off the Empire's walls, gilded sconces were ripped out of their sockets; even the star dressing room door, covered with decades of autographs that were themselves a history of the theatre, was unscrewed and carted away.

Fans are unto themselves. Once, during the run, I was in the lobby of the Empire, waiting for Shirley as she signed an autograph. "This is the playwright," she said.

"Who cares?" said her fan.

The Met was home for Ballet Theatre's New York season. I was ushered through its backstage doors by Dwight Godwin, an ex-dancer in the company, now a photographer in my company at Astoria. There were always free ballet tickets at the USO but few takers, and I was not one of the takers. Free tickets to plays? Oh, yes, please! But except for *The Skin of Our Teeth,* which I saw three times, very little that was playing was worth seeing. The other reason I let Dwight pick up two freebies and drag me to Ballet Theatre at the Met was that merely walking through the lobby doors into a theatre excited me, and if there was the sound of an orchestra tuning up as we entered, I was thrilled. This time, it wasn't tuning up, it was playing when we walked in: an omen.

That first program featured Nora Kaye in Antony Tudor's *Pillar of Fire*—an almost unfair introduction to ballet. *Pillar* is a rare work of art and Nora Kaye was a unique artist with extraordinary emotional power. I was hooked—by Tudor, by Nora, by ballet as theatre, by the music, by the glamour, by the exacting combination of art and craft—hooked and knocked out, but not balletomaned. I loved language too much ever to be that.

Into my life came Nora Kaye and close behind, Jerome Robbins. Nora's contradictions bewildered me, though not the ballet world. She was a superb actress, a dramatic ballerina, internationally known as the Duse of the Dance. Opening night of *Pillar of Fire,* she took nineteen curtain calls. She was reading all of Proust since Tudor was going to make a modern ballet of *Swann's Way* (he never did), while simultaneously preparing her first *Giselle* to prove she was a classical ballerina.

The Duse of the Dance on tour with Ballet Theatre:
Nora Kaye flanked by Janet Reed and Muriel Bentley.

My favorite photograph of Nora Kaye, perhaps because I took it.

Then there was the Nora who loved to shop for any bargain, especially cut-rate furs, and was also known as the Red Ballerina. Her parents were born in Russia; her father came here for Amtorg, the Soviet Trade Commission; oddly, he was the balletomane, not her mother. Her high artistic standards came from him, her politics from her mother, her sharp intelligence from both.

Like most ballerinas, she walked like a duck; unlike most, she had slightly nasal New York speech and was a wickedly funny camp. She lived on Fifty-second Street in a walk-up over a jazz club across from the old Tony's (its bar was largely gay) which was a hangout where she loved to drink and laugh and listen to Mabel Mercer; or to Tony singing while standing on his head; or, on occasion, to a loaded Anna May Wong doing comic monologues in Chinese. It floored me to see how much Nora could drink, how much all the dancers could drink and still dance brilliantly the next night—until I learned most of them were on amphetamines to get through the season. Nora was so connected to Tudor and Hugh Laing, Tudor's strikingly handsome lover and her partner in Tudor ballets, that when Hugh walked into Tony's one night with a mynah bird on his shoulder, someone called out: "Now what have you done to Nora Kaye?" Her nickname for Hugh was "Huge Wang"; before going onstage, she touched it for luck.

Although she was married to Michael Van Buren, grandson of the president, she wore no wedding ring. He lived in Mexico for his asthma and his furniture company but once in Mexico was enough for Nora. At the time she and I were happiest in our affair, Michael came to New York to discuss divorce. Nora, who was not above behaving as though she was in one of her treasured MGM movies, arranged for the three of us to meet over tea at the St. Regis. Her circular brimmed hat was bigger than the table.

She usually denied it but she had a "hubby," as she would say, prior to Michael: at seventeen, she had married James T. Farrell, the author of the Studs Lonigan trilogy. One night and back she ran to her father. That was the most she would tell. I was fascinated by her from the first; I admired her, then I enjoyed her, then I loved her. Rupture occurred after quite a while and was never final.

Jerry Robbins was another matter. The change in Nora came very late. My affection and respect for her were diminished but both ran so deep, the slippage was not irreparable. The changes in Jerry could not have been as radical as they seemed; there must have been signs early on but I didn't see them.

Before *Fancy Free,* Black Jerome, as he came to be called, was fun—an imp with a high-pitched giggle who loved to play parlor games, the sillier the better. Shrewd and quick, highly intuitive, drawn to intelligence, to learning, and to talented others. An insecurity about his Hoboken origins and limited education contributed to a shyness, a sweetness.

When I would turn up backstage, he mystifyingly lit up, referred to me as a romantic figure, a "dark prince." Why he was so happy to see me I didn't understand. I liked him, I enjoyed him, but I wasn't at all attracted to him. I thought that was clear; I knew the importance of physical attraction was crystal clear to both of us. However, we became good friends and he called me "baby." As time went on, that's how I knew when we were friends—when Jerry called me "baby."

A model of the set for *A Clearing in the Woods* with
Kim Stanley who starred in it; Oliver Smith who designed and produced it;
and Joe Anthony who directed it and was afraid of both of them.

A small group of his ballet-world friends—Oliver Smith, the designer;
Leonard Bernstein, the Lenny; as well as dancers like Johnny Kriza and Muriel
Bentley—circled around Jerry without kowtowing to him. Everyone knew his
as yet unproven talent was real but he was also a natural leader; and again, he
was fun. Nora was and was not in the circle.

She had arrived in Tudor ballets; there was the understanding that she
belonged to Tudor and Hugh. But she and Jerry were closer: they shared being
Jewish and ambitious. The difference in the depth of their ambitions was a difference I was late in seeing. Not Nora; she must have seen it from the start, for
no one knew Jerry as well as she did. When he was debating whether or not to
become an informer for the House Un-American Committee, she advised him:

"Save yourself the agony. You're going to inform sooner or later, you might
as well do it now." And added to me, "He'd inform on his own mother."

That was her style: statements like that made flatly and factually but non-
judgmentally. If she colored them, it was only with humor. When Jerry did
inform, she merely shrugged as though to say, What else is new? And they
remained close friends, exemplifying a moral gap between Nora and me that

widened to include more than Jerry and informing or, later, Beverly Hills and tchotchkes. I suppose it was always there, the snake in our garden: I was too judgmental for her, she was too accepting for me. But it was more than that. When we became lovers, I asked her:

"Why don't you demand more?"

"What for?" she answered with the giggle that served as her cover.

Did that mean she accepted me as I was or that it would have been futile for her to ask for more? Or was she ensuring she got only as much as she wanted? We both preferred laughing and drinking to the frightening aspects of talking.

With *Fancy Free* came Jerry's early paranoia. His enormous overnight success was not to be enjoyed, certainly not to be shared. Success was the mother of his suspicion: everyone in ballet and/or on Broadway lusted to get something from him. Old friends and/or new lovers sought his friendship, his penis, his ass, his company only because he was a success. Success was good, though, success begets power: at an unexpected moment—everyone giggling, laughing, having fun playing one of those silly games—he would swivel his head to fix a beady eye on an old dressing room pal from the old circle. The old pal didn't know what he had done but he knew the meaning of that glare and became, then and forever, a scarified ass-kisser. Jerry's friends became acolytes on demand.

Suspicious people, of course, are the people to be suspicious of. I didn't want anything from Jerry but he wanted me to write a musical about the ballet with him, so he still called me "baby." I had not, for the moment, turned into a Palestinian. After *Fancy Free* he began to suspect everyone of being a Palestinian; it was hard for him to be anyone's friend because it was harder, if not impossible, for him to trust anyone.

His success had an odd, unexpected effect on me: it made me question whether my notions of art and artistic integrity weren't naive. *Fancy Free* was enormously enjoyable. I admired its inventiveness, its theatricality. Like Jerry himself, it was full of energy and vitality; it was funny, sexy, exuberant, and shrewd, perfectly timed for wartime. But was it more than a mini–Broadway musical? Weren't its slight characters and thin story ordinary musical comedy? And—a pointed question with perhaps too sharp a point—was it driven by anything other than a desire for success? Nora, Jerry, Tudor—especially Antony Tudor—these were artists who showed me art through ballet; I envied them their existence in art. Perhaps I was too unknowledgeable about ballet, ignorant even, so perhaps *Fancy Free* was art. But if it was, then wasn't the Broadway musical art? What was art, anyway?

. . .

Sutton Place had a little park on the river. I didn't sit there meditating the answers to these questions; I didn't even cruise there, I didn't have to. Nor were they in my mind when I went back to watch *Fancy Free* or why I went back. If, watching that ballet, I'd had a question about art, it might well have been, Is sex art? Because the reason I returned again and again was Harold Lang, one of the three sailors and the best sex I'd ever had. He was the sailor with the ingratiating boyish grin and the white pants molded to Nobel-worthy buttocks. How could the answer to "What is art?" compare to Harold Lang's ass?

He came from California, was of Mexican descent, originally with a bad nose and bad acne—not a winning combination in the homosexual lottery. Desperate to be held, he went to bed with anyone who wanted him and discovered he was mad about sex—the best way to become good at it and Harold was better than good. Add that to a new name, a new nose, and incredibly clear white skin—bingo, eureka, excelsior, open sesame! And joy to the world, which he was. Desired and had by as many as he wanted—and he wanted hordes, but he only wanted them sexually. Emotionally, he gave himself to no one which, as the night follows the day, made him more desirable. Inevitably, also as the nights follow the days, turn is turnabout. Once, without preface, when we were drinking by candlelight, listening to Judy Garland—yes, but who better?—Harold asked, "You could never be in love with me, could you?" The question was rhetorical. In that way, he was like Nora.

No one suspected that anyone who partied as much as Harold did and drank so much (he died of alcoholism) could be as ambitious as Jerry and Nora, but he was. Coolly objective about his limitations in ballet—his body was more perfect for sex—he began howling in vacant lots to strengthen his vocal chords as he took endless lessons: in how to sing off the vocal chord, in acting, speech, tap. To say he "worked his ass off" would be inappropriate in his case (and unfortunate), but the hard work paid off: he starred on Broadway in a successful revival of *Pal Joey*. His last Broadway appearance was in 1961, when I cast him in *I Can Get It for You Wholesale*, which I directed. Whether Harold told anyone else of his ambitions, I don't know. I do know he never told anyone about us, nor did I. I was overlapping him with Nora Kaye.

Being gay mattered to me, not to her, not to anyone in that ballet world. It made absolutely no difference there. Diana Adams, a beautiful ballerina, had an affair with Hugh Laing with Tudor's blessing, and Tudor was not only Hugh's lover, he was his choreographer. Ballerinas and would-be ballerinas fell or thought they fell in love with their gay onstage partners. Occasionally, they got lucky and got them into bed; once or twice, they even married. Most of the boys, though, were open and out and saw absolutely no reason to be otherwise. Nor did anyone want or expect them to be. As acceptable as the straights in the company (a minority), they were uncomplicated and healthy. It wasn't as simple for the girls: convention was reserved for lesbianism. It had to be furtive, hidden, concealed, even denied when a female choreographer and her favorite ballerina were caught in flagrante.

Later, in my screenplay for *The Turning Point,* I wrote a gay subplot without commenting on it: I wanted to let the audience decide. I felt strongly that it was important and deluded myself that I had embedded it so deeply in the story that it couldn't be removed or weakened without weakening the film. Herb Ross, the director and coproducer with me, told me not to worry, he'd handle the studio. When the gay elements began to be sanitized, I assumed it was the studio; when shooting got under way and I was on the set, I saw it was Herbie.

He was married to Nora who was no longer dancing; she was more interested in houses and Beverly Hills status than in ballet and artists. Their polyurethaned house was replete with Beverly Hillsian features: a cutting room built on to the pool house, the inevitable lanai and powder rooms whose toilets were difficult to find because they were covered with the same wallpaper as the walls. That bamboo-and-chintz lanai was the scene of an almost farcical confrontation. I detailed some of the emasculations in the screenplay, the ones I felt truly important. Herb took a drag on the cigarette in his holder and held that hand out toward me, palm up, fingers curled.

"Nobody in the ballet is gay anymore," he said.

I looked at Nora; just looked, no overdramatic eyebrows or open mouth. She had begged me to write a picture about the ballet; *Turning Point* was the picture, I had written it to please her. She and Herb and I had known one another intimately for over twenty-five years. Intimately: who, what, where, when—all of it. And each of us knew exactly what was going on now and exactly why.

Nora flushed and giggled. "It's like walking on eggs around here," she said in that nasal tone she always employed to lighten the atmosphere, and left the room. My hopes for the picture went with her. So did a piece of my respect.

After the *Fancy Free* season, when Ballet Theatre went off on tour, I was left at the station with a feeling new to me: missing someone. I missed Nora. I missed Harold, but there were sexual replacements for him if I chose. There was no replacement for Nora. And the desire to be with her was increasing almost in direct proportion to the desire for sex as sex was diminishing.

The radio plays I was writing were stronger, praise was louder, but my discontent with the medium was sharper. I was impatient with not extending my horizons as Jerry and Harold were extending theirs, with continually talking about writing the play everyone thought I was writing while continually going to another party and another. It was safer to be promising.

Then a sentence was spoken exactly when I needed to hear it. The speaker was Martin Gabel, an actor-producer who had started with Orson Welles, looked like a foreshortened, stubby Welles and spoke in a Welles-like plummy basso with a Mid-Atlantic accent until he got drunk. Then he'd announce he was from Pittsburgh and laugh before anyone else could.

"My dear boy," he said to me basso profundo, "if you don't stop coming to these parties, you'll never write that play."

It was all in the timing, the most necessary element in just about everything. The next night, I took a photograph out of the drawer I had kept it in for months and began writing a play. For nine consecutive nights, I stayed home and wrote a scene a night until I finished *Home of the Brave,* a play in nine scenes.

I don't boast of the speed. The play rushed out because of a desperate need to write to validate myself. How fast didn't concern me any more than arriving while still under thirty. That was considered a major achievement by some; to me, it was irrelevant. The achievement was the work.

The photograph in the drawer, the photograph that started *Home of the Brave,* was an army shot of some GIs in a South Pacific jungle looking at the mutilated body of a buddy. The faces of the boys, the specifics of the mutilation were difficult to see. No details, no information came with the photo. With the certainty of the amateur, I had always sworn I would never write a play set outdoors—the sets are unconvincing, obviously painted, patently fake. Nor would I ever write a play with a same-gender cast—too limiting, no variety, no sexual tension(!). But that photograph haunted me. I pilfered it from the army files and kept it in my drawer. I didn't know why I knew it was a play but I did.

It wrote fast, in part because the characters, the language, and the situations were similar to those I'd been writing forever in the army radio shows. The theatrical device that frames the action, narcosynthesis (the injection of sodium pentothol to obtain the truth), I had researched in an army hospital. I'd never used it in a script, but it too haunted me, it too was waiting.

My first question about a play was, What is it about? That came from John Howard Lawson's Marxist *Theory and Technique of Playwriting.* What *Home of the Brave* was about was simple: Underneath, we are all the imperfect same. I

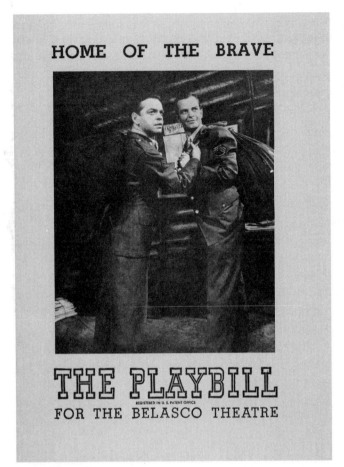

HOME OF THE BRAVE

THE PLAYBILL
REGISTERED IN U. S. PATENT OFFICE
FOR THE BELASCO THEATRE

Joe Pevney, who went on to become a Hollywood director, and Alan Baxter, from the Group Theatre, played the leads.

dramatized this by showing that any soldier who sees the man next to him get shot instantly thinks: I'm glad it wasn't me. Never having been in combat or near a shooting, I didn't know where I got that. It was true, though, and it always has been: it's what every soldier thinks at that moment.

For dramatic conflict, I needed a reason for my soldier-hero to feel guilty that he'd been glad it wasn't he who'd been shot. And so he became a Jew named Coney who thought his buddy Finch was about to call him a "yellow Jew boy" just before Finch was shot. A valid reason to make Coney feel glad Finch was shot, and then feel guilty that he had felt glad.

Innocently and unintentionally, I clouded my theme by using epithets uglier than "yellow Jew boy" in scenes of blatant bigotry never before seen or heard on the Broadway stage. They were so harsh, they stuck out so glaringly that *Home of the Brave* emerged for too many as simply an angry play about anti-Semitism.

Proof that it wasn't about that came late, as it usually does, and from an

odd source: the movies. In the screen adaptation produced by Stanley Kramer, the Jew was changed to a Negro. When I asked why, Stanley replied: "Jews have been done." He was referring to the movie *Gentleman's Agreement,* in which Gregory Peck played a gentile (no stretch) pretending to be a Jew (only in the movies). The picture's moral was Be nice to a Jew because he might turn out to be a gentile.

The film version of *Home of the Brave* was highly acclaimed and was a commercial hit. Not a critic, not a vocal soul was bothered that there were no racially integrated units in the Army like the one in the picture. It was a movie.

Where was I in *Home of the Brave*? The hero is a Jew, I was a Jew. He is confronted by anti-Semitism, but what Jew isn't? He is overly sensitive—was I? He has a big chip on his shoulder—did I? Or did I, as playwright, theatricalize the character?

The play has an echo of the moment in the barracks at Fort Monmouth when Bob Hopkins punched our anti-Semitic sergeant. That echo puzzled and troubled me. Onstage, the soldiers are in a tight, confined space in a clearing in the jungle; the men are close to each other. The non-com calls Coney a "lousy yellow Jew bastard"; Coney's buddy Finch punches the non-com and Coney just stands there. In life, in the large barracks room, I was one of three or four Jews; the sergeant was several beds away from me and Bob Hopkins was standing next to him. But Bob Hopkins wasn't a Jew and I didn't even move. Why didn't I?

Throughout the play, there are specific connections with my life that are readily apparent. A line, for example, said by hero Coney to best friend Finch—"I never met any Jewish boys til I got in the Army"—is instantly traceable to freshman year at Cornell. I'm standing at the marble urinals of the Ithaca Hotel next to a tall blond Aryan who will become my best friend for four not-very-happy years. "You're the first Jew I've ever seen," Alan Willson says. He came from Canandaigua in upstate New York, where it was well known that Jews had horns.

Another speech by that hero whose closeness to me is elusive. Coney says, "I heard something in the middle of the night once. Some drunken bum across the hall from my aunt's yelling: Throw out the dirty sheenies. That was us. I was used to it by then. What the hell, I was ten. That's old for a Jew."

"Sheeny" wasn't yelled from across the hall but I was ten when I heard it.

I am standing on the sidewalk under a huge sycamore heavy with leaves, waiting for a trolley car on Ocean Avenue in Brooklyn. A car races by, a man yells "Sheeny!" at me. The word is new, I don't know what it means but I know it's a slur meant to hurt a Jew. How? How did he know I was a Jew? Brooklyn

is the City of Churches, the neighborhood is not ethnic, I was in shadow. How could he know? They just know, I decided, they know and they don't like you because you're Jewish.

I carried "sheeny" with me until I put it in my first play.

The trolley line soon took me to high school, my father's alma mater— Erasmus Hall! It warrants the exclamation point because Erasmus was grand and formal and unexpected in the middle of an ordinary Brooklyn neighborhood. Its campus resembled that of a small Ivy League college: a large stone archway provided a dramatic entrance to Gothic stone buildings, a grassy quadrangle governed by a statue of Erasmus, and the ivy-covered walls of a stone chapel with stained-glass windows. The stained-glass figures made me wonder why a public school had a chapel.

I was drifting off, gazing at those figures through the open windows of French class one gauzy spring afternoon, the teacher's drone barely filtering through. Miss Desmarais was dumpy, with puffy cheeks and puffy white hair, always covered to her chins in a puffed-out dress of what I called bombazine because I liked the word and it seemed probable. I was only vaguely aware her French drone had shifted to irritated English when I heard:

"You [something] never pay attention. You [something] always spoil my class. You Jews poison the air."

Of the other four poisoners, I remember only Miss Kleinman with her annoyingly perfect Palmer penmanship at the blackboard. We all sat very still, caught like gnats in amber until Marian Hall, a minister's daughter, stood up and marched out of the classroom down to the principal's office. As we later learned, Marian turned in Miss Desmarais who was summoned and suspended.

When Miss Desmarais returned to class to mumble her apology (in French), a large cotton-and-gauze bandage was taped over her left eye. Marian was biblically triumphant: Miss Desmarais had been struck blind by the Lord. I was uncomfortable but relieved they didn't know it was all my fault: I hadn't been paying attention and I was a Jew.

Age fourteen, in new long trousers, I again wait for the trolley in that same spot on Ocean Avenue early one evening. This time, I'm trying to thumb a ride to Marian Hall's party, where we're going to play Post Office and Spin the Bottle despite her father, the minister. A nifty sports car stops for me. The door opens: snap-brim hat, collegiate collar ad. His hand finds my knee, then my crotch, then takes out my thing. An appreciative *Mmmmm.* My handker-

chief is ready in time. But how did he know? They just know, I decided, they know and they like you—well, they like your thing.

That, of course, doesn't turn up in *Home of the Brave,* but homosexuality does—unintentionally. Finch and Coney's relationship is homosexual; the portrayal is psychologically accurate but unconscious on the author's part. Had I realized that the friendship could be construed that way, I would have worked overtime to clean it out.

An agent recommended by Jerry Robbins found a producer for the play. Not Herman Shumlin or the Theatre Guild or any royal I'd hoped for, but Lee Sabinson—the Humpty-Dumpty in the brown suit that was his good suit. He wore it to our first meeting: lunch, not at Sardi's as I had always imagined before going to sleep, but at a little Italian restaurant with tablecloths that were not unclean but not white, either. Lee was enthusiastic and decent, immediately likable, dabbing at the film of sweat on his beaming moon face. But when he lowered his voice reverentially and said he would be "honored to be allowed to produce *Home of the Brave,*" my heart did a little flip-flop. Surely he knew how many producers had rejected the play, surely he knew how badly I wanted any producer. "Honored"? Something was wrong.

He invited me to dinner at his home which wasn't the house I had imagined, either. It was an apartment in a noisy high-rise on Queens Boulevard in Queens. No drinks. Dinner cooked and served by his wife Billie on a gateleg table opened out for the occasion. My seat was on the daybed/sofa. Both Lee and Billie were sweet, kind; friends of Karl Marx and the Common Man but they weren't Lawrence Langner and Armina Marshall of the Theatre Guild. It wasn't that I was a snob, it was a sixth sense telling me something was wrong. Exactly what became clear as Lee launched into a lecture on the State of the Theatre. Translation: He didn't have the money to produce the play. He wasn't bothered; he was convinced he would get the money. I pretended he convinced me. I wanted him to be able to produce the play for him as well as for me. And for Billie. She loved Lee, she believed in Lee. "He'll come up with it," she said as she cleared the table and offered little colored after-dinner mints.

Lee scraped up enough money, God knows how, to formally option the play, hire a director, and start casting. The casting director, Jane Broder, was the best in the theatre, known for refusing to handle a play unless she really liked it. That was more encouraging than Lee's front money. She really liked *Home of the Brave,* she liked me, she more than liked the young actor she had found to play Finch. So did I.

He was sitting in her reception room reading the script the first time I saw him. He looked up, he smiled, and I knew fantasy was going to become fact.

Unbelievably, it was mutual; more unbelievably, it would happen. He was everything the role and I wanted. Including pure in heart.

He doesn't want his named used so I'll call him Randall West. He never did play Finch in *Home of the Brave.* Before Lee got the money, Randall was snapped up by Hollywood for a career that started high in a serious picture adapted from a respected Broadway hit but all too soon went into a mud-slide beginning with a movie where he wore a white Eisenhower dinner jacket in the Far East. That sent him into psychoanalysis. Before the couch, Randall radiated sweetness and modesty but lacked the aggressiveness he thought necessary for tackling a movie career. Acting ability, he assumed he had a-plenty. A little analysis did make him aggressive but so much so that he became hostile without realizing it. Directors and producers turned away. He quit acting, became a psychologist, and got married.

Several years later, I was on the Coast for the Oscars. Randall called my hotel—there'd been some publicity in the papers. Could we have a drink? We could—curiosity more than anything else. Aggressiveness was now the least of it; he had added arrogance and smugness. As soon as I politely could, I apologized for needing an immediate nap before facing the long evening ahead. "Right!" exclaimed the licensed psychologist, and jumped up and went down on me. I didn't accuse him of hypocrisy but I didn't stop him, either.

Lee Sabinson had to postpone production while he went digging for gold. He postponed again. And again. The fear common to playwrights metastasized: "The play will never get on!" Randall was in Hollywood but Nora was back in town and I introduced her to the Sabinsons. She had a marvelous knack for suiting her behavior to the people and the occasion. With Lee and Billie Sabinson, she was the Red Ballerina with bunions. With my parents at dinner at their apartment in Brooklyn, she was the simple, unspoiled artist, so much so that I got nervous. I waited for her dry humor to come out of the closet and out it came. She began flirting with my father, joked about retaining him to handle her divorce from her "hubby south of the border." Hubby? South of the border? A Mexican? No, no, a president's grandson. Impressive—but the undisputed fact was that Nora was a married woman.

My mother, whose color was normally high, went vermilion—a giveaway that she had confided in her two dearest friends, who were also at the dinner, that Nora and I were going to get married. But to a divorcée? A divorcée in the family? My poor mother. Nora was oblivious, too delighted with her new conquest—my father.

She and I had actually begun to talk marriage soon after we began having sex. Adequate sex. I loved her as much as I could love someone I wasn't physically attracted to. Her ballerina's body was too much like a boy's for me. Even Harold had more curves, more flesh to hold on to. And when he and I saw each other, we wanted each other no matter who else was on the scene for either of us. The power of sex? Yes, and a wonderful power it is. Randall was writing and calling from the Coast, which was flattering but without as much of that power as Harold had. Once he phoned in the middle of sex with Nora and I made the mistake of answering the phone. That deflated that moment. Nora didn't know Who but she intuited Why.

"I wouldn't mind if you were unfaithful with a woman," she said, "but a man, I can't compete with."

For me, it was both more and less complicated. To be unfaithful to her with a man left me with disgust at my immorality. Yet what stood in the way of marrying her was fearing—no, knowing—I would be unfaithful to her with a man. I didn't believe the ability to have sex with women made me heterosexual or that the fault to enjoy it fully was Nora's body.

In Hollywood a very few years later, I began an affair with Anita Ellis, as extraordinary a jazz singer as Nora was a ballerina. But also an extraordinary sexual partner. I didn't tell Nora; I knew better than to test her disclaimer that another woman wouldn't bother her.

Anita had an incredibly beautiful body; she brought no baggage to bed; she knew all about me (and the affair I was having with Farley Granger then) and didn't care. That made our times in bed free and glorious. Our times out of bed were less so. She was so openly accepting, I was embarrassed. I suspected she liked the setup. Which made me complicit and I didn't like that. There was really no way I would let myself win with myself.

Loving Nora was always contradictory: it gave me a new security and yet upset me. I had never loved anyone. To be linked as Arthur-and-Nora made me feel I belonged and made me proud because Nora was an extraordinary being even without the dancing. That she loved me made me prouder, so I tried to love her more than I did. I wanted Arthur-and-Nora to be more than we were.

My friends in radio and the theatre were friendlier when I became half of a couple: their doors opened wider. I understood why. I was grateful for acceptance but not being good at self-deception, I disliked myself for being grateful, for being angry at why their doors were open wider, for leaving my own door still open for Harold and Randall and others, for being so insatiable, so greedy. I sensed I was driving down a potholed road to a breakdown.

The end of that road came in sight at Pilgrim State on Long Island, an army hospital for psychoneurotics while I was still a sergeant for Uncle Sam. I checked in for a few days of research for an upcoming *Assignment Home* script. Only two top officers were aware of my true status. I slept in a big dormitory with shell-shocked soldiers in real trouble. I roamed the halls with them and played crazy card games with them. I stood in line with them in the morning when pills were handed out (I palmed them) and in the evening when they were doped for the night. I began to fit in too easily, so easily I began to wonder whether I didn't belong there.

Serving pills was the extent of the psychiatric treatment. The staff were so ignorant, they allowed the USO to "entertain the boys" with a performance of Noël Coward's *Blithe Spirit*. When the stage lights dimmed for the first séance and the ghost wife appeared, the screams from the battle-damaged GIs were horrifying. The men scuttled to hide under the wooden benches from shells and grenades they could hear coming to blow them apart. The attendants gave them more medication.

In the middle of that night, I was awakened by a hand on my thigh, moving over the covers to my crotch. I froze in stark terror. He was big, rawboned, blond, attractive; his eyes pleaded like a dog's. I mouthed "Tomorrow" and stayed absolutely still, almost not breathing, waiting. An eternity. At last he nodded, patted my crotch gently in farewell and crept carefully across the aisles to his own bed.

The next day, he talked as we walked around and around, keeping to the mumbling halls so that no one could hear him. He was pathetically eager to talk but words came haltingly. He gulped air, he stuttered; he had held back for so long but now he had someone it was safe to tell. He was from rural Pennsylvania, hadn't finished high school, was not smart but smart enough to palm the pills because he didn't want to die a vegetable. He had survived he didn't know how many battles and had seen he didn't know how many buddies killed or maimed. But neither battles nor buddies nor war was why he was at Pilgrim State. For more than two years, he'd been celibate, had never touched another man, had fought his raging desire for a cock until finally his nerves cracked. The Army thought it was shell shock. At this point in the telling, his legs began to shake so badly, he had to sit down. He was terrified that what he'd attempted the night before he would attempt again and this time, be caught and sent to Leavenworth.

When it was dark enough that evening, we had sex in the bushes on the grounds of the hospital. Afterward, he cried and thanked me. He felt safe, sure now he could hold out til he was discharged. I was sure of nothing. I knew I hadn't done it entirely to help him, I knew I was crazy to have done it at all, I knew I had to stop doing it with men or I would end up permanently in Pilgrim State—but wasn't I there anyway?

Paranoia struck incrementally: the top brass had completely forgotten I was in Pilgrim State only temporarily; I deserved to stay there permanently and would. I would never get out. Never, and nobody would know because I was mad. I was in a state of total, irrational terror.

From a phone booth, I called William Menninger. He was the head of Army Psychiatry in Washington and had originally arranged for me to get into Pilgrim to do the research for *Assignment Home.* When we met in his office, he was amazingly straightforward and clear. His ideas were so advanced—malingerers (goldbricks), for example, should be discharged, not jailed; he was so approachable and compassionate, I had confessed to him I was homosexual. He discussed it as the Army's problem, not mine.

I got through to him easily and the moment I heard his voice, I calmed down a bit. He could undoubtedly hear the terror in my voice, for he kept talking, assuring me I was not forgotten and would get out, discussing my options when I did. He was a truly great doctor but the Army didn't listen; they weren't in favor of the purpose of Menninger's profession: to change.

In my more than four years in the Army, I'd never taken the furlough Menninger recommended. My radio show colonel/boss was reluctant to give me one but agreed. It was March, it was cold, it was bleak. I drove up to the Cape—which was senseless but in my state made sense to me: a seasonal hair shirt. On colder, bleaker Nantucket, where I'd never been, my room in the bed-and-breakfast had a linoleum floor like the linoleum floor of the whorehouse in Elmira, New York, I was taken to at sixteen, in my freshman year at Cornell, to lose my virginity. (I didn't because I wasn't up to it.)

The next morning, as I walked down Nantucket's main street, a voice hailed from the general store: Gottfried Reinhardt, on his honeymoon with Silvia. They insisted I come back to their rented cottage for lunch. It must have looked better in summer but the Reinhardts weren't bothered. They had come for a purpose, they were there on a mission. On the living room floor were piled stacks of books on Alcoholism and Brain Damage, How to Stop Drinking, How to Save Your Liver. Silvia went to find the right glasses for the absolutely last, final, farewell batch of dry martinis, which Gottfried was stirring in a huge pitcher. It wasn't even noon. Without any excuse, without a polite word, I walked out of the room and fled Nantucket.

In New York the next morning, I ran into Frances Chaney, my closest leftist friend since Eve Merriam had married. It had been rough for Frances when her husband, David Lardner, was blown up in Europe; then she married his brother Ring, Jr. She was in many of the *Assignment Home* plays, excellent at playing warm, endearing, compassionate women, women like Frances herself.

Slavic cheekbones, my sister's auburn hair—she was so lovely. Not one question why I was so desperate for help, just a list of psychoanalysts to call. It could have been a list of witch doctors. I knew nothing about them either and I trusted Frances completely.

It was illegal to go to a doctor outside the Army. I also knew that if the brass found out my reason for wanting psychiatric help, they'd heave me out with a dishonorable discharge. I didn't care, I was willing to take the risk. I didn't know what I was looking for, I had no frame of reference, I knew nothing about psychoanalysis, so I auditioned seven analysts. The analyst I did choose—I thought he resembled my father—couldn't take me. Like a bird dog, I ran back to the one I had a sense would do me in, and he almost did. His name was Theodor Reik.

A recent refugee from Vienna, analyzed by Freud himself, Reik named his son Arthur for papa's best friend, Arthur Schnitzler. Arthur Reik, therefore, had to be a writer. But Arthur Reik didn't respond to Schnitzler or his father. The world, as any fool knows, moves in not-so-wonderful, mysterious ways, and in Reik's new world, along came another Arthur who did want to be a writer—Arthur Laurents, poor shmuck. Reik, in his thick German accent (somehow Japanese in my imitations), exploded with joy: "I vill make you ze greatest playwright in America!" Then, less joy and an admonition: "But you are too zelfish!" Yes, yes, I am, I am! How can I atone? "You can give me ten perzent of vot you make." Take, take! He took.

The free association he insisted I perform dredged up a memory that brought trouble to analytic paradise, a memory of awakening in the middle of the night when I was six or seven. I had to pee and on my way to the bathroom at the end of the hall, I looked down the stairs. Fierce, hard, threatening eyes glared up at me; I scurried back to bed. I had seen a burglar. Reik disagreed contemptuously. "A screen memory," he diagnosed, explaining that what I had really seen at the bottom of the stairs was my parents having intercourse.

I saw my parents doing it? My parents? Oh, I doubted that. Reik airily dismissed my doubt: the patient always doubts, the truth is too embarrassing and too shameful to admit. The shaman knew. It made sense that I might not want to admit that my parents did it. From there, I moved on to Well, all right, I might have seen them doing it; from there to, I guess I did see them; to Yes, I saw them. But then common sense induced a minor rebellion. I couldn't have seen them: a baby grand was at the bottom of those stairs. My parents could not have been doing it on top of a piano! Ada and Irving on top of a baby grand? Never!

I now clearly remembered the house really had been robbed that night, there had been a burglar. I did the analysis of the "screen memory" myself. Scared to death at seeing the burglar, I had run back to bed without waking the household as I should have. The memory persisted because I was ashamed of having been a coward.

"Prezisely!" Reik exclaimed triumphantly.

To the victims of abuse, add reclining figures on couches. What I didn't analyze for him was the connection between my not moving against the burglar and not moving against the bigot in the barracks at Fort Monmouth and Coney's not moving in the *Home of the Brave* jungle. I didn't deliberately keep it from him, I just didn't make the connection then myself. The discoveries that I thought I behaved like a coward or even that I was a coward, that Coney in *Home of the Brave* was a coward, that that part of Coney was me, those discoveries only came together when the play was produced. "Coward, take my coward's hand" had more meaning than intended.

Reik's main interest, and mine, was my sexuality. Unlike me, he had neither ambivalence nor doubt: I was heterosexual. All my problems would fall away once I became exclusively heterosexual. He had only one small problem: to convince me. He set about that by imparting details of the sex life of other patients, one in particular: a young editor at *The New Yorker* who was making great progress in crossing over into the sexual majority which was desirable, of course. That the editor's pattern of going on the hunt for sailors and rough trade was very different from mine, Reik ignored. A homosexual was a homosexual was a homosexual: adolescent, masturbational, temporary. Just get it up for females, keep it down for males; piece of cake. The poor frightened boys are basically straight. I, too, was straight as a die, straight as an arrow, straight as John Wayne—well, there were tales about Wayne (real name Marion) and look at his walk—but he was straight and basically, inherently, so was I. Which was devoutly to be wished. Life would be so much easier—and it would be. I could have Nora. I didn't think: And I could have a wife and children. Just: And I could have Nora. Proof of the possibility existed: the editor had found a girl, he married her, he succeeded. Not alone, not on his own but aided in the achievement of what had once seemed impossible by the man sitting in the chair behind me, the same man who had asked me, "Why do you keep turning around?" and I had answered, "Because I'm afraid you're going to kick me in the head." Prescient?

The newly married editor took me to lunch around the corner from his magazine. He was happy to do that, to encourage, to help. He was the most gentle of men: delicately humorous, kind, intelligent, and above all gentle, amazingly gentle. I wanted to ask how much Reik had told him about me, I wanted to talk openly for the first time about my sexuality with a person, not a professional. The opportunity to talk to another male who had been where I was and gotten to where this sympathetic, compassionate man sitting across the table had gotten was a godsend. Yet I didn't ask anything, not one thing. I was awed and impressed by the Harvard Club, by *The New Yorker,* but what muted me above all was that he was so overwhelmingly gentle. John Cheever once described him and his wife as "two does emerging reluctantly from the woods." He did have the eyes of a doe; it was impossible for me to look into them and mention sex of any kind, even to say the word itself. To do so would have been improper, if not offensive. We talked writing and reading, about his wife and about Nora, never about what was sitting there on the table between us: sex.

I didn't realize it was unethical of Reik to relate intimate sexual details of other patients or even to introduce us to one another. I didn't know the rules of psychoanalysis, I talked little about it to anyone although Anthony Tudor told me it would ruin my talent. But even if I had been told flat out Reik was unethical, I wouldn't have cared. I would have said he was unorthodox and pointed to the miraculous proof of what he had achieved. I didn't know what a transference was but I had a beaut.

Then Lee Sabinson got the money to produce *Home of the Brave.* The war was over; peace was not an auspicious time for a war play but he did get the money. It was named William Katzell and got us a theatre, the Belasco. That got us black farce: gangsters running up and down the aisles and backstage during rehearsals.

Lee's last Broadway production, *Trio,* had been thrown out of the Belasco. It was a good play with only three characters. One and a half of them, alas, were lesbians, which sent the Catholic Church foaming at the font. The Cardinal demanded the city close *Trio;* the city kissed the ring, closed the show, and the Belasco's lessor lost his lease. He vowed revenge on Lee Sabinson; midway through rehearsals, he regained his lease.

His lawyers moved immediately to throw us out of the theatre but *immediately* is a word unknown in the legal process. So gangsters were hired to break Lee's legs in the meantime. Not to be intimidated, Lee and Katzell hired gangsters of their own to break the other gangsters' legs. The aisles became running minefields, constantly interrupting rehearsals.

All this activity was one more problem Michael Gordon, our director, didn't need. A Group Theatre alumnus of limited standing, he was determined to make Harold Clurman and Lee Strasberg regret they had underused him. Neither the Group nor the Method, unfortunately, had prepared him for dealing with gangsters who had no subtext. Or for a fellow alumnus in the cast who remembered him as an underling in the Group and treated him as one.

Or for dealing with my complaint that he was looking too hard for subtext where there wasn't any and blind to it where there was. I thought the play was getting heavy and portentous. My writing was elliptical: I trusted the audience to hear what was unsaid, Mike didn't. The closer we got to the first public performance, the less patience he had for the gangsters, the playwright, the producers, the actors, and finally, the designer. At dress rehearsal, a window shade fired the shot that started the war.

Ralph Alswang's revolving sets were stunning but he lit them himself to supplement his design, not the director's blocking. The first scene, in the doctor's office in a Quonset hut, had a bed beneath an open window. Ralph had the shade up, allowing his tropical sun to pour in from his jungle, visible outside. Mike wanted the room dark when the doctor began narcosynthesis. He ordered the stage manager to pull down the shade. The scene was barely under way when Ralph's long, lanky figure emerged from the jungle to reach into the room and pull the shade up. Mike sent a gofer with a message for Jimmy Gelb, stage manager: the shade went down. A few more lines and a long bony hand reached around the corner of the Quonset hut to pull the shade up from outside. Mike bellowed to Jimmy: the shade went down. Several more lines, then a coconut tree began to shake: a skinny figure was crawling on his belly over the jungle floor, a hand reached up to the shade, which shot up with a snapping rattle. At that, Mike shot out of his seat, screamed to the world and kept screaming as he ran up the aisle, out of the Belasco, into the night. The producers were out scrambling for "end money," Jimmy was eager for time to rehearse scene changes with the understudies, and there I was.

Chutzpah is sometimes desirable; when you're young, you don't even know it is chutzpah. I had read Stanislavsky on Acting and George Bernard Shaw on Directing; I knew the rhythms of the dialogue; I knew what was to be thrown away, what was to be pointed up; I was articulate and I wasn't afraid of the actors. Egged on by Jimmy, who had his money on me, I seated the cast in the big dressing room that served as their greenroom and as they went through the play, I clarified and simplified, helping them make their moments. I had the sense to thank each actor individually for making his character more than I, the author, had imagined. Given compliments and some freedom, they thought I knew what I was doing. I was in a daze.

In that era, it was ritual to take a play out of town for two or three weeks of testing and polishing, but there wasn't enough money even to preview *Home of the Brave* in town for a week. Only three previews could be afforded and the first was almost the last. The Anti-Defamation League came to it and threatened to picket because the play was anti-Semitic. But it was against anti-Semitism, wasn't that clear? Yes—but. But what? But the Jewish hero was neurotic. To portray a Jew as neurotic is anti-Semitic; ergo, the play was anti-

Semitic. This from a group we thought were our friends: liberals and progressives we had counted on for theatre parties! This was, however, the Anti-Defamation League, which ipso facto had to be correct politically.

Panic. The producers canceled the second preview and came quivering to me with red and yellow pencils. I was bewildered. I couldn't understand the brouhaha. I thought the hero behaved as he did because that was how Jews behaved in the face of the prejudice the ADL itself was always battling. And what if he was neurotic?

I didn't think he was, though. He was very sensitive and defensive about being Jewish—but was that neurotic? I didn't think so then. What I think now is expressed in a speech from *My Good Name,* the third in my recent quartet of plays. The central character says: "I'm Pavlov's Jewish dog. When the bell rings, I come out fighting. I think that's what any Jew worth being a Jew does." I know a producer who thinks that's neurotic; maybe the ADL would, too. I don't.

Mike had come back to see the first preview. He made a few cuts to appease the ADFL but the actors sensibly refused to rehearse the substantial changes he and the producers wanted. Not on political grounds: it was simply too late. They pulled themselves through the second and final preview, then did what good actors can do, and when they do, a playwright is forever grateful: they came through and performed so magnificently on opening night that the audience was on its feet and cheering, and I was lifted onto the stage for a bow. Standing ovations were rare in 1945, but there was Jimmy Gelb's moon: Was it out or not? I knew—how I knew, I don't know, but I knew—that on that opening night the moon was not out.

The reviews were mixed—a terminal word that meant in this case that Lewis Nichols in *The New York Times* was equivocal. Brooks Atkinson, so generous to me in my later work, was in China, alas. All the same, the play created a stir. It drew enthusiastic, if modest, audiences, and notables like Thornton Wilder, Montgomery Clift, and Harold Clurman who wanted to meet me; I won an award from the American Academy of Arts and Letters and shared the Sidney Howard Playwriting Award with Garson Kanin (for *Born Yesterday*); and George Jean Nathan, John Simon's predecessor, wrote that I was "the most overrated dramatist of the year." I was flattered by that, I hadn't thought anyone noticed. The prestigious Drama Critics Circle Award went to *State of the Union* by Howard Lindsay and (my nemesis) Russel Crouse, and *Home of the Brave* closed after sixty-nine performances. Seventy, if you count the two that were given simultaneously closing night: the box office sold the house out twice. The second audience jammed the aisles and hugged the walls upstairs and down, and when the final final curtain came down, everybody rose and roared as though we had won the World Series. But it was over; my first play was finished; the roars died down very quickly and there was hardly an echo.

The opening night party at the beery tavern next door to the theatre was like dinner on Billie Sabinson's gateleg table: no more the stuff of theatre dreams than the reviews were. Some were glowing, some qualified; it was all over too fast. A smile congealed on my mother's face. I kissed her, bringing tears that annoyed me. My father said, "Bad timing, but it's a good play." He watched the party stagger to a halt but would not leave until I did. I left earlier than I should have because I couldn't bear to look at the disappointment for me in my father's eyes and my mother's smile for her friends.

Opening nights, particularly dismal ones, are great occasions for substance abuse but I barely finished my drink at that fizzling opening night party. The remainder of the night, spent with Randall at his hotel, was also more or less a fizzle. He was generous with compassion for the playwright, less so for the below-par lover. Which was understandable. He was primed, he had flown all the way from California and in 1945 that was a long, bumpy flight. I tried but as with everything else that night, I couldn't quite make it come off. *Home of the Brave* hadn't succeeded but it hadn't failed, either. What was disheartening was not so much that its disappearance seemed imminent but that as the night went on I decided it was deserved.

No matter how well or how badly a play is received initially by critics or public, time is always the true arbiter. I knew that. I knew all about the long view; I tried to hold on to it. The movie sale was encouraging; so was an offer from London but to me *Home of the Brave* was a flop and I wasn't much of a playwright.

A week after opening night, I flew to Chicago, where Nora was dancing with Ballet Theatre. I brought *The New Yorker* to read on the plane. In the front was a listing of what was on in the theatre—and there it was: "*Home of the Brave* by Arthur Laurents." I looked at the few lines, the small print; I stared at the listing, I read it over and over. Same type, same size as the other plays by the other playwrights: I was listed with my peers. I, too, was a writer of plays. Even though the moon hadn't come out, I was considered a playwright among playwrights. The feeling that flooded me was like no other; it expanded my chest, it showed me where happiness was to be found. I was proud and that listing, small as it was, was the encouragement I needed to go on and try again.

In Chicago, sex with Nora was better than it had ever been, we were closer than we had ever been, and I got an idea for a new play.

CHAPTER TWO

Hollywood University

Mrs. Selznick, Messrs. Litvak,
Hitchcock, Cukor, and Ophuls

WE CHATTED FOR A FEW MINUTES. He complimented me on *Home of the Brave* and at his request I described what happens visually when sodium pentothol is taken. The visual, of course, was his major interest, but why he was interested in the drug, I didn't know. Then he asked me to write the screenplay of *The Snake Pit,* a novel set largely in a state mental asylum. Like the Army's asylum I had checked out, that particular state asylum also treated madness with sodium pentothol.

He was Anatole Litvak, famous in Europe for directing *Mayerling,* in this country for controlling Bette Davis in *All This and Heaven Too.* We met in the leather-chaired office of Bennett Cerf, president of Random House. Litvak was there to seal his purchase of the movie rights to the Mary Jane Ward novel; I'd been summoned from down the hall where I was going over galley proofs of my play with Saxe Commins. Commins was Random House's most distinguished editor, better known than many of his patients. He worked briskly, red-penciling all my attempts to help the reader hear my dialogue. Double punctuation like ?! made him glacial. I didn't protest much: I was cravenly grateful to Random House for just publishing the play.

To Litvak, I said no politely too quickly, with not enough reverence for his Hollywood rank. Still, how do you slow down a no? Particularly to a man in an obviously bespoke cashmere topcoat. His white hair, however premature, made him seem younger than I first thought he was, his carriage made him seem taller; his pale blue eyes had an amused glint that belied his very gracious acceptance of my rejection. Those eyes said, It's your loss, and dismissed me.

I didn't think I was passing up an opportunity. I'd read *The Snake Pit* as soon as it appeared in the bookstores because it dealt with psychiatric treatment and I was still floundering on Theodor Reik's used couch. The tale seemed autobiographical; I suspected the author/heroine was cured of her psychiatric problems in order to finish her book and probably would end up back in the Cookie Jar. That wasn't why I didn't want to write the screenplay, however. My reason was simple: I was a playwright and I had a new play, *Heartsong*. It even had a producer.

I've never included *Heartsong* in *Playbill* biographies or *Who's Who* or similar sources (how accurate is any history of anything?) but it's included here to introduce a very dear man who brought me up in the theatre and a dysfunctional woman who inducted me into the Beverly Hills circuit. And because it's a cautionary tale.

In my basement is a cardboard carton crammed and bulging with versions of *Heartsong,* circa 1946, before and during rehearsal and performances throughout the helter-skelter pre-Broadway tour. To be put in chronological order, all the versions would have to be read, and carefully. They never will be, not by me anyway, I'm not a masochist. I don't know what the play was, I'm not even sure what it was meant to be. I can only guess from a scrapbook buried in the carton, a scrapbook my father kept of interviews with me and reviews by motley critics in the cities we dragged our wagonload to.

Evidently *Heartsong* began as a high comedy in the fairly successful first two acts, then collapsed under a load of uncertain drama in the third; it ended, three cities later, not so high a comedy in the first two acts and bland in the third. Its theme—according to an interview with me—was the same as *Home of the Brave*'s: the necessity of accepting one's imperfect self. How that connected to the plot—a young couple's marriage foundering because of an abortion—I haven't a clue. My guess is that the abortion is in the play because, dramatically, I needed a secret from the young couple's past, a socially unacceptable secret that could damage their marriage. My suspicion is that I wanted to use homosexuality but was afraid to, not because the subject was taboo—that would only have encouraged me—but because I couldn't deal with it myself. I didn't know what I felt about it, what it meant to me, how much what the world felt about it meant to me. I thought a play had to know the answers and present them. Ambiguity was not for me or my plays then: I wanted certainty onstage and off, and I wanted it badly. I had no firsthand experience of abortion but at least I knew what I felt about it.

In 1946, abortion wasn't in the headlines; it didn't have the status of a civil right. It wasn't mentioned; it wasn't considered shocking, just unpleasant. That nugget comes from the reviews of *Heartsong*: critic after critic asks, Why did the author sully his sparkling comedy by bringing up that untidy subject? My knowledge of the untidy subject at the time I wrote the play was limited to an experience at Cornell.

Early in our senior year, I sat with a best friend while he sweated out a back-alley abortion being performed on his girl. They were crazy about each other sexually. *Crazy* is the operative word: too soon after that first abortion, they parked in his car in the woods just off campus and soon she needed a second abortion. Then too soon a third; so soon, it was very dangerous. So they got married and too soon, they weren't so crazy about each other.

He had fallen in love with journalism in high school. At Cornell, his love was requited: he was editor in chief of the *Sun* (I was assistant editor). He came from no money but he prepared for a journalism career which would allow for that. And indeed, the job offer he got for after graduation didn't pay much but it was just the job he had aimed for. A good job for a bright young single man but not for a bright young father with a family to support. So he went into the insurance business in Hartford and they lived unhappily ever after.

Almost a decade later, about a year after *Heartsong,* I had a more personal connection with abortion. I had moved to California but was in New York on a visit, staying at the Algonquin. I'd always dreamed of staying there—it had such a glamorously literary reputation which the lobby and ground floor rooms lived up to. But I was housed on an upper floor in a room that bore no resemblance to the lobby or anything on the ground floor, not even to a bookcase. I brought Nora back to that garretlike room late my third night back in New York.

We were in an on-again phase of our on-again, off-again affair and we'd been drinking. We were always drinking but we never wondered out loud why we were always drinking. We walked carefully, I think I even bowed a little as Nora entered the room before me. I wanted the owner of the Algonquin to be sentenced to a week in that discouraging room. Meager and shabby, the rug was threadbare, the wallpaper was curdling; everything needed mending, nothing was without something unwanted showing through. Nora and I had been on the subject of marriage again and I was hopeful when we opened the door. Less than five minutes after we sat down, the ugly ambience seeped in like gas. Conversation choked and died. A very empty pause, then Nora mentioned she'd had an abortion.

I was sitting on the edge of the lumpy bed, she was sunk in the lopsided gut of an overstuffed chair. Blood rushed to my head in a mix of anger and wounded pride. The anger is easy to figure but the pride? Why? What was there to be proud of? Proof that I was, after all, a man?

"How could you?" I asked.

She lit a cigarette and blew the smoke out very theatrically. "What makes you think it was yours?" she said.

I think my hand moved. I must have wanted to hit her, she so obviously wanted to hurt me. And she kept on trying. She offered the names of a couple of other candidates. She threw a sop: None of them knew, she hadn't told them, not yet—and here, I go blank. I can't see, hear, remember anything until a knock on the door. Then more knocks, harder. Then the night manager's voice, unforgettable: "Get that woman out of that room!"

Nora rolled her eyes. Only Nora Kaye could roll her eyes like that at a time like that. We both laughed, then quickly covered our mouths. But we had become fellow conspirators in silence, which made us, at that moment, closer than we had been all night.

Until the knock on the door, I had been busy believing I was what I knew I wasn't quite, what I was therefore trying hard to sort out in psychoanalysis in California this time around. "Get that woman out of that room"—said to me? How could I not laugh? Especially with Nora. Her ability to find the humor in anything—onstage in a classical pas de deux gone amiss, offstage in a bedroom pas deux gone amiss—was her most enchanting saving grace. It saved her, too—until she went to live in the flatlands of Beverly Hills, where she lost her humor and became what she herself would have laughed at: an upscale yenta. That may seem an oxymoron, but not in Beverly Hills. The producer of *Heartsong* came from Beverly Hills but she was no yenta. She was royalty—Hollywood royalty, that is.

Irene Mayer Selznick was the name she decided to use as a Broadway producer, a serious name to be taken seriously. "Mayer" was inherited from Louis B., head of Metro-Goldwyn-Mayer, father of Irene, pride of the Republicans if not the Republic. A few triumphant years after *Heartsong,* Irene was in London producing *A Streetcar Named Desire* with Laurence Olivier and Vivien Leigh. Husband and wife, one starring, one directing, both calling Irene several kinds of a cunt daily. (What kinds? Green, for one. A green cunt? Why? Only Olivier knew.)

Irene was a not unsophisticated woman; she talked too much and drank too much and chuckled constantly because she was aware she rarely got the joke. But there was no way she could take being called a cunt every day, week after week, as a joke. Her controls went and she burst into tears. Her London partner, Binkie Beaumont—actually, his name was Hugh but he was English—tried to make peace.

Irene Selznick going dutch with Jack Benny.

"You are absolutely in the right," he soothed. "But dear, dear Irene, do try to understand. The Oliviers are the King and Queen of the English theatre."

Irene pushed him away and drew herself up. "But I," she roared, "am the daughter of an Emperor!"

She wasn't kidding. That was how she behaved, even when her Emperor lost his studio and was stripped down to new clothes.

"Selznick" was David O., husband in name only since they separated, producer of *Gone With the Wind,* former executive producer of MGM under Louis B., now owner of his own studio, Selznick International. Both Louis B. and David O. sought Irene's advice and counsel regularly, but both always walked ahead of her and she knew they always would: she was a daughter, a wife, their girl. David O. may have driven her into psychoanalysis with his manias, as she claimed, but it was psychoanalysis that got her to leave him because of those manias as she also claimed, entirely overlooking his affair with Jennifer Jones, whom he married the minute he was legally free. Irene's mirror always told her she was the fairest.

David O., like his father, was a chronic gambler, always losing, always in debt. Louis B., in a divorce settlement engineered by Irene, forked up much of his fortune to be free of her mother. That left Irene, whose money came from the two men in her life, richer than both combined. With her two sons more or less out from under, there was no reason for her not to leave home, strike out on her own, and make both her moguls say uncle. Which was what she wanted above all else. When I met her she was living in a new city, New York, using "Mayer" and "Selznick" to open theatre and literary doors for her new career: theatre producer. Which was, to begin with, producing a new play by her very own new playwright—me.

Heartsong had landed on her desk via Harold Freedman, a Welsh Jew who became my representative during the last days of *Home of the Brave*. Harold couldn't be called an agent, not with the pejorative taint to that word. His roster of playwrights ranged from Clifford Odets to Noël Coward to Thornton Wilder, all the way down to me. A rotund, dignified man who spoke quietly with an impressive accent, he did most of his business over the telephone. The first question he asked me was, "What kind of playwright do you want to be?"

"How do you mean?"

"Good or successful?"

"Both."

"But which first?" He looked straight at me.

"Good."

"I had to ask," he explained, "in order to know how to handle you."

Not words to engrave in stone but engraved in my memory. They set the pattern of our professional life and the course of mine. He brought me up in the theatre. He taught me always to cooperate with management because the producer and the playwright have the same goal. Everyone in every department of the theatre has the same goal but everyone in the theatre behaves as though everyone else was the enemy. Harold worked hard to prevent that; sometimes, he even succeeded.

He was the most decent man I ever met in a community that thrives on envy and backbiting. To his decency, add honesty, integrity, compassion—all the unglamorous attributes. Glamour was left to his playwrights if they cared about it; Harold didn't. Each of us got equal attention; what he thought of each of us, only each of us knew. We all knew one thing, however: Harold Freedman would do the one thing necessary for any playwright—he would get the play on. Somehow, he always got the play on.

With Irene, he weighed her pros and cons for me, warned me that, being from California, she would be possessive, paranoid and provincial as well as rich, but she was intelligent, she understood the play, she would get it on and she would fight like a tigress for her cub.

From the outset, I liked her, she liked me, and we had a good time together. I enjoyed watching her sweep into her office, minions scuttling fore and aft, getting down to work on producing the play à la Louis B. and David O. after calls to her business manager and her ex-analyst on the Coast. Irene boasted she had never been part of the Hollywood scene or influenced by it. She was delighted I was in analysis; she was psychoanalyzed to the gills.

In Hollywood, she knew everyone; in New York, anyone she didn't know and wanted to know, she got to know. Moss Hart often helped. He was a friend who was mentoring her theatre career innocently—he didn't know Irene had ideas of her very possessive own. She shoved *Heartsong* at him just to read but she wanted him to direct. Moss was a man who managed to be exceptionally kind and still be funny. When the three of us met in Irene's office to discuss his directing the play, he radiated charm and, oh, such enthusiasm; he was so complimentary, he made us laugh so much that it wasn't until he was out the door that we realized he had turned us down. His tactful reason was that he wouldn't have time to direct the play because he would be too busy marrying Kitty Carlisle. Which he did soon after.

The Carlisle-Hart honeymoon was spent playing in the Kaufman-Hart comedy *The Man Who Came to Dinner* at the Bucks County Playhouse. Irene was invited to join the celebration and got her playwright invited. Bucks County's large theatrical colony was full up for the weekend. She stayed with the white folks at the Harts', I stayed nearby at George S. Kaufman's.

The prospect of meeting these near greats I continually read about in the columns was exciting even though I knew from seeing my own name in a column that what an item conjured up in the imagination was Einstein miles from reality. The first time I saw my name in Winchell—the item read, "Playwright Arthur Laurents and Ballerina Nora Kaye seen going into '21' "— was like finding out Santa Claus drank. Had the playwright and the ballerina had other names, I would have imagined him in black tie, her in mink, and a chauffeur helping them out of their Bentley. In life, the playwright and the ballerina left her third-floor walk-up and were straggling across Fifty-second Street to "21" (as guests of a moneyed balletomane) when Mrs. Wolf, her landlady, bellowed for the whole street to hear: "Miss Nora Kaye, you haven't paid your rent. And stop leaving your key under the flowerpot!"

The cold-water ghost of Mrs. Wolfe hovered over that weekend in Bucks County. What I imagined was not what I encountered; what I did encounter was unsettling.

I was prepared for George Kaufman's acerbic wit; I looked forward to it, I hoped for a quote, but he was only kind and generous to me—sweet, actually. George S. Kaufman sweet? Yes; unfortunately, he was rarely in evidence at his house that weekend. My hostess was his witty daughter Anne, assisted by two young fellows my age: Irving Schneider, Irene's general manager, and his friend Clinton Wilder. Clinton was to be an assistant stage manager on *Heartsong* in order to learn how to produce. (He later coproduced most of Edward Albee.) All three had an accent that was racing toward the Mid-Atlantic: Anne's was the slightest and sat well on her; Clinton's made some sense—he was a Princetonian and rich; Irving was from the Bronx. The two boys shared a position in the house and a relationship to Anne I couldn't quite fathom. Their efforts to put me at ease made me uneasy the very first night.

One by one, beginning with the hostess, each tapped on my bedroom door, came in to say good night, then sat on the edge of my bed and asked if there was anything I needed as a hand with a life of its own made its way to my ankle and fiddled. By the last visit, Clinton's, I was remembering a play I'd reviewed as drama critic for *The Cornell Daily Sun*. It was performed at the Ithaca College of Music, Drama, and Physical Education and was called *Gallia Placidia, or The Odyssey of a Bed in Fourteen Scenes*. Each scene ended with the Roman princess Gallia (or maybe Placidia) draped over the edge of the bed while a member of the phys ed department, clad only in a helmet and a strategic shield, kissed her ankle and started to work his way up. As the princess commanded, "Come higher," the curtain started to fall. By the fourteenth scene and the end of the play, the curtain fell just in the nick of time.

There was no need for a saving curtain at the Kaufmans'. Nothing happened and it was clear nothing would: the water was just being tested. Why was I unsettled then? That I wasn't attracted to any of them wasn't the answer. And surely I'd had more sexual experiences than my three night visitors put together. At least I thought I had to have had more—and there, suddenly, was the explanation: it was impossible for me to conceive that these three young people in this social and economic milieu—George S. Kaufman's country house and Mid-Atlantic accents—it was impossible that their sexual proclivity could be anything but conventional, respectable, "normal." Homosexuality was reserved for pariahs, an attitude fostered by Theodor Reik.

Not only had Reik decided that my position as America's best new playwright was going to be confirmed by *Heartsong*, he had also decided I was not a pariah despite the evidence of Randall West, Harold Lang, and other males. They were still in the picture—but fading fast, Reik said. He plunged ahead, ever onward, ever upward, ignoring or unaware that I was lagging behind in guilty confusion. Small wonder that that first night at the Kaufmans', I felt like the farmer's daughter in those traveling salesman jokes.

The next day, when we went over to the Harts' for the afternoon's honeymoon party, my concentration was on seeming to belong in Bucks County; sex was nowhere in my head. Not for long; but when it arrived, it was not by my choice and I wished it hadn't.

. . .

Moss Hart had long been in analysis with Lawrence Kubie, who specialized in the theatrically famous. Like Reik, Kubie introduced his patients to one another; unlike Reik, he brought them together to write shows together. From his matchmaking, Moss and Kurt Weill gave birth to *Lady in the Dark,* which I'd seen while I was in the Army and newly on Reik's couch. Its weak book trivialized psychoanalysis but it was very glamorous to look at, had a pretty score and best of all, Gertrude Lawrence and Danny Kaye.

Nor was Reik a matchmaker like Kubie, quite the opposite, in fact: he split Jerry Robbins and me. Working with Jerry, I had finished a detailed outline for a musical about the ballet which I called *Look Ma, I'm Dancing!* Reik said it was beneath me, I was trying to be unnecessarily versatile, I should drop it instantly to concentrate on *Heartsong.* I apologized and obeyed. Jerry blew up but collected himself long enough to get me to sign away my rights to everything for nothing. Since I thought I had indeed behaved badly, I signed Jerry's quitclaim. To no avail: he stayed angry and there was a long caesura before he called me "baby" again.

Rumors are quick about a man who marries late as Moss did. Kitty married late, too, but not a whisper; there rarely is about a woman. Watching them work the room together and separately at his splendid Bucks County house, I thought late might even be better than early. The friends who filled the house were almost as happy for them as they were for each other. But not all the friends. A trio of wicked witches huddled on a sofa I was standing behind: three ex-girls of Moss's, two actresses and a woman. Until the wedding, each of their names had been used in turn as the kicker in a Sardi's joke, as in "Ah, here comes Moss Hart with the future Miss Edith Atwater." Kitty, as bride, had effectively killed off the joke; the kicker names at the party, now permanently the future Misses Whoever, were taking revenge by being bitchy about Moss. The more they made one another laugh—admittedly, they were funny—the bitchier and more explicit they got.

My imagination replaced Kitty and Moss with Nora and me. If Nora and I married, how would she feel at a similar celebration? How did Kitty feel? How did Moss feel? How did I feel? Guilty, a fraud, and other helpful things. I couldn't stay in the room and went outside.

I wanted to go home; short of that, I wanted to go back to the Kaufmans'; short of that, I wanted to disappear. But then along came Clinton Wilder in swimming trunks, heading for the pool with a little pitcher of martini "dividends." We had brought our suits, he told me to get into mine. The sun was warm, water washes, water cleanses—I went for my suit.

Four or five young men were around the pool, sunbathing and drinking. I took a swim, then a sip of Clinton's dividend, and was warming in the sun when Moss walked up, dressed. He sat down in a deck chair. After a moment, he said: "There are no girls around. Why don't you boys take off your suits?"

No one did. No one moved. No one said a word. It was as though someone had gone up in his lines. Then a heavy boy belly-whopped into the pool and thrashed around noisily. Another boy dove in and began to do laps. After a bit, Moss got up and went back to the house.

I sat there. Then, because I didn't want to talk, dove into the pool and began swimming laps, forming and re-forming questions. Didn't "cured" really mean repressed? And hypocritical? And while it made for an easier life, did it make for a better life? I couldn't wait to get back to the city and challenge Reik. But when I walked into his office, I was so glad to see him, I asked no questions. He had all the answers anyway; he would give them to me in due time. In his office, on his couch, I was safe, I was patient, I was docile. No one who knew me would have known me.

Irene had been going over the text of *Heartsong* as though it were the fine print she loved in contracts. There was validity to her criticism. I began revising and rewriting—too quickly, as was my habit. The minutiae were easily dealt with but as she kept coming back for more and more, it began to seem something major had to be wrong with the play. Was there a basic flaw? If so, did she know what it was? I certainly didn't so I listened carefully; unfortunately, she talked so much, she was hard to hear. Late at night, the phone would ring; before I finished "Hello," she was off and running, words tumbling nonstop over ideas at an amazing speed for a woman who had the remnants of a stutter. Sometimes I wondered if it would have made any difference if a trick had answered the phone while I was in the bathroom. Probably not because I would fall asleep for five or ten minutes while she was talking, once for thirty-four minutes by my bedside clock, and she was still talking when I snapped awake. Lost in logorrhea, Irene hadn't missed me at all.

One day, long after *Heartsong* closed, she told me, without recrimination, that she had discovered the play's fatal flaw while we were still in rehearsal but I hadn't paid attention. In fairness, that was possible, very possible I hadn't heard because of the Niagara of words. Her solution, however, was a little simple: I should have gotten rid of the young married couple. Since the play was about them, that would have meant getting rid of the whole play—except for

The first stop on a three-city tour of hell.

the Shirley Booth character—which didn't occur to Irene. She had also conveniently forgotten that that was more or less what I did in the bitter end.

From Louis B. and David O., Irene got an insider's knowledge of how to produce a movie. She applied it to producing a play. Before *Heartsong* went into rehearsal, she fired Donald Oenslager, the scenic designer, because he wasn't all hers and only hers. Since we were unable to get Moss or any name director, she chose to gamble on an unknown she knew from back home: Phyllis Loughton, a very nice not-so-young woman who was the acting coach for Irene's good friend, Olivia de Havilland of Hollywood and *Gone With the Wind*. Three days into rehearsal with Phyllis, Nancy Coleman, the experienced leading lady, quit because of "her mother's illness." We recast; I rewrote again; the madness that presages disaster was firmly in place and no one could stop it snowballing.

This was my learning experience with the foremost reason for failure in the theatre. The signposts say STOP but the show continues anyway. Why?

Because it started. It may get better, sick productions often do, but better doesn't make it good.

No playwright could have asked for a more comprehensive out-of-town tryout than Irene gave me: New Haven, Boston, and Philadelphia. Shirley Booth, a godsend to the play, was one of the few who lasted through all three cities. Playing an alcoholic, her dry delivery, her vulnerability and her timing from God made her big scene the one surefire scene in the play. In rehearsal, she said if she got a hand on her exit in that scene, she would know she had failed as an actress. She failed every night and loved it. So did we.

In New Haven, the leading man was replaced by Lloyd Bridges, I wrote a new third act and Irene asked if she could send for Reik. She had a hunch he was treating the play as well as me and wanted to catch him red-handed. Not a prayer, as Irene, an old hand at analysis, should have known. With my permission, Reik came, approved what he saw—the play, not me—and sent Irene a whopping bill, even including the cost of his train fare to New Haven. She was furious. For a mad moment, she looked at me as though contemplating asking me to pay half. But Reik had spoken only to her and he was getting ten per-cent of my royalties anyway. ("You're zelfish!" "Take, take!") Not that Irene knew that and not that she was going to know: I was too embarrassed. It had dawned on me belatedly that a transference in psychoanalysis didn't mean a monetary transference.

Whenever Irene felt stymied, she went to what she regarded as her real strength: her fingers. She was born to massage. Now she pounced again on the actors, particularly the women, in the wings, in the dressing rooms, in the cor-ridors of the Shubert Theatre in New Haven and massaged them into submis-sion. On the railroad station platform for the train to Boston, Shirley saw Irene approach, cracking her fingers. "Duck! Here she comes," she warned, ducking into safe haven of the ladies' room.

In Boston, Phyllis was fired after Irene called home to Hollywood. Mel Ferrer was recruited as the new director; he arrived bringing new hope. His suggestions for revision made sense to me, although what I regarded as sense by then was suspect. I was in Mel's suite at the Ritz-Carlton taking notes when the clock on the mantel chimed: time for his massage.

I was in my junior suite, plodding through yet another revision, when the clock on my mantel chimed: it was my time, and for more than a massage. Randall, in the East on a publicity junket, had contrived time off to fly up to Boston. I turned off the phone, locked the door, pulled down the shades, and away we went. The clock kept chiming but I didn't hear it, I wasn't at the Ritz, I wasn't in Boston. Irene came pounding on the door: "Where's the rewrite?!"

The rewrite? I hadn't gone this wild since the great nights of the war. She's pounding on the door, I'm pounding away in bed. "I know you're in there! Where's the rewrite?" What rewrite for what?

After it was all over, after Randall left and I was back at the Ritz in Boston, I felt refreshed, renewed, once again ready for the fray. *Heartsong* came into perspective: there was life after the theatre and outside the theatre. One thing about sex: it enables you to see clearly afterward.

In Philadelphia, we opened yet another new version but without our old leading man, Lloyd Bridges, and his nameless leading lady. They were replaced by Barry Nelson and Phyllis Thaxter, indentured servants at MGM who had been boxed and shipped to Irene by her father. A bit embarrassed to look at them when we met, I was surprised to find they were delighted, even ecstatic. Hollywood scripts, they enthused, didn't have dialogue this wonderful! That, in a way, was the mainspring of the problem: the dialogue, like a good wig, deceived too well. It made the play seem better than it was.

Irene's ex-husband-to-be flew in from California. In a Philadelphia hotel room, he wasn't David O. Selznick, he was David Selznick, a flabby, bespectacled businessman in a rumpled gray suit. None of his famous memo-mania; only one slip of paper in his hand: a list of screenwriters available for collaboration with me. I was generously allowed to choose. When I objected pro forma to the notion of a collaborator, Selznick argued without much conviction and Irene busied herself fixing herself another drink.

All the long, tortuous road from New York to New Haven to Boston to Philadelphia, she had wanted so badly to come up with the magic solution herself, to save the day herself. It was her production, her first venture, her validation. Pride, and her pride was enormous, had to be swallowed before she could send for the husband she had left to prove herself on her own. But he was David O. Selznick, he would know what and how, he had the magic. If Irene was sure of anything, she was sure of that: she believed the myth. But even if it was true, if David O. did have any magic, it was for the movies, not the theatre.

The next morning Irene didn't answer her phone, not, alas, for the reason I hadn't answered mine. I went to the Walnut Theatre and waited for her in the lobby. Friends of hers were arriving from Hollywood to applaud her triumph and cheer her on. I knew Irene was valiant and would face them with the smile of the week no matter what her stomach was doing. She walked in as the lobby was filling up for the matinee, an excuse I was tempted to use for not saying what I knew I had to say. It would be unlike a playwright to say it and unlike normal theatre behavior because it would be behaving sensibly.

I led her to a corner away from the well-dressed mainline women who were sure to walk out before the end. Irene's angular good looks made her seem tough but her eyes begged; they almost made me back off. I hadn't rehearsed, I just let the words come out: my play wasn't good enough and I couldn't fix it. I told her it would not do her or me or even Shirley Booth any good to bring it into New York. I asked her to close in Philadelphia, to let it die.

The matinee ladies were pouring in now, giving the play the deceptive appearance of good business and success. Irene stared at the ladies but she didn't see them. She turned back to me and said, "You cost me seventy-five thousand dollars." Today, that might cover the costumes; then, it was the cost of the entire production and every cent was hers.

Claudette Colbert, all bubbling, enchanting enthusiasm, glamorous even in the afternoon, came swinging through the doors. Irene went to hug her. Other friends had come to Boston and Irene had proudly introduced me. Not to Claudette Colbert, not in Philadelphia. In Philadelphia, Irene pointedly turned her back.

Her crack about money didn't score. Insults about money only score with people who have money. The snub did score, though. It reminded me that the theatre was a business and business is first about success and I had failed. Failure is not welcome at the table. Moreover, I might be contagious.

Nothing nourishes self-pity more than a grubby train ride. I reveled that the seats in coach on the train back to New York were hard and grimy, that the windows were dirty, that there were only a handful of other passengers and they were dirty. I wallowed in feeling more alone than I had ever felt in my life and in being without a future. That lasted fifteen minutes. Then I switched over to the ritual I used whenever I was in trouble. I took a look at me in the third person as a character in a novel I was reading.

The playwright was lonely and miserable; the bottom had fallen out. OK: why? Because his play had failed? No, because the play deserved to fail and he had to acknowledge that. Whatever he would like to blame on the producer, he couldn't blame that on her. It was his work; he didn't know how to fix his play. He still didn't know, so he had better stop wasting time hunting down the answer. Anyway, he's too mixed up and confused to recognize an answer even if he saw one. Maybe he'll never know, maybe there isn't one; dwelling on it is getting him nowhere and making him an unsympathetic, tiresome pain in the ass. Deal with now. Living is now. Where is he now? What is he going to do now? I didn't know. I went over what I did know: I was lonely, I was broke and I had to stand up to Theodor Reik, a prospect harder than standing up to Irene Mayer Selznick.

There was a character in *Heartsong* actually called Uncle Ted. It's astonishing Irene didn't object: he was the wisest, most benign, most charming, most everything lovable this side of Vienna. For that alone, Reik got ten percent of my royalties. In that grimy train, I had a small epiphany. Beneath my mea culpa, I had always resented the royalty arrangement; repressing the resentment had intensified it. Had I unconsciously wanted the play to fail? Possibly; probably; yes. Too Freudian? A way to put the blame on my unconscious and restore my confidence? Perhaps, but it was helping and instinct told me it was true. God knows had I been in my right mind, I would never have written the role of Uncle Ted, that saccharine old fart.

I was angry. For two years, I had been manipulated by Reik and had trusted that he knew what he was doing. True, he had started the analytic thinking process and that does have a helpful life of its own. But I'd been force-fed values that had begun to screw me up worse than I'd screwed myself up. That was what I was really angry about, very angry, but too shaky to attack Reik about. When I went into his office, I didn't lie down on that seedy couch, I sat up.

The power an analyst can have over a patient is unfair and frightening and sometimes dangerous. When—long hairs in his great nose, longer hairs in his pendulous ears—Reik held up six volumes and claimed he had written them about Flaubert, I knew it was cockamamie but I didn't really see the humor in his pretense. Until you see the humor, you're not safe. I wasn't quite safe yet but I was calm.

I told the Viennese doctor who wasn't recognized as a doctor of any kind in America that I thought he had a thing about money. He pondered that but while he was pulling away at the hairs in his nose, I brought up the bill he had sent Irene and—finally!—the ten percent of my royalties. It was then that he said there was a legitimate explanation that he would give me if I gave him my word of honor as a gentleman never to repeat what he divulged. He had told me I had an overdeveloped sense of morality; I proved him right and gave him my word. With a great, sad, wheezing sigh, he told me his wife was dying of cancer and he, a refugee just getting established, was forced to do everything humanly possible to make her last months on this earth comfortable. I believed him. Nevertheless, when he sent me a bill for the hour, I didn't pay.

With Harold Freedman, I summed up where I thought I was and then listened. Concentrating on the practical was marvelous therapy. I was broke; that had to be dealt with and Harold did so immediately. He got me a contract at Metro. A detour from becoming a good writer—but for $2,500 a week for sixteen weeks, I could force myself to take the detour. Moreover, for the first time in my life, I didn't want to be in New York. I loved the city but in my New York, anyone who failed became invisible. I began the good-byes with Irene who, it seemed, had not failed.

Heartsong paid off handsomely for her. Audrey Wood, who was Tennessee Williams's agent, gave Irene the rights to produce *A Streetcar Named Desire* because she had done such a splendid job of producing *Heartsong*. Not too long after, Audrey Wood had a new house in Connecticut. One hand washes and if Tennessee wasn't included, he wasn't hurt and all the money for the production was guaranteed.

Irene invited me for a drink and sympathy as though she had not been the producer of *Heartsong*. Pleased I'd left Uncle Ted, delighted I was going to her hometown, she assured me the future was music for both of us, as she handed over a copy of *Streetcar* to please read immediately. The following night she was on the phone again as of yesteryear. What was my opinion of the ending: wasn't the rape too much? She explained at length how Tennessee Williams could change it. Happy with her rewrite, she shifted her focus to how fortunate it was for me that she was going to the Coast to cast her (sic) play because she could pave the way for me at her father's studio and introduce me to Hollywood and get me set with a really good analyst this time and and and . . .

While she chattered, I pushed the copy of *Streetcar* across the bed and pulled over my maps. In a few days, I would be driving from New York to Los Angeles in the same car my father had driven from Brooklyn to Fort Benning to bring me back home to New York. Glad to be leaving home, I was uneasy about moving to Hollywood. Not about working there. A company town, even one with bosses like Louis B. and David O., didn't intimidate me nor did writing screenplays. I had seen a lot of movies, I learned fast, and if I was anything, I was a craftsman. Living in a foreign land in the midst of transplanted palm trees and leprous poinsettias, that was what I was uneasy about. I hoped the East Coast view of the West Coast was born of cynicism and envy, but I couldn't give much credence to that hope.

What I would really need in Hollywood were friends. I knew some of the people at the left-wing Actors Lab, but only slightly. And what I would really need was a gay friend; I knew nothing about the attitudes toward homosexuality in the city of Los Physically Desirable. There was Randall who after our Boston marathon might be even more than a friend. However, when I telephoned my imminent arrival, he didn't shout Welcome! When? Great! You've got a sublet on Doheny? Terrific! But that wasn't Randall anyway; he was always Southern-subdued except in bed. We did make plans: I would call as soon as I arrived, we would have dinner, he would be a friend. That George

Cukor might be one, too, didn't occur to me. In any case, when he left the Army and returned to Hollywood, he didn't leave his phone number.

One thing I looked forward to was driving across the country alone. I liked being alone. Four or five days in a time capsule, where no one could get to me, where I could drop the last of *Heartsong* by the roadside, where I could just be with myself—that would get me ready for Hollywood and it would be an adventure. It was spring, April showers bring May flowers, the weather would be good, I would see the purple earth of New Mexico. That was all I had to do, enjoy the scenery and not get a flat tire or a ticket.

"Don't cross the desert during the day. You'll fry and your car'll overheat," the gas station attendant warned. "Drive by night and take extra water." On the backseat of the convertible was my life: a foot locker with my clothes and a carton with my scripts and a few 78s of my army radio shows. I didn't take extra water, I put the top up. I wasn't very good at maps and I had no sense of direction: if instinct told me to take the right fork, I took the left and did better. I crossed the desert without knowing it was the desert and arrived in L.A. ahead of schedule. The omens were good.

It was early evening when I shot out of a canyon, honking like mad because the brakes were gone as I hurtled across a main street that turned out to be Sunset Boulevard. Fortunately, there wasn't much traffic, so I kept going, using the emergency brake, honking when I crossed the tracks at Santa Monica. The air was soft, the light was nostalgic, I was ready. By luck, I was where I wanted to be, in West Hollywood; by luck, I found Randall's street while the emergency still held. He was expecting me to call but I didn't want to push my luck with the car. I managed to come to a stop and park according to his directions.

He had told me he lived in the guest house of a main house. I walked down the driveway of what didn't look like anybody's main house. The guest house at the end of the drive was so small, it looked like an outhouse. There was light in the window: he was home—another good omen. No doorbell, so I knocked.

When he opened the door and saw me, he blushed. He had very smooth, butter-colored skin (golden tan now), so the red stood out. He was having supper, a meal he had cooked himself for his guest. The guest was clearly a friend, to use the euphemism. I walked into the one room which became overcrowded in every way. It didn't bother me, I wasn't embarrassed, I didn't feel rejected, I was in heaven. Whether Randall had switched affections before my phone call announcing my imminent arrival or in the intervening days didn't matter. My romantic fantasies switched in five minutes. His friend was Farley Granger. We looked at each other and I was ecstatic to be in Hollywood.

I arrived in the Last Days of the Glamorous Empire. Louis B. gave a huge, gala celebratory sit-down dinner in honor of Irene after *Streetcar* opened success-fully on Broadway. Streetcars were as prominent as the letter *R* in David O.'s *Rebecca:* the dessert was an enormous sorbet streetcar. I was seated next to Louella Parsons, the powerful gossip columnist who sent her chauffered car all over town at Christmas to pick up the Christmas presents everyone was afraid not to give her.

"What picture are you in now?" Louella asked.

"None," I answered. "I'm a writer." She turned her back and never spoke to me again the entire evening.

Everybody in town was in pictures or wanted to be in pictures. The aircraft industry was booming and paid well but nobody knew anybody in airplanes except Howard Hughes—who owned a movie studio. The oil wells on Signal Hill pumped day and night, there was even one pumping away smack in the middle of La Brea Boulevard in West Hollywood but nobody knew any-body in oil, either. There was no smog, everybody played tennis, and every-body drove everywhere in convertibles to get a tan and flirt at stoplights. Everybody had hamburgers at drive-ins called Dolores where the waitresses were pretty girls who lingered when they brought the orders. Everybody saw the sexy boys thumbing a ride at certain corners along Sunset Boulevard as soon as the sun went down.

The house I rented was just below Sunset in Beverly Hills where all the houses were facsimiles of Tara or Monticello or Versailles. Mine, barely in Beverly Hills, was a facsimile of a house on Ocean Parkway in Brooklyn. It was on the right side of the wrong street, Doheny Drive. The east side of Doheny was déclassé: it was in West Hollywood. The west side, the side my sublet was on, was in Beverly Hills but only technically. I didn't know that when I moved in and didn't care when I found out. I hadn't lived in an unattached house since I was ten; the sublet on Doheny was a whole, two-storied house and it was all mine, for the moment, anyway. There were more boxy rooms than I needed and a barbecue in the backyard, but in the living room, a shag rug, a baby grand and a scarred coffee table told me I would be at home with the owners.

I hadn't met them nor did I know who they were, only that their name was Chaplin. Not the Charlie and Oona Chaplins but I was playing tennis on their court weeks before I met the Sol and Ethel Chaplins who owned the house on Doheny. They had sublet it to their friend Sono Osato which was how I got it.

Sono was a friend of Nora's—they were roommates on Ballet Theatre tours—and of Jerry's: she was the impish, exotic leading lady in *On the Town*. She had come to Hollywood to make her fortune, a foolish expectation for a half-Japanese, half-Irish girl. The Japanese in California had been interned during the war and were barely beginning to emerge from ostracism. As for the Irish, in movies they were either comics or maids, usually both. Sono vented her disappointment on the weather. She claimed it only drizzled in Southern California, didn't really rain, not Eastern rain, not rain with balls. She was packed and waiting with her umbrella when I turned up to free her by subletting her sublet.

Very soon after I moved in, I saw what a real house in real Beverly Hills looked like: the house of Irene Mayer Selznick. She phoned in need of immediate advice because I knew the New York theatre, and oh yes, to welcome me to California. Her street, aptly named Summit Drive, was in the fashionable foothills above Sunset; Doheny, of course, was below.

When I drove up, walked to the door, and entered the house, I had a continuing sense of déjà vu. Two minutes and I knew why: I had seen all of it before in MGM pictures set in tastefully overchintzed English country houses. The difference was that Irene's had a pool and tennis court where the stables would have been. No butler but yards of maids who could walk over the gleaming dark wooden floors without making a sound. My shoes squeaked as I was hushed to the library.

Irene managed a hello before she began fulminating against Elia Kazan as she paced up and down, stopping every now and then to freshen her drink. Kazan was going to direct *Streetcar*—Tennessee's choice, not hers. She had no choice, she had to take him. And allow him to take a big piece of her producer's share. Otherwise, he didn't acknowledge she was the producer, his producer. He ridiculed her suggestion about eliminating the rape ending. Not that Tennessee went for it either but that was because Gadge (Kazan) had poisoned him. Another drink fueled her anger; she was down to the last straw: Kazan's billing demand. What was my honest opinion? Be brutally honest, please. Which would be best for her: billing that read "Irene Mayer Selznick Presents The Elia Kazan Production of *A Streetcar Named Desire* or billing that read "Irene Mayer Selznick Presents An Elia Kazan Production of *A Streetcar Named Desire*"?

It was hardly news Irene had no sense of humor; I remembered she'd been given *Streetcar* to produce because of the splendid job she had done producing

Heartsong. I also remembered "You cost me seventy-five thousand dollars" in the lobby of the Walnut Theatre in Philadelphia. Still, she had been treated with contempt and she was close to tears, however booze-encouraged. I tried to take her dilemma seriously.

But how do you do that? You can't and you don't. How do you tell her that? You don't and you can't. Choosing between "The" or "An," absurd as it was, nevertheless was the only act Irene Mayer Selznick, daughter of an Emperor, could perform at that moment as the producer. It was her only validation that, like Tennessee and Gadge, she too had a contribution to make to *Streetcar.* What she wanted was acceptance as a member of the community, not as a celebrity. That, in Beverly Hills, deserved respect.

For the better part of an hour, I played devil's advocate as she took one side, then the other of the nonquestion: Would "An Elia Kazan Production" or "The Elia Kazan Production" be better for Irene Mayer Selznick? By the time she decided, she was three sheets to the wind and felt much better. She took me out to the pool to introduce me to her house guest, the author of *Streetcar.* Tennessee had just finished swimming laps. In one breath, he said: "So you're Arthur Laurents you're not much taller than I am." And he had had *The Glass Menagerie* and soon was going to have *A Streetcar Named Desire.*

My first Memorial Day weekend in Hollywood, Irene called, again in need—this time, of an escort. She had hired a yacht, really, I think, to play buccaneer on the high seas and chase down David O., who was on John Huston's yacht, possibly without Jennifer Jones. She never got him, not even on the telephone.

The yacht she rented was 125 feet long, carrying a crew of eight and four passengers, Katharine Hepburn, Spencer Tracy, Irene Mayer Selznick, and me. We sailed from Balboa, on the California coast, for Catalina, hardly a seafaring journey, but I was so in awe of Hepburn and Tracy, I was seasick the entire voyage. The few times we dropped anchor, I went swimming with Hepburn and retook my stomach. My eyesight returned to normal and I noticed that Hepburn's green eye shadow didn't come off even in the water. Self-invented, she was flamboyantly unadorned. The eye shadow was her only makeup. She did bring two huge, bulging fortnighters for what was only a weekend; all day long, she changed into identical spotless, patched white ducks and spotless patched white shirts.

The rolling sea, which got me, didn't bother her or Irene or Tracy. On the way back to town, he told me the seafaring girls had started on Dramamine before they set foot on board. He hadn't needed it. He was on booze and stayed nicely crocked the whole trip, lolling in a chair as Hepburn patted pillows behind his back. For the return drive from Balboa to Los Angeles, we switched cars: Hepburn rode with Irene, I rode with Tracy. It was Memorial Day, when traffic was bad and accidents frequent. Hepburn and Tracy couldn't afford to be caught in the same car. He was married and a Catholic but they both feared the press even more. Once, he kicked Hedda Hopper in the behind for merely printing his name and Hepburn's in the same sentence in her syndicated column.

He didn't talk much on the drive home or anyplace else as a rule. One night, though, he held forth briefly; he was articulate, emphatic and disappointing—to me, at any rate. The Progressive Citizens of America held a big rally at Gilmore Stadium for Henry Wallace as part of a drive to stem right-wing attacks on unions and the arts. The huge turnout was a surprise. The liberal part of town wanted a rallying point which turned out to be not Wallace so much as a mystery speaker. At the most dramatic moment, at the peak of excitement, a very high platform was hit with blazing spotlights and there was Katharine Hepburn in a red Valentina gown. The stadium roared. Hepburn's grin carried to the top of the bleachers and she delivered magnificently a speech fighting the destruction of culture. The crowd wouldn't stop cheering. Henry Wallace could have been elected president if Katharine Hepburn, in that red dress on that blazing tower, could have been transported from city to city all over the land.

Afterward, she, Tracy, Irene and I went back to her house on Tower Drive, high in the Beverly hills. She was euphoric, proud of her speech. I had been one of the writers of that speech but it wasn't my first time with a star and a speech and a rally. Authorship didn't matter; what mattered was that Katharine Hepburn had made the speech and made it land as no one else could have done. Speeches, like plays, are written to be performed.

Tracy was bothered by the speech, more that she had made any speech at all. Actors had no place in politics, period, according to Spencer Tracy. I'd heard that before, I was sure I'd hear it again, but I never once heard it from a liberal. Only from the most conservative—and Spencer Tracy, congenial and pleasant as he was, was a right-winger. So was Louis B. Mayer. So were Cecil B. DeMille and Sam Wood. So were Barbara Stanwyck and Ronald Reagan and George Murphy, John Wayne, Ginger Rogers—stars born on the wrong side of the tracks who thought playing footsie with conservatives would allow them to cross over. Like the homosexuals back in New York who were Republicans because they wanted to belong.

When I reported for duty at Metro, I was greeted by huge billboards proclaiming MGM had more stars than there were in heaven or at any other studio. Louis B. loved stars; he screamed at them to prove it. He also made them sit in his lap. His domain was a feudal, prisonlike fortress behind stone walls in Culver City on the road to the airport. On the upper floors of the Irving Thalberg Building, the fiefdom where the writing serfs were impounded, were offices designed to make clear our status and our future: they overlooked a mortuary. That mortuary, by refusing to sell out to MGM, sent a message the studio would not accept: You could stand up to it and survive. In a relatively short time, I discovered that myself.

The first "property"—the umbrella word for anything on one or more pieces of paper—I was assigned to adapt, I couldn't finish reading, and there I was, in trouble from the outset. But how could I adapt what I couldn't even read? I wasn't looking for material for a movie I would want to see myself, I knew better than that. I'd been hired to do a job and I wanted to give the studio its money's worth. It was investing X million in a movie, that meant X number of people had to go see it. I was confident I could write a screenplay to that end but not one based on the property assigned me; that could only make a movie no one would want to see.

I revved myself up before I went in to see the story editor, William Fadiman, brother of the famous Clifton and a very nice man. It was tricky to explain why I thought the story would make a bad movie without implying he, as story editor, should never have bought it in the first place. I plowed in, said my say, and waited for the ax. It didn't fall. Instead, I was given another assignment.

I refused that one, too. No ax. Then another; no ax; then another. I began to wonder whether I was only being given projects other writers had thumbs-downed. I continued to refuse assignments but Metro continued to pay my salary. That, oddly and surprisingly, was studio policy. It was the one advantage those of us at the bottom of the totem pole had over those at the top: stars were suspended, writers were not. The policy wasn't dictated by benevolence but by practicality. A writer who wrote a screenplay only to be sure he got his check would do a bad job. That would be a waste of Metro's money but worse, as they had learned from bitter experience, the screenplay might find its way to the screen. So my checks continued but a troubleshooter was assigned to accompany me to story conferences.

Because I'd had a play produced on Broadway, I was somewhat in demand, not that the man who hid behind the desk necessarily knew the play or what it was about or whether it was good or even its name. Just to have had a play produced on Broadway automatically made me more talented, more intelligent, better looking than the Hollywood writers. Even they themselves agreed. The town was built on all sorts of myths—one reason it kept falling down.

My troubleshooter was Albert Lewin, a producer and director himself of movies of artistic ambition. *The Picture of Dorian Gray* and *Pandora and the*

Flying Dutchman, like all his work, were visually elegant, noted for their symbolism and beautiful floors. A sweet, gentle man, well past middle age, he used a hearing aid and wandered in his own thoughts as we went from producer to producer, switching from Haitian painting, which he collected, to the erotic patterns in floors. I assumed he took me on to be sure he would get his salary. Usually, he agreed with my assessment of the assigned property and was helpfully subversive. Once, to my dismay, he said nothing and gave me no support whatsoever, and a real dog was on the table. I had to sink the assignment by myself. When Albert realized this later, he was terribly embarrassed and explained: he had forgotten to turn on his hearing aid.

My social life developed slowly, at first through Irene. Weekly, her chauffeur delivered an envelope containing the program of the movies to be shown that evening at her house. She transformed her library into her cinema: curtains were drawn, guests were settled into deep armchairs with side tables for food and drink arranged earlier by staff, the hostess pressed a button to lower a movie screen over one of the paintings from her collection. Lights dimmed at 5 sharp for the first showing: screen tests. During these, drinks and snacks were served, and careers were started or stopped. Then an unreleased major feature, followed by a break for a quick gourmet dinner—an oxymoron but a fact—then the main feature, this one not only unreleased but unpreviewed, a distinguished provenance.

She also gave me a list of parties: A+, A, A–, B+ and B. Anything below B, I was not allowed to attend. Such a list didn't seem unusual coming from a woman who had hired a tree-climbing instructor for her younger son, a woman, by the way, who'd asked me to read a play about a little boy who cuts up his mother with a pair of scissors. Irene's tree-climbing son was the author; she wasn't concerned with what might be going on inside him, she wanted my opinion of his talent as a writer. So much was unreal or surreal; so little was real.

It was extremely unreal to walk into a house and see Marlene Dietrich. Marlene Dietrich didn't belong in a house. It was peculiar to have her sit by me, tell me how much she worshipped writers, to be sharing her admiration for Edith Piaf and then have Greer Garson sidle over. It wasn't so peculiar to see Greer Garson in a house; she was Mrs. Miniver in a house, a fatuous Mrs. Miniver trying to horn in. Dietrich smiled slyly at something fascinating on the ceiling and then, not very sotto voce, asked me, "Shall I be a gentleman or shall I kick her in the ass?"

At large black-tie parties, the stars became more real because their endemic need for attention led them to get up and perform and lay unglamorous eggs. Possibly believing their singing was justified by the content of their songs,

Eddie Albert (on guitar) and his wife Margo (in serape) regularly offered the likes of "I Dreamed I Saw Joe Hill Last Night."

They were the opening act at "Positively the Last Farewell Party for Moss Hart," as the sign on the front door of Harry Kurnitz's house proclaimed. Kurnitz was a very popular screenwriter well known for his wit and his girl-friend's name: Blossom Plum. "Joe Hill" was followed by Edmond O'Brien with "Oh, that this too too solid flesh might melt!"—not a wise selection for a man fifty pounds overweight in a jacket he couldn't button. In for a penny, he then announced his Brazilian wife, Olga San Juan, was going to sing in Portuguese a "sad folk ballad of unrequited love in the slums of Rio de Janeiro." She sang "Tico Tico."

The evening picked up with the successful parlor trick regularly done by Jeff Kessel, brother of the noted French novelist, Joseph Kessel: Jeff took bites out of a martini glass until he had eaten the whole glass. Humphrey Bogart, no drunker than usual, took a good bite out of his martini glass to prove he was as macho as any frog sissy. Blood gushed, his mouth glittered with shards of glass; Bogie just grinned a bloody grin and went for another bite. The boyos around him knocked the glass from his now bleeding hand and wiped him off. True ass-kissers, they marveled at his derring-do and reveled in his humilia-tion. Just as they marveled at his old buddy John Huston at another party and watched, silent and still for too long, while he "put on the gloves" and pounded the shit out of a kid—Manny Robinson, Edward G. Robinson's lighter, shorter, teenage son. Movie males defined masculinity as they played it or directed it on celluloid.

One of the biggest parties on Irene's list was a triple-tenter: John Huston, Jean Negulesco, and Charles Vidor celebrating their wedding anniversaries to their bevy of wives. Irene phoned: "What time are you getting there?"

"I'm not going."

"Didn't you get your invitation?"

"Yes, but I've had it."

She was astounded. "How can you not go?"

"How can you keep going?"

"Because tonight, it might happen!" As he does for Cinderella in fairy tales and movies, so Prince Charming might turn up for Irene.

There was an endless, vicious circle in Hollywood that limited both the quality of life and the quality of movies. Life in the movies was based on the life of the people who made movies who based their lives on the life they saw in movies.

That was why Hollywood did best with pictures with no pretense to real-ity: comedies like *The Awful Truth* and *The More the Merrier,* romantic dramas like the original *A Star Is Born* and the original *Love Affair,* fantasies like *The*

Wizard of Oz (and *E.T.*). Entertainment skillfully, even artfully crafted but without a center, without a core. Shadows without substance. Rarely did Hollywood make a picture of substance: *Citizen Kane* was a marvel of style and technique, not content. When Hollywood tried for substance, it got pretentious or nobly simple or diffused in key lights on chiseled faces. The movies that stood up were hot fudge sundaes like *The Manchurian Candidate* or *The Godfather* or *Jezebel.*

Driving home from the party where I met Dietrich, I stopped at one of the corners on Sunset for a hitchhiker. He looked even better in the car. He was wearing jodhpurs and riding boots but had no more interest in horses than he had in conversation. We were driving along Franklin Avenue, which had few street lamps and lots of tree shadows; he was going down on me, though, because of the steering wheel, not with the ease we both would have preferred. Preparing to park by the curb in the shadow of one of those trees, I slowed down and turned off the lights. At that moment, I saw a police car approaching; I switched the lights back on, pulled away from the curb and picked up speed. Instantly, the police car made a U-turn and came after us.

There was just barely enough time to zip up my pants, exchange names with the trick, tell him our alleged destination when the cop was yanking open the door on my side and flashing his light on my crotch. In vain: I was so frightened my penis had already crawled up inside me to hide.

In New York, when I went to the Actors Studio, I watched them improvise. To me, the value of improvisation was overrated: it wasn't so much a question of thinking as the character as it was of just thinking fast on your feet. I was good at that. When the cop asked why had I started to park, I had an answer: I was going to get out and take a leak—"urinate" would have been a giveaway, "pee" would have been a confession—but I saw the police car coming. The cop bought it. He bought that we were headed to the Pancake House on Hollywood Boulevard. In the rearview mirror, I saw his car turn around but I drove to the Pancake House anyway. I went in—alone. I even ordered and ate pancakes.

Was it Marlene Dietrich who primed me to stop my car to pick up that trick on Sunset? Although she was all about sex—her "Hello" was "Want to have sex?"—she was very, very funny and humor is not exactly an aphrodisiac. Ah, but power is, and being chosen and favored by Dietrich gave me power and the confidence that what happened when that sexy boy got in the car was exactly what would happen: I was emanating rays. Then why did I put my car into arrest-me mode when I saw the police car? Where did the guilt come from? Those were questions for a psychiatrist; by then, I was going to one.

Dr. Judd Marmor. He soundproofed his office after he caught a writer-producer eavesdropping on his wife who was a patient.

. . .

His name was Judd Marmor. It was Irene who got me to him—the best thing she ever did for me. Marmor was a Freudian psychoanalyst; he put my life into turnaround. In the movie business, turnaround is a pejorative: a screenplay put into turnaround is a screenplay thrown back out into a cold world with every prospect of freezing to death. In the living business, turnaround is a positive, hard to attain: a life put into turnaround is a life put on the right track. Judd did that for me.

Back in New York, when Irene said she knew the perfect analyst for me, she meant the famous May Romm, who had been her analyst. When we walked into Dr. Romm's living room–like Beverly Hills office, a short, stocky, motherly lady with a broad smile on her face stretched out her arms to Irene. Irene raced across the room and swept her up in her arms, whirling her around and around, the analyst's little legs flying out as though she was the female half of their dance team.

In her backyard, Dr. Mother Romm gave me metaphoric chicken soup, lamenting we were both too close to Irene for me to lie on her couch. There was, however, a new young doctor in town, a very talented man whose office was in Beverly Hills. I gathered the importance of the location: although this Dr. Marmor's office was more legitimately situated in Beverly Hills than my sublet on Doheny, it still wasn't in a really good part of Beverly Hills: i.e., Marmor would be less expensive than Romm. Years later, Judd reversed that. He was worth it: he became president of the American Psychiatric Association, and during his regime homosexuality officially ceased to be termed an "illness"—a great boon to gay liberation.

At our first meeting, Marmor didn't look either impressive or compassionate. Nevertheless, when he asked me why I was in his office, the reply came right out with no hesitation: "I'm afraid I'm homosexual."

"Why afraid?"

"Because I don't want to be."

"Why not?"

Why not? What was wrong with him? "You know it's dirty and disgusting."

"I don't know anything about it," he said. "I just believe whoever or whatever you are, what matters is that you lead your life with pride and dignity."

I had never heard anyone say that. Even though I could see he meant it, it was hard for me to believe he meant it. Hard to believe anyone could or anyone else did. Hard to believe it was true, hard to believe I could do it. Yet I was elated. Why? I didn't know why, but then, I didn't know that sentence had put me into turnaround.

No one had to tell me that sexuality is where we all begin. The woods were full of homosexuals trying to hide from themselves and to live a lie. I could see them all too clearly. I didn't much like them which was probably why I couldn't see myself as one of them. But just what was my sexuality? I wavered, I seesawed. What I had to learn was that the sooner I accepted whatever I was, the sooner I would start to grow up. Slowly I made my way with Marmor's help—help, never insistence or bias, one way or the other. When what had been obsessive behavior became occasional, I realized the process was working. Realization didn't come in one holy effulgent moment as it does in *Snake Pit*. It came after the fact, after I had stopped behaving like an adolescent.

I went to Marmor three times a week; by the end of the third week, he bore a remarkable physical resemblance to my father. The analysis spread over almost four years, though during that period I went to Europe for the first time and to New York two or three times, one of them for several months when I was doing a new play, *The Bird Cage*. And of course, like all analysts, he went on vacation in August. What is it about August? In California, it can't be the weather; I think it's Eastern envy.

Although he was a Freudian, Marmor didn't believe in orthodox Freudian analysis. For one thing, he thought it took too long and wanted to start group therapy but there were no takers then; for another, he dealt with my daily life and didn't delve into childhood until an intractable problem seemed to originate back there. I learned to interpret my dreams myself. Very overrated: the meaning of one recurrent dream was a mystery never solved but when I left analysis, I stopped having the dream.

It was important to me to know Marmor's frame of reference; for example, that he was liberal, a progressive. Think not? Then live through the Hollywood Witch Hunt with an analyst whose political stance and morality are unknown to you, or unfriendly and even threatening. Abe Burrows—who was a friend, went to an analyst named Phil Cohen—Phil Cohen who was rumored to be an FBI agent. Abe Burrows turned informer. False syllogism? His new wife, another patient, named friends she merely suspected. Despite all I thought I knew about Judd, a political obstacle surfaced in my analysis near the end, around the time that I was blacklisted.

At the outset, there was a lesser, nonpolitical obstacle: he asked me about my analysis with Reik and wanted me to repeat Reik's explanation for his greed. Marmor was my analyst: that meant no secrets, no hiding, no lying, no omissions. I understood all that but he had to understand I had given Reik my word of honor. Six months later my father sent me a newspaper clipping: a picture of Reik and his wife, with "Uncle Ted" holding a big, angry cat. The caption said Mrs. had divorced Mr. for throwing the cat at her. I told Marmor all.

He focused on my sexuality because it troubled me so much it limited my ability to love. He didn't bother much with my attitude toward Hollywood, perhaps because he didn't share it: he remained there and, inevitably, its values took their toll on him. Before that, however, he certainly nailed me on mine.

"I'd like to point out something," he said one session. "I'm not being judgmental but I'd just like to point out that every time you say the word 'movie,' in the next sentence you say the word 'shit.' "

True. But by then, I loved being in California. I was having a wonderful, paradoxical time: going to the beach and playing tennis while publicly (and happily) excoriating the House Un-American Committee at a Thought Control Conference held at the Beverly Hills Hotel, and living on Lookout Mountain Road in Laurel Canyon in a crazy little house I shared with Farley Granger.

My first weeks in Hollywood, Farley and Randall were the only homosexuals I knew. I didn't see them often, usually at the house on Doheny, which was sort of a second home to Farley. Fate or coincidence, the Sol and Ethel Chaplins, as I found out later, were his best friends. Ethel called him Farfel. He loved it. He wished he was Jewish; the people he loved most were Jewish. That, of course, got to me. I didn't speculate what he would wish he were if the people he loved most were Scientologists.

I looked for his smile when he came by Doheny with Randall and it was always there. Twice, I went off to an A party while they stayed on and had an X-rated party that they didn't keep secret from me. Nor did I object. Farley lived with his parents, Randall's landlord was a snoop; as consciously rising young stars, they had to be careful about being seen together. I was their beard, but that was OK. As intended, my magnanimity impressed Farley.

The first time I saw him without Randall was at Gene and Betsy Kelly's house on Rodeo Drive. I had met the Kellys through Sono Osato before she left town. Farley became the main reason I continued to go there. A Kelly regular, he had been brought into the group by a boyfriend whom he had dumped for Randall whom I wanted him to dump for me. That didn't stop me from seeing him as pure in heart and elsewhere. Well, I was in analysis, wasn't I?

Gene and Betsy held open house for what the movie colony called, literally, the "Real People." Only in Hollywood. The house was modest for Beverly Hills, furnished not with bad taste or tastelessly, just with an absence of taste: uncertain colors and islands of plaid. The Real People didn't dress up, they sat on the shaggy rugs; they talked politics as well as movies (that was Betsy); they were liberal (also Betsy); and only the exception made a sexual pass (that was Gene). There were slapdash potluck meals for the faithful: writers and directors, actors and dancers. The intellectual level was not a challenge but they were all young, all on the way up and every last one hell-bent on arriving now, this minute. Although there were always two or three stars, no ass was kissed except Gene's and there was a line of assistants and secretaries for that. The core stars were Peter Lawford, Louis Jourdan, and Lena Horne.

Lena was quiet, not wholly there; usually just sitting, sipping brandy near the piano where her husband, Lennie Hayton, doodled at the keyboard—on his face a gentle, brandied half smile. Ignoring the yachting cap he always wore, she called him Daddy, not Commodore. Lennie had conducted the band at Leon and Eddie's when I was a Nitewit; luckily, he didn't recognize me and I was not about to remind him. Although he was a musical director at Metro, his whole focus, professional and personal, was on Lena. He radically changed her career as a singer.

It happened overnight, not in pictures—she was the wrong color for pictures—but at a downtown club called Slapsie Maxie on the night it opened. Los Angeles had a downtown then where frustrated creative energy could be released even on the legitimate stage. The Biltmore Theatre was used by frustrated movie stars like Gregory Peck and Dorothy McGuire to act in plays for a brief run. Slapsie Maxie, after that opening night, lit the spotlight for performers who'd been rusting since the end of vaudeville.

There is such a thing as cabaret history and it was made at Slapsie's in one night. Everybody lucky enough to be there (I was one of them: the Kelly group went to support Lena) saw fireworks explode twice. First from the heat of Jack Cole and His Dancers: three highly sexual males, three highly sexual females, dancing unlike any dancers anyone had seen anyplace before. The first number, "Spy," set to Benny Goodman's "Sing, Sing, Sing," fixed the tone—intense and erotic—and the style—angular, slashing, knee slides, tipping hats, twisting torsos and pelvises. That tone, that style, the moves and steps themselves, unseen until then, became a permanent part of the choreographic language of the Broadway musical. Bob Fosse is credited but it all began with Jack Cole in a town that drained and discouraged and finally destroyed him. One of his dancers was Gwen Verdon who became Bob Fosse's closest collaborator. Well, nobody waits, nothing stands still, everything has to start someplace and if it's good, it'll go somewhere better.

The closing act at Slapsie Maxie's was Lena Horne with a trio led by Lennie Hayton. She wasn't Metro's Lena Horne, she wasn't the Helena Horne I remembered from the Savoy-Plaza, she wasn't the Lena who sat removed and bemused at the Kellys'. The voice deeper, the lyrics almost bitten and spat out, the eyes glittering, this was a new Lena. This Lena was angry sex.

I gave the credit to Lennie because that was all I knew then. What Billy Strayhorn did for her, I learned only after I met him with her at the Hotel Trémouille, April in Paris, 1954; what Ralph Harris, her white manager, meant to her I factored in during the late Fifties, again in Paris. Jeanne Noble's sudden, fiercely black influence I felt full force in New York in the Sixties, when it derailed, besides the personal, "Hallelujah, Baby!" which I had written for Lena. Credit for turning the lady into a tiger doesn't matter; the angry sexuality was always there, uniquely hers, just growling while it waited to be let out of her cage.

In the early Sixties, when we were so close, I asked her what was in her head when she came out on the elegant floor of the Waldorf in New York or the Fairmount in San Francisco. She bared her teeth in the smile those expensive audiences waited for.

"Fuck you," she said. "That's what I think when I look at them. Fuck all of you." She meant it figuratively, they took it literally.

Sex with Farley was secondary to me. As Marmor pointed out, I separated sex and love like church and state. With Nora, it was love without the need for sex; with Harold Lang, it was affection, even candlelit romance, but wonderfully abandoned sex without love to get in the way. With Farley, I wanted sex to validate what was going on silently and unacknowledged between us at the Kellys'. We never had a conversation at the Kellys' without other people present; we touched once by accident and reacted as though it was foreplay.

It was exciting that no one at the Kellys' had a clue anything was happening. How could they? They were all battling hard to please the lord and master, and survive the competitiveness. Competition was lifeblood to Gene, as was too evident the night Noël Coward dropped by to meet the Real People.

Elaborately dressed down, a baker's dozen of us gathered at the Kellys', sprawling over the floor more than usual, ostensibly to make us more Real than ever by displaying indifference to the superficial, Mayfair elegance Coward would undoubtedly display. The guest of honor was so tardy that we were finishing a picnic-lunch dinner when he swept in wearing black tie and waving a cigarette in an elegant holder.

"Sorry," he said, exactly like Noël Coward, "I've just been to a wingding at Joan's."

His delivery, the word *wingding,* the subtle disparagement of Joan Crawford in his pronunciation of her name made us laugh: we were his and happy to be. He held us, chatting away like a hedge clipper, no interruptions until one of the more militant subversives, wanting attention, moved aggressively to politics. Success is the great deceiver; Coward was high on it, hubris equally high. He rattled, unmindful of adages like Give a man enough rope. He started splendidly: The world's greatest problem was overpopulation. Ahead with that, he went on to take aim at the solution. He not only missed the target, he shot himself down.

"War is the solution," he instructed us. "That's why we need wars. The bubonic plague used to do the job. Now that we've been clever enough to do away with plague, we must get rid of these unnecessary people with war."

Noël Coward had played to too many audiences not to know instantly that he had lost us. It didn't faze him. He wanted us back and he knew how to get us back. He went onstage. For one hour, that indestructible entertainer sat at the piano and sang his own songs to the enemy. He was funny, he was sweet, he was bittersweet, he was poignant, he was incredible. His politics were limited to satirizing himself through his countrymen with "Mad Dogs and Englishmen" and "The Stately Homes of England"; our politics went out the window. So did our objections, our values, our anything that wasn't adoration. He turned a plaid-and-shag rumpus room into his own elegant drawing room; he turned us into his guests; then he turned the room into his shrine and us into his worshipping sycophants.

Gene couldn't stand it. Before we had stopped applauding, even as he himself applauded, he was on his feet, taking over the floor. Not only did he sing, he danced. In his own house on a shaggy rug he knew was not for dancing, Gene Kelly tried to dance because that was what he could do best and Noël Coward couldn't do very well. The secretary-fans were with him, everybody was. We all wanted it to work. Noël Coward wanted it to work; Gene was so needy, even I wanted it to work. If it weren't for the rug, it might have but it didn't; it was embarrassing. Betsy gracefully saved him and the party was over. The competition for the Real People was won by an old master, Noël Coward.

Because of Gene, games were played night and day at the Kellys'. I loved the Game—charades played in teams—because I was good at it. Usually, I was captain of one team; Gene was always captain of the other. It was not happy hour when he lost.

He never lost at volleyball, which was played in the backyard. His secretary-fans gasped if he merely picked up the ball. To give him his due, however reluctantly, he was terrific at volleyball. He took it so seriously, he decided there would be two games: an A game for players like himself and Stanley Donen the director, and Richard Conte the actor, a B game for duffers like Farley and me and Betsy. The first time out with A and B teams resulted in disaster and a cast change in *Easter Parade,* Gene's next movie.

His A game was played first: swiftly, ferociously, silently except for a "Shit!" a "Fuck!" an adoring "Oh, Gene!" When the game was over—Gene's side had won, there was a God—the players flopped on the grass to recover while we played, but the tension was so great, we began to laugh like bad kids. Which made it difficult to play. Which made us laugh even more. The harder we tried to stop, the less we succeeded and the longer the attempt at playing the game went on.

We didn't dare look at Gene. Even the air on the court trembled at his rage. He was rested, his teammates were ready to return but the end of our nongame was nowhere in sight. Laughing made it difficult to score. The more points we missed making, the more infuriated Gene got. Then the ball flew off the court and hit him. That ended the game and life in his backyard.

He sprang up like a geyser. We were a bunch of lousy spoilsports! We were deliberately staying on the court so he couldn't have his second game! We offered to stop. Oh, it was his fault we were quitting? He didn't play fair? Did we think he was like us? Who the fuck did we think we were anyway? Roaring at the top of his high tenor, he thrashed his way back to the house, flung open the kitchen door, and swiveled for one final curse. "Faggots!" he shrieked and like Rumpelstiltskin, stamped down so hard on the doorsill that he broke his ankle. And that, dear cineastes, was why Fred Astaire replaced Gene Kelly in the leading role of *Easter Parade,* which was scheduled to start shooting the next day.

Probably Gene didn't really yell "Faggots." That raspy, high tenor made whatever he did yell indistinguishable. It wasn't purely perverse wishful thinking that made me think "faggots" when it wasn't. Gene made faggot jokes constantly. Why? Particularly with me there and Farley there, why did he make them?

There were whispers, there always are, but the whispers about Gene were about him during his time in New York as a chorus boy—an appellation that gave unfair automatic credence to the whispers. But he flirted with men as well as with women—which, never mind unfair, was disgusting, however much due to his overblown narcissism. Whether or not he had played around in New York, he was now a movie star but unfortunately, a dancing movie star. Astaire didn't have the problem, but then, Astaire was sexless and Gene wasn't. I understood Gene had to be more macho than John Wayne even though if he wore boots, they had to be soft so he could dance in them. What I did not understand was, Why the fag jokes? "Methinks the lady . . ."? Not that sexual bigots had to have homosexual experiences. Paddy Chayefsky hadn't.

Thirty-odd years later, after a meeting of the Dramatists Guild's council, Chayefsky asked for my help with a play he was writing. It was set in a time and place I knew firsthand and he didn't: Hollywood during the Witch Hunt. Chayefsky's problem was how to write a homosexual suspected of being a Communist. He knew little about homosexuals but admitted having been prejudiced until his wife went to work on him and got him over it. He chuckled. "Not entirely over it, but getting there."

We were walking in Central Park; it was a lovely day, whether early fall or late spring I don't remember. I can still hear his voice, though, when he used the word *bigot* about himself. That surprised me. I barely knew him, but he was intelligent, a writer; he lived in the theatre world and he was a Jew. The anger I ordinarily would have had to work to hold down was fairly easy to keep in check: I liked him for being open. It seemed a compliment that he felt he could be open and I would not be offended. Then I wondered—his voice was so gruff and he was so blunt—if the truth was that he didn't give a shit whether I was offended or not. He needed to research what happened to fags in the Hollywood Witch Hunt. What better way than talking directly to one who had survived?

I helped him: his imagination had put him on the wrong track—homosexuality had never entered into the Hollywood part of the Witch Hunt. I gave him the answers needed to put him on the right track; then it was my turn. I asked where his prejudice came from. From his family, his upbringing, he said, his neighborhood. An answer, but not a satisfying or complete answer. After all, my father was brought up by prejudiced Orthodox Jews but ended up completely without prejudice, a humanitarian. Why? My mother was brought up by tolerant socialists. Why, married to my father, did she become what she had not been before marriage? Why was she prejudiced against gentiles? Why was Paddy Chayefsky prejudiced against homosexuals? In analysis, I was busy trying to find out why I was homosexual. Judd Marmor didn't know. At one session, I offered up the summer of my thirteenth birthday, not because I thought that was when my homosexuality began but because that was when I connected love to loving a man.

His name was George, he was eighteen, a natural athlete, and straight—let that be clear. The girls in the sister summer camp across the lake were all over him; he could pick and choose and he did. Not that he was handsome—he was slightly walleyed, but I found that sexy along with his full ripe lips, high cheekbones, big strong nose, and the way he walked. I suspect it was more that walk, like a graceful panther, that made him seem so sexy; I'm not sure, I was only thirteen and he was a junior counselor, assigned to my group at the camp I had gone to for the first time the summer before.

I hated camp. I was an outsider again: every other kid had been there from the age of seven or eight; every one of them hoped that after he was a senior, he would be allowed to stay on as a junior counselor. Summer camp didn't end Labor Day. The campers saw each other constantly in the winter in the city, even after they were married and middle-aged. If they'd had to move out of town to Connecticut or Florida, they visited.

Everything was a competition. Not just races and games and the end-of-summer Color War; anything that could be made competitive was. The privilege of raising the flag at morning assembly, the distinction of having the cleanest bunk, membership in the honor societies—that was the holiest of holies.

My first summer, they were all set to tap me the second week. An older boy, whom it had taken three years to be chosen, exercised his privilege and said he would blackball me unless they hazed me to find out what I really was like. They did and I spent the summer crying in the woods. When the next summer came around I pleaded but my mother thought the sister camp had been wonderful for my sister. I knew what she really found wonderful was the hotel for parents on the top of the hill above the camp. Back I went, dreading the summer ahead.

George fell in love with me, why, I don't know. Slowly, he set about making me the boy athlete, and he succeeded. I was tapped for the honor society and ended up president. Beyond my quick reflexes and speed, he didn't have too much to work with at first. He was so careful, no one knew he was giving me what amounted to private tutelage. At a tennis match, as he retrieved a ball, only I could hear him urge me to just go for it and how. I went for it, I won the point, I trusted him. I began to be good, camp began to be fun, I began to love him back. He was with me as much as possible; he let me be next to him when he had bull sessions with his buddies his age, but he was protective. "Not in front of him," he would say but I hadn't a clue what they were talking about. I wasn't listening, not consciously; I was content just being next to him. I loved him.

I loved my father and I knew he loved me, but I knew it was different with George. Mother's threat was always that she would report to my father whatever crime my sister and I had committed. The threat was empty, of course. He never punished us, he always loved us. But we rarely saw him when we were kids. He was often away on business, and even when home he was a bit removed because he was busy. Or perhaps I'm just granting him being busy. During my freshman year at Cornell, I told him I didn't want to be pre-law as we had planned. I was telling him I didn't want to follow in his footsteps, that I was rejecting him. He asked only what it was that I did want.

"To be a writer."

"Fine. Good."

He gave his full support and never wavered, not even while I was a Nitewit. He loved me and I loved him, but it wasn't like it was with George. Nothing ever was but then, I was never thirteen again.

We had three physical moments; only one was sexual. The first was early in the summer. I was in a play for the first time, a summer camp classic called *The Crow's Nest*. I got the part because Bob Sidney, the dramatics counselor, judged I was smart enough to remember the lines and agile enough to shinny up the unsteady mast while saying them. Bob, who later directed *This Is the Army* and then became a Hollywood choreographer, had the whole camp camping without knowing we were camping—subliminally absorbing the notion it was not only OK to be homosexual, it was fun.

Everyone in my bunk had gone on to the social hall to see *The Crow's Nest* when George came in to wish me luck. He kissed me. Nervous about the play, I pushed him away. Later in the summer, I was always waiting, hoping he would kiss me again. He did once more, at the end of that summer of arousal, the summer that kept me coming back to that camp until I was a senior, then a junior counselor, and finally the dramatics counselor. But I didn't camp, nor did anyone else.

The third physical moment with George, the sexual moment, resulted indirectly from a lesson from another teacher. The bed in a far corner of my bunkhouse was occupied by a waiter. The dining hall waiters at camp were college boys older than the junior counselors. They worked harder and were paid more but were treated snobbishly by the kids. Our waiter was a notch up because he was a smash basketball player. In later life, his picture appeared daily in the tabloid that featured his sports column.

Occasionally he talked sports in the bunkhouse after taps, giving us pointers or telling stories about legends. One rainy night, with the shutters closed down, making the bunk pitch black, he sat on my bed for his talk. About what, I don't remember because he took my hand and put it on his penis, then reached under the blanket and took hold of mine. We hardened together and came together. I enjoyed it and felt no guilt. Nor did I wonder why he picked me; I understood without entirely understanding.

That was a one-night stand but a few nights later, Jesus Christ—our name for the counselor in charge of our bunk because he looked like Jesus although he wasn't Jewish—took us and his telescope outside to look at the stars he loved. What we loved was being out of our bunkhouse after taps when all the other kids were stuck inside theirs.

I was standing in the shadow of a tree, looking up at the stars through the branches when George appeared. It was his day off; in my ear, he told me he'd been unable to stay away. He was wearing thirteen-button navy blue sailor pants. The waiter had inducted me. I played with a button, then slid my hand over George's penis. He let it stay there for a second, then gently took it away in his but I felt him starting to get hard. That was it and that was all; again, I understood why without entirely understanding. I don't think George understood entirely, either.

Back in the city that winter, he took me to the theatre a couple of times, once to see Earl Carroll's *Vanities,* which he liked more than I did—personal affection didn't affect me as critic. My parents must have approved, possibly because I was regarded as a little adult but probably because, in their eyes, no one connected to camp could do wrong. Parents don't listen.

George didn't come back to camp the next summer. In the fall, I heard that the college he'd gone away to was in Edinburgh, where enrollment was much easier. But it was so far away and he never said good-bye. Put the ache in a box and bury it: I learned that at fourteen. There's always a little residue, of course, and it surfaced many years later when I ran into him.

I was back from California, living in New York again, in an apartment high up on East Fifty-seventh Street. The elevator door opened and a man walked in. He was wearing glasses, he was older but he was George, older.

The difference between thirteen and eighteen is a generation; at eighteen, he had begun to grow into his face, I hadn't grown into mine until years after he knew me.

"Hello, George," I said.

It took him more than a moment. Then he said: "Your pictures don't do right by you."

Through the summer camp grapevine, he knew I was a playwright; I thought he was an anesthetist with a wife and a son, but the grapevine was behind. He was divorced and had been visiting his son who lived with his ex-wife. We chatted as we walked through the lobby, thawing out.

"Do you have time for a drink?" he asked.

"Sure. We could go up to my place."

His obvious wariness—I had said I lived alone—was annoying; more than annoying because I sensed he was wary of what had crossed my mind and he was right that it had. "There's a nice little bar around the corner," he suggested.

We went to the nice little bar where I waited to find out why he wanted to have a drink. He had no interest in theatre or movies. Finally he got to it.

"I've always wondered—well, worried . . . Did I—Is it because of me . . . ?"

"No," I said. "You were very good to me. And for me. But I like what I am, George."

That was the last real sentence either of us said; it effectively ended his concern and my ache.

In telling this to Marmor, I realized my homosexuality, contrary to what I had once thought, wasn't traceable to George. Where it did come from, I had no idea. I didn't think Freud or Jung or Marmor did either, though Marmor, at least, admitted it. And when he came back from a psychiatric convention in Chicago, he told me all the bigwigs agreed: they didn't know where homosexuality came from either. Oedipus and Momma were out of the running.

Farley was my idea of the last candidate for analysis. Uncomplicated, he was all the easier to love. In Hollywood, beauty like his was so common it didn't make life and love easier. In the gay world, it was like being born rich. I never liked what I looked like—the only photographs of myself I liked were always taken years earlier. As striking and improbable as Farley's looks were, he seemed unaware of them; and once you knew him, what you marveled at was his sweetness. He was generous with praise for his peers and with presents for his friends as though he himself wasn't enough to give. His enthusiasm was unlimited, especially for music, and endearing but ill advised for his own

Farley in bedroom slippers in front of the two-way fireplace in
the house we shared on Lookout Mountain Road in Laurel Canyon.

singing. Physically uncoordinated, he stormed the tennis net, tripping over his
own racquet on the way. But he was the first to laugh.

He tried to supplement his skimpy California high school education by
reading the right books and sitting in on discussions about the right issues—
"right" as defined by me, of course. Not by his parents, who were reactionary
bigots he lived with in a small house in the Valley. He was their only child and
meal ticket. As a kid, he had often slept in the doghouse with his dog to escape
his father's drunken ranting but his childhood didn't seem to bother him, his
parents didn't seem to bother him, nothing seemed to bother him except Sam
Goldwyn, who was his boss and therefore supposed to bother him. It took me
a long time to realize that where Farley was really a good actor was offscreen.

I was never happy if I wasn't writing, so while not writing screenplays at
Metro, I started a new play. It wasn't going well; the distractions that had come
with moving to California and living in this new world of movies finally

couldn't prevent the failure of *Heartsong* from catching up with me. I had thought I had put it behind me but failure is vengeful and patient. Until fully acknowledged and accepted, it will do what it was now doing so efficiently and effectively: killing my confidence. I would embark on a new scene; one or two pages and then the murderous question was not Could I write it? or Would it be any good? but Would it make the play a success? Even though I couldn't stop myself from asking it, I knew that question was a sure way of ensuring failure. So I tried to concentrate on the most important element in any dramatic work: the characters. But they were eluding me and interrupting all thought was Farley.

Whether my inability to concentrate on the play was making me fantasize about him or whether desire for him was making me unable to concentrate on the play—chicken or egg, what difference, it was irrelevant. I wanted him and I had to let him know I did.

Once, someone on Fire Island said to me: "Why don't you ever make a pass at someone you can't get?" He was in the wrong sexual loop. Passes are made by the clumsy, it's all done with the eyes. Don't dance til the music starts. If the eyes connect, the music starts sending a rush to the groin without a word— that's what's exciting.

Contact with Farley had been made at the Kellys'. The next step was the how, when and where of the first move. Not by whom; I knew that was my role but I was hesitant, unsure whether Farley wanted the move now, whether he preferred it some vague time in the future, even whether he wanted it made at all. But I never could stand suspense; better the worst than nothing. So late another wasted afternoon at the typewriter, I called him at his folks' house.

The words tumbled out just as they did on yellow legal pads or my typewriter: too many and too fast but felt. Being a beard was over, I told him. Looking at him sitting next to Randall (this was the first time I'd even thought of Randall) on the couch at my place on Doheny, that was over. And I was going to stay away from the Kellys'. I only went there to see him but just seeing him wasn't enough so I wouldn't anymore.

He was bewildered. He refused to accept my self-banishment: we had to see each other. That was all the encouragement I needed. I slowed down, calculated, huskied my tone, played the strings: told him I couldn't pretend I could just be his friend because I knew I wasn't capable, I cared too much. All of it was not entirely true before I said it but as I said it, it all became true. And worked. It was as though he had been waiting for the signal, all he needed to jump into his car and come barreling across the canyon. I barely had enough time to shower and shave before there he was, running through the door, and then, there we were, rolling on the floor. On the shag rug in the living room of a sublet on the wrong side of Doheny Drive in midafternoon, me and my movie star. Oh frabjous day!

My sexual motor went out of overdrive and moved into a more normal gear. Love was going to make my life fuller and calmer and keep me off the boulevard. We had to pretend we weren't lovers because we didn't have friends with whom we could be what we were. There were people we called friends, familiar faces from the Kellys' or from Charlie Chaplin's, but being gay was not something anyone talked about openly unless it was disparagingly about someone else. Chaplin was an exception: he censured no one.

I met him because of his tennis court. He loved having young people use the court; it ensured his having a game whenever he wanted one. He gave the golden California boy who gave lessons to all the Chaplins the use of the court for lessons to other pupils, like Farley and me. All the pupils and their tennis-playing friends participated in what was called the Cockamamie Tennis Tournament, a round-robin played at Charlie's and at Willy Wyler's next door. Whether you played or watched, you were welcomed into the circle, which at the Chaplins' included Bill Tilden for a time.

Tilden had done time at the county farm for an incident involving an underage boy. When he got out, the man who had been the most famous tennis player in the world was broke and broken. Charlie, of course, knew how vulnerable fame can make a star. He himself was famous for unpopular things, very famously for being tight with a buck but he came to Tilden's rescue. He hired him to give tennis lessons to all the Chaplins and to any of the rest of us who wanted lessons. At his expense.

Tilden was a curious, dour man. His instructed me to stop and retie my laces whenever an opponent was ahead. That learned, he set about giving me a forehand. Charlie also let Tilden use the court to teach his new protégé while in the overlooking tennis house, the boy's mother sat knitting, not watching: the Court mandated a parent had to be there. The boy was never going to be a champion, and even at fifteen his lush features were beginning to thicken, but Tilden hit with him as though it was a privilege. The boy's name was Arthur; every time Tilden said it, I was embarrassed.

Charlie never mentioned Tilden's small scandal; he didn't find him very interesting and he wasn't. He only talked of Tilden as Tennis Past. Charlie liked good talk. After doubles—he was a good player and a cheerful partner—he enjoyed discussion on almost any subject before he went up to the main house to work on his script for *Limelight*. That we were so much younger pleased him. He didn't use his age or that he was Charlie Chaplin or even that it was his tennis house and his court. Nor did he sermonize or lecture: he talked with us, exchanged ideas and beliefs with us—*then* he sermonized. He was completely nonconformist, with a belief or two traceable to George Bernard Shaw but not to any political party. His ideas were idiosyncratic, pure Charlie. He was all for the common man, in theory and his movies, anyway. I once overheard Kate Hepburn explaining Communism to her friend Fanny Brice.

"It's very simple, Fanny," she said. "Everyone shares."

"Yes, I got that part," Fanny said. "But will I be able to keep my jewelry?"

Charlie would have been right there with Fanny but he wouldn't have had to ask, he just would have kept. There wasn't much he thought he couldn't answer and he was very generous with his help. *Rain*—seminal play of my childhood—was being rehearsed at a little theatre his son Sidney had started on La Brea and the actress playing Sadie Thompson was in trouble. Charlie went to help. He directed by demonstrating: he played Sadie by becoming Sadie. In his tennis clothes, with his white hair and a napkin, he walked, gestured, moved, spoke, and there she was: Reverend Davidson's downfall, Sadie Thompson of Pago Pago. Charlie was marvelous but the actress never got it.

Afterward, I asked him how he did it, what he used to become Sadie. He smiled coquettishly and said:

"I always wondered if I'd been given a little push . . ."

Untrue, Charlie, but thank you. He liked me, he was an actor, actors want

At the Chaplin tennis court with Norman Lloyd and Charlie.

to please. They also flirt. Charlie adored Oona, beamed when she appeared. More than twice her age, he had twice the energy she did. She was ready to leave a party long before he was. His passion for her, however, didn't prevent him from being aware of sexuality, anyone's and everyone's, and being interested in it whatever it was. But his interest wasn't personal, he didn't judge. Clearly, he knew I had a relationship of some sort with Farley, but it was equally clear that he regarded it as none of his business. Unlike others—a toad called Julian Claman, for instance, a would-be writer and a freeloader who practically lived at the Kellys'.

Julian dropped by on a very high horse one afternoon, white and twitchy, sanctimonious and upset. Because he had seen Farley's car parked all night in front of the house on Doheny. That was very, very bad for me, Julian announced.

For me? Farley was the actor; if anyone was going to be hurt by gossip, it would be he. But none of it was any of Julian's business anyway. My dislike fed my anger. Why had Julian made it his business?

The first time I saw him at the Kellys', I thought he was gay. I learned he had a wife and children living in an orange grove in Ojai; I still thought he was gay. What else had put this bug up his ass? Was he being Reverend Davidson and playing my protector because he was hot for me or, more probably, for Farley? I didn't say any of this; I just sat and listened until I didn't give a shit why he was a self-anointed Legionnaire of Decency, he was a sanctimonious snoop. I was primed to blast away when the doorbell rang.

There was no vestibule, so Julian could easily see the uniformed chauffeur in the doorway and watch him hand me a package and hear him say:

"From Miss Dietrich."

I thanked him and put the package on the piano.

"Aren't you going to open it?" Julian was salivating.

"I know what's in it," I said. "I have to get to work." I held the door open and he had to exit. A small triumph.

I did know what was in the package—Piaf records—and I did have to get to work: finish reading the screenplay of *The Snake Pit.*

The shooting date was set, Olivia de Havilland was set, there was a completed screenplay written by Millen Brand, a novelist, and Frank Partos, a Hungarian. But Anatole Litvak wasn't happy with the screenplay. Darryl Zanuck was less happy and he was the head of 20th Century-Fox, the studio committed to making the picture. Zanuck and Litvak lunched at Romanoff's together, smoked Havana cigars together, played gin rummy for enormous stakes together, but it was Tola who was in a jam.

He and I had seen each other a few times through Irene and her best New York friend, Dorothy Paley, the ex–Mrs. William S. Paley. Dorothy, who had Tola dangling, had come to California to say yes or good-bye. Like all Paley women or wives, she was intelligent, cultured, beautiful and beautifully dressed but like Irene, psychoanalyzed to the gills and a Freudian missionary among the savages. Litvak, I suspected, was making *The Snake Pit* to please Dorothy. She and I had laughed together in New York—Irene had even gotten our jokes once—so I made the obvious fourth for dinner.

Litvak stood on no Hollywood ceremony of agents to approach me again about doing *The Snake Pit.* He simply picked up the phone, explained the situation, and asked was I interested. Risking a second rejection didn't bother him, or perhaps he factored in all the scripts I wasn't writing at Metro and my sessions with Marmor. If he did, he was right: Metro and Marmor tipped the balance, at least so far as my agreeing to read the screenplay. It wasn't bad, it just wasn't good; it was flat and more than a little ponderous.

The screenwriters had made the mistake of being too faithful to the book. A book can proceed leisurely, it can take its time; a screenplay can't. The center of a book is its narrator (a character or the author) who has a vocal viewpoint and is fluent; the center of a movie is the camera (the director), which has a visual viewpoint and is mute. In the troubled screenplay of *The Snake Pit,* the story unfolded too slowly, relating the events of the book without editing, heightening and above all, dramatizing them. If the screenwriters had any personal experience with analysis, they kept it a secret: their psychiatrist was a pipe-smoking stick. And in their blind fidelity to the book, they left the heroine with the same problem that had bothered me when I first read it: her cure at the end was phony. How could she be cured when neither she nor the psychiatrist nor anyone else knew what was wrong with her in the first place? On paper, the author managed, just, to finesse the question with vague language. In dialogue, it couldn't be finessed, it was highlighted.

One week after I reported to Metro I knew that no screenplay is written without "input" from the director and/or producer. What I didn't know was whether Litvak had already been inputting and if so, to what extent. Nor did I know what delicate maneuvers were necessary to find out and I did have to find out before deciding whether or not to redo *Snake Pit.*

I braced myself for the customary meeting at the Studio. I needn't have: it didn't happen; Litvak did everything in his own style. The meeting was over lunch at his house in Malibu. He sent his secretary, Ann Selepegno, to pick me up and drive me there. Sleek as her convertible, glinting black hair pulled tight in a bun, precise gold earrings, a constant cigarette—we all smoked like factories but it added to my picture of her as tough and forbidding. I was wrong. The house she drove me to—a red door in a small stretch of gray fence—

looked like a shack from the Coast highway. I was wrong there, too. It was on the beach but it wasn't a beach house; it was the house Tola Litvak lived in and it said so eloquently once you went through the red door.

A startling concoction of glass and wood cascaded down the cliff to a deck cantilevered over big rocks, then continued flowing down until it finally came to rest on the beach. The design was so dramatic it was duplicated for *Mildred Pierce,* but the movie beach house didn't have sunny pastel Dufys hanging in the entry hall that looked out to the vast Pacific Ocean or Rouault Judges in the upstairs living room, Klee squiggles in the downstairs game room, or Tola's imprimatur in all the rooms (except the guest room, which had been the bedroom of his ex-wife, Miriam Hopkins, and looked it). Nor did the movie house have quiet Calvin and Esther who took care of him and his house as long as he lived there or Ann, unquiet but his wherever he was and wherever he went. The love and devotion all three had for him was remarkable in view of what a formal, undemonstrative man he was.

His clothes were never casual nor was he. Ann called him Colonel (the rank he earned making army films). He was polite always, remembered small things and appreciated small things. He could be caustic when irritated, could suddenly laugh, be intimate for a moment, open up like a window, then close down but not tightly: a breath of air remained ever after.

He was born in Russia, upper middle class. A teenager when the revolution broke out, he hid in a brothel where he was so well known that the girls sheltered and mothered him (and more) until he escaped to Paris, which was paradise for him and home forever. It was in Paris when we were making *Anastasia* that something I had long known finally came out in the open: both he and Ann were compulsive gamblers.

I'd watched him play gin rummy with Willy Wyler, John Huston, David O., Zanuck, even Sam Spiegel and lose twenty, fifty thousand dollars in a night. He shrugged off my clucking, saying that at the end of the year they all came out even. Oh, maybe one of them lost ten, twenty thousand but that was all. He knew I knew that was nonsense. He didn't care but I did. I hadn't been through a revolution and escaped from a brothel. I was from Brooklyn and my father was cautious. On the other hand, I'd watched my mother play bridge for a penny a point, her face flushed with pleasure.

Perhaps that was why I tried gambling my freshman year at Cornell. More likely, I was trying to act older; I had started smoking for that reason and chug-a-lugging beer with the big boys until I threw up. Downtown Ithaca had the XYZ, a club where you had to knock on a door with a peephole and be looked over before being allowed to enter a dark hole with a table of moldy food that enabled the proprietor to claim the hole was a restaurant. I played blackjack and lost all my room-and-board money in one night. Since I didn't dare tell my parents, I went to work reading proof for both the Ithaca newspaper and *The Cornell Daily Sun*. The camaraderie with the Linotype operators, who treated me not as an outsider but as another worker, was so warming that I enjoyed the job. But learning the value of money cured me of gambling.

Ann confessed her gambling addiction during the shooting of *Snake Pit* only because she was in a panic: the bookies were going to break her legs unless she forked up two thousand dollars in twenty-four hours. From her terror, it was apparent she'd been through this before and knew the boys weren't kidding. And she didn't just play gin, she played the horses, the numbers, anything playable she played anywhere she could. I loaned her the money, she paid me back in installments. That was to be the pattern over the years until Paris and *Anastasia*.

After a night shoot, Tola and I were sitting in his car outside the Hotel Trémouille where I was staying with Tom Hatcher. It was his first visit to Paris and Tola was wonderful to him. Usually, he just dropped me off but that night, he turned off the motor and sat, humming tunelessly. Then he chatted away about his wife, Sophie, his house in St. Tropez—would Tom and I come and stay?—and then:

"We have to make an agreement not to lend Annie any more money," he said. "It's the only way to get her to stop gambling."

The remark seemed to come out of nowhere but of course it didn't; remarks like that never do, especially Tola's, it was his way. It had taken him a long time to get to it because he knew he was giving me an opening. I took it. Trying to sound casual, as though searching for the answer for Ann, I asked what would make him stop his gambling. Oh, well, that was different. He was different, he had it all under control, he had money. And then, very irritated:

"For Chrissake, Artur, I can't stop."

"OK," I said. This most formal of men, never a toucher nor to be touched, then put his hand on my shoulder and pressed hard for two or three seconds, touching me forever.

I settled for helping Ann, agreeing not to lend her money until I discovered he had started to do so all over again. No confrontation, he wouldn't allow one; he merely shrugged when I called him on it. It was one of the few times I was livid with him.

What maddened me both times we worked together was his insistence on correcting idiomatic speech in my dialogue. This Californian, with a bastard French-Russian accent he couldn't hear, would change every *don't* to *do not*, every *wasn't* to *was not*, every *wouldn't* to *would not*. But I loved him and I didn't blow up.

·   ·   ·

Fox had fewer stars than Metro but each writer had a little semidetached, rustic cottage instead of an office over an old funeral parlor. I preferred to work at home which was fine with Tola. His input on the original *Snake Pit* screenplay had been minimal: he had given Brand and Partos free rein and regretted it. He and I had enjoyed discussing their screenplay because any time it suggested a topic that interested either of us, off we went wherever that topic led us. We wound up in happy agreement about what my screenplay was to be. Working with him was going to make me happy in Hollywood.

How many times can a writer meet with a director and lose his virginity once again? Over and over, the meeting ends and the writer is on air: enthusiastic, excited, elated. At last someone with insight, someone who speaks his language! Then the script gets put on its feet on a stage or a set and the writer is appalled, depressed, even frightened. The idiot is word-deaf; he's going to fuck the script.

In my discussion with Litvak, there was neither confusion nor ambiguity about two things important to me: the ending would be hopeful but the heroine would not be cured, she would not skip down the yellow brick road at the end. And incest—taboo and more difficult to handle because of Hays Office censorship—would be present and identified delicately but clearly as the root of the heroine's trauma.

Time was scarily short. The shooting date was imminent; casting, budgeting, sets were all on hold. None of it fazed me, not after whipping out all those radio shows for the Army. Actually, I rather enjoyed the pressure: it was familiar. My first move was to get released quickly from my Metro contract. I walked into Fadiman's office, confident and cheery: at long last, I would make MGM happy. They'd be rid of me and save money in the bargain. I wasn't cheery when I came out but they were happy because they could loan me out to Fox for a thousand dollars more a week than they were paying me and pocket the difference. It was a fine-print lesson: I was still their serf.

Writing *Snake Pit* was a strange experience, not because it was my first movie (since *How to Carve a Side of Beef*) but because it was the first time I felt removed from what I was writing. I wasn't just adapting someone else's original material, I was adapting someone else's screenplay which itself had been adapted from someone else's original material. Normal in Hollywood, routine, but not to me. What removed me even further was an inability to really connect with the love story because I didn't believe the main characters in either version. Well, was I as good a craftsman as I supposed or not? If I wasn't, I was sunk.

When he read my pages, Litvak thought I was. He was pleased that so much that had been unworkable was now both dramatic and good. Not to me: I just thought it was serviceable and worked. I did better with some elements I could connect with and use: my time in the Army's Cookie Jar informed the madhouse scenes; my feelings for Judd Marmor gave some life to the psychiatrist; what I was learning from Marmor helped me devise behavioral patterns for these thin characters. Not for the husband's, which was too bad. Nobody, from the author of the novel to the pretty but wooden actor who played the part, had a clue who that husband was, what he was or why the girl married him.

I tried. Perhaps if I had cared more I would have tried harder, but it was just a movie. All the same, I wanted it to be good for Tola and I had some pride in my work, even this hackwork. What did me in—and I did it myself—was that I was so facile: the same sort of deceptive dialogue that covered holes in *Heartsong* covered holes in *Snake Pit*. My excuse to myself was that it had to be done fast—and fast I was.

At the end of the day, I'd rush the finished pages to Litvak at Fox, he and I would go over them, Ann would retype them on a stencil so they could be mimeographed and sent to the various departments, including Brand and Partos. More often than not, Tola and I would go out to dinner afterward and talk—a little about the picture, a little about ourselves. We began to reach the easiness with one another that is called friendship, but while he talked about Dorothy, I didn't talk about Farley. I was afraid. I didn't want to know whether he knew I was gay although I was sure that he did—correction: I was as sure as I could be without taking the risk of putting the subject on the table. Which I didn't because, I told myself, distance suited him, he preferred it. I wasn't about to force him to come closer.

While I was busy writing *Snake Pit,* Farley was making *Roseanna McCoy*—I think. He was constantly making one earnest Goldwyn drama or another, usually with Ann Blyth, so our time together was limited. I was learning to cook, courtesy of Ann Selepegno—Ann who said "you and Farley" as naturally as others said "Mickey and Judy." Food in Hollywood restaurants, with an expensive or exotic exception like Trader Vic's, was really bad. The popular restaurants on nearby Restaurant Row were "cock" restaurants, i.e., the Tail of the Cock, the Bantam Cock, the Cock and Bull, the Golden Cock, et al. Although the neighborhood was stealthily gay, "cock" only signified a menu of steak, baked potato, and salad. I stepped up my cooking efforts for Farley; it was part of nesting.

I wanted a nest, I always had. When I lived with my folks, my dream was an apartment of my own in Greenwich Village but when I finally got to live in the "City," it was only in a sublet—not conducive to nesting. Doheny Drive was a sublet of a sublet but there was a difference: I had someone to make a nest for. True, he stayed there only on occasional nights but that suited me; I didn't want to think why. Marmor did, however, which meant I had to and eventually did.

The first complaint about my screenplay for *The Snake Pit* came from Olivia de Havilland. She took her role very seriously, researching everything she could about the inmates of psychiatric asylums, including what they looked like. That led to her most successful discovery: makeup that would make her character look her worst when she was at her worst—totally insane, at the bottom of the snake pit. The solution was no makeup except false eyelashes. They sunk her eyes and made her face a death mask, a look guaranteed to get an Oscar nomination.

To keep her happy, Litvak gave her pages of the new script to work on. She came a-hugging and a-kissing until a stage direction induced a tantrum. I had described her as coming downstairs for a date with her future husband wearing a dress with a bow in front. The bow was to be loose; her father (played by the attractive Leif Erickson) was to retie it, his hands grazing her breasts.

"Disgusting!" was Olivia's overreaction. "He's her father, he's—old!" At the time, she was married to Marcus Goodrich, the novelist, who was old enough to be her father. A cigar may be just a cigar but the piece of business was cut. Just replace it, Tola said. With what, he didn't say. Leaving me to figure out what replacement could show subtly what the father wanted, what the daughter wanted, and not run foul of the censors or the studio or Olivia. She was the toughest to please: she didn't want the girl to want what she herself wanted.

The next complaint came from Litvak and threw me. He asked for the very scene we had agreed not to have: a climax where everything would come clear for the heroine in one holy effulgent moment. It wasn't rewriting a scene in the other version or adapting one from the book. The scene didn't come from another script, it didn't come from the book; above all, it didn't come from life. But Zanuck wanted it and Litvak wanted it. I didn't. I didn't even do much battle. I hadn't been a studio hand very long but long enough to know it would have been pointless.

The sad truth was that I wasn't surprised: we were making a movie. Blinding revelations just before the end of movies on serious subjects were par for the course; endings were to satisfy the audience. That tenet didn't come from cynicism or snobbism: it was a fiscal fact to be faced or get out of the business.

The real problem, the practical problem, was how to write the scene with some conviction. The setup was fairly easy: Olivia in the kindly doctor's office again; her brow unfurrows as her pipe-smoking psychiatrist (he did smoke a

The lunch celebrating the end of shooting *The Snake Pit*: Betsy Blair peering
around an unidentified man, Tola Litvak, his secretary Ann Selepegno,
Olivia de Havilland and the uncredited screenwriter.

stereotypical phallic fucking pipe in the picture) leads her gently toward that
last truth—"How simple it is if we just let go!"—and she reaches it, as illustrated by the totemic doll in her hands that turns out be . . . "Why doctor, it's
only a handkerchief!" I didn't hate myself in the morning but I did hate the
scene.

When the script was finished, there was time off to worry while Zanuck
read it. Happily, he liked it; unhappily, he wanted some twenty-odd pages cut.
He gave us a week: if the script wasn't cut by then, he would cut it himself.
Precisely which pages, he didn't care. All that mattered was that the correct
number be cut because the cost of shooting each page each day was budgeted
with amazing accuracy: twenty-odd pages would send the picture twenty-odd
thousands of dollars over budget. Left alone, I could have cut thirty pages in
thirty minutes, beginning with that soppy ending. But it wasn't my call. We
didn't cut that scene, we didn't cut any scene, not one. That was not how
Hollywood cut a script.

For circumcision week, Tola, Ann and I arrived at his suite of offices at Fox
early in the morning before most of the studio came to life. Ann sat at her
typewriter with a stencil while Tola and I dictated cuts and re-cut the cuts.

First, stage directions were trimmed, even eliminated if possible. No one entered or exited a room because cutting "enters" and "exits" saved two lines on a page. If dialogue went over one line into two or three words on the next line, my job was to keep the thought but get rid of the three words so another line could be saved. We cut reactions; we cut CLOSE UP, LONG SHOT, CAMERA PANS, MUSIC IN; we cut helpful descriptions of what the madwomen were doing down to one brief phrase. Ann cut by being stingy with her spacing, extending every line to the margin and keeping it as close as possible to the lines above and below without losing legibility. It was painstaking, it was hard, it was endless, it was ridiculous.

When we thought we were finished, we were seven pages over. Back we went—and finished still two pages short of Zanuck's magic number. Everything squeezable and cuttable had been squeezed and cut; to have to re-stencil the whole bloody, bleeding mess would take too long. So we misnumbered a page, making the script one page shy of the commanded number and prayed Zanuck wouldn't catch it.

What was truly insane about the whole procedure was that we were subverting its basic purpose: to limit the shooting so it would not go over budget. Since no action had been cut and no scene had been cut, the script was going to take exactly the same amount of time to shoot as before it was "cut": it was going to go over budget. Tola knew it. He also knew once he started shooting, Zanuck wasn't going to stop him. He would protest, mildly, but Zanuck knew the drill. It was all ritual, standard Hollywood. Alice could have taken lessons for Wonderland.

Exhausted exhilaration the night we finally finished may have been responsible for Tola's letting down his guard. It was well after midnight, he wanted a drink but most of unseedy Hollywood closed down early: everyone had to be up at dawn to look gorgeous at work. On the Sunset Strip at the edge of Beverly Hills, Ciro's, the most elegant of clubs, was still open. I was surprised when Litvak drove us there because some weeks earlier, I'd merely mentioned the name Ciro's and he had snapped at me for the first time. Ann busied herself sifting papers. When she and I were alone, I asked, What was that and why? Normally, she'd tell me anything, even her age, but she clammed up. I was not to ask and never to "mention Ciro's in front of the Colonel" again.

Are there any sexual secrets anywhere? Not in Hollywood. In Hollywood, there is always someone eager to tell all. Someone? Everyone, not only Irene. I felt like the last-to-know deceived wife. It was old news throughout Beverly, Brentwood and Bel Air that Anatole Litvak was famous for performing cunnilingus on Paulette Goddard one night in Ciro's.

I couldn't visualize Anatole Litvak at it under a table anywhere, he was too formal. Bespoke suit, dressed impeccably, hair perfectly groomed? No, it wasn't his style. And then I remembered a lunch with Litvak and Billy Wilder that in turn made me remember a touching moment in Clifford Odets's play *The Big Knife* when a little contract actress laments "those rainy afternoons" at the studio. This was a rainy afternoon at Romanoff's. Tola and Wilder had a phone brought to the table and began calling girls. No luck. Little address books (very good leather) came out; more calls, no answers. One of them got up and went to the phone in the men's room, where telephone numbers are penciled on the wall. More calls made, none answered; rain or no rain, the boys were out of luck.

Well. So it wasn't only gays who demeaned themselves, went off the rails for sex. It is a democracy we live in: the common denominator is sex. Comforting thought but not entirely true. Hollywood was no democracy and Hollywood was where we were living. Hollywood aggrandized sex on the screen but belittled it off, had contempt for it, really. Popular, almost quotidian behavior was to telephone new arrivals without introduction or intermediary: stars wanted sex with new stars on the cusp. When Farley and I lived together, the phone rang with invitations to a romp with a male and/or a female in twosomes or threesomes or more. When I happened to answer, the poor caller sputtered. Once it was Montgomery Clift whom we had both just seen at the Kellys' an hour earlier. The "Hello" of people living together gets to be very similar. Mine was answered with:

"It's Monty, Farley."

"Farley's in the shower." He was. "It's Arthur. Would you like him to call back?"

Pause. Long pause. Then he stammered: "No, that's OK." Click.

At the time, I didn't wonder where or how he had gotten our number. I did know why, though.

Lana Turner telephoned John Garfield before they started *The Postman Always Rings Twice*. Both were married, both were famous, where could they go? They made out in the backseat of a car in her garage. (Source: Garfield.) Hardly beneath the surface, Hollywood was as sexually wild as New York was during the war but not as pleasurably. For us in wartime, it wasn't about conquest, it wasn't about having movie stars, we weren't chasing sexual images. We wanted sex because we loved sex.

When Tola and I walked into Ciro's, the captain kept his eyebrows in place and led us to a table as though Tola had been there the night before. We drank to celebrate the end of the non-cutting of the screenplay, we drank to the screenplay itself, we drank to his filming it, then Tola had enough to drink.

"It was there," he said, indicating a table against a banquette not far from us. "Paulette dropped her napkin under that fucking table. I bent down to pick it up. Too much champagne made it take longer than it should have. For Got's sake, I have asthma!"

He finished his drink and sat still, humming some Russian song off-key. I was busy working out why he had taken me to Ciro's, why he had brought up Paulette Goddard, why he had explained what was embarrassing and painful for him. Because he had snapped at me and was sorry. That was as far as Tola Litvak could go in apologizing to someone he cared about, that was his way of saying he was sorry. OK. I was ready to cut all the *don'ts*, *won'ts*, and *wouldn'ts* he wanted. I am a toucher; I was ready to hug him even though he would have hated it, but his asthma inhaler was out and he was spraying away.

Preparation for shooting went into high gear: actors were tested, sets were built, budgets were rebudgeted—it was all a fascinating hustle-bustle that Tola enjoyed watching me watch. He loved being mentor, a father without senti-ment. Then Irene telephoned with her bad news voice. She had gotten a copy of my screenplay of *The Snake Pit* from Fox. Not a word whether she thought it was good, bad or indifferent, she was too overwrought—angry, actually, at Tola. Why? And at me, too. Why? Because Tola had allowed it and I obviously hadn't objected. To what? She was stuttering badly. I waited. Idiot! My name wasn't on the screenplay, I wasn't credited as author. Not even as co-author with Partos and Brand. I didn't know? Well, now I did, so call Tola immediately—and she hung up.

I knew she was being a good friend but I didn't share her concern. So my name was omitted. An oversight Tola would correct. Everyone knew I'd worked hard and long, everyone knew I had rescued the troubled screen-play—did everyone know Farley and I were lovers? I could pretend that ques-tion popped into my mind simply because I'd been meeting with Hitchcock about doing the screenplay for *Rope* and two male lovers were at the center of the story but the truth was I constantly worried whether anyone, everyone, knew of my affair with Farley. It was always on my mind.

Hitchcock had told me Fox was so high on my work on *Snake Pit* that he'd contacted me the moment I was done to be sure he got to me with the first offer. But he took it for granted it was "Screenplay by Arthur Laurents" and I took it for granted that Tola would waste no time ensuring that was how the credit would read, despite my usual it's-only-a-movie attitude. *Rope* was also only a movie but one I did want to work on. Hitchcock and the subject intrigued me, and Farley was set to be one of the stars. That was titillating, even providing a feeling of a little power. The credit for that screenplay I thought I could be sure of. I was, but there was a small hurdle, as there usually is in the snake pit of screenwriters.

Basically, I didn't understand the practical importance of the credit on *The Snake Pit*. Nor did I have a clue that someday, four decades later, despite all the movies I had written, I would not be entitled to health benefits from the Writers Guild because I didn't meet the credits requirement. The *Snake Pit* credit could have tipped the scales.

The Guild's health coverage is substantial but its complicated, arcane rules have a paradoxical result: benefits become unavailable just when they are most needed. Screenwriters who haven't gotten a credit for too long and are sliding over the hill and seeing doctors too frequently are the very screenwriters who lose the health coverage paid for by their union just when they really need it.

I wrote no more screenplays after my experience with *The Turning Point*. Five years later, when I became eligible for Medicare, I found I had been too long absent from the celluloid scene to be eligible for supplementary coverage from the Writers Guild. Moreover, credits I did have for pictures I had written were deemed insufficient or even nonexistent: documentation that I had written *Rope* was not in their files—Transatlantic Pictures, the company that had produced the movie, was long gone, as were its records.

"The picture's on video, look at it!" I told the union folk.

"Not in our purview [sic]," they answered.

Of course, I could afford to go elsewhere for health coverage and did, to B'nai B'rith which has excellent insurance. And those who couldn't go to B'nai B'rith because they were of the wrong persuasion? Ah, persuasion! I've had a fondness for that word used as it wasn't intended ever since the Modern Language Award for Best Usage was won by Arnold Saint-Subber at the time he produced *Kiss Me Kate*.

His lawyer's wife, Carly Wharton, invited Saint to a grand party. He lusted for grand parties and this was to be very grand. But:

"May I bring my—friend?" His normal stammer became very pronounced because he was unable to say "boyfriend."

Carly heard the omission. "Why, of course," she said.

"But he-he," stammer stammer.

"But he what, Saint?"

"But he's of colored persuasion."

"Who on earth persuaded him?" Carly asked.

Obviously, that was long before PC, when everyone was funnier, even Communists.

. . .

Until *The Snake Pit* and the Writers Guild, I thought writers were the chosen people. Even screenwriters, but experience taught me to qualify that. Not only did I not understand the importance of a credit to a screenwriter, I did not believe what some screenwriters would do for a credit until it was shoved in my face.

Under the Guild's rules, credit is determined by the percentage of the shooting script written by each writer who contributed. Some contributors have been known to use a thesaurus to change enough words on a page to get credit for writing that page. Disputes are settled by a Guild arbitration board to which the parties involved submit the evidence of their work. With *The Snake Pit,* Partos and Brand submitted copies and carbons of everything they had written. I had nothing to submit except their final script and my final shooting script, and let the difference speak for my claim. But was it "my" final shooting script? I hadn't made any carbons, and after Ann copied my pages onto a stencil, I threw them away. Why keep a copy of a revised version of someone else's screenplay adapted from someone else's book? Not for any archives I might have.

Litvak was brusque with Partos and Brand, dismissive of their "absurd" claim to be the sole authors. From the set, he dictated an impatient letter to the Guild in my support. How the arbitrators made their judgment, I have no idea—it would be easier to get clean files from the FBI—but the percentage I needed to get credit was finally narrowed down to one scene: the scene I had hated to write, the scene of the heroine's phony epiphany that had never been in any version of *The Snake Pit* before I wrote it, however unwillingly. OK, then, my credit was secure! Poor Candide. Partos and Brand claimed authorship of that scene. For proof, they produced a carbon copy they had somehow overlooked when they first presented their evidence.

Litvak was enraged. What was obvious to him and should have been to the arbitrators was that anyone with a copy of the script could fake a carbon of any page in any script. But the Guild was insulted: How dare a director (the enemy) question the probity of a writer! His written statement that the scene hadn't existed until I wrote it was hardly sufficient; he would have to testify in person. Now Litvak was insulted: How dare they question his integrity! How dare they demand his appearance! He was in the midst of shooting, he was behind schedule, he had no time for the goddamn Guild! They had his statement in writing, take it or leave it.

They left it. I got no credit.

Irene was angry because I wasn't angry at the Guild and Tola. I was too happy with my life to be more than disappointed about a movie credit; even then, I wasn't as disappointed as Ann and Farley thought I should have been. I never said anything to Tola; it was too late, this was no J'accuse. He never said anything either, but he felt badly. He hosted a celebratory lunch for Olivia at the studio with me and the publicity department on hand to take photographs and send them to the press. No Partos, no Brand. And after the picture opened, he gave an interview to *The New York Times* crediting me for writing such a remarkable script. The Writers Guild made him retract. But he'd tried to make amends—late, but he tried.

I never accepted the Guild's ruling. They based it on total belief in Partos and Brand who were duplicitous. They jump-started my injustice motor and I got angry at them. That pleased Irene who raged that it was bad enough to be cheated out of credit on any picture but this picture was of a kind all too rare in Hollywood: classy, thought-provoking, distinguished. But was it really?

The subject matter had importance, was controversial, had never been dealt with before—I was as aware as anyone of that. The subject was hot in Hollywood where half the town was in analysis; there was an envious buzz about the movie and I had been proud to be working on it. At the same time, my own experience on Marmor's couch kept raising niggling doubts about how the movie was handling the subject, doubts I brushed aside while writing the screenplay because there wasn't time to debate them even if Tola had been willing to. Besides, as I went over the screenplay with him, I was learning what was wanted in movies, what he wanted in his movie: the epiphany scene, for ghastly example. I began to doubt my conviction that it was wrong because what was psychiatrically wrong seemed to pale beside what was cinematically right. On the set, more doubts arose and they weren't so niggling.

Litvak rode a crane with the camera racing after Olivia through the corridors of the asylum. As she ran, madwomen rhythmically scattered out of the way of machinery until the camera caught up and zeroed down and in on its terrified, screaming target. Visually, the shot was exciting, the magic of movies. But was it necessary? Willy Wyler, during one of our Cockamamie Tennis Tourneys on his court, told me he tried never to move the camera unless absolutely necessary. His style was to put an object—a vase, a lamp—in the foreground to give depth to the shot; then he let the actors do the moving.

Those actresses in the path of that crane shot—whose idea of madwomen and their keepers in an insane asylum were they? What kind of actresses were they, anyway? Ham, I thought. I had described in detail to Litvak the behavior of the inmates in the army asylum I'd been locked up in; he and I had visited a California state asylum where we'd observed the behavior of psychotic women and the nurses who watched over them. In the movie asylum, there was no difference between patients and nurses: all were self-indulgent actresses acting up a tropical storm. Not one of them was believable for one minute.

One element I didn't doubt was my dialogue. From radio, it had been my strength and still was but as I heard it spoken on the set in scenes being shot, I began to doubt that, too. Olivia was a star; Mark Stevens, her leading man, was a future star according to Zanuck himself. I rationalized: all the booms and tracks and cables made it difficult for me to see and hear; acting on a movie set was new to me; perhaps on the screen and edited, it all would look very different.

The first time I saw *The Snake Pit* was at a screening in a projection room at the studio. As the lights went down and out, my excitement grew: it was the first movie I had written. See the first performance of anything you've written—in a rehearsal room, on the stage, or on the screen—your eyes fill up or you giggle. It has nothing to do with whether the scene is sad or funny, everything to do with seeing your work brought to first life. At the end, when the lights came up, the studio suits clustered around Tola, hyperventilating with enthusiasm. I was glad nobody cared what the writer thought because I thought the picture wasn't very good.

From the first scene to the last, it was tainted with artificiality. Everything written in dramatic form is written to be performed; nothing, not even *Hamlet,* is so good that it can weather bad performances, and the performances in *The Snake Pit* were bad and bogus. The leading man couldn't act; he was made of wood and made all his scenes with Olivia wooden. Nor was she much help in her early scenes with him: her eyes were either the shining eyes of a musical nun or the darting eyes of a scared shoplifter. On the big screen, the asylum scenes were anything but wooden; the wild overacting came off even wilder than it had on the set. Only Leo Genn, as the psychiatrist, gave a respectable performance. He was an English actor; American Method actors may sneer but at least the English are masters of restraint.

And then there was Olivia. A woman of much intelligence and varied interests, an extremely nice, generous woman but like most movie stars, untrained and unskilled. Her acting was based on and limited by the quality that made her a star: sweetness, in her case. In *The Snake Pit,* she was saccharine; her sugary vocal monotony cried out for insulin. The word around town was that Olivia de Havilland was Duse. Playing a character crippled in one way or another invariably gets that appraisal; often, even the Oscar; at the very least, a nomination.

The director, in the catbird seat on any movie, is responsible for the performances. I didn't offer my opinion of Olivia or the picture to Tola or Ann or anyone. Whatever I felt about the director, what I felt for the man wasn't diminished. But he had no need for my sympathy or empathy; applause was coming from all sides. To my bewilderment, the studio, and therefore the town, was high on the picture. Wait until it's released, I didn't say, and a good thing. The reviews were wonderful, Anatole Litvak was a heroic pioneer!

Quotes from those old reviews are on the box the videocassette of *The Snake Pit* comes in. *The New York Times:* "A fine, mature piece of work . . . Courage, intelligence and fine dramatic power." The *Los Angeles Times:* "Powerful . . . Poignant . . . One of the most challenging pictures of all time." "Of all time"—ah, well.

What critics pan invariably begets angry, attacking letters; it's what they praise, however, that gives them away, especially theatre critics. Movie critics don't have much influence except on one another. And there are so many of them that a good review from a radio station in Northsouth Nowhere can be dug up for a quote for an ad. Fortunately, the movie public has a stubborn mind of its own, determining in advance what it will and won't see, a decision largely unaffected by reviews or ads.

It was almost fifty years before I saw *The Snake Pit* again. When I ran the videotape, I was curious whether my opinion of the picture would stand up. It didn't. Initially, I thought the picture wasn't very good. I was wrong. It's no good at all. Particularly, alas, Olivia, who is terminally sweet. As for the critics back then on the *Times* (on both coasts) who gave themselves away with their unwarranted praise—who were they? Oblivion is justified.

But doesn't taste change? Yes, though not as much as one might think; besides, allowance is unconsciously made for that. What does change is what is acceptable to us as audience: outdoor scenes shot on indoor soundstages are no longer acceptable because location shooting is taken for granted; heroines waking up in bed in the morning in full makeup were acceptable and still are—but not to anyone with taste; the acting in those *Snake Pit* asylum scenes was never acceptable and is now embarrassing. But at least, in the context of that time, wasn't *The Snake Pit* brave to deal with its subject and to have a madwoman as its heroine? Yes, but that only makes it an ambitious picture, not a good one.

Some weeks after filming of *The Snake Pit* was finished, word came from New York that my landlords, the Sol and Ethel Chaplins, were coming home sooner than anyone had expected and I had to move out. A new musical had taken them to New York for what they expected to be a long stay since the music Sol had written was for lyrics and book by Betty Comden and Adolph Green. The show was called *Bonanza Bound,* but it wasn't. It had opened and was closing in Philadelphia, not my favorite city either. I had to find a new place to live fast.

A house turned up rather quickly. It was on Lookout Mountain Road in Laurel Canyon, a quirky little wooden cottage, hidden from the road and the neighbors by a tamed jungle that gave complete privacy. The house had lots of light, lots of wood and the rental price was right. What sold me was the fireplace. The living-dining room must have been two rooms originally, for the fireplace was dead center and opened on two sides with its stone chimney going through the vaulted ceiling. The moment I saw those two hearths, I wanted to move in fast. Happily, the owner wanted to rent and move out just as fast. His name was Millen Brand.

He was a mild man, rather colorless and passive or maybe just embarrassed. Our business was over swiftly. Then, haltingly, he apologized for faking the carbon copy of that scene. He was mumbling so much, I had to ask him to repeat what he said. Neither he nor Frank Partos had written it—he knew, of course, that I knew that—but Partos had pressured. The credit was important to Partos: he was a career screenwriter. Millen's wife had pressured: she liked

At the Dutch door of the house, holding my screenplay of *Rope.*

movies, he didn't; she wanted him to be a screenwriter, he didn't. He was a novelist, he wanted to return to writing, to be a novelist again.

I didn't thank him for telling the truth, albeit belatedly. I didn't say I understood. But I felt sorry for him, so I told him I, too, wanted to be a writer again and was hoping to finish a new play in his house. He'd been unable to do any real writing there but he wished me luck and I wished him luck. We shook hands and I left, feeling as though I'd been vindicated. Which was a good feeling.

Moving day brought trauma. Farley was helping, loading his car with whatever I couldn't jam into mine. I was transferring clothes I had dumped on the bed to the more than ample closet when I noticed Farley propping up some sheet music on the upright piano in the living room. It was a piece by Poulenc he was going to pretend to play in *Rope*, finger-synching. He had been using the baby grand in the house on Doheny to learn the fingering. Listening to him practice was less than pleasant, but *Rope* was to start shooting soon; he wouldn't be around all the time. Then I saw him unload an armful of shirts from his car and carry them into the bedroom—his shirts. Then his jackets, his trousers, his tennis gear. There was a second bedroom, a sliver of a room squeezed in behind the kitchen, but Farley wasn't moving in there. Unasked, he was moving in with me. We were going to live together. We'd never talked about living together. That was what lovers did and I did love him, but I didn't want him living with me. The thought frightened me.

He had talked a lot about getting away from his family but he'd never suggested, never even hinted at moving into Doheny Drive. Perhaps because the house belonged to his closest friends (although he had no compunction about having sex in the bed they slept in). Or perhaps he was moving himself in because the house in Laurel Canyon had no memories and was new for both of us, a beginning of a time together. I wasn't sure whether I resented that he hadn't asked or that he took it for granted that I wanted him there. I did want him there; it made me happy to see him happy unpacking his things but it also scared me: he was forcing a commitment I didn't want to make. I knew that, but there was something more than fear of commitment watching him unpack; something else was really scaring me. What?

That I wouldn't be free to trick on the side? To breakfast with the newspaper without having to talk? To sit and read undisturbed whenever I wanted? To write—no, it couldn't be that because Farley made himself invisible when I was writing or reading. As for tricking, at the moment, I didn't want to but if and when I did—all right, when I did—I wouldn't do it in the nest. No, I knew what I was afraid of, it now was no surprise. I was afraid Farley moving in would be announcing I was gay. Whatever people might think, they didn't know. Now they would.

But didn't some of me want them to know I was living with a movie star? Cary Grant and Randolph Scott famously lived together as bachelors; to prove it, they double-dated. The comparison got a smile out of Marmor but Farley and I did double-date: his beard was Shelley Winters, mine was Anita Ellis or Geraldine Brooks. Shelley pretended she didn't know; Anita and Gerry knew and didn't care. Except that Gerry, who lived higher up our winding road in Laurel Canyon, thought Farley wasn't worthy of me. Well, she and I loved each other from the first day we met to her last, and I didn't think Budd Schulberg, whom she married, was worthy of her either.

Judd Marmor agreed that my reaction to Farley's moving in showed I was still uncomfortable with my homosexuality, but his comment ended with three dots, not a period. That, of course, irritated because it meant he thought there was another, deeper reason (another reason was always deeper). What that reason was, he didn't say, just hinted. That was how the game of psycho-analysis was played: the analyst hints, the patient bites, tries to solve, does solve and they both hope peace is on the way.

But Judd wasn't an orthodox Freudian. Since he believed the whole process took too long, he prodded and he pushed, concentrating on the present. The worst was when he said "We're on a plateau." Which meant we weren't getting anywhere. Which meant I was stalling—I would say that, not he, because I knew the fault was mine, any fault was mine and had to be mine: I was in analysis, he wasn't.

Eventually, I came to realize I would not rise from the couch with a halo; all my problems were not going to disappear. What analysis could do was make me aware of what my problems really were as opposed to what I thought they were—which problems could be gotten rid of, which avoided, which handled and dealt with. Acceptance of homosexuality was a large one, obvi-ously; another was the need for recognition (the subject of *Gypsy*); and then we get to Judd's deeper reason that Farley's moving in upset me: I was afraid that if he lived with me, he would know me.

I had never let anyone know me—not Nora, not Harold, not Randall, not Irene, no lover, no friend, even no analyst until Marmor. Even Reik was on to that. He tried to unlock my door by getting me to free-associate: relax on his cracked, imitation-leather couch and say whatever came into my head with no editing.

I shrugged. "You won't learn anything. Everyone's mind is like a seven-layer cake and mine works so fast, I can serve you a slice from any layer that appeals to me and you won't be able to tell the difference."

He felt impugned. Freud would not have put up with a recalcitrant patient and Reik had been analyzed by Freud: I had to try. So I did; for Reik and Freud, I tried, hard. Reik threw in the towel. Not every mind had seven layers, he said, just mine. With Marmor, I got down to four or five layers—not a deliberate cover, just the normal number as I walked and drove through daily life—but he kept at me to dig up why, specifically, I didn't want Farley or anyone to know me. He knew, of course, but it was the game not to tell me; I had to discover the reason myself. And finally I did. I was afraid he'd find out I was a fraud.

At Erasmus Hall, a teacher marked a paper of mine A+−, writing in the margin: "You are either a genius or a brilliant fraud." I knew I wasn't a genius, I doubted I was brilliant, but I was certain I was a fraud. I had not lost that certainty. It stayed with me through college and after, all the way to *Heartsong,* which proved that as a playwright of worth, I was a fraud. Sexually, my fraudulence was obvious: I only pretended to be a man. Etcetera, said Marmor.

Alfred Hitchcock was fun to work for and fun to be with. He was a tough businessman; otherwise, he lived in the land of kink. Initially, I thought he was a repressed homosexual. Repression was necessary: he was a Catholic; being grossly overweight and thus unattractive made it easier. Bad breath helped, too. The actual word *homosexuality* was never said aloud in conferences on *Rope* or on the set, but he alluded to the subject so often—slyly and naughtily, never nastily—that he seemed fixated if not obsessed. Which indeed he was because he was obsessed with what Alfred Hitchcock was always obsessed with: the subject of whatever movie he was making. Homosexuality was at the center of *Rope,* its three main characters were homosexuals. Thus the seeming obsession.

Sex was always on his mind; not ordinary sex, not plain homosexuality any more than plain heterosexuality. Perverse sex, kinky sex, that fascinated him. In *Rope,* not just homosexuals and not just murder but a murder committed by homosexuals for a bizarre reason. He himself didn't strike me as ever having much sex or even wanting sex. Those cool blondes he was supposedly so mad for—I doubted he wanted them for himself. I thought he wanted to put them with a man sufficiently ambiguous to provoke a perverse situation. The Hitchcock who was reputedly berserk about Tippi Hedren was not the Hitchcock I knew. But then, no one knows for a certainty all the contours of someone else's sexual landscape. There were probably other Hitchcocks I didn't know; I was happy with the one I did.

The camera was his true obsession: essentially, he was a voyeur; *Rear Window* could have been his epitaph. He was consumed with his camera and the infinite possibilities in intricate maneuvers: how differently he was going to use it in this picture this time; what tricky, difficult shot he was going to pull off. Although his objective was to highlight the story, he could become so fascinated with the technical challenge that his camera got in the way of the story. I think that's what happened with *Rope*.

When Hitchcock liked you—and he got to like me very quickly while we worked on the screenplay—you became part of his extended family. Dinner at his informal house in upper-strata Bel Air was with that family: Alma, his wife, and Pat, his teenage daughter, along with Ingrid and Cary and other stray Hitchcock stars. Ingrid's husband, Peter Lindstrom, always brought an extra shirt to change into after working up a healthy Swedish sweat jitterbugging with Pat. Cary was married to Betsy Drake, pretty but very annoyed she wasn't taken as seriously as an actress as she thought she should have been. She said so and at length. Crocked as usual, Hitch listened like an impassive

On the set of *Rope*. A comparatively thin Hitchcock directs while
the screenwriter, faceless as usual, observes from behind the camera.

Buddha, then leaned across Betsy to Cary and me and said: "Full of shit, isn't she?" Cary smiled a smile that meant something different to each of us and made all of us feel the remark was funny; even Betsy did.

Hitch took me on a little Toonerville Trolley plane—you rang a bell when it came to your stop—up to Santa Rosa in Northern California where they had a country house in the hills. No house party, no parlor games, just family: Hitch (in his business suit, shirt and tie), Alma, Pat and me. They were very much a family, very much a laughing family, even laughing at his familiar puns.

"Don't come pig's tail." Translation: "Don't come twirly." Further translation: "Don't come too early."

And his familiar jokes.

Cockney girl flirting with cockney boy who is trying to guess her name: "What clings to a wall?" He: "Shit." She, indignantly: "No, Ivy!"

And his descriptions of new drinks he liked to mix for me: "A new martini—gin and menstrual blood."

Alma: "Oh, Hitch!"

Pat: "Oh, Daddy."

Both giggled indulgently and he was beamish. It was lovely being with people who loved each other.

The picture was based on an English play by Patrick Hamilton that stemmed from the Leopold-Loeb murder case in Chicago, but that was never acknowledged or discussed. Hitch emphasized his desire that I totally Americanize the play even as he paradoxically cast two English actors, Cedric Hardwicke and Constance Collier. Hardwicke, like Leo Genn in *The Snake Pit,* gives the most effectively understated performance in the picture. Lest that be dismissed as an English specialty, Constance Collier throws restraint to the wind and is insanely over the top. Hitch was concerned with her performance, but more that her lower register made her sound like a lesbian.

Americanizing the play really meant Americanizing the characters which was harder than I anticipated. George Bernard Shaw said England and the United States are two countries separated by a common language. The language only seems the same: usage, locutions and idioms can be very different. Add differences in background and behavior and the result is quite different characters. There is a thin American line between upper-crust and effeminate, between cultured and precious. I drew from some silver-and-china queens I had met briefly in New York who played squash and were raunchy after dinner in my effort to Americanize English homosexuality—a major task, not aided by fear of censorship by the Hays Office.

At Warner Brothers studio in Burbank where *Rope* was shot, homosexuality was the unmentionable, known only as "it." "It" wasn't in the picture, no character was "one." Fascinating was how Hitchcock nevertheless made clear to me that he wanted "it" in the picture. And of course, he was innuendoing to the converted. I knew it had to be self-evident but not so evident that the censors or the American Legion would scream. It's there; you have to look but it's there all right. Without it, motives and relationships would have been altered and that, neither of us wanted. Casting, however, destroyed a motive and a relationship unintentionally.

Hitchcock was more than happy with my way of bringing Patrick Hamilton across the Atlantic with my dialogue. During shooting, he had me on the set writing party dialogue that was continuous in the background, some of it better than that in the foreground. Only once did we have a disagreement. In the picture, food for a buffet supper is served on a tablecloth-covered chest housing the murder victim. Hitchcock wanted a bottle of wine spilled accidentally so he could zoom in on the blood red of the wine staining the white cloth. When I pointed out that the dead boy in the chest had been strangled with the eponymous rope, Hitch pouted. He had once enlightened me on the importance of what he termed the "icebox trade":

"The film is over, they are home. She opens the icebox and as she gets him his beer he says, 'But why didn't they call the police?' "

I wondered why they didn't call the police when I saw *Strangers on a Train*. But here it was plain that when the icebox was opened, he or she would say, "The fellow was strangled, there was no blood, for Pete's sake!" That derailed Hitchcock only for a moment; then he lit one of his enormous cigars, getting happier as other ideas puffed out. His delight was almost sexual, centered in his very red lips as he described himself zooming in with his loved one for a close-up of that deadly length of rope at unexpected moments. He was back in form.

One other disagreement I never mentioned because it came too late. After the picture was shot, he inserted a scene of the actual murder. I thought it better to let the audience guess whether there really was a body in the chest. I also thought the actor playing the victim deserved the rope around his neck.

On the screen, there is a credit to Hume Cronyn for his adaptation of the play. My agent, Irving (Swifty) Lazar, had to stop him from claiming credit for writing the screenplay in publicity interviews but I'm not even sure what the adaptation credit means; I was never shown what Hume did. I suspect, since he and Hitchcock were old friends, that he was used to help work out the details of Hitchcock's innovative plan to shoot *Rope* without any conventional cutting. Each reel was shot continuously without one cut, ending with the camera going to black, usually by closing in on someone's back. It was then reloaded; the next reel began with a close-up of the same back as though there had not been a cut; the camera then pulled back and away and action resumed as though without interruption. To me, the device often looks obvious and rather crude on the screen, but the stunt was very difficult to pull off—precisely why it intrigued Hitchcock.

It did add one value to telling the story: screen time is actual time. Otherwise, it handcuffed the director and the actors. So many noticeably peculiar lineups—one actor physically unable to talk directly to another, shooting a look sideways or over his shoulder—because of the positioning of the camera. What was most awkward and interfering, what isn't noticed and can't be noticed because it's offscreen and thus invisible, is the intricate, choreographed footwork forced on the actors. Constantly, they walk sideways, backwards or even cross-legged to get out of the way of the ever-moving camera and its heavy cables. Fear of tripping may be at least one reason why scenes meant to be played lightly and comedically are heavy and awkward.

Everything in any movie is to accommodate the star; in *Rope,* the camera is the star. Before shooting, there was a press session at the studio for journalists; because it was Hitchcock, they came from all over the world. He had the same degree of control over the press as he did over his pictures: total. At his *Rope* session, he was regaling them with minute details of how carefully he'd had to rehearse this challenging picture when the usually mild Jimmy Stewart blurted out: "The only thing that's been rehearsed around here is the camera."

Hitch wanted me on the set for rehearsals but there was time for a holiday before that. I hadn't seen my folks and I missed them. I missed the theatre, I missed New York, and as soon as I got there, I phoned Nora.

It's not unusual to love two people at once, particularly when each makes the other more desirable and when what's greedily wanted is a combination of both. Unlike Farley, Nora was a peer; we had a history, however condensed; we were both bred on all the challenges that make New York the First City; and heterosexual was better and easier simply because it was what society mandated. Farley was beautiful and my eager pupil; we were beginning to share lasting friends; California was living in the sun I loved at the beach, on tennis courts, driving in convertibles. And hardly last, hardly least, he was male.

Just one New York night of going to the theatre, drinking at Tony's, listening to Mabel Mercer, all with Nora, and I was back, wanting to stay and wanting her. Time was so short, self-deception was so easy, even with the confrontation in the Algonquin about her abortion. Why not get married? we asked each other again, she more seriously this time because she thought Ballet Theatre's future was shaky and felt she had none without Ballet Theatre. We may not have been ardent—we weren't—but we were loving and affectionate. We planned a wedding when she came to California or when I came back to New York but didn't make plans for either.

So although it was a surprise, it wasn't a startling shock to read in the newspapers a few days after I was back in Hollywood that Nora had married Isaac Stern. Normal reaction would have been a mix of disappointment (yes, but I understood), rejection (yes, but I could hardly blame her), and anger (yes, I was angry because she must have been planning with Isaac while she was planning with me). Mainly, though, there was a hollow sadness. Did Nora always take us less seriously? Was she less romantic, more realistic, more practical? Just calculating? And the one that hurt most: Did I really know who she was? Of course, she could have asked that of me and my answer would have been, No, not for sure, not yet. But her answer?

I knew if we had gotten married it wouldn't have lasted long and I knew why. It didn't last with Isaac, either, but for the opposite reason: he was too straight for Nora.

When I returned to the studio, the Hays Office had stumbled on the presence of homosexuality in the screenplay of *Rope* and been slashing away—not at what I had written but at what had been interpolated by Sidney Bernstein, Hitchcock's producer/partner in Transatlantic Pictures. Before I left for New York, Sidney had lectured me that "every line must be a gem, my dear boy. Literature, that's what we want, literature!"

I thought it was a screenplay we wanted, a screenplay for a movie, not literature and flew off to New York. Sidney returned to the original English play. Unlike Shaw, he couldn't hear the difference between English English and American English; he didn't even know there was a difference, a dangerous one in this case. He inserted "my dear boy" before or after speech after speech, sending the Hays Office into a censoring lather. Every word, every sentence Sidney took from the Patrick Hamilton play and inserted in the script was furiously blue-penciled and marked HOMOSEXUAL DIALOGUE exclamation point. Since Sidney himself either began or ended everything he said with "my dear boy," he was mystified. Not at all embarrassed, he asked me to undo the damage. I did more: I took a little stab at an elegant phrase here and there to make Sidney happy because I liked him.

As English as Hitchcock but upper-class and elegant, Sidney was tall and lean, made more handsome by a nose that looked as though it had been broken in the ring. Cultured as well as rich, an anomaly in the movie business, he nevertheless felt it was a privilege to take Hitchcock to dinner.

One strange night, dinner was at his rented house in Beverly Hills. He and his wife must have quarreled before the Hitchcocks and I arrived because when we did, Zoe had wrapped herself in silence—not even a "Good evening"—and was on her way to being shit-faced. By the time dinner was over, she got there. Whenever Sidney spoke, she squinted at him balefully; when he finished, she laughed like a barking dog. The Hitchcocks left early; Sidney showed them to the door, went upstairs, and didn't come down. Time for my good nights. I stood up, she squinted balefully at me, barked her laugh, and then spat out a sentence:

"He's in love with Farley, too, you idiot."

I flinched. I had no idea whether Sidney was or wasn't bisexual although he was English, of course. Nor did I care. What bothered me were the depressing implications in his wife's single sentence of the night. Despite Marmor, I worried continually.

Privately, I had assumed Hitchcock had hired me to write *Rope* because it was to be filmed as a play and I was a playwright, and because its central characters were homosexual and I might be homosexual. I worried about the latter on and off until the Saturday night before the start of shooting. He invited me to dinner at Romanoff's with his wife Alma—it was always Romanoff's, always steak, red wine, a huge cigar and brandy.

When Farley told me he'd been invited, I assumed the other leads, Jimmy Stewart and John Dall, had been invited as well. And perhaps Joan Chandler, to add a pretty girl to the table. Farley and I drove to Romanoff's in separate cars, my idea though I needn't have bothered. Hitch and Alma were already there at a table for four. My jig was up. "Might be"—as in I was hired because I "might be homosexual"—went out the window.

Since Farley and I weren't living together when he was cast in *Rope*, I doubted Hitch knew at that time that we were lovers. He certainly knew now, not that he showed it that night or ever by even a glance or an innuendo. It was very Hitchcock: it tickled him that Farley was playing a homosexual in a movie written by me, another homosexual; that we were lovers; that we had a secret he knew; that I knew he knew—the permutations were endless, all titillating to him, not out of malice or a feeling of power but because they added a slightly kinky touch and kink was a quality devoutly to be desired.

It was now plain he didn't give a hoot in hell whether I was gay as I should have realized earlier when we first talked casting—I would have been less edgy. The three central characters in *Rope* are homosexual. Brandon and Phillip are lovers who carry the Nietzschean philosophy learned from their former prep school teacher, Rupert, to its outer limit: a murder committed to prove superiority. Rupert is a good friend and probably an ex-lover of Brandon's; his is the most interesting role. Caustic with a sardonic sense of humor, overly cynical, he is caught off guard by having to face the appalling result of what he taught and professed to believe. Hitchcock wanted Cary Grant for Rupert, Montgomery Clift for Brandon, the stronger of the two lovers, and Farley for Phillip. Dream casting.

Cary Grant, arguably the finest screen actor of his time, had deftness and humor, was always sexual, usually ambiguous. When we became mildly friendly through Hitch, he told me he threw pebbles at my window one night but was luckless—I wasn't home. His tone made it impossible to tell whether he was serious or joking, but his eyes and his smile implied that even if he were joking, he would have liked doing what we would have done had I been home. That was all and it was enough for me: fantasies are better left fantasies. Monty Clift shared the New Boy in Town pedestal with Marlon Brando. I preferred Monty: more variety, more nuances, more vulnerability. And whatever his sexuality was, it was intensely romantic.

Both Grant and Clift said no. According to Hitchcock, each felt his own sexuality made him too vulnerable to public attack. It was very, very unfortunate. With those two, the picture would have been so different, as compelling and fascinating as it should have been. The lesson, once again and always, was the enormous importance of casting—in any dramatic medium.

Instead of Cary Grant, we wound up with Jimmy Stewart; instead of Monty Clift, with John Dall. There wasn't a word of dialogue that said the lovers were lovers or homosexual, but there wasn't a scene between them where it wasn't clearly implied. John Dall and Farley played Brandon and Phillip's sexuality truthfully, and that took courage. I don't know whether it ever occurred to Jimmy Stewart that Rupert was a homosexual. Hitchcock didn't say anything but it wouldn't have mattered if he had.

Jimmy Stewart was Jimmy Stewart, which meant not a whiff of sex of any kind. He does dominate the picture, though, with ease and authority. His Rupert is intelligent, attractive, laced with humor—teasing, though, rather than sardonic. And Stewart's inherent folksy quality—he went to Princeton, maybe that's where he got it—made his denial of any responsibility for the crime too plausible and uncomplicated. He is conventionally appalled but if Rupert is anything, he is unconventional. Sexless, Stewart is interesting as the detective on the case but not as Rupert. That he was friends with two boys who were lovers makes no sense at all. Being gay, being any minority is a bond, and Stewart has none in the picture except with an old maid who is literally the maid. The actress who played her, incidentally, was treated like a maid by the other actors when they sat around the set.

The attitude of the stars toward playing homosexuals was no surprise; the attitude of the studios toward real-life homosexual stars was. Samuel Goldwyn had Farley under contract and often asked me to write for him. I never did: I didn't think any of the proffered glop would make a good picture for Farley or his boss. It never occurred to me (because I wouldn't have let it occur to me) that Goldwyn might have had a close-to-home reason for asking me to write for Farley. Nor that it wasn't just happenstance that his wife would invite both of us to dinner but never on the same night.

Nothing Frances Goldwyn did was happenstance. She had eliminated any sign that she had begun life as a Ziegfeld showgirl along with Marion Davies. Now she was the wife of the most distinguished independent movie producer in town and her old friend was the mistress of the most despised newspaper publisher in any town, William Randolph Hearst. Both ladies appeared at my first Goldwyn dinner party.

Irene, not without self-interest, alerted me that martinis would be served out of a mason jar Frances kept in the bar fridge; to get a second, I would have to down the first as fast as I could or the jar would be closed. After dinner, just as Irene was jostling for a brandy and we were all settling down in the library for the new Goldwyn movie, a wraith appeared in the doorway: a distraught Marion Davies in her nightgown. The room really did stand still; everyone in it really did freeze like a still frame. Ripping the silence was an agonized "Frances!" from the ghost figure in the nightgown but a man in a white coat popped out behind her and Marion Davies vanished like a joke. Irene, who knew everything, filled me in: Hearst was dying and kept Marion confined to her bed in order to make her die with him. She had outfoxed him at San Simeon when he tried to stop her drinking and she was using an alcoholic's cunning to keep alive in Beverly Hills: she rolled on her bed, on the bedroom floor, on the bathroom floor; she walked and stumbled around her room any chance she got; she sneaked out to the grounds; she even sneaked drinks—anything to outlast the old man who had been her protector since she was a showgirl with Frances. And she did outwit him. Marion Davies survived.

Frances Goldwyn invited me to tea. She went to the studio every day but the invitation was for tea at their house. Proud though she was of the Goldwyn Studio, she wouldn't set foot in its commissary, she said. The food there was poor and overpriced; she brought her lunch from home in a paper sack. Couldn't she afford a lunch box? As easily as she could afford a pitcher for martinis—she glanced up from pouring to let me know she was way ahead—but did I know why she and Mr. Goldwyn had money? Because they knew how to hold on to money. Then she shifted with no sequitur to the reason she'd invited me to tea: Farley. I could feel myself blushing so I dropped my napkin to the floor and picked it up to explain the rush of blood to my face.

Frances continued on even with my head out of sight. She and Mr. Goldwyn, Sam, considered Farley fortunate to have me as his best friend. Did I know that? Oh yes, they felt very fortunate, too. And very appreciative of all he was learning from me. (More blushing but the napkin could not be dropped again.) Would I, could I do them a favor? Gladly. Good! Well—the cake is homemade, try it—if Farley felt it necessary to take a girl with him when he went out in public, would he please take Ann Blyth instead of Shelley Winters? Miss Winters was too brassy, too blowzy and too old for his image.

Image was all. Very sensible, very understandable in an industry whose business was image making. Homosexual, lesbian, bisexual, adulterer, molester, rapist—nobody was concerned so long as the studio could keep whatever it was out of the papers and whoever did it out of jail. There was no moral judgment: image was all. Occasionally, a mistake was made. A sunny male star caught performing in public urinals once too often was ordered by his studio to get married. His best friends, a young comedian and his wife, divorced so he could marry the wife. The studio was pleased, the three friends were pleased, the public wasn't pleased. To the fans, their star had stolen his best friend's wife. That image was enough to dim his star.

That was understandable. What wasn't, for me anyway, was that the images themselves bought their own images. They knew full well they were only images but they bought them as the reality. They all knew who was gay and who was lesbian, whose marriage was arranged and who arranged gang bangs, who rented tricks, male and female, but they all pretended gracefully that they didn't. The hypocrisy was considered sensible, even admirable.

No one else found this at all confusing, or so I felt. Perhaps because I had been in Hollywood such a short time, or had been lovers with Farley such a short time. He wasn't confused, no one who knew us was confused. Our accepted image was mentor and friend; that was it, that was real even to our very close friends, on the surface, anyway. But at the same time I was pretending friends didn't know what I didn't want them to know, I was speculating whether they speculated on what Farley and I did in bed. I was good at confusing myself.

Accepting that image was everything should have made it easy for me to live as I wanted. It would have if I had known how I wanted to live. The explanation that I did know but couldn't accept it because I was basically a nice Jewish boy from Brooklyn was too simple and really not true anymore. I had lost Brooklyn—I would never lose Jewish—but even Brooklyn is middle-class America. And middle-class America, I knew, would accept Farley as a movie star and me as a playwright but would not accept us as lovers. I knew that didn't matter and wouldn't matter once I had the "pride and dignity" to live as I chose. But that was hard, that meant more than just accepting what I was

even though I still believed I would be better off if I weren't. It meant prefer-
ring what I was.

Hitchcock was all image: he pretended to wink at his own while flaunting
total control of those he put on the screen. Unlike other directors, he never
looked through a viewfinder on the set; unlike everyone else, he knew precisely what would be in every frame of every scene he shot before he shot it.
That was true for *Rope*, but he was uncharacteristically nervous. He couldn't
sit back as usual, fold his hands across his belly, and just concentrate on what
his cast was doing within those immaculately planned frames. The demands
of shooting in one set with a constantly moving camera, allowing only one cut
to a reel and that cut dictated solely by coming to the end of the reel, made it
necessary for him to watch the camera like a stage mother. The actors were
scanted, they had to fend for themselves too much; worse, there was one technical aspect that wasn't under his control. In fact, it was altogether out of control: the color.

Rope was Hitchcock's first picture in Technicolor. On his meticulously
designed set, the decor and the clothes were carefully muted, almost mono-
chromatic. On the screen, it was fiesta time on Olivera Street in downtown
Mexican L.A. His pride had been the New York sky seen outside the wide windows of the apartment where all the action takes place. He had taken every
precaution to paint and light the backdrop of that sky so that the changes
from pleasant late afternoon to uneasy twilight to macabre night were subtle
and gradual. Bubbling with excitement, he waited in a screening room to see
the test reel of his first color picture. The shot began with curtains covering the
wide windows, they were pulled back and there was the New York sky in late
afternoon sun. That was the first and only time I saw him explode with fury:
it wasn't his sun in his sky, it was an atomic fireball setting the city ablaze.
Alfred Hitchcock did not control color, Natalie Kalmus, High Priestess of
Technicolor, controlled color. His picture was in her gaudy hands! Natalie
Kalmus was the enemy, Natalie Kalmus might have to be killed off-camera,
but Alfred Hitchcock was going to be in control. Print after print after print
was ordered—at her expense, not his—until he got what he wanted. He got it
and he deserved to: he was Hitchcock, it was a Hitchcock picture.

In that realm of the magic lantern, the stars were the kings and queens. But
Hitchcock was a star, too. He was one of a handful of directors who got star
billing and were kings—kings paid by emperors like Zanuck and Louis B. and
Jack Warner to whom they were therefore subservient and from whom they
therefore withheld the loyalty they expected from their subjects—the writers.

After a family dinner with the three Hitchcocks and Sidney Bernstein (sans wife) at which they all giggled over a secret I wasn't in on, Hitch gave me a novel called *Under Capricorn* to take home and read immediately. I was flattered: he wanted me again and furthermore the picture was for Ingrid. His timing was serendipitous: I was stymied by *The Bird Cage,* a new play I'd started. I didn't need an excuse to put it aside, I wanted one. That night, I began reading *Under Capricorn.* I stopped early, limped through it the next day. What Hitchcock saw in that novel was a mystery. What Ingrid saw in it was another, although maybe she saw Hitch and had evangelical faith. *Under Capricorn* was wrong for both of them, certainly for me, and it didn't occur to me not to say so to Hitch.

I hadn't told Litvak what I thought of the finished *Snake Pit* because it was too late and because I loved him. But I was always outspoken and had been about the phony ending in both the novel and the Brand-Partos screenplay. True, we wound up with that absurd epiphany scene anyway, but at least I spoke up—no regrets as opposed to all the regrets about not speaking up about the ham acting. Tola and I were friends; friendship made me timid when it should have made me direct. Even if he had disagreed, he would have heard an opinion rather than an echo.

Hitch and I were friends; it was early: there was only the novel. I wasn't a total idiot, I wasn't going to play bull in the china shop and ask, What in God's name made you buy this thing? I rehearsed speaking frankly with a view to possibly being of some help but I heard the danger of sounding superior. Double-talk was out, I was no good at pussyfooting, so I decided the hell with it: say as little as possible and see how it goes. When we met, I simply said I very much would like to work for him again but I was wrong for *Under Capricorn,* it wasn't my cup of tea—and that was as far as I got. He interrupted and I was excommunicated.

Later in the day, Sidney put his arm around me and friend to friend, for my sake, tried to persuade me to recant. I had hurt Hitch, I had offended him by my disloyalty. Loyalty was an unquestioning yes; no was ingratitude. For me, however, recanting would not be an act of friendship, it would really make me disloyal. Hitch didn't see it that way. I never sat at his table at Romanoff's again.

A hard, early lesson in friendship: we had never really been friends. That bewildered and hurt. Friendship was serious, it was to be treasured; Hitch confused friendship with blind approval or at least acquiescence. He wasn't the last friend who did that.

There was a sequel—there were two, in fact. He asked me to do *Torn Curtain* for Paul Newman and Julie Andrews. Not directly: the offer came through Swifty Lazar, at that time a star-to-be on his road to fame and fortune for himself as well as his clients, if not before. As Swifty got more famous, his half-glasses got bigger, his *A*s got broader, and his name became Irving. Going through Swifty was Hitchcock's way of signaling I was on probation. But *Torn Curtain* seemed exactly what he didn't need at that moment: another ill-fated venture. I didn't want to go through Swifty, I wanted to talk to Hitch myself, to explain with such care and so well that I would sit at Romanoff's with him again. He wasn't interested in anything but a yes or no via Lazar. So: same reaction to the material from me, same reaction to me from him, same reaction to the picture from the press and public: failure.

Years later—I was long gone from Hollywood—he made one last offer. He was visiting my next-door neighbor on the beach at Quogue. I went over gladly, eagerly but oh Lord, the movie was *Topaz* and I'd barely been able to finish the book. This time he did ask, he did listen, he did let me explain. And he accepted my opinion; he wasn't cold or brusque, he was pleasant, almost warm, even regretful. Progress, and I was so pleased. But he quietly made it clear he was not a friend. We were not as we had been and we never would be again. A king in the realm of the magic lantern can be like that, especially when the crown is slipping.

Anatole Litvak and George Cukor were also kings. Professionally, Litvak may not have been in Hitchcock's class but once we became friends, loyalty was never a subject: we stayed friends until his last day. George Cukor was another king and another who expected loyalty—of another kind, though.

Through Irene—he and she were as close as she and her sister Edie weren't—we resumed our army friendship shortly after I moved into the house on Doheny, but except for our wartime classic *Resistance and Ohm's Law*, we never made a picture together. Unlike Hitchcock, George didn't dump me when I said—several times—a project wasn't my cup of tea.

"Don't insult me with that crap!" he would bark. "What don't you like? Why not? Do you think it can be fixed? Could So-and-so write it? Should I go ahead with it? Come to dinner tonight."

Like many of the kings, he was possessive of his subjects. He allowed Hitchcock in my life because he respected him and because he thought Hitch was "socially retarded"—i.e., no competition socially. Litvak he was mean about. He didn't like his pictures, resented that he traveled in Irene's A+ circles and was annoyed that both Irene and I really liked him.

"What kind of a name is that: Anatole Litvak?" he asked testily. "It's like calling yourself Anatole Kike." He laughed at what he thought was a joke. He laughed at similar jokes about homosexuals. He, of course, was Jewish and homosexual and hated being both. It never occurred to me to wonder whether Tola was Jewish. He never said what he was, maybe his name did, but I knew he wasn't anti-Semitic just as I knew George was anti everything he had received at birth, especially his face. Apparently, he had decided that if he was grand enough—as the years went by, his *A*s, like Swifty Lazar's, got broader and broader—he would rise above being an unattractive Jewish queer by becoming an elegant silver-and-china queen and a Republican.

The other side, the attractive side was that he was cultured, well read, very knowledgeable about theatre and was funny—bitchy, yes, but very funny. And his parties! Famous, especially the Sunday brunches around the swimming pool at the bottom of his terraced gardens. A high wall hid the quietly grand house and the unexpected extent of the grounds which had a staircase descending to street level. By the door in the wall there was a telephone: a visitor had to identify himself to be buzzed in. From my first visit, I wondered why George felt the need for that protection.

The brunches always starred women who were either beautiful or witty. Men, stars or husbands, served as an appreciative audience. Regulars like Kate Hepburn and Ruth Gordon gaped with the rest of us one afternoon when Garbo came down the path. In shorts, with a scarf tied over her hair and a straw hat over both, she said: "The old boy didn't have time to wash his hair." I turned to Hepburn and said, "Now I can leave Hollywood." Kate asked, "Why?" and when I answered "Because I've met Garbo," she clearly was pissed off. Garbo pissed off many people, especially when she insisted on being introduced as "Harriet Brown."

At tea at Constance Collier's—she was tutoring Kate in Shakespeare—the phone rang. Feeliss (Phyllis), Constance's English secretary, answered in the next room, then came back. "It's her."

"What's she calling herself?"

"Harriet Brown."

"You tell her I said if she's Harriet Brown, I'm not home."

Cukor's famous black-tie parties were a very far cry from charades at the Kellys'. I felt as though I were in one of his glossy movies: drinks in his expensive expansive library where every surface overflowed with autographed photographs in silver frames of every theatre celebrity since Booth; candlelit dining on the terrace; brandy and coffee in an elegant oval pigskin-lined drawing room that was either formal or stiff, depending on your take. His cast, pace Irene, was a mix of stars old and new—Ethel Barrymore, Ronald Colman, Norma Shearer, David Niven, Rosalind Russell—and writers old and new—Somerset Maugham, Donald Ogden Stewart, Garson Kanin, Lion Feuchtwanger, me. Very impressive but I wished it had been less so once when I died a death of embarrassment in that library.

Irene was angry with me because I hadn't given her my new play (*The Bird Cage*) to produce, so she cut me dead. Her pal, Kate Hepburn, went her one better. Arriving late at Cukor's with a guest who had to be introduced around the room, she stopped when she got to me and said: "I always forget those little boys' names."

I pretended I hadn't heard; if I hadn't heard, then nobody else had heard. I wasn't sure whether she'd said "those little gay boys' names" but I knew she'd implied it. After she said it, she gargled the little Ah-ha-ha she always did when she said or someone else said something that might have been funny but she wasn't really sure. She was completely humorless, I knew that; not a whit of humor about herself. But she didn't mean this to be funny; it was cruel and she meant it to be cruel. Loyalty, yes: she was Irene's friend, she was being loyal to Irene, I recognized that. Maybe she had learned from Irene, Irene had also been cruel in the Walnut Street Theatre lobby and God knows was also humorless. The two friends also played a good game of tennis. They were two women who were uncomfortable with being women; it made them peculiarly dissatisfied. I recognized that. It was no excuse but it did take out some of the sting. Years later, it was my turn with Hepburn and I took it; some years after that, it was my turn again but by then, I didn't have the need to take it.

There was another kind of party George invited me to that wasn't at all famous; in truth, it was almost secret. When his secretary said "casual dress," I knew I was in for dinner in George's smaller but still elegant dining room with a very different cast of just four: me to converse with George, an old queen to reminisce with George, and a hustler to fuck with George. The old queen and I would be kicked out at 10 sharp. Those evenings were insulting, much as I tried not to admit it.

The same white-aprons-over-black-dresses staff served those dinners with the same facial paralysis they served the more kosher glamorous ones. Whether they also served the very large all-boy parties where George showed pornos, I never knew because I was never invited. He had his own rules for his guests; he drew the lines I, for example, could cross and not cross.

I was always aware of his piss-elegance and his hypocrisy. It was what I didn't like about some of his pictures, what I tried not to hear in his conversation. I kept playing dancing monkey at those dinners for four because I wanted the Sunday brunches and the all-star black-tie dinners, but Hepburn's vicious little jab did more than just embarrass. It made me look and listen; then, of course, I saw and heard the piss-elegance and hypocrisy present in the starriest parties.

But George was kind, generous and very supportive of me to everyone. I genuinely liked him despite the chichi. I was beginning to have new friends, more like those I'd had in New York, but George was a friend. A diva, to be sure, but divas were vulnerable as well as demanding. I wanted to back off gently, without hurting. George would have said: "For Chrissakes, just tell me to fuck off!" I wouldn't have had the nerve if we hadn't had a dustup about something completely unforeseen: hustlers.

George knew about my affair with Farley but ignored it. In his world, young men didn't have love affairs. If they went to bed with each other, it was briefly and only if one of them was a piece of trade or a hustler. Occasionally, he tried to foist a hustler off on me. Not that he called them hustlers; instead, they were young out-of-work actors who gave massages for money. The third time I said hustlers were not for me, George got very angry. To be fair, he honestly did not and could not believe I was uninterested in hustlers. What homosexual wasn't interested?

Over the years, other friends—well-known literary and academic figures—have gotten seriously angry at me for the same reason: they would not believe me when I said hustlers weren't for me. In one instance, a close friend, a university professor and respected essayist—all right, admittedly, an alcoholic and he was drunk—got angry enough to end our friendship. He and the others thought I was being judgmental; I thought they were angry at themselves.

George's anger helped me: it was so unwarranted that it gave me the guts to refuse the next "casual dress" invitation. His secretary was scarcely off the phone when he was on, sputtering in an absolute rage.

"And what are you doing that is so fucking fascinating you can't come to me?"

"I'm having dinner with an old friend."

"Which fucking old friend?"

"Mitzi Green."

"Mitzi Green? MITZI GREEN?? You are having dinner with Mitzi Green rather than with me?!!"

Mitzi Green was a child star in the movies who became a musical star on Broadway overnight by stopping the show with "The Lady Is a Tramp" in *Babes in Arms*. She was on the Coast to visit her husband, Joe Pevney, who had played the lead in *Home of the Brave*. Joe was now a movie director; he and Mitzi were good friends from New York and I adored her—which made me as angry at George as he was at me.

"Yes," I snapped. "I would rather have dinner with my friend Mitzi Green and her husband than with you and one of your piss-elegant old queens and a dumb, fucking hustler."

"Fresh as ever," George said and hung up.

I was never invited to another "casual dress" dinner with an old queen and a hustler. But not too much time passed before I was invited to a Sunday brunch. I went. A Saturday night black-tie—I didn't go. Invited to another, I went. It continued: sometimes I went, sometimes I didn't, until the Un-American Committee so changed the temper of the city that the cast and content of even George Cukor's parties changed.

If the Austrian director Max Ophuls was a king, it was of a very small country of cineastes, cinephiles, and sadists. His Hollywood-made *Letter from an Unknown Woman* with Joan Fontaine garnered him some respect in this country but not nearly as much as he got from his fellow refugees, and they didn't like him. As his agent, Paul Kohner, another refugee, said at lunch: "Max, but for a small blemish, you would have been the archest Nazi of them all."

Max laughed happily. He always laughed happily at a reference to his sadism. He laughed when he told how he had sent an assistant director to a Paris brothel to pick up some whips for a scene in a picture he was shooting.

"Three days, it took him!" Max cried. "Three days before he came back, and when he did, he could not sit down for three more!" He laughed happily.

The picture I did with him was called *Caught*. James Mason's first American picture, costarring Barbara Bel Geddes and Robert Ryan, it was made for the brave new Enterprise Pictures, and therein lies a prototypical Hollywood tale.

Enterprise was the creation of Charlie Einfeld, previously the most successful press representative in Hollywood. His new approach was Big Stars in Big Pictures, stars like Ingrid Bergman and John Garfield, whom he did sign, and Ginger Rogers, who said she would sign if Charlie bought a novel called *Wild Calendar* for her. He did but she didn't.

Max was to put his distinctive touch to Abe Polonsky's screenplay based on the novel. He invited me to lunch to discuss a small rewrite for big money, at least according to Swifty who hadn't read either. Nor had I.

"Don't," Max instructed. "I'm not going to make a picture from that lousy book. I'm going to make a picture about Howard Hughes."

"Why?"

He laughed merrily. "Because I hate him."

Lynn Baguette, a very pretty, sweetly sympathetic girl with the long legs grown in Texas, met Howard Hughes once—when she was flown by a Hughes pimp to Las Vegas along with some other candidates. Each girl was given her own hotel room plus one hundred dollars in gambling money. They were told Hughes would observe them from above the tables and make his selection. Lynn ordered a big room service and stayed in her room. She was finishing the last of the best steak she'd had in a year when Hughes knocked on her door. He was curious why she wasn't downstairs gambling. Lynn's simple explanation that she couldn't afford to lose a hundred bucks kept Hughes in the room; he sat down and discussed the relative value of money for almost two hours. He impressed her, she liked him but he got sleepy and left without saying good night. Also without giving her another hundred, which she could have used, or even a ten percent tip. She never saw him again.

At the time she told me this story, she was taking a course in Great Books as part of an effort to keep alive a bad marriage to Sam Spiegel, the producer. Much later, divorced and in Paris, she made a small name for herself by being kicked in the ass by Marian Shaw at an expatriate cocktail party. Lynn had been having an affair with Irwin, Marian had broken a leg skiing and was on crutches. The leg she kicked Lynn with was in a hard plaster cast and it really hurt.

"Why didn't she kick her husband?" a bewildered Lynn asked.

The men understood, the women clutched their men tighter, the gays brought Lynn a chair and a drink.

Lynn and her anecdote about Howard Hughes were the nucleus of the picture about Hughes I wrote for Max Ophuls. (There is a screen credit— "Adapted from *Wild Calendar*"—that allowed Enterprise to write off its purchase of the novel. A protest to the Writers Guild was ignored, not to my surprise.) During the writing, Max's only concern was his vendetta. Hughes had given him a rough time at RKO; Max wanted me to give him a rougher time in the picture for Enterprise. He was all exclamation points:

"Make him an idiot! An egomaniac! Terrible to women! Also to men! Make him a fool! Make him die! Kill him off!" He wasn't kidding. Then he cackled. "Have fun."

I did, actually, with evading the strictures of the Hays Office. According to those rules, a man and wife had to sleep in twin beds; if he even touched her bed, his feet had to stay on the floor. In *Caught,* the wife is seen on an enormous bed after what had clearly been, judging from the ecstatically disheveled state of her nightgown and the bedclothes, a very active night. No man in sight, however, so no Hays rule violated. To rub salt, when a man does enter the room, he sits on the bed, he reclines next to her but keeps his feet safely on the floor.

Divorce was a trickier proposition. No wife in a movie could ask for a divorce, period; no exceptions for any reason. In *Caught,* the wife had a cornucopia of reasons; more important, the story needed her to ask for a divorce. Dilemma: How can she ask without asking? Simple, blessedly simple: He does it for her and the Hays Office is circumvented.

"You want a divorce, don't you?" he asks.

"No, I don't, I don't!" she protests tearfully. But we know she is lying; even he knows and consequently has a heart attack that kills him. Max loved it.

Unfathomable was why James Mason chose *Caught* as his first American picture. His role was a young pediatrician on New York's Lower East Side. To justify the accent, I added a rejected Park Avenue family. Mason didn't need justification for anything. Whatever he said, whatever he did, he was believable and riveting. He made movie acting an art yet was alive to anything accidental that might happen on the set: watch him in a largely improvised nightclub scene, dancing with Barbara Bel Geddes, breaking up and making it work for the moment. To top it off, the camera loved him: he was a star.

Offscreen, he was likeable, quiet; he would even have been unremarkable had he not been the apex of a triangle with his wife Pamela—a smart, bosomy Englishwoman with a tongue that could slice meat—and a sexy ex–Jersey City cop who, whatever else he did for the Masons and neither bothered to explain, was always on hand to strap James into the false torso he wore beneath his shirt. The resultant visual increase in bulk visibly increased his intensity and his sexuality on-screen. Mason was completely unself-conscious about the falsie; not a qualm about the cop strapping him in right on the set in front of all and sundry. One of the sundry was a carpenter, five or six years older than I, attractive enough to be in pictures himself. He caught me watching him watching Mason and winked. At the end-of-shooting wrap party, we went to my darkened office on the lot and used the couch. Farley was living with me, the carpenter was married, neither of us had had that much to drink. We wanted to do it because we knew it would be good and it was. I didn't feel guilty about it, not even when I told Judd Marmor who made no comment one way or the other.

When the two other leads were cast, Howard Hughes became a problem. Barbara Bel Geddes and Robert Ryan were both under contract to RKO. Before agreeing to loan them out, Hughes had to vet the screenplay himself. Max blanched: his sole reason for making the movie was to destroy this man and now this man could and undoubtedly would, Max was sure of it, destroy him.

Beyond Lynn Baguette's anecdote and Max's injustice collection, I had done almost no research. Inadvertently, however, I had hit upon truths about Hughes. No Barbara Bel Geddes, no Robert Ryan unless the coincidences were cut. Most were characteristics easy to remove: Robert Ryan would not wear only sneakers, would not drink only milk. Excising one situation on Hughes's shit list wasn't at all easy, in fact, it would derail the whole story.

Neither Max nor I had a solution. It was right there, though, right in front of us, we just didn't know it: James Mason.

Unknown to me (or anyone else), Howard Hughes had had an anonymous first wife who dumped him for a dentist—a poor dentist, which was doubly infuriating and exactly what I had invented, I thought, for the screenplay. Hughes went glacial. It was timidly pointed out that the character in the movie was not a poor dentist, he was a doctor—a doctor who came from Park Avenue and money. Then that James Mason was to play the doctor. James Mason? Signed? No out clause? OK, muzzle the attack dogs. James Mason was class; it was understandable a wife might leave her husband for James Mason; James Mason made Howard Hughes happy. Max could have Ryan and Bel Geddes but the dailies had to be delivered to Mr. Hughes in person at his house at midnight by the editor.

The editor was Bob Parrish, the most amiable man in Hollywood. He was a good friend; he and I and his wife Cathy often played in the Chaplin-Wyler Cockamamie Tennis Tournament. After a match, you would never know whether Bob had won or lost; with Cathy, you always knew. Bob was the perfect fellow to deliver the film to Hughes; he could make his midnight delivery, wait outside for Hughes to say yea or nay, and not suffer. But Max did. Max, not Bob, succumbed to Howard Hughes–induced stress. Just before the start of shooting, Max came down with shingles.

John Berry took over the picture. Why? Whose idea? A mystery. I knew Jack slightly from the Kellys', where he was a devout progressive but so macho he always seemed to have arrived on a horse. His first day on the set, the wife became a dumb blonde bimbo out for a buck. She even chewed gum. I went home.

Barbara Bel Geddes, one of the best young theatre actresses, had a good-girl-but-I-want-it kind of sex appeal that had made her Maggie in *Cat on a Hot Tin Roof* steam. To date, she hadn't been steaming in pictures and hadn't gotten very far, so she eagerly combined Marilyn Monroe, Jane Russell, Jean Harlow—name them and watch the wiggle-walk. For twelve days, she wiggled. Then Max recovered from the shingles.

He ran Berry's footage and emerged from the projection room in a rage but with his priorities clear. First, Barbara Bel Geddes had to be his again. As usual, she arrived at the studio at dawn and went to Hair for her Berry-chosen style. When she arrived on the set, Max gave one appraising look and sent her back for a new hairdo. A delicate moment but Bel Geddes was a professional. Back to Hair, back to the set, ready to rehearse her scene with an Ophuls over-actor named Curt Bois, playing the piano and delivering nasty cracks out of the corner of his mouth until she stopped him with a slap across his face. Max, as annoyed by the overacting as Barbara, had her slap Bois twice as hard twice across the face; then he sent her back for a change of hairdo. She glared but she went. A new hairdo approved, she slapped Bois harder and got sent back to Hair. It went like that all the very long day; new hairdo, slap Bois harder, back to Hair; new hairdo, slap Bois harder, good, back to Hair. At the end of the day Barbara Bel Geddes belonged to Max. Curt Bois's face looked like raw liver but he was still overacting. I think he was Hungarian. Max laughed, then got down to serious business.

Out went all twelve days John Berry had shot. Max Ophuls made Max Ophuls pictures and was going to start fresh. Unfortunately, there was one not-so-little hitch: the cupboard at Enterprise was bare. The studio had produced too many big expensive flops like *Joan of Arc* and *Arch of Triumph;* there was barely enough money to reshoot four days. Enterprise was finished. *Caught* was to be its last release.

Could I condense twelve script days into four? A rhetorical question: I had to do it. And dug up a memory from the theatre that salvaged the night scene where Bel Geddes first meets Ryan.

As the girl based on Lynn Baguette, Barbara is waiting on a dock for someone to take her to a party aboard Howard Hughes's yacht out in the harbor. He arrives in a motorboat and they play their meeting scene on the dock overlooking the misty harbor. The scene on the dock could be managed with smoke pots, but the four-day budget didn't have a penny for renting a motorboat, let alone the yacht.

Bob Parrish supplied the yacht: a stock shot of a distant boat with glittering lights. Add music and there was a party on the yacht. But where was the motorboat to approach the dock from the misty sea with Ryan aboard?

That's where that memory entered: a production of *Anna Karenina* in Paris in which Anna's suicide provided one of those moments in the theatre that make the entire evening worth attending. On a small stage, in full view of the whole audience, Anna Karenina went to her death by jumping off a bridge into the path of a fast-moving train. I had gone backstage to find out: What was the bridge? What was the train? How was it done? Answer: with an economy to marvel at and remember. It's amazing how often in the theatre, a marvel is accomplished because there isn't enough money. Backs must be to the wall for us to find we have more imagination than we imagined.

A crude wooden arch upstage was the bridge the actress stood on; smoke billowing from a little machine in the wings obscured half of the arch and much of the stage that wasn't lost in darkness anyway; a recording of a locomotive getting louder and louder, played over a backstage mike, made the train run closer and closer. But the real coup was the train itself: a stagehand in black with a spotlight on his head. The light cut through the smoke that hid his body as he came from the wings in a curve, then walked downstage, his light, the locomotive's light, shining straight out at the audience. Just before he passed under the arch, the actress jumped, her body flailing in his light. Then, lost in the smoke, she was buried in the roaring sound of the train that killed her.

In *Caught,* Bel Geddes waits on a dimly lit wooden platform against a black velour backdrop, party music in the distance. Stock shot of the yacht at sea; quick cut back to Bel Geddes looking out to sea with the sound of a motorboat getting louder and louder. A stagehand in black, with a spotlight on his head, bobs up and down: the bouncing motorboat coming closer to the dock through smoky murkiness. Bel Geddes goes to the edge of the platform; the sound of the boat's motor sputters and dies; the light goes out. She leans over to talk down to Ryan who is heard from below. Then he appears, climbing up onto the dock where they can now play their meeting scene. It cost almost nothing and it worked.

Later in the picture, there is dancing in a nightclub Ophuls created out of a stock bar, that same black velour, gauzy black chiffon curtains and more smoky murkiness. Pauline Kael, the cinema oracle, praised Ophuls for the murky darkness he created throughout the movie because to her, it symbolized the murky darkness of the characters.

Two contributions to *Caught* came from my personal experience: one, the light worn by a stagehand; the other, light from a psychoanalyst. The former brought Ryan, who made a good Howard Hughes, to the girl on the dock; the latter got him to marry her.

Plots whipped up for the occasion tend to have hidden land mines—in this case, the absence of a sensible reason for the Hughes character to marry the girl. Since a psychoanalyst was resolving my personal plots, I brought one in to resolve this one. Not the pipe-smoking Englishman in *The Snake Pit* but the real thing, personified by Judd Marmor, naturally. Max cast Art Smith, who usually played union organizers; I apologized to Judd. But when I saw the couch scene, I saw contradictions in my feelings about Judd I hadn't been aware of.

Ryan as Hughes marries because his analyst tells him he will never marry and he will not allow anyone to tell him what he will or won't do. The analyst points out that he is destroying Bel Geddes and himself just to prove the analyst wrong. "That's your opinion," Ryan says and walks out, saving himself money.

It's crystal clear to us that the analyst is right in his assessment. He deserves our respect and he gets it. Still, a question lingers: If he is so good, couldn't he have stopped his patient? Then another: Isn't it he who drove his patient to do the wrong thing? Isn't he responsible?

Reik through Freud might have leapt on indications of some ambivalence toward Marmor. Or at least, some confusion about what I, as patient, was doing. What I was doing was confusing enough to me.

After telling Farley he didn't need analysis, I had gotten him into analysis. More accurately, I had driven him there: we slept in the same bed but I wouldn't let him touch me. Everyone we knew and liked was straight; I was going to go straight and so, therefore, was he.

We were part of a group of loving friends. Being necessary to them made a difference in my life. Having them and giving to them lessened the need for having Farley and giving to him. Like him, like me, like everybody in that company town, all the friends were in pictures and psychoanalysis even though they were straight.

We all smoked during meals, got drunk on Saturday night, ate in one another's houses, barbecued in the backyard and picnicked on the beach at Santa Monica. I played less tennis because those I played with were not in the group. Music was a shared love; so were rallies and fund-raisers for progressive causes, and sneak previews.

Our center was the house on Doheny, now repossessed by its owners, the Chaplins—Sol, Ethel, and their daughter Judy. All three were in love with Farley. Look, how gorgeous! they caroled, even Sol. Farley's best friends, and no wonder, they were mine now, too. Sol—a tall, skinny, almost albino stork with thick glasses—was a member of MGM's legendary music department. He didn't laugh, he howled; he didn't like, he adored; and he lived almost exclusively at the piano: four hands with Ethel or Judy, or solo, to play the house favorite, "Porgy and Bess," which we sang around the piano. Anyone who came through the door joined in.

Ethel held the group and the house together. From New York's Yiddish Lower East Side, here she was with her little tip-tilted nose almost living in Beverly Hills; Comden and Green were her pals; she was in and out of Gene Kelly's house the way Judy's friend Marilyn Letterman was in and out of hers—imagine! She cleaned, she cooked, she chauffered Judy to ballet lessons (although even off pointe, Judy was too big for ballet), she did everything housewives and mothers did but it was hard to believe she was either. Maybe because what she cooked was chiefly tuna delight. Or maybe because the house constantly needed to be yanked together. Or maybe because her passion at the piano didn't relieve her sexual discontent.

Judy, who dreamt of marrying Farley (with me as a backup) but grew up to marry Hal Prince, wore the clothes of a ten-year-old which enabled her to sit unobtrusively in a corner of the living room, hearing everything the adults said, even some of what was unsaid. I treated her as an adult and wrote a one-act play called *Queen Lear* for her birthday. It required a large cast, much dancing to a score by Sol, and had only one speaking part: Judy as Queen Lear. Her supporting company was made of friends like Marilyn Letterman who were accustomed to their lowly place. *Queen Lear* opened in the Chaplins' living room and was such a smash, it continued on to play the Beverly Hills living room circuit.

Two New York actors were emeritus in the Doheny group: Buddy Tyne, who was to become Ethel's second husband, and Stanley Prager, who also, as he put it, "took from Marmor." Buddy, ruddy and hearty with wild hair, was a great straight man for Stanley, called Stash. He was an adorable, chubby comedian, one of the few who were truly funny in the living room, much more so than his friend, Abe Burrows. Abe had tics and twitches even when singing his own comedy songs like "The Girl with the Three Blue Eyes." He worked hard to be

Farley and I spent a lot of time with Millard Kaufman *(right)*—
ex-Marine, screenwriter and reader of dictionaries for pleasure.
He loved to share the meaning of *merkin.*

funny so he was not appreciative when Stash got more laughs. One night at Abe's, Stash was down on all fours playing a frozen dog; we were all laughing, which made him laugh which made us laugh even more. Abe emptied a glass of ginger ale on Stanley's head. Somehow managing to attain dignity despite ginger ale dripping down his apple cheeks, Stanley said quietly, "That isn't funny, Abe."

A few years later, when we learned Abe was an informer, we didn't speculate whether he had informed on Stash. That would have been unbearable.

Stanley introduced me to two other, very different friends I knew immediately I had to hold on to: Lorry and Millard Kaufman. Millard, the author of the screenplay for *Bad Day at Black Rock,* was a tall, bony, bighearted ex-Marine who used "fucking" where anyone else would use "very," yet read dictionaries for pleasure. When he talked in his fucking loud voice, he would get up and pace around the room as though he felt unsure of getting everyone's attention.

Anita Ellis, the legendary jazz singer who stopped performing because of acute stage fright. While she was the voice of Rita Hayworth in *Gilda,* she was studying philosophy at UCLA.

Lorry was quiet: quietly pretty, quiet spoken, quietly observant; she even giggled quietly. An anthropologist, she also "took from Marmor." She was studying psychology to switch over and be a therapist. Neither of us said anything memorable to the other at our first meeting but, to use E. M. Forster's word, we connected. There was a sexual undertone, unmentioned by either of us, but I was sure she was as aware of it as I was. Every so often—exactly why, I don't know—that undertone has been there between a woman and me. It doesn't get anywhere but it makes the connection lasting.

Everyone in the group was part of a couple. Farley and I were a couple. So were Buddy and Stanley but Stanley was having an affair with the California Mattress King's daughter, who was very sexy, wild about him, and—essential for real interest—a progressive. Stanley, then, was straight; Buddy was straight; Karen Morley, Lloyd Gough, Sid and Cora Zelinski—all were straight. And although there was never a sign or a sigh to intimate Farley and I were not, I was sure they all knew why we were a couple. Oh, Farley was adored for more than his looks—for his enthusiasm, his eagerness. There was much to adore, but I knew they could hear him parrot me and parrot Ethel because I could hear it. They overlooked that, they pretended we were just friends, accepted us as just friends, but knowing we were the only people in the group who were not straight was too difficult for me, so it wasn't coincidental that when I met Anita Ellis at the Chaplins', we fell into bed.

She was becoming a jazz legend. She had her own radio show every week; sometimes she dubbed for stars, most famously for Rita Hayworth, singing "Put the Blame on Mame" for her in *Gilda*. She laughed—an infectious musical trill as lovely as her singing—when she described Harry Cohn's *Gilda* party in his house for his exhibitors. The Columbia Pictures mogul wanted Hayworth to lip-synch "Mame" in the dining room while Anita sang through the kitchen door behind her.

Dubbing for Vera-Ellen at MGM, Anita met Sol. He was so knocked out by her singing, he brought her home as a gift to Ethel and Judy, who were equally knocked out by it but also by "crazy Anita" herself. She became part of the group, but only when it suited her. And she resisted singing at the Chaplins': it made her nervous to be stared at while she sang. Whenever we could, though, we got her to sing "I Love You, Porgy": it was spectacular. She took philosophy courses at UCLA, she rhapsodized equally about nature and her Canadian family, transplanted to L.A., particularly her brother, Larry Kert, who also sang but did back flips and stood on his head while he did; her own mother; and her quasi mother, Salka Viertel.

Salka was the wife of the Austrian director Berthold Viertel, who had returned to Vienna, and the mother of Peter whom she admired for his writing and his wife, Jigee, and scorned for his tennis and movie friends. She was a writer of sorts herself, at least on Garbo movies, and had been Garbo's lover, perhaps still was, but surely was the trusted friend of the "old boy," as Garbo referred to herself. Salka's house in Santa Monica was a salon for intellectual refugees like Thomas Mann and Hanns Eisler and one of the Reinhardt sons, Wolfgang, who produced *Caught*. Anita and Salka talked philosophy and life; Anita gave Salka singing lessons and Salka, an actress in Poland, gave Anita acting lessons. Neither profited and I wondered what I wondered but I was enormously fond of both.

Anita had been married to Frank Ellis, an Air Force pilot—very handsome in the photograph she had—but divorced him because she hated the military. There was a young doctor in her life, very attractive in the flesh, with whom she was and wasn't having an affair. I was making a bet with myself that he was gay when she told me he was and laughed as into bed we tumbled again.

We didn't see each other on any regular schedule; neither demanded nor seemed to expect. I wasn't quite sure of that, though. She confided in Lorry Kaufman whom she admired intensely but Lorry would never be a messenger. There was something slightly but profoundly loony about Anita that made her vulnerable and dear. It also removed pressure.

The sex, so incredible and natural, was why I thought I could go straight. Tola had given me the key to his Malibu beach house when he left for his beloved Paris to movie-make in Europe; being able to take Anita there eliminated awkwardness with Farley who had moved into the sliver of a second bedroom behind the kitchen. If going straight was what I wanted, going straight was what he would do, with enthusiasm. There was no apparent tension on Lookout Mountain Road.

We double-dated; I was often with Anita, he was always with Frances Goldwyn's nemesis, Shelley Winters. They liked being seen together: each week, the fans screamed louder, the photographers clicked faster, they both lapped it up. Believing adulation is like believing rave reviews: when you do, you're dead. In public, Shelley was the blonde bombshell in black with her mouth half open to look sexy and to hide her overbite. Farley tried to look older and protective but he was stuck with his boyish grin. He and Shelley talked very seriously about Acting and the Method and costarring first on the Stage and then on the Screen. They had a good time together, and an occasional sexual foray gave their image a little reality. Still, when we double-dated and went to Mocambo, Shelley would table-hop or work the bar and come back with a cute little offering for Farley. If her intention was to do me in, she surely didn't think she was doing herself in as well. She seemed to go along with our pretense that we were not what we were. But Shelley was too shrewd; she knew. Her goal was to drive a wedge rather than simply to please Farley.

Gerry Brooks shortly before she read her tarot cards
and left Hollywood for Italy.

The blonde bombshell Shelley was a joke to me, but the no-makeup Shelley I liked a lot. We were members of the same Marxist study group led by an Australian recently named Harry Carlisle. What I enjoyed most was learning how to read the *New York Times*—from its point of view, from the left-wing point of view, and from all points liberal and reactionary in between. Shelley enjoyed parading her credentials as a striker against Woolworth's back in Detroit, but Harry was a wonderful leader. He managed both to let Shelley talk and feed her ego and to shut her up before the rest of us struck.

Sometimes when I double-dated with Farley and Shelley, I brought Geraldine Brooks, whom I had known slightly in New York. She was under contract to Warner Brothers where, as Joan Crawford's daughter, she was smacked by our Joan across the face with a hairbrush and sent tumbling down a long flight of stairs. Attention-getting stuff for a beauty, but because she was very young and quite small, she accentuated her girlishness and hid the intelligent, sophisticated woman she was but was never cast as.

Words were unnecessary with Gerry: she knew who and what I was; whatever I chose was fine with her. She saw no reason for me to push myself to go straight but she didn't want to be part of Ethel's group. She loved Stash, he made her laugh, but the group was too possessive and too unsophisticated for her. And serious though she was about acting and politics, she was also serious about sex and knew she wasn't going to find any on Doheny Drive even if I had. We had no sexual undertone but we didn't need it. The love was mutual.

One new arrival from New York was an old friend who was gay: James Mitchell moved into a house on Lookout Mountain Road between Gerry's and ours. Earlier, back East on a juicy weekend in 1946, Jerry Robbins and Oliver Smith asked me to rush up to New Haven where they were trying out a new musical, *Billion Dollar Baby,* starring George Cukor's rival, Mitzi Green. The leading dancer was James Mitchell. He and I had flirted during the run-throughs in New York; that New Haven weekend, I rotated between meeting with Jerry and Oliver in their suite in the Taft Hotel and sneaking down the back stairs to Jimmy's room, where we giggled before and after but not during. Sex and the giggles begins a good friendship.

In his next show, *Brigadoon,* Jimmy's career really took off. During my New York holiday before *Rope* started shooting, I took my mother to a matinee. Ingrid Bergman was sitting next to me, I introduced my mother, *Brigadoon* became the best show my mother had ever seen after *Home of the Brave.*

Brigadoon brought Jimmy to the Coast, where he and Farley were in the same acting class. When Farley started going up to Jimmy's to rehearse a scene, I wondered if they were giggling before and after but not during. Speculation stopped when Jimmy announced he, too, was going straight, starting Saturday night.

Sunday, Farley and I were having a big Sunday breakfast, when Jimmy walked in, strangely deliberate and frozen-faced. Drop-dead handsome, he was known in New York as the Great Stone Face but that morning, he looked carved in granite. Dropping silently into a chair, he yanked a lampshade off a lamp, put it on his head, and said with utter contempt:

"Disgusting. She didn't even bring her own toothbrush."

All three of us went: we howled and howled and that was the end of going straight.

The absurdity did it. The absurdity plus my jealousy. Plus my desire for same sex. My problem with being gay in a straight world wasn't solved but If You Can't Fight 'Em, Join 'Em didn't seem a workable solution.

Farley came back from the little bedroom; we were back, though not exactly to where we had been. The difference was small but quantitative. We said nothing but we both knew; at least, I assumed he knew.

Anita's radio show folded and she took off for New York and Paris. The next week, Farley was off to New York. Carried away by his celebrity, he made what I thought was a serious career mistake. He had come to hate the kind of picture Goldwyn stuck him in—with or without Ann Blyth—and decided to risk crossing Goldwyn by turning down one more of the same. Sam Goldwyn was adept at killing careers: he loaned Farley out to Metro for a B picture. The picture called for location shooting in New York which made Farley danger-ously delirious. He didn't give a hoot in hell how B the picture was; he'd never been to New York, he couldn't wait to get there. Leaving me alone in the house in Laurel Canyon with the double fireplace and an empty bed.

At first, I liked being alone. I had the friends and I had to revise *The Bird Cage*, which Walter Fried would be producing on Broadway with Harold Clurman directing. Long distance, they arranged a meeting for me with Melvyn Douglas, whom they wanted to star in the play.

The screen plays tricks with height: I had no idea Melvyn Douglas was so tall. It made him very impressive. His intelligence and relaxed charm made him more impressive, he was nicer than any movie star I'd met and yes, he was a progressive. Married to Congresswoman Helen Gahagan Douglas, he'd have to be. But he asked some probing, unsettling questions about the play; I answered glibly and tried to divert him by talking about how unfairly Nixon had treated Mrs. Douglas during her failed reelection campaign.

At that time, I had asked her—she had fought for Marian Anderson's right to sing in Constitutional Hall—if she would fight for the fascist Gerald L. K. Smith's right to speak in the Hall. When she answered Of course, I said: You're going to lose. Which she did.

I was fairly confident Mel—he made it Mel very quickly—would do the play but had a sensible hunch it would be for the wrong reasons: he was in danger of being blacklisted in movies and he wanted to work with Clurman.

With the house to myself, the revisions went well, but when the work was done for the day or night, there I was. I could go to Chaplins' or the Kaufmans' and I did, but when I got home, there the bed was and there I was, alone in it. Farley called when he first arrived in New York, thrilled to be stay-ing at the Plaza! The next time, he was thrilled he'd seen Betty and Adolph in their New York, New York! And meeting their friends! Then he had night shooting and the time differential knocked out calling until he was back on a regular schedule. Then he stopped calling.

When I called him, it was six o'clock in the evening in New York; he should have been back from shooting, having his drink. There was no answer in his room so I left a message. When I was having my drink, he should have been back from dinner, so I called again. And left another message. At ten and eleven o'clock at night his time, I called. He hadn't picked up his messages; maybe he was on a night shoot again but I didn't think so.

At midnight, at twelve-thirty; at one; at two, his time. Now it's midnight and one and two my time. I can't sleep. I take a pill that I don't think will work so of course it doesn't. I'm embarrassed that the night operator at the Plaza knows it's the same person calling; she can hear everything in my voice but the hell with her. Not knowing is the worst; suspense is the worst; no, possessiveness is the worst. I didn't know jealousy, I didn't know anger, and I've never known such pain.

At daybreak, I'm exhausted but not enough to be numb. I shower slowly, dress slowly, make coffee slowly, drive slowly, everything slowly so that Sol will have left for Metro and Judy will be at school when I get to Doheny Drive. Ethel is in the kitchen, doing the breakfast dishes. I have neither pride nor shame. I tell her the whole night: all the calls, all the no-answers, all the agonies. She cares and she'll understand.

"Where could he possibly be?" I ask her. "Where?"

She turns from the sink. "With Lenny Bernstein, of course." There's the slightest smile of triumph on her face.

That smile shocked and hurt almost more than anything Farley had done.

When he came back from New York, he confessed he had never gone to the analyst. He was sitting on the living room floor, I was on the window seat; it was daytime, the sun was filtering in—not pouring in, not flooding the room, just giving it light. Confession had been the mode all night and we were both done in. I was no longer in control and fear of losing him made him desperately desirable.

"What did you do when you were supposed to be at the analyst's?"

"Drove around until the hour was up."

"Why did you say you were going?"

"To please you. I never thought there was anything wrong with being gay. I always liked it!"

Guiltless, gorgeous, and gentile—God, he was lucky! Well, what about smart, talented, and Jewish? And sexual and funny? Nothing can match "guiltless." He had no guilt about Lenny. He loved the music, Lenny loved the face, each loved the other's star. It was being in New York, it wasn't an affair. How could he have done it whatever it was? He was pure!

"I was never pure!" he cried, pounding on the floor. "Only in your crazy head!"

Had there been others then? A carpenter like my carpenter? And like a couple of more that I'd had? It was different for me, of course: just sex, over and forgotten, no emotional connection. But he was different, he was pure!

"Only in your crazy head!"

I didn't believe that. That might be what he thought but I knew better. I wanted him to be the image I fell in love with up there on the screen in *The Purple Heart*. I could tell Judd Marmor movies were shit and mean it, but emotionally, I was a movie fan.

Which was not Farley's fault.

And finally, I realized that.

After the Sturm und Drang, we drove to the Chaplins' in one car, a couple again. That was what the group, particularly Ethel, wanted us to be. And what we wanted to be. But both of us were growing up and, inevitably, gradually growing apart. We both knew that but we held on for quite a while.

CHAPTER THREE

Master Class

With Harold and Stella, Shirley and Kate, Steve and Dick

THE NEW HAVEN OPENING NIGHT PARTY for *The Bird Cage* was given at the old Taft Hotel which must have been born the old Taft Hotel. The decor of the room the party was held in could never have been new but nobody was noticing, least of all the ebullient director surrounded by a bevy of adoring actresses, all cast by him. I managed to reach through and tug at his sleeve.

Shyly: "Harold."

"Enjoy success, my boy! It's a hit!" The magic word didn't work for me.

"Harold, can we please talk?"

"Enjoy!"

"Harold, I think there's something wrong with the play."

"You worry too much. Stop being young! Learn to enjoy yourself!"

Verbally, Clurman himself was a passionate enjoyer, blowing his cheeks out like Triton working to make waves, rubbing his hands like a genie over a bottle, and talking, always talking, rarely leaving a space for listening. Not even to the pretty women competing for his attention. He adored pretty women, all the actresses he cast in *The Bird Cage* were pretty with the exception of Stella Adler: Stella was beautiful.

She swept into rehearsal for the first reading of the play all in beige: suit, shoes, gloves, little hat with little veil over her ash-blonde hair. A little kiss for Melvyn Douglas, a little flirtatious smile and a little pat on his cheek to acknowledge he was not her leading man, she was his leading lady. Factually, she was one of two leading ladies but Stella ignored the other one. Seating herself center stage, she read like royalty visiting a hospital, accepted compliments,

Clurman, Kazan and Maxwell Anderson at a rehearsal of *Truckline Cafe,* the play that booted *Home of the Brave* out of the Belasco Theatre in February 1946.

left for lunch and never came back. She was feuding with her husband, the director, who waited in vain for her to return. I was not surprised.

Harold was always waiting for Stella. In Venice two years later, she told me she had finally married him because the gangster she was obsessively in love with had walked out on her.

"Gangster?" Stella in love with a gangster?

"In jewelry! A vulgarian from Jersey who never heard of my father!" She was on all cylinders now, her eyes flashing. "He used me up and when he was finished, threw me in a ditch by the roadside! And there was Clurman—waiting. So I said, All right, Clurman. If you want to marry me, you can marry me. I don't love you but I need someone to take care of me."

In Harry's Bar in Venice, another Stella—there were several—sketched a pencil portrait of Harold on the back of a menu: a room with walls lined top to bottom with books; in the center, a nude man sitting on a plain chair, a big cigar in his mouth and a big penis going down to the floor, across the room and out the door.

Maureen Stapleton, a recent petitioner in the offices around Shubert Alley, replaced Stella opposite Melvyn Douglas. He played the performer-owner of a nightclub like Leon and Eddie's; she was his alcoholic social register wife. A very Irish girl from Buffalo and too young for the part, Maureen was further handicapped by having to wear a coat of Persian lamb (all the production could afford) rather than the mink the role called for. No matter: she made the audience believe she was wearing sable, was social register and alcoholic and anything else she wanted.

The supporting cast was headed by a neurotic survivor of the Group Theatre, Sandy Meisner. He too could make the audience believe anything he wanted but he couldn't make himself believe he was any good. Each rehearsal began with Sandy begging Harold to fire him. Totally irrational, as only actors can be. Harold dealt with it by ignoring it.

I had my own problem with an irrational actor during rehearsals, one who wasn't even in the play—my friend Judy Holliday. At least, I assumed we were friends. I played a friendly game of poker at her apartment with Judy, her ex-

Sanford Meisner and Melvyn Douglas in *The Bird Cage.* Sandy made the Neighborhood Playhouse arguably the finest acting school in New York.

girlfriend, Yetta Cohen, and Yetta's new girlfriend, Ruth, while Judy's husband, David Oppenheim, sprawled on the couch like a beached whale, dead to our world. It was Judy herself who told me—I knew the story, those stories get around—that when she scored in her first Broadway play, the play that got her *Born Yesterday,* Yetta, a policewoman, walked into her dressing room and said:

"It's over. You're going to be a star. Go to a psychiatrist."

They remained friends even after Judy married David; he became a friend of mine, too, and was an observer on *The Bird Cage.* I thought that was what Judy wanted, so when she banged into my room at the Hotel Elysée looking for my head on her plate and told me I had wronged her, I didn't get it. She was more irrational than Sandy.

"David was right there, sitting next to you, sitting in the same theatre with you and Harold—how could you?!"

"How could I what, Judy?"

"How could you dare let Alec Wilder write the music for your play?!" David was a clarinetist, a very good clarinetist but all the same, a clarinetist, not a composer. Usually the convoluted workings of Judy's mind fascinated me; not this time. She didn't let me say much of anything, she was too clever, she ranted nonstop: tears, vows that this was the end of our friendship, and out the door she stormed—quite happy with the scene she had played was my guess.

Our friendship wasn't over, I knew Judy. I had more than an inkling that she had come to the Elysée because of the state of her marriage, but like Harold, I ignored that, I ignored everything. It was very tough to call Judy on anything: she was too cagey and too quick; she inspired fear as easily as affection.

Harold ignored Sandy because he knew Sandy so long and so well. Sandy's performance grew and grew despite Sandy but never enough for Sandy. Eventually, acting became such torture that he turned to teaching and made the Neighborhood Playhouse a landmark school of acting in New York. He gave his students the confidence he couldn't give himself and doing that, kept himself alive in the one world he could live in—the theatre.

The other leading lady, Eleanor Lynn, was the quirky, fascinating thief who stole Harold's Group Theatre production of Odets's *Rocket to the Moon.* Paradoxically, one of the offstage attractions of this beguiling elf was a dangerous mouth. She was in good company: all the pretty actresses had mouths so dangerous that in New Haven, the stagehands complained about the language of the ladies in the company. A preview came early on:

During rehearsal of a scene between Mel, who was well over six feet, and Eleanor, who was barely five, Kate Mostel, Zero's wife, was heard to say in the wings, "Well, she can always go up on him."

Giving notes in New Haven, Harold told Maureen: "Darling, you don't look as though you know what you're doing in that scene." Maureen rolled her eyes heavenward: "Harold, I don't know what the fuck I'm doing in the whole play."

The coup de grâce came in the midst of a violent game of charades.

Maureen: "Will you cocksuckers shut up so we can get on with the game?!"

Eleanor: "But that cunt called me a peasant!"

Language was their bubblegum. The stagehands were offended, Harold shook his head in not-so-mock despair, the rest of us waited eagerly for the next breath of foul air. It sweetened the longest day.

Clustered like geishas around Harold at the party in the old Taft Hotel, the actresses radiated security: they were in a success. After all, Harold said it was a success. But did he know? Elia Kazan said Harold should direct the first three days of a play, then go home and stay there. Harold, unsurpassed at explicating the text, was not very good at blocking or staging or directing the actors.

Still, it was Harold, not Kazan, who was one of the founders of the Group Theatre; it was Harold who nurtured Clifford Odets and directed *Awake and Sing;* it was Harold who taught Kazan. Harold did know plays; he swung high on my seesaw.

It was Kazan, however, who was changing what had been a playwright's theatre to a director's theatre, Kazan who evoked performances that burned up the stage with a ferocious intensity, Kazan who made the plays he directed so dazzling that holes and evasions were successfully covered over—as with the issue of the hero's homosexuality in *Cat on a Hot Tin Roof.* And sometimes he successfully subverted the author—as with his electrifying, wildly theatrical production of *A Streetcar Named Desire.* Jessica Tandy was sacrificed: Blanche was made the villain, in part because of the shock of Marlon Brando's intensity, in part because of Kazan's feelings about women. In Harold's production with Uta Hagen and Anthony Quinn, Stanley was the villain, in part because of Uta Hagen's exciting abandon, in part because of Harold's feelings about women, in part because for Harold, the play was the thing. His production was gripping but it used Kazan's staging.

The movie of *Streetcar* settled the villain question merely by existing on the record: Stanley is the villain even though Kazan directed. He had to be the villain or the Hays Office would not have allowed the picture to be made. He probably would have been anyway because Vivien Leigh is Blanche, and beautiful, fragile Vivien Leigh is one of a handful of screen actresses who can legitimately be called great. Seen today, she dominates Brando: hers is the performance that stands up; her Blanche is the heroine she is meant to be and thus, the play is the thing.

On the page the play is the thing but plays are written to be performed. I had to learn how few people, even in the theatre, can read a play, and how even fewer can differentiate between play and performance. When I was eighteen, in New York on a vacation from college, I took that course in two nights.

On the first, I saw John Gielgud's production of *Hamlet;* on the very next, Leslie Howard's. Gielgud took the play out of the classroom and out of the dust. Completely mesmerized, I forgot I was seeing a masterpiece. It wasn't until after the performance that I understood, really for the first time, why *Hamlet* was a masterpiece.

In Leslie Howard's production, the actors recited in black tights and brown robes. Howard himself was a gentle Hamlet in the big arias, even a charming one in the recorder scene. A gentle, charming, weak Prince, he was personally a very brave man. At the curtain call, he stepped forward and asked the embarrassed audience: "It wasn't so bad, was it?" "Yes, it was," I wrote in my review for *The Cornell Daily Sun* (proving I was qualified to be a professional critic). But the performance was bad because it relegated *Hamlet* to Required Reading, put it back into the category of a musty play about a vacillating prince that made for a long pre-examination night in the theatre.

Harold, unable to mesmerize like Gielgud or dazzle like Kazan, was nonetheless directing *The Bird Cage.* As the author, I had to believe that if the play was there on paper, it would come through and hold the audience. And Harold did know the play. With me always was a five-page single-spaced essay on *The Bird Cage* he had written and which I had used as a blueprint for revisions. He'd put knowing fingers on the flaws and so eloquently, I went racing to the typewriter—certain now the play would be everything I had hoped.

What I saw on the stage of the Shubert Theatre in New Haven, however, had me tugging his sleeve: "Harold, I think there's something wrong with the play."

He didn't think there was. Or did he know there was? Did he know but not know what to do about it? My heart thundered; I went cold, shaken by a premonition of an imminent disaster, precisely what, I didn't know but something scarily important was hovering, I was sure of that and I wanted to run before it got me. I put down the drink I had hardly touched—I never drank unless I felt good—and ducked out of the party, hurried down the drab hallway of the Taft Hotel to my room as though I was being followed, pulled my clothes off as I closed the door behind me, got into bed as quickly as I could, turned out the light, pulled the covers up to hide me and broke out in a cold sweat. Because I could go no further, there it was, there was the disaster: Daddy didn't know, Daddy couldn't help me.

Whatever was wrong with the play, I was going to have to discover myself, to fix myself: the only person I could count on was myself. I was not ready but it was my play and I wasn't going to give up on it.

In the morning, I went to Harold's room. He was on the phone, listening to Stella, not replying. I whispered I was going back to New York and would meet him in Philadelphia with the rewrite. He heard—he nodded—but his face was unfamiliar. No "my boy," no "enjoy!" Was he distracted because of Stella? Had she been telling him the play was troubled? Had he realized it himself? Was he frightened, too? Was he embarrassed because he was without the answer? Whatever he was, he wasn't Harold, my mentor, my answer. He imitated a smile and waved me on my way.

On the train from New Haven back to New York, I kept pushing and pulling at pieces of *The Bird Cage* I had been pushing around like a jigsaw puzzle the sleepless night before. Back I went to the beginning, to the origins of the play, trying not to let terror intimidate concentration. The jumble finally began to take some shape. Leon and Eddie's had been the starting point: the world as the nightclub world. *Heartsong* hadn't had much plot so I had clutched at Lillian Hellman's intricately plotted *The Little Foxes* as a model—ah, there it was! *The Bird Cage* had too much plot. And as a result, was schizophrenic. The antihero Melvyn Douglas played was supposed to be the protagonist as Regina was in *The Little Foxes;* the piano player in the club—a combination of drunken Addy Bailey and idealistic me—was supposed to be the hero as Alexandra was in Lillian's play. But Alexandra barely existed; was my hero stronger than my play could support? Was he the real protagonist? Should he be? There couldn't be two.

By the time I got off the train at Grand Central Station, I had a handle on what was wrong. Back at the Hotel Elysée, I sat down at the typewriter to make it right.

In Philadelphia, the Harold directing the company in the new scenes was the Harold who was all enthusiasm, blowing his cheeks out like Triton, rubbing his hands like a genie. The actors glowed with visible enthusiasm as they rehearsed on Boris Aronson's two-tiered set. Everyone was excited, even the usually phlegmatic Boris, though it was not the revision that excited Boris. He was quivering because he had found the one, final, heretofore missing touch to complete his set.

On the top of a gleaming black upright piano on the cantilevered upper level, he reverentially placed a silken orange evening slipper with a spike heel. The shoe was the one note of color in the all-black set.

"Vell, Harld?" Boris added Borisisms to a strange Russian accent: he gargled the *r* and omitted the *o*.

Harold stood up in the auditorium. "Now it's art!" he proclaimed.

"Now is art," Boris agreed.

Art; fine. What about the play? Not art but did it work now? Listening to the actors speak the new lines, I heard what I hadn't written; watching them perform the new scenes, I could see a curtain coming down to a spattering of applause once again. The sinking in my stomach was too familiar. Oh, I'd survive as I had before, but how many times could I do it? How many chances would I get? The play was better now, I had accomplished that. But as I knew from experience, better doesn't make it good.

Harold had never known what he didn't have. Shortly before rehearsals, he had written Stella's daughter Ellen, who was living in Paris, that he was going to be directing two plays this season: one would be a hit, one would be a flop. *The Bird Cage* was his pick as the hit, the flop was going to be *The Member of the Wedding*.

Our reviews were kiss-of-death mixed. Harold's own review was also mixed. Oh yes, he reviewed this play he himself had directed. He wrote that he was asked—by whom?—why he had directed the play. His answer was that he wanted to encourage the promising young author. My note in response was brief.

"Dear Harold: The ship went down with all hands on board, including yours."

Clifford Odets once accused Clurman of incurring resentment by setting himself up as an impossibly omniscient father. Harold told me that himself some months after *The Bird Cage* closed and casually asked if he had set himself up as a daddy to me, too. Of course I said he hadn't although of course he had. While a director has to be captain of the ship, it's in the nature of some of the beasts to ratchet that post up to dictator or, as in Harold's case, to omniscient teacher/father. But collaborator? That was bypassed, no matter how much they themselves lectured that theatre is collaboration.

I had no desire to accuse Harold of failing to be a collaborator. Unlike Odets, I felt not resentment but disappointment, which thinned as months passed, selective memory went into high gear and it was summer. I was born in summer, I thrive in summer, summer is when I am happiest. It would be very hard for me to be disappointed in summer, and that was no ordinary summer—it was my first in Paris. Who could hold on to disappointment the first time he saw Paris?

If *The Bird Cage* had succeeded, I might have stayed in New York. But there was Farley waiting in Hollywood. I didn't look forward to returning there with my tail between my legs, but when I got back there the focus all over town was on Paris, not on New York and a flop no one cared about. The Viertels and the Parrishes were already across the ocean, following their sun (Irwin Shaw) and also taking advantage of the income tax break available to anyone who stayed abroad for eighteen months. It wasn't the tax break that got me to Paris, though, it was a combination of two unrelated events: the dissolution of a marriage and an act of Congress.

The ending marriage was Sol and Ethel Chaplin's—not unforeseen by the group. Her restlessness was matched by her obvious sexual dissatisfaction. The piano couldn't compensate and over the top she went when she and Buddy Tyne fell in love. Sol knew, Farley knew, Lorry and Millard Kaufman knew, the Kellys knew; Ethel's mother and father didn't know but her sister did. And Judy, her child and Sol's, Judy knew. In Hollywood, divorce or separation would have followed with no ado—in movie Hollywood, that is—but this was Doheny Drive Hollywood where they had supper, not dinner, where Ethel shopped at the Farmers Market and she and Sol had a kid like Judy who was shlepped to ballet class. Judy was the only one playing the piano in the Doheny house now, pounding it, really, to vent her anger at all three points of the adult triangle that had no place for her.

Farley had been providing a shoulder for Ethel while I was in New York; they were closer than ever. But when sex is the motivator, reassurance is never sufficiently abundant. He was in her pocket anyway and movie star or no, I was higher in the pecking order of desirable friends with shoulders. After the rejection of New York, I lapped up her need. With Farley, I drove her around and around Beverly Hills, up and down the canyons as she cried and asked for advice though we knew what she wanted was encouragement to go for what she wanted: she was going to go ahead whether the encouragement was there or not. As lagniappe, her need for Farley and me brought the two of us closer. Then Buddy was added in, then Judy, communal daughter like it or not, and the little family had a child. For we were a family.

The taking of sides, an integral part of any marital split, made life in their community uncomfortable and awkward for both Ethel and Sol—more so for Ethel because the other women didn't want a free-floating threat or a vivid reminder of a viable alternative. It appeared cut-and-dried that one or the other, Ethel or Sol, preferably Ethel, had to vanish. Then Congress passed the Mc-Carran Act over Truman's veto.

The Internal Security Act of 1950—its official name—authorized fingerprinting and registering of all Communists, all members of Communist organizations and all "subversives" on the Attorney General's list as well as the construction of "relocation camps" for "emergency situations." The reaction of the Hollywood left was the same as that of the Hollywood left, right, and middle to a new movie: hyperbolic. They pounced with joyous martyrdom on "relocation camps": unquestionably a euphemism for concentration camps, the buzz went over the phones. All the fault of Harry Truman who deserved the blame. Hadn't he opened the Era of the Witch Hunt with his Loyalty Oath for Federal Employees? Wasn't he responsible for the Hollywood Ten going to prison with his appointment of the two new, reactionary justices to the Supreme Court, the shits whose votes made it a majority that upheld the constitutionality of the unconstitutional contempt citation? The liturgical singers of "I Dreamed I Saw Joe Hill Last Night" were so busy enjoying their rage they almost overlooked the dangerous item in the McCarran Act that was of personal practical importance to us: passport restrictions on anyone deemed "subversive." That meant me, for one, Buddy, for another.

My subversive activities were itemized in a sleazy, far-right-wing bible called *Red Channels,* published by three ex-FBI agents. Nora waved a copy in my face, teasing because I merited only half a page whereas Stella Adler, like several of the 150 show folk listed, got a whole page.

Buddy wasn't listed in *Red Channels;* he was on a worse list, the Attorney General's. Not that anyone had actually seen that list, it was just a rumor, but we lived by rumors those days and some died by them. What mattered in any event was that the McCarran Act was warning us to See Europe Now or Never—or Until the End of the Cold War, which might well be never. Time was running short to get passports while they were still gettable.

All five of us ran like bad kids to get them, the excitement making us forget politics, forget everything but what the passports were for: Paris! Farley wanted to fly over. I encouraged him—it would make him independent, I said, half believing I meant it and wasn't again resisting being lovers publicly—and booked passage to sail for France with the others. Like ignorant idiots, we threw into suitcases whatever anyone advised us to pack: drip-dry shirts (which we heaved into the garbage when they turned out either to freeze or to sweat), pocket English-French French-English Hugo dictionaries (for Ethel and me), toilet paper (for the Congo?), cigarettes by the carton; but we did remember to get international driver's licenses. And to top it off, gave ourselves a slam-bang farewell party at the house on Doheny Drive with every leftover bottle of anything that had a breath of alcohol.

Food and booze out and ready, dustballs brushed under the sofa, we went to grab a bite, leaving Judy to hold the fort in the unlikely event any guest arrived on time. Two arrived early. We sauntered back to the house and walked in to find Judy, with total command, playing hostess to Gary Merrill and his new girlfriend. None of us had met her; all we knew was that he was going to bring his latest heartthrob and her name was Betty. Except one look and we saw it wasn't Betty, it was Bette.

She was terrific, very lower case. She really talked that way; she really walked that way (try imitating a bear walking and you have the walk); she sang with the rest of us around the piano, danced on the shag rug, boozed, laughed, listened—at one o'clock in the morning in the kitchen—to an equally loaded Karen Morley praise the charms of the Communist Party.

The evening was a smash, everyone said it was. At the end, real tears and hugs for the Kaufmans and Stash and Sol—yes, Sol, why not? What has pride to do with love? We were really going to miss our friends and they would really miss us. All the same, they knew we couldn't wait to start traveling and get to Paris.

When the boat train from Le Havre pulled into the station in Paris, the sight of Farley running along the platform made me dizzy with happiness; the surprise of Peter and Jigee Viertel running with him—they had come to welcome us—made me even dizzier. The porters in smock coats of that singular French blue; hearing nothing but Gershwin taxi horns and French as we emerged into the sunlight and saw Paris: P-a-r-i-s! We had arrived, Lafayette, we had actually arrived in Paris and unbelievably, it was all we expected!

The Viertels led us—we weren't capable of doing anything but gaping and following—to where they and we were staying: the Hotel May Fair, in a little side street on the Right Bank near the Étoile. Discovered by Irwin Shaw, the May Fair wasn't a proper hotel. An impoverished baron had chopped up his *hôtel particulier* into odd-shaped two-room apartments; mine was on the top floor, half a flight up from the fifth landing where the rickety iron lift stopped. Jigee Viertel, who was always putting her mark on me, had put some tiny flowering plants on the window ledge in my sitting room. I knew before I looked past them that I would be looking out over the rooftops of Paris, but there is no preparation for seeing those rooftops, not on film but in three-dimensional life for the first time. Tears do come.

Room service was limited to coffee and the best omelettes we ever tasted;

The rooftops of Paris as they were supposed to look from my window—and did.

the cook also worked the switchboard, which was the worst we ever encountered—who cared? She and it were French, we were in Paris. That first night, we ate in a bistro, then got lost walking along the tree-shaded streets trying to find what we knew we had to see, were determined to see but where was it? I ventured to ask a woman walking her dog; everyone in Paris had a dog.

"Pardon, madame. Où est la Seine?"

A contemptuous shrug but a contemptuous French shrug; she flounced off with her dog. Had I unintentionally insulted her in French? Had I been terribly stupid? What? Half a block and we saw what: we were there, we were at the river. We leaned over the wall and we were looking at the Seine! There was one of the elegant bridges with its gilded lamp! There was another bridge! And another and then—there was Notre-Dame. All on the first night!

Harold said we had come to Paris too late. We should have been there after the Great War, in the twenties with Hemingway and Fitzgerald—that was when Paris was Paris. But just around the corner from the May Fair was a furrier's shop. In the window, a silver fox stole with diamond earrings reclined languidly on a little gilt chair before a gilt dressing table and gazed at her reflection in the oval mirror—that was Paris.

Farley posing for me on the Right Bank, 1950.

Harold himself took Farley and me for a walk through the city, pointing out all the streets named for writers—that was Paris.

We went to dinner with Harold and Stella at Le Grand Véfour, the famed restaurant in the gardens of the Palais-Royal graced by Napoléon and Josephine. When Stella walked in, the maître d' handed her a single, long-stemmed rose and said: "The most beautiful woman in Paris has graced my restaurant." That was Paris.

Scott and Zelda danced to jazz bands in clubs where Negroes did the Charleston. On the Left Bank, we went to a cellar in Saint-Germain-des-Prés where Gordon Heath, a black actor from New York, sang to his fans. Huddled on low stools, they had evidently been trained by word of mouth to applaud by snapping their fingers: Paris. On the Right Bank, where the vogue was candlelit supper clubs with White Russian doormen, silver (plate) settings, and half a dozen strolling violinists, I literally waltzed Uta Hagen off her feet: she collapsed and lay down on the dance floor. Instantly, a gold-braided Cossack was there to place a pillow gently under her head. Dancing with a glamorous actress I barely knew, seeing her out cold on the floor with a satin pillow beneath her head while Russian fiddlers fiddled away—that, too, was Paris.

Challenging Uta Hagen in the Bois.

.   .   .

"It's like the Eiffel Tower: you have to see an exhibition," said Jimmy Lipton, whom we had casually known in New York's theatre world. Apparently he was doing better as a sex guide in Paris. He handled all arrangements including the financial; in quick time, Ethel, Buddy, Farley, and I were sitting at the foot of a large bed in a room in Montmartre, trying not to appear nervous or eager. Jimmy sat up near the head: good posture; the man in charge.

A nude couple appeared from behind a screen in the corner. Thirtyish, fairly attractive, not very sexy, they sort of bowed like stars acknowledging entrance applause, then, with no warning, embraced madly. Tongues darted in and out of gulping mouths; they carefully collapsed onto the bed. Wild thrashing accompanied by extensive moaning and groaning preceded a huge pelvic thrust and a mounting. He then fucked her athletically as she gasped and bucked like a bronco. Of course, it was Let's Pretend, and Members of the Comédie-Française, they were not; the simulation left something to be desired. But A for effort could not be denied them.

Their first appearance—mutual reactions checked out afterward—from behind the screen was erotic. When the performance got under way, Jimmy's face flushed; his heavy breathing was too audible. For the rest of us, the paying audience, it was embarrassing; then giggles had to be choked off; then, as the simulated fucking went on and on, boredom set in. Not unbelievable if you've ever seen one of these sad, not even degrading performances. We waited, tried not to fidget because the chairs creaked, and at last patience was rewarded by a yip indicating orgasm and the end of the act: Curtain! The actors retired behind the screen.

"Wonderful, no?" said Jimmy, agent/manager.

"Oh, wonderful . . . wonderful."

The sound of running water from behind the screen stopped and the actors emerged in dressing gowns. We could have been in the Lunts' dressing room: we congratulated them on their performances. Modest disclaimers as hands were shaken all around. Thanks, good-bye, *merci, au 'voir,* and out. Jimmy stayed to settle up. We emerged into shabby daylight. None of us had sex that night.

I suppose that, too, was Paris, always was and probably still is.

Sitting at the Flore and the Deux-Magots, sipping *fine à l'eau* as the little chits piled up under saucers may also have been for tourists but we were tourists and sat for hours, loving it. Neither Sartre nor Beauvoir ever showed but we weren't watching for them, we were just watching. One attempt to smoke a Gaulois, and back to American cigarettes, so grateful they were easily obtainable on the black market, thanks to Ann Selepegno.

Unable to speak a word of French and uninterested in learning, Ann had put down key money for an apartment in Paris. She was staying on because The Colonel was staying on and The Colonel was her life. Just as her closest friend, Gladys, was staying on in Dublin because The Major (John Huston) was staying on in Dublin and The Major was her life. Ann had a longtime boyfriend back in the States, but Bob didn't need her the way she believed Litvak did. Being needed kept her alive. It was so out of proportion, the way she was made happy by my need for American cigarettes which she knew where to get: from the man who ran the best black market in Paris.

A very old Russian Jew, Mr. Landau was a refugee from both Stalin and Hitler. His transactions were performed in a rat hole upstairs in a creepy building in the Lido arcade on the Champs-Elysées. The ground floor entrance was between huge photographs of bare-breasted beauties in feathers and lipsticked musclemen in lamé loincloths. Three flights up, at the end of a dark, dank corridor, Mr. Landau worked and lived. Only one window—and that almost opaque with dirt—faced an areaway: his escape route should the gendarmes ever catch up with him. Two years later they did. He had said so often he would jump if they caught up and he did. He landed three stories down on cement and broke his spine.

Money was Mr. Landau's main moneymaker, not cigarettes. He showed us how to check a roll of black market franc notes for newspaper cuttings used to fatten it at the center. Though the dollar was so strong Americans could live well for very little without black market money, Landau francs were a boon for Ethel and Buddy. They had no income and a limited bank account. Which Farley and I mistakenly thought was none of our business. If anything can affect a relationship more than sex, it's the need for money; even more, the opportunity to get money. Buddy and Ethel had the need, Tola Litvak had the opportunity, and I knew Tola.

He was in preproduction for *Decision Before Dawn,* a war movie. Which meant soldiers. Which might have meant a role for Buddy except that the cast was to be mostly European—cold-watering one hope but firing up a new one: Buddy as dialogue coach? I volunteered to ask Tola. I had gotten Betsy Blair, Gene Kelly's wife, a part in *The Snake Pit* simply by asking. Betsy was my friend, Buddy was my friend; Tola liked Betsy, Tola liked Buddy; Buddy got the job.

Unfortunately, the picture was to be shot in Germany, in hated Munich.

Tola and Ann discussed everything except each other's gambling addiction.

Farley and I with Janet Wolfe, who finagled free trips everywhere with anyone
of note. She once had a radio show, broadcast from the old Copacabana, on
which she introduced herself as a "retired failure making a comeback."

Ethel wasn't too happy about that, none of us were; besides, it was going to
split up the family. But Buddy needed the job; good faces were put in place.
Farley and I promised to visit in Munich and we all sat down to discuss what
was immediate and practical: How were Buddy, Ethel, and Judy going to get
to the Fatherland? The most desirable way was the cheapest way: by car. I
loaned them five hundred dollars with which they bought a secondhand Qua-
trechevaux because Ethel believed in it.

Departure morning, Judy was too busy busily arranging her nest in the
lumpy back of the car to kiss anyone good-bye but when Buddy started the
engine, she came flying out to be hugged as tight and as long as I could. Finally, they took off. Watching the overloaded old car sway down the street
away from the May Fair was like growing up.

· · ·

Judy Chaplin with Ethel and Buddy Tyne. Notice the ballerina foot.

I bought an English car, a little Hillman Minx convertible. The idea was to rack up enough mileage on a Grand Tour so it could qualify as a used car and be brought into the United States duty free when shipped home. Harold and Stella approved—"Splendid idea, my boy!"—and offered help in accruing mileage: a weekend at Deauville if I drove them there.

When I picked them up at their hotel—the elegant Prince de Galles, next door to the even more elegant George V—I anticipated chauffeuring the Stella Adler who had studied privately with Stanislavsky in Paris: Isadora Duncan scarves, hatboxes, scorn for the size of the car. What I got was the Stella Adler who had used Paris as headquarters for running guns to Israel. Tying an old scarf around her head, she piled into the backseat saying: "I'm going to sleep. You boys sit in front and talk."

Harold talked.

A one-question prompting and off he launched into the history of the Group Theatre, every bit of it fascinating, the history of a theatre that both reflected its time and changed it told in detail by a man who was one of its makers. When he was done, I asked: "But Harold, why did the Group die?"

Stella in Venice. In New York, in addition to the dogs, there were
always student volunteer handmaidens her family called "pouks"
after the Indian boys who fanned their rajahs.

From the backseat, Stella reared up. "Because I killed it!" she roared. "It
was time!"

Justifiable homicide perhaps, with revenge her motive. While she was in
her thirties, Harold had cast her as a fifty-year-old mother in Odets's *Awake
and Sing* and again in his *Paradise Lost.* Lavishly praised, Stella had still not
been happy; she'd smoldered, festered, gotten angrier and angrier. Lorna
Moon in *Golden Boy* was demanded as her reward for her service in the
trenches. Instead, Harold and Odets cast Frances Farmer.

The Hillman Minx. Imagine Stella Adler huddled
in the backseat with her luggage.

Male arrogance? Hot pants? Whatever, it was amazing that those two in
particular could have underestimated that woman. They hadn't just met her
and even if they had, meet Stella Adler and in two minutes you knew she was
a formidable whatever she decided to be, including your enemy. Whether
their cavalier disregard was why she killed off the Group, whether she really
did kill it off, I don't know. Harold didn't rebut her claim, but contradicting
Stella was not his long suit. He just beamed proudly at his artistic murderess.

In Deauville, Stella introduced me to friends unlike any I'd ever seen her with:
improbable accents, improbable husbands, beautifully groomed and bejew-
eled, languid hands emphasizing Chekhovian sadness. Not fools: one of them
remarked that the only country that won every war was Italy. Italy always had
the sense to switch sides at the last minute. As I suspected these women did.

Saturday night of the weekend, there was a gala in the Deauville casino
with a prize for the most beautiful evening gown. Each of Stella's ladies was
stunningly chic in haute couture. Stella herself was elegant in dark blue taffeta,
one bare shoulder making her white skin lewd. She had pilfered the dress from
MGM, where she had worn it in a Thin Man movie. (When the studio
changed her name to Stella Ardler, her brother Luther asked why it hadn't
been changed to Beverly Wilshire.) She knew what that dress did for her, how
to wear it, and perhaps Stanislavsky helped, but it was Stella who won the

prize for the best gown at the gala. She laughed prettily, pretending surprise to her glittering friends but she wasn't surprised for one minute. Winning over them was a lighter version of killing off the Group Theatre.

Hemingway, Fitzgerald, Stein, Toklas, Clurman, Adler—not one of them or any like them had or could have had the Paris experience I did: Paris celebrated my birthday. *Tout Paris,* all Paris, the whole city. *Le quatorze Juillet,* Bastille Day to them, was July Fourteenth to me, my birthday was also theirs—the throngs in the street, the rejoicing in the air, of course it wasn't for me but it was. A feeling I wish everyone could have, a feeling Jule Styne must have had every New Year's Eve because that was his birthday. He could have it anyplace; I could only have it in Paris. That was limiting but better because that made it more special.

To celebrate, that year, the city was throwing a star-studded gala party on a floating stage in the middle of the Seine. Stella organized a double birthday

Ellen Adler in Paris, 1950. She lived, loved and cooked like a Parisienne to the delight of Stella and Harold, who considered himself her father.

party group that included her daughter Ellen and Ellen's French lover, René Leibowitz. Ellen's intelligence was as formidable as her beauty; she loved music, René was a noted cerebral musician—which pleased Harold—yet I wondered why she was living with a man more than a decade older when she could have had Marlon Brando—which would have pleased Stella.

Seats for the gala—cushions on temporary bleachers on one of the bridges facing the floating stage—were at a premium. The air tingled with excitement and anticipation. Once we were settled in—seating by Stella—erect and beautiful, she surveyed the crowd and the scene.

The scaffolding on the stage was still being adjusted by workmen with no indication that they were going to take it down. It blocked the view, not leaving much room for the promised stars to perform, but presumably it was for spotlights. To shine on whom where? The workmen left, replaced by officials who walked around, pointing here, there, and abracadabra: spotlights went on! The crowd cheered. Stella squinted at the scaffolding with a practiced fish eye.

"No show," she announced.

A motorboat approached the stage; the crowd was silent with hope, the pilot turned up the throttle and zoomed away. The banks of the river, where there were no seats but masses of room for standees, were now jammed. Fitting for Bastille Day, it wasn't the expensive cushioned behinds who started taunting the officials on the stage, it was the standees who hadn't paid.

A fireboat came tearing down the river, bringing expectant silence again. The officials almost fell in the Seine getting in the boat, but once they were safely on board, the boat sprayed the stage with a torrent of water. The crowd cheered; then they realized that wasn't the show but simply the stage being doused.

"No show," Stella repeated.

The crowd began to boo lustily. A rather elegant man near us threw his cushion into the river. Then another cushion went in and another and with the third came the call "*Remboursez!*" It was picked up by the mob on the banks which hadn't bought a ticket entitling a refund, but good Bastillians, they howled their hearts out:

"*Remboursez! Remboursez!*"

Cushions were flying into the river; the sansculottes on the bank were throwing anything they could get their hands on: bottles, cans, bricks. It was another Bastille Day and it was wonderful! Who could have asked for a better birthday?

· · ·

"JE SUIS UN NÈGRE"
Bon pour la chair à canon......... mais pas pour le reste !!
PARLANT FRANÇAIS

The French title for the movie of *Home of the Brave*
in a cinema just outside Paris.

Soon after, Farley and I took off on our own Grand Tour. While I fluctuated, certain only that I didn't want anyone else to have him, the Hillman held us together. It was the link between where we were and where we were going. If something turned a little sour in some room in some town, back in the link of the Hillman there was time and scenery to sweeten the air again.

We left on a lovely summer morning, the convertible top rolled back so we could catch the sun on our faces. Exiting Paris through the suburb of Villejuif, I wondered if the sign registered as Jew Town to the French or merely as a two-syllable name. We were headed for the coast to put the car on a ferry that crossed the channel to those white cliffs we connected with Greer Garson.

On the English side, the scars on the land from the war were less noticeable than they had been on the French side. The stubborn perverseness of the British prevented me from really taking them in; my concentration had to be on driving on the wrong side of the road. Any destruction I saw was peripheral until we reached London; then I could look and what I saw was shattering. Doubly so because only the blind and the English would go about their business as though that magnificent city, their city, wasn't the ravaged victim of a war they had won.

They crossed streets, went into stores, came out of offices, oblivious to the craters and bombed-out sites in Picadilly, along Jermyn Street, everywhere;

there wasn't anywhere they weren't. The few signs of rebuilding were pathetically half-assed, and the food—well, austerity was the watchcry and they had won the war. Their reputation—the stiff upper lip, the taking it in stride, the gallantry, the whole kit and kaboodle of their legendary behavior—they lived up to it. The drinks were tiny but plentiful; they flowed and the pubs overflowed. The city was gay, in both senses; and in one sense the word took on a new dimension.

Farley had been there earlier in the summer, doing publicity for Goldwyn; when he came bubbling back to Paris with too lavish a present, I knew he had tricked. I had been unfaithful in my way: I had been relieved to be without him. Being with him in London induced a different feeling because he was an even more popular movie star there than he was at home. Especially with the gay world which was gayer than any I had ever seen at home. Not sexually: with two or three notable exceptions, I never found the English sexual. But gays were certainly ubiquitous. Married, not married, young, old, all shapes and sizes, all classes in a country still obsessed with a caste system, gay men were so many and so evident that I wondered were there any Englishmen who were totally straight.

Kensington was the capital of the upper gay crust. We went to a party in Walton Street given by the noted Bunny Roger—lean as an umbrella, a Ronald Searle sketch for a Ronald Firbank novel, highly intelligent, cultured, genuinely witty, and nobility to boot. When there was a purge in London—too many guardsmen had been caught with too many paying patrons—it was said the times were so bad, Bunny Roger was wearing his daytime maquillage at night. His brother Sandy didn't look stereotypically gay: he was ruddy, hale and hearty—well-named Sandy. But Sandy had had only two "stand-ups" (i.e., erections) in his life: once when he dressed as Marie Antoinette for a costume ball and looked in the mirror, once when he dreamt he was Queen Elizabeth II.

Bunny's drawing room had apricot chiffon curtains and mauve silk upholstery. When Farley and I arrived at a party after the theatre, most of the guests like Freddie Ashton were doing Scottish reels for onlookers like Terence Rattigan. The dancers were deadly serious; there was no suggestion of camp until the music ended and they sat down. Then there was patting of brows with scented handkerchiefs, followed by application of a light dusting of powder to glistening noses. Until Emlyn Williams arrived, without his wife, and the party screamed to life.

Emlyn was appearing in a play in the West End; he must have hit the bottle the moment the curtain came down and kept hitting it in the taxi that delivered him. He was roaring drunk when he lurched in the door. He sized up the scene, let out a great whoop and yelled: "Isn't anyone going to suck a cock?"

They flew up the apricot curtains. Emlyn didn't give a shit: he had spied Jack Rose—a dark, sexy Lithuanian-born actor—and growling hungrily, went for him. Jack Rose laughed and ran in a circle from one room to another. The rest of the evening was like watching a Marx Brothers picture where Harpo keeps chasing a blonde all over a ship. Emlyn kept chasing dark Jack Rose from room to room until the much younger actor wore him out and he fell over a mauve ottoman and gave up the chase.

Years later, "Jack Rose" changed his hair to golden brown and his name to Laurence Harvey. Not his sense of humor, that never changed: no one laughed louder at Larry Harvey than he did.

There was another side to the chiffon curtains and the Scottish reels and the general piss-elegance characteristic of but hardly limited to gay English: they went to lengths to make us feel comfortable. That they didn't quite succeed with me was because of the fluttering fuss they made over Farley whom they knew better than I had supposed. It's difficult being at a party as an accessory to a celebrity; and if the party is gay and the celebrity a gorgeous movie star, the accessory can become invisible. Bunny Roger was aware of that and I was grateful for his lifeline. He was one of the funniest men I have ever met; his humor was effortless, for apparently he was born witty, droll, and kind.

The play Farley and I saw the night of Bunny's party was Anouilh's *Ring Around the Moon.* Peter Brook's beguiling, very high-style production featured an ethereal, talented young leading lady. By English standards, she hadn't done much: a season at the Bristol Old Vic, two or three plays in the West End, studied here, toured there. For an American actress, that would have been a career; it was continually astonishing me how much training through experience English actors had. The young actress so impressed me that when I was back in Hollywood where Charlie Chaplin was searching for a leading lady for *Limelight,* I recommended Claire Bloom.

Charlie flew her over, she got the part and a great deal of publicity and everybody was very happy as they always are in the beginning. By the end of shooting, when Charlie mentioned Claire to me, she was "your friend." In London for the English premiere, he and Oona invited me to have dinner with the beautiful Claire in their suite at the Savoy. After the meal, they left us alone but eavesdropped discreetly.

"I've been very remiss," Claire murmured. "I've never thanked you."

"Oh, all I did was recommend you."

"You're so right!" she said.

. . .

Having the Hillman enabled us to drive to Stratford and see some of the English countryside on the way. Three *p*s: pretty, pastoral and above all peaceful; and perhaps imagination working overtime, an awesome sense of history I never felt driving across America.

It was a Gielgud season of Shakespeare. The first night, we slumbered through a *King Lear* that was Noguchi-designed and -destroyed. The second night, a performance which I shall never forget: John Gielgud and Peggy Ashcroft in *Much Ado about Nothing*. Set in a ravishing Venice, directed by Gielgud as though the entire company had been born to bewitch, that *Much Ado* was the most brilliant high comedy I had ever seen. It still is.

Farley and I were on air when we went back to the Welcombe Inn where we were staying (in separate rooms) for supper. The extremely handsome waiter in full fig who had served us dinner served supper looking more handsome and more available—it was later and the hour was witching. There had been flirtatious but discreet (sneaky) maneuvering during dinner; there was more during supper, more specific and sneakier. Farley and I said a very cheery good night with exaggerated happy yawns. I had just gotten my clothes off when there was a light tap on the door: the waiter with a prearranged brandy on a tray.

No time wasted and not much time spent but very satisfying. So I washed, brushed my teeth and then decided to put my shoes outside my door. Very quietly and carefully because of a hunch what I would see. Exactly what I did see: the waiter entering Farley's room with a brandy on a tray. I chuckled delightedly.

After I shut my door, I laughed out loud. Why? All the way back to London the next day, I was in high spirits. Why? Because I knew and he didn't? Because I realized what was sauce for the goose and what did it matter anyway? Yes, but I think because finally accepting he was a busy boy put an end to infatuation, an end to being his registered lover. That I was no longer with him as his lover removed guilt at being with him publicly. I was free to enjoy just being with him. Clear? Well, to me, it was.

Before returning to the continent and crossing into Germany, we had the Hillman serviced. We knew austerity in England but Germany lost the war so we were taking no chances on what we would run into there. In Munich, we ran into schlag—everything was mit schlag, great gobs of pure whipped cream piled on any likely candidate. All food was plentiful, real and plentiful. Rebuilding was everywhere, real and plentiful, mit schlag but also mit that German precision which overlooks the purpose. In the men's room of the Hotel Fier Yaritzeiten, under the new urinals were shiny new pipes not yet attached

Stopped at the entrance to the Linz-Vienna highway. From then on,
all the signs were in Cyrillic, which was oddly scary.

to drains. So the piss emptied directly onto the spotlessly clean floor. *Sieg heil!*

We had caught up with Ethel and Buddy in Munich and the Viertels as well—Peter was working on Tola's picture, too. His friend Bob Capa, the photographer, joined us for drinks in the hotel bar. War was Capa's passion and métier; war was what he loved to photograph; war was what he loved; war was exciting! Ethel's lips were pressed tight, she listened quietly for as long as she could, but when Capa said he loved war, he fired her cannon.

"You love war? War is exciting? Killing people is exciting?"

"For me, it's life," he said, and they went at it.

At the end of that summer, we were all back in Paris. Fouquet's was the hangout. We were drinking there late one afternoon—the Viertels, the Shaws, the Parrishes, Capa, and I—when Ethel and Buddy came walking down the street.

"Ah!" Capa exclaimed. "Here come the North Koreans!"

Austria had also lost the war, Vienna was also a schlag heap, but Farley and I kept listening and listening for waltzes we heard only in our heads. Oddly, my strongest memories of Vienna are of a pianist in an intimate little restaurant and an article in *The New Yorker*. The article described life in a Vienna divided into four zones, each administered by one of the four powers that did win the war. They had been the Four Allies but now new phrases were at work—Iron Curtain, Cold War—and Russia was the bogeyman. We met him face-to-face before we even got to the city.

The only road from the West, the Linz-Vienna highway, ran straight through the Russian zone. At the point of entry, a barrier was guarded by a silently ominous Russian soldier; a few feet away was a large hut for unseen others, a fact equally ominous. We felt like spies and got overly excited. The guard stood by the barrier, smoking as if we weren't there. No comrade came out of the hut to inspect us and lift or not lift the barrier. Evidently the road wasn't much traveled: not one other car showed up. We sat and waited, baby and me and the soldier made three, all of us smoking and nothing happening. It was no longer exciting.

At last a non-com ambled out of the hut and approached the car. He knew about the Cold War, too: he thrust a printed sheet at me, a thick finger pointed to his watch, then to the time entered on the sheet—our departure time—then to a blank space for our arrival time in Vienna. I nodded broadly as though he was deaf and smiled ear to ear. He rejected the smile. A finger pointed to that empty Vienna arrival-time slot; he glared; I nodded once, barely. He signaled. The guardian of the barrier raised it and waved us through. Unthreatening and undramatic but we were on our way.

After a few kilometers, it did become exciting. Signs began to pop up in Cyrillic Russian. The effect was magical: we weren't in Austria, we were in Russia! I wanted to stop and take pictures of a sign and whatever village it was identifying but Farley had a fit. The Russians knew exactly how long it took from Linz to Vienna, they'd nab us when we arrived late, they'd find the camera, they'd think we were spies—oh, come on, Farf! What if we had a flat and had to stop to fix it? But I wasn't immune to Cold War paranoia either. I drove on, faster than I should have. At the Vienna end of the highway, no one even asked for the time sheet.

The hotels recommended to us were in either the American or the British zone, enviably first-class but jam-packed with military. Luckily we had the Hillman: we did a lot of driving from one booked-up hotel to another, seeing a lot of Vienna in the process of getting nowhere. Every Allied officer in Vienna had gotten to every hotel first until we stumbled on the Weisse Hahn.

Small, not first-class, but the room was almost charming and the twin beds were large and comfortable. The hotel was just inside the Russian zone—a small Russian flag on the corner said so. Each zone had the flag of one of the powers at the corner where its jurisdiction began. You didn't always see it; this one was less than a foot high and stuck in bare ground. We weren't clear what

Austrian with a tourist vengeance: Tyrolean hats in front of Schönbrunn Palace.

Farley playing *The Third Man.* Not as menacing but better looking.

difference it made what zone we were in anyway until our third day at the Weisse Hahn and I was on my bed with *The New Yorker,* reading that article on Vienna by Joseph Wechsberg before dinner.

Well, sir, Miss Bankhead, as Fred Allen used to say, Farley and I were pretty damn lucky we weren't in Siberia. According to the article, the zones were separated by barbed wire; the unfortunate American who stumbled into the Russian zone by mistake would in all probability disappear, never to be seen again. We'd been safe for three days, we were not about to pack up, we stayed put at the Weisse Hahn.

We had also been warned, though not by Mr. Wechsberg, that an American passport was worth a small fortune. Hold on to your passport at all costs! Sleep with it! Farley lost his, probably while we were slinking around the Ferris wheel made famous in *The Third Man,* taking pictures of each other as Orson Welles or Joe Cotten. As we arrived at the nearby polizei station to report the loss, a jeep with the customary four MPs from the four powers was just pulling out.

"The sergeant has it," the American said laconically.

How and where Farley's passport was found by whom, we never found out. It was on the sergeant's desk, though. But this was not the Vienna of barbed wire, it was closer to the Vienna of the waltz and at last, we heard one.

It was played by the pianist at the intimate little restaurant but didn't quite count since it was by Noël Coward. His repertoire was show tunes—Coward, Rodgers and Hart, Cole Porter—none of the Strausses, but a sign of some life in this dead city and it gave us our first good evening even if it wasn't Viennese. Brandy helped; so did the pianist. He played very well, he was very attractive, and he kept smiling over at us. Because we liked his music?

There are those of any sex who can flirt and have sex with anyone anywhere; there are those who can separate a sexually attractive trick from their beliefs; there are—to get right down it—gay Jews who are attracted to Nazis, even seek them as lovers. I had an experience in Israel which at least was of use in my playwriting, specifically in a one-act called *A Loss of Innocence,* but more subtly elsewhere, too. Writers are cannibals.

Israel in the mid-Sixties, my first night in Tel Aviv. I was staying at the Hotel Dan. After dinner, I wandered around the lobby, then strolled aimlessly out the glass doors at the back end. They had to lead somewhere and they did: to a croisette overlooking the Mediterranean. A warm, dark night; a sky dotted with stars; a sea splashed with reflections; and a balustrade I leaned against, aware shadows were passing behind me. No, they couldn't be cruising, Jews were notoriously antihomosexual. But when I took out a cigarette, a hand was there with a Zippo. My first night in the Promised Land!

The steady flame gave each of us a good look at the other. He was a knock-out: blond with high cheekbones and a sunburn. I apparently passed because he stayed to chat, and after he learned I was an American, invited me back to his flat.

As we walked, he talked easily and freely, answering anything willingly. He was a major in the Israeli army, a Sabra (born in Israel) and an engineer in civilian life to which he would soon be returning. Not here, though. Not here in Tel Aviv? No, not here in Israel.

We were in the flat by then; foreplay had begun but I stopped. He was leaving Israel? Where for? If he hadn't answered, if we had just resumed, it would have been a very different evening. But he was eager to answer, his future made him happy. He was leaving Israel to emigrate to Germany. Germany? Yes, Munich. Munich?! Yes, his lover lived there. His German lover? His German lover.

They were the same age, even to the month—wasn't that remarkable—and the lover was on the West German Trade Commission to Israel. That was how they had met, but his work was now finished and they were going to live together in Munich.

Israelis tended to be arrogant, Sabras took arrogance to an extreme. His arrogance allowed him to assume that he was so attractive—even more without clothes, which he was—that I would have sex with him no matter what. Or that nothing he had told me—neither the existence of a lover nor the identification of that lover as a German whose age certified he had to have been brought up as a Nazi—none of it had anything to do with a primal sexual attraction between two adults. And beyond arrogance, what he considered simple practicality, I suppose: punish yourself afterward if you must, but afterward.

If he had told me he had a new Jewish lover and was emigrating to Minsk to be with him, I wouldn't have been thrilled but I would have done it with him. He read me right for that; he was not stupid. Nor all arrogance. He explained he couldn't stay in Israel any longer. It was his homeland, he was a Jew but there was no place for him—not as an engineer, not as a major in his own army. There was no place in his country of Jews because a Jewish homosexual was undesirable, unwanted, beyond the pale—trafe.

But did he have to go to Germany?

"I want to be with my own kind," he said. His lover had a large group of gay friends; Germans were tolerant of homosexuals.

He was, as I said, extremely attractive nude but I couldn't have managed an erection no matter what he or we did. I was a homosexual and less of a Jew than he was but I was a moral Jew and the moral Jew took over. Neither of us said a word while I dressed. He didn't call me a prig or a fool or a waste. How could I call him anything? He was an Israeli, he was a major in the Jewish army, he had fought for the Jews in a war. The common denominator was sex. That was not a surprise; the surprise was learning it wasn't always true for me.

It wasn't true for flirting with the pianist either: I couldn't. He was even younger than Farley and I were; he must have been a teenager at the time of Anschluss. If he hadn't been a Nazi, how had he gotten through the war? This was a city of old men and war-made cripples; what was he doing in Vienna now?

Questions like that weren't asked of Europeans but there was a challenge in Farley's voice when he asked if the pianist knew anything from *Porgy and Bess*—implying it was a work written by a Jewish American about inferior Negroes. The pianist was bewildered.

"You are Americans, aren't you?"

"Yes."

"But you like this music?"

"Yes. Why not?"

"It's for Negroes."

"Do you object?"

"Me? I love all Gershwin."

He played *Porgy* the way Sol Chaplin used to. We might have been singing around the piano at Doheny Drive instead of around the piano in the little Viennese restaurant, singing Gershwin's music for Negroes with the pianist until the place closed.

Afterward, he took us home with him to his flat where his wife was waiting. They were an enviably matched pair: looks, age, intelligence, culture; both born in Vienna and both Jews.

His parents were foolish socialists—his phrase. Foolish because they were so blindly optimistic: when Hitler came heiling in, they stayed but he, the teenage boy, fled and escaped to London. He never saw his parents again. Her parents were well off but too complacent. She had been in boarding school in Paris when she fled to London rather than to Vichy. Her parents in Vienna let the last minute go by.

It wasn't in London that she met the pianist, though; that happened in Jerusalem. Paper Jews, neither brought up religiously, they were converted into militant Jews by the combination of Hitler, the Holocaust, and the life of refugees in England. In Jerusalem, fighting for a home state for their people, they met, fell in love and married. Life was good there: they enjoyed their work, they were doing well, they were happy.

But why, then, had they come back to Vienna?

Ah, well, that. The answer was simple: They wanted to see Vienna. All their lives, they had heard about Vienna but they had never really seen it. They had been too young and then Hitler had come. So they had returned to see Vienna—only to find that Vienna had gone.

The war, of course.

No, oh no, it wasn't the war; that was what hurt so much. Vienna, the Vienna of every Viennese's dreams, hadn't gone in this war, it had gone in World War I. The waltz had stopped being played before they were even born but their parents hadn't told them, they hadn't wanted to admit it. No one wanted to admit it, even now.

Now they were saving their money to go back to Israel but they felt cheated. That had nothing to do with being Jewish, it had to do with being Viennese. Even Israeli citizens, they would always be Viennese—but where was Vienna?

The Hillman overheated on the Italian side of the Alps, on the border between Austria and Italy. While we waited for it to cool down, we sunbathed in a field

The *ragazzi* were too fascinated by a convertible that broke down crossing the Alps to fetch any water for the overheated engine.

of multicolored wildflowers. It was improbably beautiful to be surrounded in summer by snow-capped mountains and even a glacier glistening like blue milk glass in the hot sun. I read aloud from a guidebook to the unique city we were headed for. All on water, the book blurbed, no streets and no cars, just canals and gondolas. What it neglected to add was that Venice makes everyone a virgin again so that it is able to seduce them.

We stayed less than a week but when we left, a play set in Venice was rapidly taking shape in my smitten head. I knew everyone fell in love with the beauty of the sudden views but I was too deeply in love to let that worry me. I also knew the effect of Europe on an American had been written about before—Henry James was not merely required reading—but the effect of Venice on me, that was special and very different.

Whatever we'd heard, what we saw was more exciting, more beautiful, more fantastic, more unique, more improbable, more of more. Venice makes a tourist of any traveler. There is too much to see—within the city, out in the lagoons, on Torcello, Murano, Burano. And just sitting at a little table in what Napoléon called the most beautiful drawing room in Europe, the Piazza San Marco, having coffee on one side in the morning sun, drinks on the other in the afternoon sun, and in the front line of those tables for the *passeggio* at the evening concert watching the cruising to Puccini.

The cruising was everywhere: it seemed indigenous to the city but there was always the Italian twinkle, the humorous touch indigenous to the whole country. Farley and I didn't ignore it, it was too much unconsummated fun, but we took it as one of the sights of the city. Since you have to walk, you have to see and Venice is like one huge gallery, with so many twisted alleyways that it was easy to get lost—which we did with pleasure.

Farley always wanted to spend more time in the art galleries than I did; in one, however, I perhaps should have stayed longer. It was unusual on two counts: not a picture was rococo or baroque, all were defiantly contemporary, misplaced in Venice to me. The second count was a different kind of art: the only two other people looking at the pictures were two of the handsomest young men I had ever seen.

I'm aware it appears I couldn't go anywhere without encountering, in one way or another, very attractive young men. I can only say that they were all over Europe, especially in Venice, and the two in the art gallery, as it turned out, were famously handsome. One—Bozo (Giuseppe) Roi: dark, rich, titled family, from Bologna; the other—Bill Miller: blond, richly kept, from New York. As a pair, they enhanced each other so much they inspired inspired fantasies. Cruising was an art and a craft for them: glances, half smiles, full alluring smiles, looks admiring and erotic, not too much conversation but enough to exchange names. Places were not mentioned in my hearing.

The next day Stella invited us to swim and lunch on the beach in front of her hotel on the Lido. Farley didn't want to swim, he preferred more galleries, more pictures, he couldn't get enough. Off I went to the Lido and off he went to wherever he went. This was Venice, not England and the Welcombe Inn, but he was as beautiful as they were so why wouldn't they?

And why shouldn't he? I knew I would have (and did some years later with the Bill Miller half of the duo). That admission of being a glass-house resident allowed me to amuse and flash as usual, showing no pain to Farley or anyone else. But the painful ache from not being wanted was there, buried deep until it surfaced in that play set in Venice.

Those six days had left a vivid impression; longer would have been too much or not enough; the impression would have been fuzzy and I would not have written a play that could take place only in Venice. *The Time of the Cuckoo,* I called it; it starred Shirley Booth, who was directed by Harold Clurman, though not for long. Then it was turned into *Summertime,* a movie starring my pal Katharine Hepburn, directed by a besotted David Lean—besotted with herself, of course. And lastly, a musical, *Do I Hear a Waltz?,* with a book by me and a score by Richard Rodgers and Stephen Sondheim. The book always gets first billing; it also gets most of the blame and little of the credit.

In all versions of *Cuckoo,* the central character, a woman, is based on me. Not on what I did doing during those six days—except for the sightseeing—but on what was going on inside me. I realized that as I wrote the play.

Room 59 in the Grand Hotel had been recommended by Stella, who, naturally, wasn't staying there. Farley and I could have roller-skated in Number 59: it was a small ballroom with two balconies on the Grand Canal yet was priced as a double room. The walls were green brocade, the ceiling had gold-leafed wooden beams and the bathroom was bigger than the living-dining room in the house in Laurel Canyon.

From the first, an object on an elegant coffee table caught my eye. In the midst of all the rococo, baroque, overglitzed furniture, it was unique because it was so gracefully simple: an ashtray of amber Venetian glass, delicately shot with gold fibers. It was large and heavy but I set about testing to see if it could be stolen safely.

Each morning when we left the room to explore the city, I hid the ashtray in a different place—under a pile of clothing in a drawer, on top of an armoire but never in a suitcase: that would be proof of felonious intent. Each evening when we returned, the maids had put the ashtray back where it lived on the small coffee table. They said not a word but I gave up and went out to search the city and its islands in the lagoon and across the lagoon until I found a duplicate and bought it. There is not one piece of Venetian glass, however unique, however beautiful, however old, that doesn't have a duplicate for sale someplace in the city or on one of those islands. That undramatic bit of trivia I used, with some embellishment, to mold the plot of *The Time of the Cuckoo*.

Plot didn't interest me as much as character and the difference between American and Italian attitudes. The amber Venetian glass ashtray became a red eighteenth-century Venetian glass goblet that the American heroine wants to believe is real because she wants the attractive Italian who sold it to her.

"Is this glass eighteenth-century?" she asks the owner of the pensione where she's staying.

Signora Fioria examines the goblet. "Yes it is," she says, then, handing it back, adds: "But it is so lovely, what's the difference?"

That attitude came from two women—one Italian, one Jewish. The Italian was a shopkeeper who said a line I pilfered for the play: "Enjoy yourself, it's too late already." The other was Stella, who said as we entered a church: "I've done everything in my life except needle work." She wasn't referring to needlepoint.

We had naively assumed we could drive up to the entrance of our hotel in Venice but there's Farley, in a gondola with our luggage.

Lydia St. Clair *(right)* was a wonderful pensione keeper in *Cuckoo*. Onstage and off, she was fearless.

Shirley Booth used the natural quaver in her voice to get laughs or tears with effortless skill.

Like Venetian glass, the gondola informs the plot of *Cuckoo,* but more, it permeates the whole atmosphere of the play just as it permeates the whole atmosphere of Venice—with sex. Sex hangs in the Venetian air; it's almost palpable, even in the sunniest of mornings; its symbol is the gondola, which is used for sex, any kind, with or without gondolier. Stella brought us to lunch at the house of a man who had his own gondola and his own gondoliers to match. One look at them and we knew our host was homosexual.

Most gondoliers are hustlers. That husky, incessant "Gondola, gondola!" is a mating call from one animal to any other who has the price. As the day gets darker, the call gets more excitingly threatening. Writing "Gondola, gondola!" into the play for all its different purposes sometimes made me feel I was writing pornography. And when Shirley Booth snarled it on stage in furious sexual frustration, it sounded very pornographic.

The third day of rehearsal on the stage of the Empire Theatre, she walked off, refusing to take any more direction from Harold Clurman. *Cuckoo* was being produced by Robert Whitehead and Roger Stevens, Bob being the hands-on producer—but in this case, he kept hands off.

The honeymoon wasn't over because Harold and Shirley had never wed. He didn't know how to talk to her, nor she to him: each spoke a different theatre language—his was Stanislavsky as filtered through the Group Theatre, hers was George Abbott as filtered through inestimable experience. To me, it behooves the director to speak the actor's language; it is the director who must reach the actor. Harold was not heedless of this but in his attempt to reach Shirley, he came out with a pidgin English equivalent of Method lingo. She heard and wasn't fooled. So genial, so felt-slippers, she nevertheless could be acid and spike heels.

Shirley Booth looked like a bargain-shopper, not an actress; not even onstage where she never appeared to be acting. She was heartbreaking because she was walking vulnerability; her laughs were surefire because she had an intuitive comic talent and was immensely skilled. She knew her craft and respected it; little was accidental and if it was and worked, she put it in her bag to pluck out when she needed it. She had a theory about comedy: you got a laugh by sending it out to the audience with a rise from a chair, a turn of the head, a thrust of the hand, a flick of a handkerchief. She was not above kicking out her leg on an exit.

Her persona was warm, pleasant, reticent, but she was a tough cookie like any star, particularly women stars who don't get there otherwise in a male-dominated culture. Day One, she warned her understudy she would never go on.

"I got here and I'm staying here," Shirley told the talented younger player. "If I have to crawl, I'll go on."

She did once: with stys on both eyes, a temperature of 101, her hair burned by her dresser. What made it amazing was that she crawled on in a role that angered and frustrated her because it wasn't what she had thought it was. Harold wasn't aware of that but I was.

Shirley and I could talk; we had history, we went way back to my very first radio play and to *Heartsong*, which she had stolen in the part of Malloy. She loved Malloy, and for superficial reasons thought Leona in *The Time of the Cuckoo* was a richer version. Both women drank too much—Malloy was an alcoholic, Leona was on the equator—both were funny and both used humor to cover, but that was it. Which Shirley didn't realize until the first read-through of the play. Why she didn't realize it until then, I don't know—she'd had the script long enough, we waited almost a year for her—but even working people in the theatre often don't know how to read a play.

There is a climactic scene at a party in the second act of *The Time of the Cuckoo* where Leona is publicly embarrassed. High to begin with, she gets drunk; out of her agony, she lashes out viciously at everyone. Bob Whitehead loved the scene—"If only every scene in the play could be as good as that one," he sighed—but it frightened Shirley because it forced her to expose the Achilles' heel in her acting.

We were standing onstage, discussing the scene during a rehearsal break. Tension was high. Pointing out to the auditorium, she said, "I want them to like me." That desire was the flaw in her acting, a desire shared by far too many of her peers. It limits the actor, it's destructive to his performance and thus inevitably, to the play.

Shirley knew the party scene was good and good for her. But it pushed her to a place she had never been before and for that, she needed help; help had to come from her director, he had to have a strong hand she could trust. Unfortunately, early on, she lost faith in Harold. Comedy was her best friend: she recognized it instantly on the page; the possibility of a laugh—from character and situation, not a just a one-liner—she could sniff out and bring home; comedy was her security blanket. Harold tried to deflect her from playing a crucial scene for comedy as well as pathos and with that, Harold Clurman, director, lost Shirley Booth, star.

"A very gentle play" was Harold's characterization; the scene in question was "gently touching." Di Rossi, the Italian Leona is falling in love with, has a speech where he tells her he knows all too well what she dreams:

> He is young, handsome, rich, witty, brilliant. A gondola of his own. A duke, or a count at the very least. And—unmarried. Well,

I am a shopkeeper. Not handsome. Not rich, not young, not witty, not brilliant. No title, no gondola. And not unmarried. But Miss Samish, I am a man and I want you. But you? "It's wrong, it's wicked, it's this, it's that." You are a hungry child to who someone brings ravioli. "But I don't want ravioli, I want beefsteak!" You are hungry, Miss Samish. Eat the ravioli.

And Leona answers: "I'm not that hungry."

Harold thought the exchange touching, capable of bringing out the Kleenex. Shirley assessed "Eat the ravioli" as a big laugh to be topped by her "I'm not that hungry." The actor playing Di Rossi had no opinion. He barely spoke English: his pronunciation of "count" often came out as "cunt"—quite confusing in context. The playwright felt the scene as a whole was touching but comedy often makes a scene more touching and did so in that scene. Shirley was totally right about those two laughs. The first performance before an audience proved her case.

Di Rossi got a roar. Shirley helped him with a timed turn of her head, didn't step on his laugh but let it roll until an alarm clock in her gut went off and said Go and she did. She shot her line out and brought down the house. She helped Di Rossi because she knew it helped her but also because she was a very generous actor. The best always are.

Watching that scene from the back of the house one night out of town, I felt a stirring in my groin. I saw the Israeli major standing nude in his flat in Tel Aviv. Had leaning against the partition at the rear of the orchestra reminded me of leaning against the balustrade on the croisette overlooking the Mediterranean? I didn't think so. The actor playing Di Rossi was, to be kind, portly, middle-aged, a very nice man, in no way attractive to me, but what he was saying to Leona, his attitude toward her—it was then that I made the connection. I was Leona. The Israeli major had been telling me to "eat the ravioli"; that's where I got it, it was his attitude that I put in the play. What a writer doesn't know about himself is thrilling.

The dispute about laughs or no laughs in the ravioli scene was the last straw for Shirley; it sent her walking off the stage. Nobody said anything for a few minutes. Jimmy Gelb, the stage manager, went to her dressing room and, not too long after, they both came back and rehearsal resumed. Three lines and Harold made a suggestion. Before his sentence was finished, Shirley cut in with "No." Rehearsal resumed. Harold started another suggestion—"No." It didn't happen again; he was too wise to provide another opportunity but it was a peculiar rehearsal with a star who was not about to take direction from the director.

An impasse I thought had to be broken even if one of them had to be fired. I went to the producer but Bob was Bob: always affable, always kind, never strong. He adored Harold, Harold would come through. As would Shirley who was professional; also box office, although he didn't say that. Unfortunately, neither of them came through. She never did get the party scene and the play was damaged.

Bob muttered that perhaps he'd been mistaken, perhaps the scene he loved needed rewriting. Any doubts I might have had—what author doesn't?—were canceled by an Off-Broadway revival in which an actress named Kathleen Maguire made that scene a shattering climax to the play. Not on Broadway, not at the Empire Theatre; there you understood but you didn't feel, it seemed forced. *The Time of the Cuckoo* was a hit anyway but the play suffered, I suffered and Shirley suffered. The audiences cheered her, the critics raved about her, she got those prizes but she suffered because night after night throughout the run, she would tell Jimmy Gelb she was going to get that scene. She never really did, hard as she tried and she kept trying, but she had never gotten the help she needed.

I didn't think either Bob or Harold realized or, if they did, cared much that the play was damaged by the impasse between director and star. I didn't think they thought that much of the play anyway. A success was what they wanted and a success was what they achieved. They both talked and believed in artistic goals and aimed for them. But they were also show business which, I had to accept, was what we were in. I did wish Shirley had been able to lick that scene, though; she could have been hair-raising. Her desire for the audience to like her wasn't all that got in her way; she was very angry at Harold.

While we were in Philadelphia—unbrotherly unloving Philadelphia—I rewrote the ending of the play. I liked the ending, the ambiguous meaning of the last word: "Ciao." No one asked me to change it but watching, listening to the audience, I knew what we had didn't really work. Naturally, I thought Harold hadn't directed it right and Shirley wasn't playing it right; practically, there was no way to get the two of them together to try it my way.

Harold glanced at the single revised page I handed him—"Fine, my boy, fine"—and gave it to Shirley and the child actor who were the only two involved. She looked at the page and snarled:

"Well, he's made you as tacky and vulgar as he is."

Harold protested cheerfully. I took the page, read it carefully, then said: "I know what Shirley means." And I did. My new ending was wrong; she was wrong in being so undiplomatic but she wasn't used to being a star, she was too new at it.

I had made a cardinal mistake: I had given the curtain line to the kid. I switched the lines and handed the page to Shirley. She kissed me. "That's my angel!"

They rehearsed quickly—she staged herself, Harold staged the kid—the new ending went in and the curtain came down to bigger applause. She hugged me and ignored Harold who laughed pretend-cheerful. He took whatever she dished out.

Each evening out of town before the performance began, Shirley gathered the small cast onstage to play a game she had invented: Who knew a worse director than Harold Clurman? No matter what name was proposed, she knocked it down: No, no, Harold Clurman was worse. He was onstage once or twice to hear the game: he laughed pretend-cheerful.

If it was difficult to hold on to whatever respect and affection I still had for him, it became next to impossible after his behavior to Lydia St. Clair, who played the Italian owner of the pensione. An excellent actress, she was striking but not very pretty, not at all pretty by Harold's standards. For him, there was only one beauty among the four women in the cast—my darling friend, Geraldine Brooks, and she was miscast as an adoring but very stupid young wife. As good an actress as she was, and she was very good indeed, Gerry couldn't conceal her own intelligence—it was too luminous. But Harold wanted her for the part, she wanted to get out of Hollywood and come back to the theatre, and although I didn't want her, I didn't object. Good old show business? No, friendship. Friends didn't come any better than Gerry.

Signora Fioria, the part Lydia played, had been a bitch to cast. Gale Sondergaard, whom I had known from Hollywood and the blacklist, came in and read. She didn't get the part—she was too threatening, almost menacing—and wrote me an angry letter, accusing Harold of turning her down because of her politics. Harold was too uncommitted to have any politics but rejection was easier to take if the blacklist was allowed as the reason.

Lydia St. Clair's reading was exactly what we had all been waiting to hear. If her look wasn't what we had all been waiting to see, her style and panache more than compensated. She and Shirley worked very well together, everything was roses until a rehearsal in Wilmington when Harold Clurman said five words I would never have believed he would say, surely five words he had never said to the Group or any other actors he had directed. He had told Lydia to change a cross and sit in a different chair.

"Why?" she asked.

"Because I tell you to," Harold Clurman answered.

Lydia had said very little during any rehearsal. Now she came to the edge of the stage and spoke first to me. "Mr. Laurents"—it was Mr. and Miss and Mrs. then—"I like your play and my part but I hope you will forgive me if I say the reason I wanted to do it was because I wanted to work with the great Harold Clurman. I don't have to work. I have a wealthy husband and a house in Connecticut with a swimming pool." Now she turned slightly to address Harold directly. "Mr. Clurman, you have not given me one piece of what I could reasonably call direction from the first day. Is it because you don't find me attractive? Should I have my face changed? Lifted, redone? Tell me, Mr. Clurman, if I were more attractive, would you direct me then?"

The silence was terrible. It went on and on and on. The woman just stood there, holding herself erect as she looked down at Harold in that terribly silent auditorium. He said nothing. He left her standing there with her face waiting. He said nothing. Lydia dipped her head in a slight bow, walked to the chair he had told her to sit in and picked up the scene where they had left off. I walked

THEATRE ARTS

ANC

50 CENTS   NOVEMBER 1953

Mary Martin and Charles Boyer in Joshua Logan's production of Norman Krasna's New Comedy "KIND SIR"

ARTICLES BY MAURICE ZOLOTOW, ABE BURROWS, DAVE GARROWAY

*Complete Play—
"The Time of the Cuckoo"
by Arthur Laurents*

As the credit in the right-hand corner shows, in those days, *Theatre Arts* published a new play in each issue. Today, the magazine is gone and few new plays are published anywhere.

out of the theatre. It was difficult to look at Harold after that; I didn't want him to read my eyes.

Opening night, I was sitting at a small table somewhere having a drink with Gerry Brooks when someone—the press agent or a minion—brought us a copy of *The New York Times*. One of half a dozen papers, the *Times* was nevertheless always the paper that angered the theatre community the most because its review had the most power over opinion as well as the box office.

The audience had been very enthusiastic, the performance had gone extremely well except for Shirley's bête noir, the party scene. That played neither better nor worse than usual so it let the play down as usual. I was neither up nor down; I didn't know what feelings I was covering until I read Brooks Atkinson's review. He said I had written a lovely play for Shirley Booth which was a lovely time for everybody.

Gerry took my hand in both of hers and clasped it very tightly. The tears in her eyes reflected the unexpected tears in mine. I was unprepared for how much that review meant. If the play had been another in my string of failures, would I have gone on writing? Yes, but what? Screenplays, probably; there were offers to both write and direct. I didn't have to debate or decide anymore now. I had the two best reasons why success is important: for the encouragement to go on and for the money to live on while you do go on.

I didn't believe in fraternizing with critics in any way but Brooks Atkinson's review meant so much to me, I wrote him a brief note of thanks. In his answer, he wrote that perhaps he shouldn't be encouraging me in the path my writing had taken. After that, I didn't write to please him but whenever he gave me a good review, I hoped he was glad he had encouraged me.

During the run of the play, John Gielgud had invaded Shirley's dressing room, sat her down and told her to play it as long as possible, take it on tour, take it to London, to milk it because a play so suited to its star rarely comes along. Then Kate Hepburn swashbuckled into the dressing room—she and Shirley had become friends during the run of *The Philadelphia Story*—sat her down and told her not to go on tour, not to take it to London and most definitely not to do the movie. Hepburn won over Gielgud.

Life magazine did a big spread on Shirley—she had won the Oscar for *Come Back, Little Sheba* to no effect on our box office—in which she dismissed the report that her next picture was to be *The Time of the Cuckoo*. Oh, no: *Cuckoo* wouldn't make a good picture, she said vehemently.

"I have to be honest" was her explanation to me.

I countered with: If I told her the dress she was wearing was tasteless and all wrong for her, I might say I was being honest but was there any need for me to say it?

"You really think the dress is wrong?" Shirley asked.

The movie deal with the studio that had her under contract collapsed. It wasn't a good deal—Swifty Lazar had blithely tried to horn in on Harold Freedman's territory with no authority whatsoever. Harold called him off and despite the damage that had been done, managed to set up a deal with Alexander Korda in London. The announcement of the sale attracted attention because set to star was none other than our mutual friend, Katharine Hepburn.

"She asked my permission," Shirley assured me, "and I said it was OK."

I don't doubt that Kate asked and Shirley allowed but how did Kate explain her switch? She didn't have to explain it to me, I knew the answer: David Lean was to direct the picture. How did she explain it to Shirley? I could write the scene with one hand: Kate would intimidate Shirley with her classy New England superiority, then bamboozle her with ease because she would be bamboozling herself at the same time. She never had trouble with reality because she never had a good grip on it. That became very clear much later—in 1972—when we met regularly over several weeks to decide whether I was going to write and she was going to act in a movie based on Graham Greene's *Travels with My Aunt.*

Bobby Fryer—known as the Red Queen, not entirely for the color of his hair—was to produce and George Cukor was to direct. I would write the screenplay only if Kate was going to be in it; I didn't believe the picture would work otherwise. From her Olympus: Graham Greene had sent her his novel but she didn't think it would make a movie. She was perfectly willing to play it if I wrote a screenplay that proved her wrong. But I wouldn't write on spec and she wouldn't sign on spec. An impasse broken by our mutual agreement to meet two or three times a week to see if one could convince the other.

We usually met at her house on Forty-ninth Street, next door to my friend Steve Sondheim. He always referred to Kate as "your friend" in the same disparaging tone Charlie Chaplin had used about Claire Bloom. (My mother had used it about that boy on the block who introduced me to sex. She didn't like his parents but had she guessed?)

Kate's house was rather like her clothes: spartan and shabby. Unlike her clothes, which were mended to prolong life (theirs), the house was in need of repair. Once, the knob on the only door in the room we were in came off in her hand just as she was going to let me out. Her face registered fear, not embarrassment—fear, I think, of being trapped in a room with a man. The last time we met, she blushed when I said, "Oh, Kate, you're so paradoxical, you're adorable!" and impulsively took her by the arms as I spoke. Fear flooded her face and she jerked back as though she had been clawed by a leper.

We did talk about the book as a book and as a movie, but not too much. I knew I could convince her to do it and that what she wanted was to be courted and wooed. But I wanted to find out who she really was—if she knew. Certainly she had invented her physical self: no one was born speaking that way; no one dressed that way, wore her hair that way, moved that way. It was all affectation but carefully calculated along with her much vaunted directness and honesty. She was direct all right, and even more opinionated than I, but get to a real question, our vestal squirmed and wriggled, she could not be pinned down.

I asked her about a piece Garson Kanin wrote about her. We were down at my house in the Village where, the first time she walked in, she said "I'll swap houses" and I said "Are you kidding?" She looked askance. Refusal or rejection was not permissible; for someone else to be as blunt and direct as she was beyond the pale. She didn't want to hear about Garson's piece, which accompanied her face on the cover of some women's magazine. It described Garson and Ruth Gordon sitting at a sidewalk café in Paris with Kate and Tracy, talking about sex. Hard for me to believe, but harder still was Kate's remark (quoted by Gar): "I don't believe there is any such thing as male homosexuality."

Queen Victoria didn't believe there was any such thing as female homosexuality. Which would neutralize all the rumors about Hepburn. But male homosexuality? No such thing as? George Cukor her adored friend?

"I didn't read the article," she snapped.

"But did you say it?"

"When my father died—and he was a doctor, a damn good one—he said he knew less about sexuality than he did when he was an intern."

"Very interesting but, Kate, did you say it?"

"My mother was a suffragette, first woman to . . ." and she was off—and off the subject and stayed off no matter how hard I pursued. Finally, she simply picked up her gear and out she went.

At our last meeting, I admitted defeat: *Travels with My Aunt* was not movie material. Typically paradoxical, she thereupon cried, "No, it is, it is! You were right! You must write it!" That was when I told her she was adorable and half embraced her to her horror.

She didn't make the movie either. Before shooting began, she was rewriting and kept at it vigorously after they started with the result that one night, she called across a crowded theatre lobby to me: "They fired me! Have you heard? They fired me!" She sounded triumphant.

. . .

In December of 1954, I sailed for London to meet David Lean and discuss the screenplay of *The Time of the Cuckoo*. My mind was elsewhere, still on London but on a meeting that could turn out to be an answered prayer, a frost, exciting, ridiculous, or stupid. In New York, just before I left, one John B. L. Goodwin had proposed that he and I have a romantic affair and I had accepted. It would begin in London right after David Lean and I were finished and would be celebrated in Madrid on Christmas and in Torremolinos on New Year's Eve. Everything but a theme song.

Johnny and I were neither old nor new friends but we had been circling for a while. He was the author of a very good first novel—*The Idols and the Prey,* set in Haiti—but hadn't written another. He was too rich, too firmly entrenched in the New York version of the avant-garde which by then wasn't: everything changes but the avant-garde. He now wrote haiku, which he illustrated himself, beautifully, like Japanese painting. He was as eccentric as his clothes: in his town house, his pet ocelot was usually locked up in its own room lest it shit all over any guest it didn't like. It did cross my mind that Johnny's eccentricity could be as calculated as Kate Hepburn's but on the other side of the ledger, it was he who introduced me to *One Hundred Years of Solitude,* to pot, and to Emily Hahn who was authentically eccentric and gloriously so.

David Lean was morose, cold, detached; much more interested in Katharine Hepburn than in *The Time of the Cuckoo*. Alexander Korda's name made him producer but it was Ilya Lopert who produced the picture and did the work. Korda was effective in areas like changing the title, which he didn't like. "What was that damn fool author thinking of? Not the public," he said, not caring a whit that the damn fool author had just entered the room. Lopert changed it to *Summertime.*

Lean didn't care one way or the other unless Katharine Hepburn cared. It wasn't Kate yet but he pumped me for anything I knew that could tell him what she was like—not as an actress, he didn't care about that, he knew about that, he could see her screen mannerisms and maybe even loved them or was blind to them. The latter is more likely, for he was probably in love with her before they started shooting. During shooting, he must have been because it was Hepburn who called the shots and I do not mean camera angles.

. . .

I finally managed to get Lean back to the screenplay—i.e., what did he want, how did he see it—but not for long. He disappeared; by the time he returned, it was clear I wasn't going to be free to leave London as early as we had planned. I called Johnny who was in New York and furious: his passage was booked, he would have to sit around London for about a week. Was it so awful to sit around and wait for me with our romantic affair in the offing?

"You don't understand," he said with transatlantic impatience, "it's my clothes."

"Your clothes?"

"My clothes! In New York, they're eccentric, in London, they're old-fashioned."

That doomed it. We'd never been to bed and we never got to bed. We did set out together on an insane journey to Madrid, Torremolinos, Tangier, then back to Madrid where he accused me of being "commercial and vulgar" one time too many. The first time was Christmas Day in Madrid, in a big beautiful double room at the beautifully elegant Ritz Hotel—ten dollars a night. Such was Spain's economy under Franco.

Johnny was at me because he wanted to go to Toledo and a young man we met at a party the night before had a car and had come on to me. Johnny hadn't wanted to go to the party—he'd taunted me for being "tacky enough to go to a Christmas Eve party at the house of someone someone else told you to call." I hadn't much wanted to go but I didn't fancy Christmas Eve with my ex-lover-that-never-was in an evil mood. So I went and he sullenly tagged along. Now he was pushing for the young man to drive us to Toledo.

"If you fuck him, he will," he urged.

"I don't want to fuck him, Johnny."

"When did you become so fastidious about whom you fuck?"

It was like that. And went on like that until finally, in a crazed, vengeful rage, I fucked the young man in our grand room at the Ritz with Johnny reading a book in the elegant bathroom. And yes, I did it on Johnny's bed. Those were the days. But Toledo was worth seeing.

By New Year's Eve in Torremolinos, John had hooked up with a character I named Quasimodo while I had a connection of sorts with a character named Pepe de l'Amo—really. He would have been too pretty but for a scar in his cheek: he'd been slashed with a broken bottle in a bar in Madrid.

We were staying at a parador—a government hotel which in Torremolinos consisted of a central building for drinking and eating, and several little two-room cottages, each with a fireplace. *Fuego! Fuego!* I would hear Johnny shouting from his cottage in counterpoint to my own less angry *Fuego! Fuego!* Occasionally, a maid might bring two sticks of wood for a brief fire.

We had come to the Costa Brava for the sun but it was bleak as a cemetery, the sand was coarse, black volcanic ash and the Spaniards were all *loco.*

In the bar of the parador where a dry gin martini straight up cost ten cents, a government spy everyone was warned was a spy would sit every night ostentatiously eavesdropping like a ham actor. What he hoped to overhear was a street being called by the name it had before Franco came to power, a heinous crime for which he could make an official arrest. At a "Twenties" cocktail party in Málaga, half the guests were calling streets by their former names, not to defy Franco but to be "Twenties" verbally as well as sartorially. We were all arrested and thrown in jail, not because the old street names were used but because a permit was needed for any gathering of over twenty people and there were twenty-two of us. Fearless Franco.

Americans were released first. Johnny and I pedaled back to Torremolinos on our rented bicycles. His vision was bad anyway, but it was dark and on the way he ran into a herd of sheep, mangling the front wheel of his bike so badly, he had to walk home. He raged and ranted, threatening lawsuits, but really raged when the farmer took him to court for running over his sheep. Neither Quasimodo nor Pepe nor any of the Spaniards who hung around the parador would come to court; they weren't political but they were terrified of Franco's police. With only about ten words of Spanish between us, Johnny had to pay a hefty fine. He fumed for two days of bad weather but on the third, seven of us sardined into a taxi and drove to Algeçiras where we caught the ferry to Morocco where we sardined into another taxi that took us to Tangier. That cheered him up.

It cost almost nothing to stay in Tangier because it was under international jurisdiction administered by seven powers, each with its own currency. Just as it had its casbah—the *petit zocco*—the city had its money street, or more accurately, its money exchange street. The idea was to run fast enough from one *cambio* to another to exchange one currency for another at a more profitable rate. Each morning, hungover or not, I started at one end of the street with twenty-five bucks and raced up and down, changing dollars for lire, lire for French francs, French francs for Swiss francs for pesos for whatever, until I had made another twenty-five bucks, a day's expenses and a night's drinking at the Parade bar.

The Parade was famous as home to all the expatriates, Yank and Brit, paid to stay in Tangier by their families. Johnny and I made a beeline for it our first night but disappointingly, it was closed to honor the death of Mildred Bailey. We could hear her records being played by the proprietors who sang along as they drowned their sorrow.

The next night, the doors open, in we went to be welcomed and embraced.

Every night after that, I wound up at the Parade, usually at a corner table with an intriguing Brazilian woman—Beatrix Pendar. Her husband was a CIA agent in Rabat who was homosexual and needed a beard (this, she said) and who also married her for her money (this, she implied)—a fair deal because it enabled her to escape from her family, her first (Brazilian) husband and Brazil itself. Beatrix and I would talk for hours, those cosmic, deep-shit conversations you have while you're getting very drunk.

Behind the bar, the Parade had a big placard advertising *In the Summer House,* the Jane Bowles play that had recently closed in New York. Johnny and I had known Jane and her husband Paul in New York when they lived on West Tenth Street in Greenwich Village, so we went to hunt them up. Paul wasn't around or was around but with Ahmed, his Arab boyfriend; either way he wasn't available at the moment but Jane was, even with her Arab girlfriend, Cherifa. She rustled up provisions for the picnic-cum-tour Cherifa organized for us, and greeted us at the prearranged meeting place with an enthusiasm I'd never seen her have in New York where she'd usually been rather hazy and foggy. Cherifa was supervising bossily like a foreman from atop her donkey—it was just like one of Jane's plays. Finally we were all set, ready to take off when she looked down at Jane and shrieked at her to go home. And Jane did. Even in the short time I was in Tangier, every time East-West culture clashed, the East won hands down.

Exploring the *zocco* on my own late one afternoon—it was like being dropped in the middle of a maze blindfolded—I rounded a corner and found myself in what looked like an indoor Moorish swimming pool without water. Arches, columns of mosaic tile, broken and faded but still fanciful, and in a long alcove, a soda fountain! Grimy, long abandoned, but an honest-to-God soda fountain complete with the handles and spigots from the neighborhood drugstore when I was a kid. Wondrous! And waiting under the next set of arches beyond the soda fountain, more wondrous! Half a dozen Arabs sitting cross-legged in a semicircle smoking hash in a pipe they kept passing. I sat down at one end of the semicircle, crossed my legs and waited. They passed me the pipe. It was grade A hash.

There was a special, personal reason I was in Tangier: my passport had to be renewed and the word was that the list of undesirables (i.e., subversives) hadn't as yet reached our consulate. The attaché—or whatever his official position was—to whom I presented my dying passport was career Foreign Service,

The hashish was a bonus. I had come to Tangier in 1952 to renew
my passport because the official list of subversives hadn't caught up
with our small consulate there.

which was heavily under attack by Joe Kennedy's friend and fellow Joe, Senator McCarthy. Good for my side, I hoped.

At first, we walked on eggshells, each cautious about revealing anything
politically lest the other wrong-foot him. But that fact that he was a career
man, that he seemed to indicate it was time for him to get out, encouraged me
to take the first step and reveal somewhat where I was politically. Not completely; that would have put him in an untenable official position no matter
what his personal sympathies were. The fencing was delicate and dangerous
but it was also perversely enjoyable. And the ending was happier than expected: not only did he renew my passport but he gave me the number 33, a
number for a diplomat. For the time I had that number, when I crossed bor-

ders and went through customs, boy, did they hop to! Especially in the homeland of Joe McCarthy and Pat McCarran, the U.S. of A.

Once I had the passport, there was no reason to stay in Tangier. There was a due date on the screenplay so as soon as I got back to Torremolinos, I got down to work seriously, if not enthusiastically. When it was finished and ready for London and David Lean, John quixotically decided to go as far as Madrid with me.

We flew from Málaga in a rickety single-motor plane that carried fourteen passengers and on the luggage rack, a half dozen chickens in crates. Johnny and I were in the last two seats; as the plane rolled down the runway, the heads of the twelve passengers in front of us disappeared—they had all bent down to cross themselves. But just as the plane took off, the heads came up and the ceiling came down on them, the chickens squawking their fool heads off.

In Madrid, we checked into the Montague Hotel, known in the Spanish gay world as the Gaylord in honor of the English lord who had been caught in a homosexual scandal.

Johnny had been given the address of a gay bar where Our Kind could be found. After too many wrong turns, we got there only to find that the gay bar was a tea room for proper ladies and a few old gentlemen having tea and cakes and little sandwiches. Well, what the hell. The getting there had left us hungry, the cakes looked delicious, we were gobbling them up when the clock started to strike seven. It was Cinderella at midnight in reverse. Before the clock finished, the last of the cakes had been whisked away, the last of the ladies had disappeared, glasses and bottles were being popped up on the counter, queens were flying in the door—the tea room became a gay bar! The very gay bar, in fact, where Pepe's face had been slashed with a broken beer bottle.

Johnny and I had another tiff about nothing but I was "vulgar and commercial" for the last time. He took off for Fez, where he found a Moroccan acrobat, and I took off for London and David Lean—who wasn't there.

Mindful of the contract and movie moguls, I handed the screenplay to Ilya Lopert; he read it with pleasure that pleased me. He was cloutless but praise is always preferable, regardless of the source. While waiting for Lean, I became grateful to Johnny because I ran into Emily Hahn—Mickey to her friends and I became one. At Brown's Hotel where I was staying, Mickey, her old girlfriend, Barbara, and I were having drinks courtesy of my per diem from Lopert while Barbara's six-year-old was gorging himself on high tea. Mickey was up from Sussex, where she lived with her husband, Charles Boxer, and her daughter Carola. The two ladies and the quality of their relationship were encapsulated in the following interchange.

A week earlier, Barbara had rung Mickey, asking her to help introduce a young intern friend who was moving into the neighborhood: give him tea and have a few locals in.

"Your young intern was very nice," Mickey said, taking a big cigar from her bag.

"They liked him, then?"

"Oh yes. They were a bit startled, though. Why didn't you tell me, Barbara?"

"Are you going to smoke that?"

"Yes. Do you mind?"

"No, I was wondering whether I should have one. No, I think not. Tell you what about the intern, Mickey? Oh—that he was a dwarf?"

"No. That his name was Will Shakespeare. Come on, Barbara. Have the cigar."

"Oh, well, why not?"

"You always do."

"But they did like him?"

"Yes. He'll do fine."

David Lean still didn't turn up, which should have made me suspicious; Lopert didn't want to pay out any more expense money, which I understood. So we shook hands and that was, for the time being, the end of my connection to *Summertime,* née *The Time of the Cuckoo.*

Snow was falling in New York that winter when Kate Hepburn phoned to invite me to tea. The picture was finished, she had seen it and wanted to report.

"You won't like it but I'm brilliant," she said. She had no sense of humor whatsoever about herself or about anything else though she could be funny. And when she was dueling, which she enjoyed, she had a touch of dry wit.

A fire in the grate made her spartan little sitting room almost cozy. We sipped hot chocolate as she told me how she had gotten rid of two-thirds of the second act of the play: "Wouldn't do at all, wouldn't do at all." Her insensitivity was so innocent, I had to wonder if her lightbulb wasn't dimmer than I had thought. The party scene—"Out, out, absolutely out." And the scene where Di Rossi leaves Leona, where the man leaves the woman—"Oh, out from the very beginning."

Shirley as Leona Samish in *The Time of the Cuckoo* with the kind of inexpensive camera a tourist would bring to Venice.

Kate Hepburn as Jane Hudson in *Summertime* with the expensive movie camera a movie star would bring to Venice.

"I wouldn't give you ten men for any one woman," she announced. "All men are poops." Rattle, rattle. "The fire needs another log."

"All men are poops." I smiled at her. "I'm sure you could put another log on much better than I could."

She was ready to kill. So was I when I finally saw the picture.

The name of a character is very important to me. I go through endless candidates, searching for the one name that is the character, that suggests the character to a stranger. In *The Time of the Cuckoo*, Shirley Booth played the character Leona Samish; in *Summertime*, Katharine Hepburn played Jane Hudson. Leona came by boat to Venice on a budgeted holiday; her clothes were bought on a secretary's salary. Hardly a virgin, under the façade of fun and laughs, a romantic aching for a "mystical, magical, miracle." Kate Hepburn's Jane Hudson flew to Venice in gowns by Adrian. On arrival, she whips out an expensive movie camera and proceeds to photograph everything in sight with the expertise of a professional. She has come to Venice to change outfits, flirt archly with a good-looking man, but preserve her very-long-held virginity at all costs. She does lose it—as a screenload of fireworks in the Venetian sky tells us—and to her surprise, she likes what it takes to lose it. Now we're getting somewhere but no: at this point, Jane decides to leave Venice. Why? Because the picture has gone on long enough. Her given reason is that she has always stayed too long at a party—a line from my unused screenplay that I liked when I wrote it but regretted when I heard it on the sound track.

The picture itself is a beautifully photographed travelogue, a coffee-table book on film. What little story it tells is mawkish and sentimental, made more so by the maudlin performance of its star whose weeping threatens to overflow the troubled canals. Hepburn told me crying made her voice less monotonous. She was wrong.

At the very end of the movie, there is a moment, wonderfully shot and conceived, where Di Rossi runs frantically along a railway station platform with a flower in his hand for Jane—Jane!—who is on a fast-moving, departing train. He doesn't catch up and she is left, looking back at him, flowerless, her eyes leaking like an old faucet.

Summertime was moderately successful at the box office and Katharine Hepburn was nominated for an Oscar. The screenplay was credited to H. E. Bates, a first-rate English novelist; it should have been credited to K. Hepburn and D. Lean, true believers that stars can do anything they want, even write. In this aspect of the movie business, they were unoriginal. Bad cess to both of them.

. . .

One more note, but this time I come to praise Hepburn, not to bash her. At the end of the Sixties, the decade of change and liberation, she came to Broadway in *Coco,* an old-fashioned musical about the life of Chanel. The book and lyrics were by Alan Jay Lerner, the music by André Previn. Previously, it had been reported that Richard Rodgers was writing the music but he withdrew. Shortly after that announcement, I ran into Rodgers in London and told him I was glad he wasn't doing *Coco.*

"Why?" he asked.

"Because during the war Chanel collaborated with the Nazis."

"I'll tell you something worse," he said. "She was a part-time dyke."

Although the show wasn't well received, Kate Hepburn was; even if she hadn't been, her name was enough to make any show a hit. I took my mother and father to see it because they admired her.

By the night we went to see *Coco,* my father had severe, chronic rheumatoid arthritis. His doctor, the specialist William Kammerer, used him as a guinea pig for testing everything from shots of gold to shots of cortisone; he even appears anonymously in films to testify as to the effects. It was painful for him to walk but when he walked down the aisle of the Mark Hellinger Theatre, my mother and I hovering nervously, eager to hold, help, just touch, he walked on his own.

He sat on the aisle, it was easiest, his hands helpless in his lap; his fingers curved like claws, his knuckles big as knobs. He tried not to move: the less movement, the less pain. I asked him if he was in pain. Oh, I'm always in pain, he said reassuringly, but you get used to it. Then the curtain rose. He leaned forward a millimeter. The light from the stage allowed me to see his eyes brighten and shine. He loved the theatre.

Coco was a musical but after her first four notes, it was uncomfortably clear the star couldn't sing. To Katharine Hepburn, that was unacceptable: she was determined to sing, she could sing, she did sing, dammit! She identified strongly with Chanel who had that same determination to succeed no matter what and on her own terms: to rely on no one, to be independent, to do precisely what she wanted and to hell with the consequences. And she identified with Chanel's desperate love for her father.

"Mademoiselle" and "Coco" were her two solos in the show, two places where Kate and Chanel came together in their ferocious determination. She couldn't sing either song but she performed both magnificently. She was moved and she moved the audience. My father's fingers uncurled, he lifted his hands, he applauded—my father able to applaud and he did!—even though his applause was soundless. And when the curtain stayed down and it was time to leave, he walked up the aisle as he hadn't walked in such a long time: he walked as though he wasn't in pain.

What she had said to me years ago at George Cukor's party didn't matter any more than what I thought of her performance in *Summertime*. All that mattered was what she did for my father. When a performer can do that— how marvelous! And how marvelous the theatre is! I wrote her and I thanked her for my father.

A few years before *Coco,* in 1964, I tried to fulfill a not impossible dream for *The Time of the Cuckoo* to be transformed into a small chamber musical with bittersweet melodies by Richard Rodgers, rueful lyrics by Oscar Hammerstein, and starring Mary Martin. Not a roaring, smashing hit, I didn't envision that—no long lines at the box office, not even with Mary Martin. No, my vision was a modestly successful Broadway run that could be my blue chip stock, my annuity from future road companies with any number of eligible ladies as well as from stock and amateur productions. Not the purest motive for writing a musical; impure motives can be counted on to bake dough that doesn't rise, I knew that. But I believed the show could be good and the money would enable me to write whatever I wanted without worrying about money.

I maneuvered and cajoled and I got Dick, Steve Sondheim (Oscar had

Dick Rodgers, Steve Sondheim and I working on three different shows
with the same title, i.e., *Do I Hear a Waltz?*

died), but not Mary Martin: Dick thought she was too old and since he was the producer, he had the money so he had the final say. But never mind: a score by Rodgers and Sondheim? Savor the songs, dry the martinis, cash the checks! By 1965, *The Time of the Cuckoo* was *Do I Hear a Waltz?* and theatre parties were signing up. Then came the first run-through.

There was a song, "Two by Two," that the heroine sang while the rest of the company walked around and around and around the stage in pairs; it seemed longer than all of Eugene O'Neill's plays including *Strange Interlude* performed in tandem. I knew from that moment. After the run-through, I went out and bought an expensive antelope coat. The sleeves weren't right, either. What happened? *Mea culpa.*

Steve and I were best friends; Dick Rodgers and I were casual acquaintances but Steve and Dick knew each other from way back when probably only Steve thought they might ever be peers. When they first met, Steve was a teenage fledgling lyricist-composer-librettist under the mentoring wing of Oscar Hammerstein, Dick's lyricist and librettist by then. Rodgers and Hammerstein were legends, Steve Sondheim was a precocious showbiz kid. Among the many achievements of time is troublemaking: Steve was now a wildly successful Broadway lyricist and a threatening Broadway composer, Oscar was dead and Dick needed a lyricist. Understandably, there was tension, largely from Dick's end. That tension may have exacerbated a problem Dick had, one his family and friends refused to see. It was their elephant on the coffee table and because Oscar hadn't seen it and he worshipped Oscar, Steve hadn't seen it either.

I caught a glimpse of the elephant at a meeting Steve, Dick and I had with the first director sought for the show: Franco Zeffirelli. It was held in Dick's well-appointed office which smelled of success and shone with success in the polished statuettes and framed plaques and citations on the shelves and walls. Zeffirelli both saw and smelled as he one-upped explaining, with international charm, his scheduling problem—the Met, La Scala, MGM, *helas!* He hoped it would not stand in his way, would not prevent him from doing this wondrous show, of course it would be wondrous! Whether his interest was real, we never knew because Dick fell asleep; the great man fell asleep right in the face of the other great man. Resentment? Desire for attention? Or something else? Something else, I suspected. The suspicion was verified at another meeting Steve and I had alone with Dick at his apartment.

Usually the three of us sat by the piano in the lovely, large living room decorated by Dick's beautiful wife, Dorothy. Decorating was but one of her talents; she wrote coffee-table books and invented the johnny mop. In view of Dick's wide reputation as a womanizer, if you were of the Freudian generation, that johnny mop started a train of thought. Which went faster after a look at the office she gave him in their apartment. It was small—not just Park Avenue small, small—and while the furnishings weren't secondhand, the room, unlike everything else Dorothy Rodgers decorated, would never make *Town & Country*. Not that Dick cared; for him, the most important feature of his little office was its own connecting john.

He went so many times, my melodramatic movie mind whizzed around like the ball on a roulette wheel. One remembered shot from an old black-and-white movie landed the ball in its slot. Excusing myself, I went to the john, locked the door and very quietly, very carefully lifted the cover off the toilet's water tank. Yes, the movie was *The Lost Weekend,* the shot was of Ray Milland lifting a bottle of booze out of the water tank of a toilet. Dick's bottle was neatly stashed in the corner. He drank vodka; it doesn't smell.

When we were trying out the show in Boston, he drank in the men's room of the Colonial Theatre. Standing guard at the door so his boss could put away the vodka undisturbed was Jerry Whyte. Jerry was Dick's man Friday every day; he accepted with a shrug that Dick was boozing in the men's room just as he accepted that the music for the show wasn't Dick at his best or anywhere near it. He said as much to me, sensing, I think, that I still had hopes. Jerry was a fact facer.

Hiring John Dexter, the brilliant English director, was my idea, a lousy one. I had enormous admiration for what John did with plays, contemporary and classic; since he had also directed operas, I figured he would be great for us. Moreover, he was no upper-class, stiff-upper-lip Brit; quite the opposite, he came from below, was politically aware, bright and very funny. What I didn't know was that he hated women. Not actresses, women. Actresses, he could be wonderful for, especially if they didn't take any shit from him and lashed back when he lashed out at them with a tongue dipped in his own patented brand of vitriol. He enjoyed when they hit back but American actresses were trained in the Method, not self-defense.

That he disliked Leona Samish was evidenced by his casting of the role and his treatment of the actress he cast. Her acting sufficed but her persona was as cold as a knife and humorless. What she did have was a big voice; that was what Dick was listening for, so Dick went along with John over my objections and that was that. A collaborator and producer in one and the same person is a combination devoutly to be avoided. And Steve? At that point, he was apathetic leaning toward sour about the whole show. A professional nonetheless, he worked hard despite the treatment he got—not from the director, from the producer-composer.

One person on the show was a gay deceiver in several senses: Wakefield Poole, John's assistant-cum-choreographer for what little choreography there was. A mild, bland, nice fellow, Wake had a sweet, pretty wife which was incongruous with the bigger surprise that came long after the show: Wake made a kind of history with the first feature-length gay porno, *Boys in the Sand.* Knowing John, it shouldn't have been that much of a surprise.

Whatever interest he had in the show vanished after that first disastrous run-through. He gave up. He went through the motions: he sat with me, going over the lines for everything from laughs to intentions but he never did anything about it. For him, the curtain was down. In Boston, I threatened to appeal to Dick as producer if John didn't at least have a rehearsal. He grinned wickedly and called for one that very night—during intermission.

Earlier, in New Haven, where it was immediately obvious we were in trouble, he didn't rehearse, he wouldn't. What he did do was have a different hustler sent up from New York each night. While the hustler saw the show, John stayed in his hotel room smoking joints, having a much better time than anyone. He laughed about it. He may have panicked, being unaccustomed to Broadway knives, out-of-town tryouts and the terrifying demands of making a new musical work. Surely, though, he'd panicked before? Who in the theatre hasn't had at least one cold-sweat moment of panic? But you take a deep breath and on you go.

For John, it must have been a great relief when Herb Ross was called in to supply some real choreography. Herb arrived with Nora—his wife, by then—who immediately camped it up with John and every homosexual in the chorus. I don't know of a single homosexual who didn't absolutely adore Nora Kaye, with one exception: Wally Siebert, a dancer with Ballet Theatre when she was a ballerina and I was sleeping with both of them. What Nora didn't know, she sensed—oh, she had antennae! Wally claimed she held back his career in Ballet Theatre because of me. If she did, it was because he, a Southerner and a ballet purist, had contempt for her unclassical feet; when she danced *Giselle,* he would hiss, "Spoons! Spoons!" from the wings. Nora heard; Nora was subtle; Nora could be ruthless.

Nora's camping wasn't without purpose: it relaxed Dexter which relaxed the whole company and they went all out for Herb. She levitated the atmosphere for him his whole career. With Steve as with me, she had no work to do. Besides being old friends, we had all worked together on *Anyone Can Whistle,* for which Herb and Nora had done one of the best and funniest ballets seen in any musical. Steve and I were ready and receptive when Herb reminded us that with *Whistle* we had been breaking the musical out of the mold in which we were now stuck with *Waltz.* Delightedly, we joined hands and got down to work.

Steve and Dick wrote a new song, which had one of the best tunes in the show. Steve's lyric struck exactly the right tone: rueful, relieved by wit, and then deepened by an arrow to the heart. The song was perfect for Leona and the moment; it even allowed Herb to choreograph a dance number, limited though he was by a chorus whose main qualification was that they were good in threesomes. Dancers are far better in that category than singers, so there were a few Herb could use. He worried that the finished number resembled *Fancy Free* in form; nevertheless, it was one of the few bright musical spots in the show. Everyone was so encouraged, another new song was put in the works. When it was presented, wounds that had been festering from the beginning opened up and pus spurted out.

The songwriting procedure Dick and Steve followed was first the melody, then the lyric. Dick was at the piano on the stage of the Colonial, the whole company gathered to hear the new song to be sung by the pretty, stupid wife and her anguished husband. Dick had previewed the tune to applause. Steve came in and handed the lyric to him. I had seen it. It was not the expected boy-girl number the tune suggested; it fit the melody for the first deceptive chorus, then played against it for the second chorus with an edge that was sharp, satiric, and slightly nasty. The song was moved up and out of its conventional doldrums by that lyric. Dick read it. His face reddened; he flipped the lyric to the floor.

"This is shit!" He was furiously contemptuous. "I'm not going to let my singers sing shit like this!"

I think "my singers" was worse than "shit." The company stood frozen as a photograph—horrified, embarrassed, and eager to run to a telephone.

Temporary wooden steps from the auditorium to the stage had been set up for rehearsal. Steve came down them, down the aisle to where Jerry Whyte and I were standing in the back. Anger was no stranger to Steve—he was a very angry young man—but he had never shown it, not to me, anyway, until that moment. Even then, it was Jerry Whyte he looked at. Oh, he was angry at Dick all right, he was furious at him, but it was me he was really angry at and that anger went deep.

"I've had it," he said. "I'm not taking any more from him. I'm leaving."

He didn't leave. The song went in, though without the second chorus that gave it its point. We all continued to work on the musical numbers, fixing little odds and ends—potchkeying, my mother would have called it. Nora and Herb cozied up to John Dexter—they were vehement Anglophiles, but still—and Steve moved into that camp. Dick continued to drink in the men's room during rehearsals which were never of the scenes. The scenes remained underrehearsed and inadequately played by the two leads. After we opened in New York, I wrote Dick a letter—he wouldn't be seen in person by me or answer

Escorting Lena to the opening of *Do I Hear a Waltz?* at the theatre
that is now named for the composer Steve and I did battle with.

the phone—asking if I might rehearse the company. The cast wanted it; they
knew the show could be improved; there were a good many theatre parties: if
they enjoyed the show more, we could run longer, the company would have
jobs longer, etc. Dick barred me from the theatre. It was official: "Arthur Laurents is not allowed backstage." For *Gypsy* I had written the line "The mother
of Miss Gypsy Rose Lee is not allowed backstage." Virtual life imitating virtual art? Or merely plagiarism?

Do I Hear a Waltz? opened to a consensus of disappointment. Regret was ap-
portioned among the leading lady and the leading man (too young and no
actor), the director and the score, the music getting the worst of it. *Mea culpa*
I said before, and it was. The cardinal, the fundamental mistake I made was
pushing blindly to make my dream a reality and getting Richard Rodgers and

With Goddard Leiberson and Stephen Sondheim during the recording of
Anyone Can Whistle, Steve and I only look young.

Stephen Sondheim to work together. Dick's daughter, Mary, aided and abetted but at least her reasons were very personal. She worshipped and loved Steve; she believed he would be helpful to her father whom she wanted badly to requite her love. No, the mistake was mine.

Dick Rodgers was a famous composer I knew casually from meetings of the Dramatists Guild's council and from another, richer world—the parties Irene Selznick took me to until I saw the dog beneath their skin and stopped going. Dick seemed pleasant if imperial—he was Broadway royalty—but removed, rather melancholic. His visits to Payne Whitney, allegedly for nervous breakdowns but in reality for drying out, were not known to me until after *Do I Hear a Waltz?*

If someone had told me he was past his composing prime, I wouldn't have listened. He had moved easily from Larry Hart to Oscar Hammerstein and another level, he could move easily to Stephen Sondheim and another level with his glorious melodic talent intact. So I believed, so I wished, so I hoped.

Steve wanted the recognition as a composer he had gotten as a lyricist. I knew that. Like Dick, he too came from another, richer world, but he was younger, not yet molded, still open and basically centered on one thing: making his mark as a composer-lyricist in the theatre.

Theatre was the basis of our friendship. We saw each other or talked on the phone almost every day. A year earlier, we had survived the splendid failure of *Anyone Can Whistle* intact and proud. I had done three musicals with him: *West Side Story, Gypsy,* and *Whistle.* I couldn't conceive of doing a musical with anyone else.

Steve didn't want to do a musical of *The Time of the Cuckoo.* As much as he liked the play, he didn't think it would make a musical; he didn't believe Leona sang; and he did not want to work with Dick Rodgers. Oscar was his attachment, the man he admired, not Dick. I pushed and pleaded, Mary pleaded, and at last we persuaded him. Some thirty years later, I learned we hadn't persuaded him. He wrote the lyrics for *Do I Hear a Waltz?* because of his fear that if he didn't, he would lose me as a friend. Which is revealing about him in 1965. He wouldn't have lost me as a friend, he never did, not even when he dropped me.

Dick was twitchy with Steve from their first day of collaboration. The boy he had met with Oscar in Bucks County was now a peer—hard to accept. Worse, the boy was on the way up and Dick was on the way down. His resentment grew and he began to treat Steve as below if not beneath him. Steve rightly resented that and began to resent me because it was I who had gotten him into this untenable situation which, in addition, was headed for flopdom. *Mea maxima culpa.* There was no way that collaboration could ever have worked. From the start, I doomed the show, determined to get what I mistakenly wanted.

The failure of the show didn't bother me anything nearly as much as the hiatus it led to in my friendship with Steve. The rupture had been building as he grew up and away and restless: he didn't want to be so strongly influenced by me. He admitted that, though not to me. To me, he simply suggested we cool our relationship for a while. Rejection is rejection: I was angered and froze. There was no sneering or sniping, we were politely distant for several years, too many. Every once in a while, always when he was drunk—one occasion I remember vividly was in a London taxicab while we were there for *Gypsy* with Angela Lansbury—he would come careening back, but oh, what a high horse I got on!

In 1997, a taped recording of a concert version of *Do I Hear a Waltz?* that had just been performed in London was sent to Steve. Acted poorly, sung operatically, the show nevertheless excited him. He heard how *Cuckoo* could be a musical, how Leona was so vulnerable, she could sing; and he heard that most of the problem with the show was that most of the music was not very good. When he called to convey this, his voice rang with enthusiasm and the delight he felt because he knew it would delight me. He sent me the tape and then we discussed what might be done about *Do I Hear a Waltz?*—probably nothing which is of no matter. He had listened with the ear of a best friend.

CHAPTER FOUR

Change of Direction
I Can Get It for You Wholesale,
with Stark and Merrick vs.
Streisand

WELL, WELL. Ray Stark suddenly was claiming that *The Way We Were* began with him. When the reviews get better with time, everybody wants in on the act. To be fair, one point of origin is as good and as arbitrary as another; since he was the producer of the picture, he could say it began with him. He was the producer and the picture might have pleased Fanny Brice, who was his mother-in-law, much to her disgust.

The woman who became a star as a low-comedy Jewish clown was the same woman who collected contemporary art and antique furniture and introduced the little black dress to New York. That woman thought Ray wasn't classy enough for her daughter Fran, but Ray thrived on opposition and was determined to prove her wrong: he bought a Henry Moore for the lawn overlooking the sunken tennis court he had added to the old Bogart-Bacall house not quite in Beverly Hills, a Frank Stella for his New York pied-à-terre in a commercial block on East Fifty-seventh Street, and came close to producing something Fanny might have liked with his stage and screen productions of *Funny Girl,* the musical glamorization of her life. By that time, unfortunately, Fanny was dead and it was Barbra Streisand who didn't think Ray was classy enough.

He wouldn't and couldn't be put down by his newly minted star. Ray was always fun, even when he was being ruthless—a synonym for sensible to him. He took Barbra and her newly acquired Klimts in his usual stride. She could turn down the scripts he sent her for as long as she wanted; there was no way Barbra Streisand was going to make another picture until she made the picture she owed Ray Stark under her contract with him. Of course, they both knew they were going to make a picture, they just didn't know what picture.

Ray figured I might know so he took me to lunch in New York. He had turned to me once before to write what became *Funny Girl.* Repeating myself was always to be avoided; I had already done a backstage story in *Gypsy,* so I turned him down. Rejection was one area where Ray was like the vast majority: what doesn't come easy is an aphrodisiac. He was determined to get me this time, more so because he knew I had a history with Streisand that could help his cause.

I had jump-started her career by casting her in her first Broadway show, *I Can Get It for You Wholesale.* When she came in to audition for me—I was direct-

With the principle actors in *I Can Get It For You Wholesale* in 1961.
Top row from the left: Ken Leroy, Jack Kruschen, Barbra Streisand and Harold Lang; *below them:* Elliott Gould and Lillian Roth; *seated, front:* Marilyn Cooper, Bambi Lynn and Marilyn Lovell who was replaced by an electric Sheree North.
Standing: the first-time director of a musical.

ing—there was no part for her. One role was still open—Miss Marmelstein, the secretary to the dress company's boss. But Miss M. was a fifty-year-old spinster and Barbra was nineteen. True, with her bird's nest of scraggly hair and her gawky, disorganized body, she was a poster girl for Spinster Incarnate. Equally true was the debit side: thrift shop clothes which proclaimed eccentricity, behavior which was calculated spontaneity.

After an elaborate shedding of an old movie star wrap—all the while clutching feverishly at a slipping pile of sheet music—she clumped across the stage as though her knees had just been buckled on and dumped the music on the top of the upright piano. A whispered conference with the accompanist, a trilling giggle, then she marched center stage to the chair she had ordered. As she did, the music accordioned across the stage after her. Funny, attention getting, a good trick, and the trilling giggle of feigned surprise on its way to becoming a trademark.

Nothing she did was simple. She didn't just sit in the chair—she sprawled in it, flung her legs out, took them back, wrapped her arms around them, under them, across them, elaborately chewing gum and chattering as though we out front were the audience on her talk show. When I managed to break in and asked if she would sing, she thought about it, took the wad of gum from her mouth and stuck it under the chair before starting. After the audition I had the chair checked: no gum underneath.

A performance, all of it—some intriguing, some irritating—and then she sang. Eight bars into her first song, I knew she had to be in the show. She began with a comedy number from an Off-Broadway revue she'd been in, then "Sleepin' Bee" followed by "Soon It's Gonna Rain." I would have had her sing every song she knew just to sit back and revel in the glory of that voice. When she sang, she was simple; when she sang, she was vulnerable; when she sang, she was moving, funny, mesmerizing, anything she wanted to be. The authors were beaming, the producer wasn't thrilled but if Barbra Streisand's agent could have read my mind, he would have asked a fortune for her to play Miss Marmelstein.

Life in the theatre is very different from life in the movies. While waiting for rehearsals to begin, I sent Barbra to Goddard Leiberson, the head of Columbia Records. He listened to her sing and sent me a note saying: "Barbra Streisand is indeed very talented but I'm afraid she's too special for records." Later, when he came out of town to see *Wholesale*—he was going to record the cast album for Columbia and nobody did that better than Goddard—he signed her to a deal that cost him a lot more than it would have had he signed her earlier. She was always an acquired taste.

Goddard wasn't the only one who didn't get her early on. In Boston after a performance, some of the company would go to a club where she would get up and sing. In a movie, the patrons would stop talking, an orchestra would sneak in, and she would finish to a standing ovation. In Boston, there was no orchestra and they didn't stop talking: she wasn't Barbra Streisand yet, she was an ungainly girl singing overdramatically in a dress from Filene's basement.

When I dragged Steve Sondheim to hear her at a Greenwich Village cellar called the Bon Soir, he found her voice too pinched and nasal. When I asked her to record some of the songs he wrote for *Anyone Can Whistle,* he wasn't Stephen Sondheim yet. By then she, however, was a Movie Star; she never even replied to my note. Years later, to his delight, she recorded several of his songs, including two from *Whistle,* on her new album. Even the great need validation before life is like life in the movies.

Barbra's only stage experience before her audition was in that Off-Broadway revue, which lasted one night. *Wholesale,* her first Broadway show, was also the first musical I directed, on or off Broadway. It was also the first for a tall, shy, striking-looking young lady—I use the term advisedly—as talented in her field as Streisand was in hers and with a heart that matched her talent.

I went to see *The Saintliness of Margery Kempe,* an Off-Broadway play set in medieval times—in those days, I would see anything. Off-Broadway, Off-Off-Broadway, I saw all of it and kept going, reinforcing myself with THC as the years passed and the plays became defiantly un-well-made. I don't remember much about *Margery Kempe* except the title and the costumes. They dazzled with a color sense equaled only by Irene Sharaff's but subtler; they moved with the actors, something costumes rarely do; and, unbelievably, sixty costumes had been made for two hundred dollars. The designer had cut and sewed most of them herself—also the explanation of why they moved so well. Her name was Theoni V. Aldredge; "Aldredge" from her husband Tom, a fine actor, "V." for her Greek maiden name and the touch of Medea lying in wait.

To provide a theatricality not exactly abundant in a musical set on a sleazy Seventh Avenue, I had asked the scenic designer, Will Steven Armstrong, to do the sets and drops in black, white, and gray, each with a bold slash of a different color: blue for a kitchen, crimson for a nightclub, and so forth. Will Steven was like a lapsed monk—who else would use both Christian names? An unnaturally quiet young man, he had done very well the season before with *Carnival* for the same producer: David Merrick. Merrick, almost as famous for his classically cheap toupee as for his productions, was obsessed with red: Stop Red, Matador Red and, in his office, Blood Red. In his desire to give Merrick red and me black, white, and gray, Will Steven came up with pink. *I Can Get It for You Wholesale* was a tough, harsh, abrasive show set in the

Depression. Whatever its dominant color should have been, pink was not on the list unless as in pinko.

Merrick was not pleased. Repainting, however, cost money, so his displeasure was expressed in grunts and grimaces. Anger, he left to me. I matched Will Steven's unnatural calm with calm unnatural for me. He listened, his mouth never opening, his expression never changing, his eyes never leaving the floor. I pleaded; I joked about "Think Pink"; I lost my manufactured patience and yelled like a banshee. Nothing. Enter Theoni as Medea. Even as Medea her voice is little more than a whisper but it cuts like a German knife.

"Excuse me, sir," she said to Will Steven, "but you are destroying the show and yourself. That is your business. You are also destroying Mr. Laurents. That is my business. I will help you give the man what he wants. Where are the paintbrushes?"

The pinkish tone wasn't completely eliminated but the show received much praise for its "Brechtian look." Will Steven Armstrong had done it again. As Rose says in *Gypsy*, "that's show business." Rose—a name closer to pink but a character bloody and red. No wonder Merrick liked *Gypsy.*

He had taken a chance hiring me to direct *I Can Get It for You Wholesale.* We had worked together on *Gypsy,* which he produced with Leland Hayward. After the first run-through, he cornered me in the back of the theatre and said Jerry Robbins was ruining what was my show: I should be directing it instead. Flattering, but with Merrick, the smell of rat was always in the air. And as I found out with *Wholesale,* his producing philosophy was basic Machiavelli: Keep the creative elements at one another's throats and you'll get their best work. And he admitted it. That was what was disarming about David Merrick: he would admit anything—and then offer a disclaimer.

"Homosexuals are taking over the theatre," he complained loud and long to the press.

"One more interview like that," I warned him, "and we won't work for you."

His faux-macho general manager (with a penchant for Puerto Rican boys) signaled frantically behind Merrick's back for me to lay off. Merrick wasn't fazed.

"It's only for publicity. I wouldn't have anyone on my staff who wasn't homosexual. They have no one to go home to so they work late and don't complain."

In a taxi when we were out of town with *Wholesale,* he mused about one of his big backers: "He doesn't like girls, he doesn't like boys. I don't understand anyone who doesn't do something, do you?"

"Oh, no," I agreed. "Everyone does something, I'm just not always sure what. I imagine you masturbating over someone's dirty underwear in a closet."

He stuttered a few little chuckles to cover himself, as though to say he knew it was a joke, it had to be a joke, please say it was a joke. I wondered if I had hit on something.

One of the reasons he liked me was that he made me laugh. If he made many others laugh, it was in fear. What I liked most about him was that his love and respect for the theatre were genuine. He was dismissed—enviously, I think—as a commercial producer, which he also was. When a show was panned, he would sigh, "Time to tack up posters in the men's room again." Other producers, including those of *West Side Story,* laughed when he began tacking up his posters in the subway—until his box office sales jumped; then they all followed suit. While he produced shows he judged to be commercial under his name, he also produced artistically venturesome and controversial plays like *Marat/Sade* under the safe umbrella of his foundation. Ironically, the financial batting average for the foundation productions was higher. On a percentage basis, the investment return on the supposedly risky shows was much greater than the return on the supposedly commercial ones. A message sent but never received, to this day.

When Merrick asked me to direct *Wholesale,* curious how much faith he had in the show, I asked what the budget would be. Not much—no surprise—but I had long wanted to become a director in self-defense, figuring I couldn't do worse than the directors I had worked with. My first directorial job was *Invitation to a March,* the play I wrote after *Gypsy.* Merrick must have read the praise I got for my direction. He also must have been turned down by the big-name directors he went after first for *Wholesale.*

The book had been adapted by Jerome Weidman from his rather nasty novel: the writing was timid but possibility was there. What the show needed was a hard edge, a theatrical toughness to sweep it off the sidewalks of Seventh Avenue and let it come alive in the gutter. I thought it wouldn't be very difficult for Weidman and Harold Rome (who wrote the score) to get that hard edge—get it with my suggestions as opposed to the customary imperious, roughshod intrusion of the director on territory that artistically, legally, rightfully belonged to the authors. Ever the idealist.

Merrick had no objection to Theoni as costume designer: she came cheap. Barbra also came cheap but halfway through rehearsals he began objecting to her. By the time we went out of town, he was on my back to fire her and Elliott Gould, the antihero in the play whom Barbra had fallen in love with during intermissions. They were both ugly, Merrick complained, and that when Elliot danced, the first rows were sprayed with sweat (they were) and that Barbra wasn't funny. Which she wasn't out of town; it wasn't until New York that she found her audience. That was when she began to stop thinking of herself as homely.

Halfway through rehearsals, she had asked why she couldn't play the heroine.

"Be content where you are," I told her. I had been fattening her part. "You're going to steal the show."

"It's because I'm not pretty, isn't it?"

It was, though I didn't say it. That year, the audience wouldn't have accepted her as the heroine. Two years later, she was in fashion, a contemporary Nefertiti.

While waiting for *Wholesale* rehearsals, I helped with her debut in an uptown supper club, the elegant Blue Angel. She was rehearsing on the tiny stage, perched on a stool. "Don't look down," I interrupted.

"Why not?"

"The lights."

"On my nose."

"On your double chin."

She did have a double chin. She also had beautiful skin and exuded sex, which was very much on her mind. Contrary to all polls, it wasn't the nose that was off-putting, it was the eyes: too close together, too small and at that time, one could slip out of alignment. When she made her first record album, I suggested that for the cover photograph, she have her back to the camera.

"Because you think I'm not pretty."

"Because I think you need mystery."

She huffed and refused the advice. On the cover of her second album, her back was to the camera.

Changing fashion wasn't all that made her more attractive; what she thought of her face played an equal part. Her opinion of her looks has been the measure of her dissatisfaction far more than the accepted chilly mother who actually brought her homemade chicken soup to *Wholesale* rehearsals and very good it was. The key to that opinion was the way Barbra dressed. As her opinion of herself climbed, her outrageously outlandish clothes disappeared. These days she tends to dress with a simplicity that is stylish. Still, each morning she must look in her unrelenting mirror over the bathroom sink: Have a good day. Her gay audience identifies with her stormy self-rejection and empathizes.

. . .

Although Merrick was kindly disposed to people who came cheap, I had to do battle with him to get Herb Ross as choreographer. Herb's first Broadway choreography had been for a Merrick musical. "Too artsy fartsy" was Merrick's considered opinion; "turkey lurkey" was his appraisal of the show as a whole. Herb and he had been suing and countersuing for so long, it wasn't difficult to get both to back off. The doubts I had about Herb's choreographic talents I discarded now that he was married to Nora.

Tom Hatcher and I had been living together for more than three years when Nora told me about Herb. She and I had no romantic loose ends dangling, Tom liked her, she liked him, the three of us melded. She came out to Quogue so often I didn't realize she had a particular mission the summer weekend she sort of told me about Herbie.

We were drifting, lazing on Shinnecock Bay in a motorboat Tom and I used for waterskiing. He had taught me and we both enjoyed teaching our friends. On his first attempt to get up, Steve Sondheim threw his back out and that was that. For Mary Rodgers, bouncing along the water as she came up was a sexual pleasure. Hal Prince gave us a bitch of a time. He was determined to get up on skis. A determined Hal is a successful Hal: he got up and when he got up, he clutched the tow bar hard as he could and stayed firmly and safely in the middle of the wake behind the boat, never veering right or left. When the boat had to turn, Hal refused. He simply let go of the rope, sat down in the water, and waited for us to come around and get him up again.

For Nora, it was an exertion merely to get in the boat. Now that she had given up dancing, she didn't even want to walk. Her final appearances were in a ballet company Herb had formed around her. They did a brief, unsuccessful European tour with some ballets he had "made" for her, as the Arlene Croces have it—though why "choreographed" is disdained is a mystery to me: it's accurate, precisely descriptive. One doesn't "make" a play, one writes a play. One can "make" a movie but that's because there are so many cooks—oh, well, ballet and its language exist in a world unto itself. About the end of Nora's dancing:

Driving through the Black Forest in Germany, she threw her toe shoes out the window and almost imploded, she was so happy—happy her feet would stop hurting, happy she could stop dieting, happy to be free of her career and free to devote herself to Herb's career.

That lazy afternoon in the motorboat, she asked casually: "Would you be shocked if I said I might marry Herb Ross?"

I knew her too well. "Congratulations."

She giggled. "What do you mean?"

"You've already married him."

Tom showing me . . .

. . . how to walk on water.

She had but wouldn't admit it until drinks later and a lot of them. It's staggering how much and how heedlessly we drank at that time, and how we relied successfully on spicy-hot Bloody Marys the next morning to clean the sinuses and convince the head it would stay on.

One Quogue weekend with Nora and Lena Horne sharing the guest bedroom, to get us ready for a cocktail party at a house down the beach, Lena made Sazeracs, a specialty she had picked up in New Orleans. An hour or so later—"or so" probably means closer to two hours—the four of us wove our way down the beach to the party; another hour or two or so later, the ballerina, the diva and their hosts came crawling back along the sand on all fours.

Herb Ross had made a name with two remarkable ballets: *The Maids,* based on the Genet play, performed by androgynous men on pointe, and *Goyescas,* theatrically stunning vignettes of Goya paintings. While his cultivated visual style was apparent wherever he lived, his taste was expensive. Making a name in ballet is not making a name at Chase Manhattan so he was forced to do a lot of television in the style of the late, great June Taylor, the tube's Busby Berkeley. One of the unfortunate by-products of doing work you have contempt for is that when the chance comes to do what you want, you can go overboard with pretentiousness. Herb's chance came when Ballet Theatre invited him to participate in its Sunday Night series of new ballets at the Phoenix Theatre downtown.

Herb Ross and Nora: a good marriage.

Devoutly believing that ballet and she herself would fade away without new choreographers, Nora was generous with herself and her time. She danced a couple of regrettables for Herb; then came one he choreographed for her and Erik Bruhn, the most princely dancer of his time. Just two superb performers, the Lunts in ballet shoes, tragically doomed in a Thomas Mann *Magic Mountain* tuberculosis sanatorium, dancing to music from *Tristan und Isolde* in a room with walls of billowing white chiffon, a white bed, and a white radiator. Nora Kaye and Erik Bruhn in white—clinging, coughing and after very long lust, expiring.

"If you ever do a Herb Ross ballet again," I said in Nora's dressing room afterward, "we're finished."

She suppressed those giggles as Bruhn walked in. We were introduced, we chatted; not a word about the ballet but more than one wire crackled.

The first time I visited Copenhagen—in the early Fifties, that was—Erik Bruhn was dancing with the Royal Danish Ballet. I hesitated, then went backstage. Over wine later, we talked about Nora. He had learned so much from her about acting that he was eager to dance with her again and learn more. However aptly Nora was called the Duse of the Dance, it was her antic humor that captivated this not melancholy, alabaster Dane.

Although Danes are even more hospitable than Americans, I was surprised when Bruhn invited me to his home for either a late lunch or an early dinner, I wasn't certain which and was so pleased to be invited, didn't ask. His mother cooked and served the meal, yet I never met her. I never even saw her. She passed the plates across a pass-through between the kitchen and dining room; Erik served, we ate, he cleared. Very strange to me, ordinary to him. Even stranger, the conversation was very personal. Was it only Jewish mothers who eavesdropped?

A decision about a bad knee was troubling him. Due to serve his required time in Denmark's army, he could get a medical exemption with the knee even though the same knee couldn't prevent him from dancing if treated regularly and not overtested in dance. He was aware I had been in the U.S. Army and probably—no, undoubtedly—aware of what I thought of his fellow dancers who hadn't, he was that perceptive. Even so, he wanted my frank opinion of his options.

There was a difference: it was not wartime and while the army had no real need for him, there was a need, I said, for one of the greatest dancers in the world to dance as long as he could for himself, for ballet and—a little hyperbolic but what the hell, for Denmark. The argument made sense because it was true and because we were lying naked in bed in my room at the top of the

Hotel Angleterre. The mullioned windows were open to moonlight which really was silver and really did pour in.

Erik Bruhn didn't go into the Army. He became world famous, so revered and respected that Denmark was proud and grateful. How persuasive I'd been, I never knew. Whether he even remembered that night, I never knew either, but the memory was more than enough for me.

The book of *Wholesale* had nine principal roles, each potentially juicy, so I thought of the show as a musical ensemble play rather than a musical comedy. A Conception, that was called. "The Elia Kazan Production" vs. "An Elia Kazan Production"—such designations were old hat, we were in the era of Concept Musicals. Directors no longer just directed musicals, they Conceived them. The importance of the Conception was emphasized by the box they demanded be put around their names and by the size of their billing. More: the Conceptualists asked for and got ten percent of whatever the authors got. Not I. Not then, at any rate; by the time I directed *La Cage Aux Folles* I got the ten percent which I thought well deserved. At the time of *Wholesale,* however, I was still maintaining it was a playwright's theatre and regarded myself as a director, period. Building the nine principals into an ensemble of singing-dancing actors was a decision, not a Conception. I cast them with as many distinctively individual performers as I could get. One was Lillian Roth, a haunted woman from the past hungry for a present.

Fairly well known on Broadway and in pictures, she became a Name with her autobiography, *I'll Cry Tomorrow,* and became a Star when Susan Hayward played her in the movie. The book was honest about her alcoholism and unsparing, brutally graphic in its description of hitting bottom on Skid Row in Los Angeles. What saved Roth was a man linked in her mind to his "My name is Bert and I'm an alcoholic." Bert twelve-stepped Lillian into AA; she fell in love with him and they married. An uplifting ending for the Susan Hayward movie but not life. Not too long after the marriage, Lillian Roth's new life ended.

The book had been a moneymaking best-seller; Bert was a pilot, she had flown to Australia with him and become a seminal figure by starting AA there. For the first time in a lurid life, Lillian Roth knew what it was like to be happy. Then Bert walked out. He left her for a man, took her money, and there she was, again at the edge of the abyss AA had pulled her out of but dumped back there by the man she linked with AA.

Once an alcoholic, always an alcoholic; that was why Bert had said "My name is Bert and I'm an alcoholic." A drink would surely make Lillian feel better; if her body couldn't take the beating again, then it couldn't and so what?

Seething with anger, she went to a meeting and told them what she thought of all of them. They listened without comment and held out their hands in support; she hung on to the hands, stayed sober and came to rehearsals sober.

In the second act of *Wholesale,* Lillian had a song called "Eat a Little Something," a plaintive Jewish mother chicken soup song that didn't go anywhere. After she finished, her son (played by Elliott Gould) had a monologue in which he confessed he had betrayed his partner and stolen from him: a lump followed by a lump. I put Lillian's song and Elliott's monologue together, intercutting them. Her moment of realization that her son was a shit came in midsong. It should have been touching; it wasn't. Lillian couldn't make the moment; nothing happened outside because nothing was happening inside. We talked about her character, his character, the revelation; she understood but the moment eluded her, she was just singing a Harold Rome song about chicken soup. I asked if there wasn't something in her life she could use. She shrugged; she didn't think so; she didn't think about Bert.

I knew about Bert. I had held her clammy hand when she was so nervous about auditioning for an obviously skeptical Merrick that she couldn't stand up. She literally trembled sitting down, rattled away, spewing out any and everything that came into her head. Bert came into her head, the whole ugly, unhappy story of his betrayal poured out, I think to reassure herself nothing as bad could happen. I debated.

A Method actor can use or not use his own life, the choice is his. But I was the director, not the actor; it wasn't my life. Lillian was the actor; it was her life. Tipping the scale the other way was my desire to have her succeed in spades and, admittedly, to have the show succeed, but that was less. I wanted her to win over Bert. I went for it. I took her aside her and said:

"Think of Bert."

That was all. She went white as though she might faint. She never looked at me, just turned and walked. For one ghastly moment, I thought she was going to walk out of the room and head for the nearest bar but she didn't. She took her position for the top of the song. Elliott took his place, Lillian nodded to the pianist and they began. When she got to the moment, she did nothing, just picked her head up, looked at Elliott and saw Bert. The few people in the room stopped being bored and cried. She was magnificent then and every time she played the scene and so was Elliott. She never said a word to him, to me, to anyone, but Bert had helped her in spite of himself.

I questioned myself whether it was worth it. For the show, it obviously was: the moment was unforgettable. For Lillian, it was her comeback and possibly even an exorcism. Actors say they are the vulnerable people in the theatre because they are out there and exposed but nobody ever knew Lillian was exposing her insides. Isn't that why authors can be hurt so badly by critics? The actor is only hurt personally if his physical attributes are attacked which is rare. And the director? He's safe; he can be as ruthless as he wants; he is only exposing others.

One audition was as memorable as Barbra Streisand's, though only to me: Harold Lang's. Our relationship had never gone anywhere but had never completely gone away, either. Over the years, we had occasionally seen each other, less occasionally ended up in bed—once when he was in *Kiss Me Kate* and the last time in 1952, almost a decade before *Wholesale,* when he was starring in the revival of *Pal Joey.* Since then, though we hadn't seen each other, there were sporadic late-night calls from towns of all sizes except major; he was always affectionate and always drunk.

He had become an alcoholic. When he did get the odd job in a summer tour or a winter package, he went onstage sober, then drank himself into happy Harold after the performance. The thousands he made in *Joey* were swallowed in drinks for himself and everybody else at the bar: he was a sport. That was the casting director's report before Harold walked in. It didn't prepare me for what he looked like.

From the wings came a seedy man in a thin suit; older, with a moustache and deep lines, trying to focus. Then he felt the lights. There was the big boyish sexual grin, there were the still-eager blue eyes blinking behind what I knew were contact lenses as he came down front center stage. Suddenly I was nervous, whether because I wanted him again or because I wanted him to be good and get the job, I wasn't sure.

I went up on the stage to say hello and put him at ease. He didn't need to be put at ease, I did. Then, as I reached to shake his hand, the smell of stale booze hit so hard, I hugged him to pretend he didn't smell. I didn't want him. I could feel him sweating with so much fear, I wanted him to give a good enough audition so I could hire him.

When I asked him to read, he read better than I thought he would; when I asked him to sing, he sang almost as youthfully as ever in that imitable, Keith Davis–Hugh Martin trained voice. I couldn't ask him to dance, and Herb and Nora said he didn't have to for them.

"Hello, sweetums!" she called out.

Back in Ballet Theatre days when they were both sleeping with me, she and Harold had hardly been enamored of each other but she had called him "sweetums" anyway. He knew her and knew her power, recognized she still had it. He laughed, did a few jokey steps but they were fast and fleet; two pirouettes, steady and clean; then finished with his arms opened wide, his hands out to the audience and smiled big: Harold Lang was still here.

. . .

Rehearsals were during an icy New York winter. Harold had only a raincoat as thin as his suit so I gave him an overcoat I didn't wear much. Unfortunately, the ability to give an overcoat vs. the need for one underlined the gap between where I was and he was. He thanked me but kept his distance. Having a job allowed him to run up a tab. When he danced, the beads of sweat with which he peppered the air were scented with whiskey but always from the night before: he came to rehearsal and left rehearsal cold sober.

Whether or not he was happy, he acted happy. No one in the company was cheerier; the cast doted on him with the exception of Barbra, who was involved only with herself and with Elliott. When she asked to be excused from rehearsal to appear on a local TV channel, she was so immersed in deciding what thrift shop remnant to wear that she was totally unprepared for my refusal. My explanation—if she were given permission, everyone would have to be given permission—had a logic that escaped her. She was different, she was special, she was going to be a star—a movie star, the theatre was merely en route—she had not a doubt in the world about that. Like a future star, she bypassed me and went to Herb for permission. He was important, he was the choreographer, he was staging her big song ("Miss Marmelstein")—would he excuse her? He sent her back to me. She went to the authors: they were important, it was their show. They sent her back to me. She sulked; future stars were not to be ignored.

Trying to direct her out of her excesses wasn't easy. Her Miss Marmelstein was very funny, a bizarre collection of idiosyncrasies which came from instinct and were probably rehearsed at home. The trouble was overkill: too many twitches and collapses, giggles and gasps, too many take-ums. Plus her infatuation with her falcon fingernails which led her to fling her hands in the air like a diva, not a secretary; so often, it was becoming a mannerism. She was an original, I didn't want to lose that; what I did want was to edit, to cut out the extraneous contortions. Annoyed and irritated, she glared. I persisted and it was worth it, whether she agreed or not.

Inexperience and a low threshold of boredom made it difficult for her to repeat but when she did, she was terrific. But she had to be active. When she sang or spoke, she was alive; when she had to listen, Miss Marmelstein went home and in her place stood Barbra Streisand, uncomfortable in a costume. Her Miss Marmelstein came from the fingernails, not from inside.

Possibly the hardest thing for an actor to do is to listen. The gypsies—chorus dancers and they always know everything to be known—whispered Barbra had an acting coach stashed in the back to help her. If she did, he didn't. She was simply incapable of just standing and listening. Pointing that out produced the by then familiar scowl which meant she was annoyed, angry with me but not for long. She knew I believed in her talent. She also knew I liked her but she couldn't figure how to use that.

Her excesses were not excessive to her; her fingernails only got longer. But the ability to listen—oh, she wanted that! As shrewd and as quick as she was, she couldn't get it and the frustration left her annoyed. As a director, I learned how to trick performances; you often have to. Listening is not a trick; it requires a skill only the best actors have: concentration. I couldn't help Barbra and she couldn't help herself. Luckily, it was a musical: she had that incredible voice. But also the fingernails.

I more than annoyed Harold, I angered him. That bewildered me. We were in Philly; the show was in deep trouble but out of the rewriting had come a dramatic scene that showed him off as an actor, not just a song-and-dance man. I staged it with a theatricality I knew was stunning and would land. It did. He went about his business with the discipline only dancers have but never saying yea, nay, or thanks. My hands were too full trying to rescue the sinking ship to attempt understanding.

Once the ship was safely afloat, I went to each dressing room to thank each actor for patience and support. When I got to Harold, I had barely started when he cut me off and shot up like a rocket. His fury was brief and startling: the scene I thought pleased him was killing him. And it was my fault! He was lucky to get through it because it followed immediately after his big dance number, left him no time to catch his breath let alone change his costume but I was so insensitive, I hadn't noticed any of that!

He was right, I hadn't. But there was nothing I could do about it; there was no way to move either the dance or the scene. I apologized. I didn't ask if he would rather I cut the scene, because he was so furious, he might have said a yes he didn't mean. Nobody wanted either the scene or the dance cut: both were too good and he was too good in both. I considered apologizing again but a first apology is felt, a second is forced and sounds as lame as it is. Besides, he had heard me; it wasn't what he wanted. The empty air was full of unfinished business. Never the one to make the first move, this time he did. Abruptly, he locked the door and lowered his pants. That was the last time we had sex; "made love" would not have been an apt euphemism.

Because of the show, we saw each other occasionally; after it closed, not at all. Then, just when memory was fading to a blur, there came one of those late-night drunk and affectionate phone calls. For a few years, calls came sporadically, the last from a college town in California where he was teaching dance and loving it. He was bubbling, a happy drunk, so good humored, a little shy with his affection but it was there. When we hung up, I drifted back into sleep thinking of him—not sexually, but how sweet he was. A month later, a woman identifying herself only as a friend of Harold's called from that college town to tell me he had died, of what she didn't say. Only that she knew Harold would have wanted me to know.

My most vivid remembrance is of the first time I saw him: in his white sailor suit, grinning on top of the bar in *Fancy Free.* The grin has slowly faded but has never quite disappeared.

He came off well in *Wholesale,* all nine principals did, Barbra best of all. Her legend began there, along with invented legends, some by the legend herself. One was my first though not by any means last firsthand experience in watching an invented story get credence and acceptance as fact merely by being repeated in interviews, articles and celebrity biographies. The Gospel According to Barbra relates a battle with me over the staging of "Miss Marmelstein" that went like this: Barbra wanted to use a chair on casters, I fought her; she wanted to roll around the stage on the chair during the song, I fought her; she won the battle and stopped the show cold opening night in Philadelphia, I capitulated. In point of fact, "Miss Marmelstein" was staged by Herb Ross and very inventively. It was his idea to use a chair on casters and it was he who directed the rolling around the stage. If she really had stopped the show cold opening night, David Merrick would never have wanted to fire her, but she couldn't have: it was dead before she came on.

The City of Brotherly Love once again had no love for a work I was connected with. The show was a dud, an egg, a bomb; in short, the critics hated it. They labeled it anti-Semitic because—like *What Makes Sammy Run?*—*I Can Get It for You Wholesale* had a sleazy, unethical antihero who was Jewish. Jews did not like that just as Negroes did not like Hitchcock's *Lifeboat* because the Negro in that picture packed a razor. Personally, I prefer to confront Jewish anti-Semitism as expressed in a line in the play *My Good Name.* There, a Jewish wife is horrified to discover that her upper-class Wasp husband is an unethical insider trader on the order of Michael Milken and Ivan Boesky.

"Do you think ignoble behavior is restricted to Jews?" he asks her.

Of course, my preference is probably linked to the fact that I wrote *My Good Name.*

After the devastating Philadelphia reviews, rewriting the book of *Wholesale* was the first order of the day and Jerry Weidman rewrote fast. Up to that point, my relations with the authors had been bliss. They were happy which made me happy. They wanted me, not Herb, to stage all the songs; they gave me presents—books, records, expensive sweaters—and then Jerry gave me his rewrites.

What is the point of not coming to the point when the water level of the sinking ship has reached First Class? If I gave the pages to the actors, I told Jerry, they would laugh. "Oh, I mean them to laugh," he said, laughing himself as though the rewrites were a prank. That encapsulated Jerome Weidman for me and ended that chapter. My vows not to steamroller the authors went out the window. The first Commandment of Out of Town with a Musical is "Survive!" The second is "Survive Now!" Like the demon devil I always thought directors were, I cut, I pasted, and—*mea culpa, mea culpa*—I went beyond other directors: I rewrote.

Poison-pen notes were slipped under my door nightly until they got too fat and had to be left at the front desk. They didn't make me feel guilty, there wasn't time for guilt, but they irritated. We were drowning, for Pete's sake! Ironically, the notes weren't from Jerry but from Harold Rome, whose songs I hadn't touched—well, except for the intercutting of "Eat a Little Something" and, oh yes, converting one group number into a solo for Barbra plus group. But Harold loved Barbra's voice which was a perfect match for the plaintive Jewish wail in his tunes. The atmosphere was polluted with sensitivity, insensitivity, fear, panic, stasis, frenetic work, exhaustion—an ordinary Out of Town with a Musical but with a welcome twist: the Boston reviews were terrific. Read carefully, however, not so terrific. There was an unwelcome comment: Elliot Norton, the revered dean of the Boston critics, went all out for the show but wrote that it had my "stamp" on it.

Shortly after dawn the morning the reviews came out, the authors summoned me to their suite. I hadn't had breakfast. No excuse: we were all in the Ritz-Carlton, they would order for me. By the time I showered, dressed, and went upstairs, an enormous breakfast was awaiting me. My favorite meal kept my mouth occupied while Jerry and Harold devoured me.

Standing on their legal rights as authors, they ordered everything restored to what it had been before I went to work: every scene, every word, every piece of staging. Second, but first on Jerry's shit list of my sins, he claimed Merrick had reported that while having a drink with him at the Variety Club in Philly, I had said quote that the show was a piece of shit but I could fix it with my stamp unquote.

As though on cue—and with David Merrick, it probably was—the door opened and the quoted himself entered. Nattily dressed, he was beaming: his authors were going for his director's jugular.

"Jerry, will you repeat what David told you I said about the show?" I asked.

Hesitantly: "Well, David, you said Arthur said the show was a piece of crap."

"No, 'shit,' was the word you quoted, Jerry. David told you I called the show a piece of 'shit.' " I lit a cigarette to go with the Ritz-Carlton's great coffee.

"You're a fucking liar, Weidman," Merrick said with his usual smile of ice. "And I will repeat the four-letter word: liar."

Jerry backed down but Merrick pursued like a cat after a rat until Jerry admitted he had lied: David had never said any of it. Merrick beamed, I beamed back, foolishly thinking it was all over. Merrick sighed a long ominous sigh. As a signatory to the Dramatists Guild contract, he unfortunately had to abide by the authors' demand for the restoration of everything I had changed. I had to put everything back. Exit with wig.

This wasn't the David Merrick I knew. This was a Merrick who was ordering me to return the show to the piece of blubber it had been. My choice was to do it or quit. Weidman snickered and said he had backed down only because he thought it was best to be tactful: he had quoted David correctly, I had called the show a piece of shit. What is beneath beneath contempt? I was never able to look squarely at Jerry Weidman again.

As I walked across Boston Common to rehearsal, I visualized telling the company we were going back to the Philly version that had sunk them. I couldn't do it. At the theatre, I called Merrick and told him I was leaving.

"I'll come over and say good-bye," he said.

He didn't get it. "I mean I'm quitting, I'm leaving the show," I said with heavy emphasis.

"I know," he said rather gaily. "I'll be over."

Rejected! Unwanted! A failure! I sat in the Colonial Theatre's beautiful baroque lounge a mass of dejection, waiting for the final kick while the cast unknowingly awaited doom in the auditorium. David arrived, all smiles and bonhomie, with Jerry and Harold trailing after him.

"He's quitting because he has to put everything back," Merrick told them. "So I'll have to close the show."

"Why?" a shocked Harold asked.

David looked at Harold as though he was the idiot child. "Who do you think's going to come in and take over this dog if it's the same turkey everybody knows it was in Philly?"

Bird or beast, they got the message.

So did I. Merrick was happier than if he had sold his rights for a capital gain of a million dollars. He had produced as a producer according to Merrick should produce. Laughing like a felon, he boasted he knew he'd had to find a way to get me to quit so he then could get the authors to retract their demands. I went back to work, putting my stamp on the show. Divide and conquer, his motto and method, had worked. An illustration of the golden rule of theatre and not only commercial theatre: If it works, it's justified. A variation on Marx—Karl.

Out of town, it becomes a matter of life and death to keep a show surviving; unexpectedly, I was confronted with a matter of real life and death. I had hoped Tom would be in Boston with me. I was relying more and more on his opinion. Godfathering the romance between Barbra and Elliott made me miss him even more. But at the last minute, he hadn't come up to Boston because of Geraldine Brooks.

The three of us always spent New Year's Eve together as part of a group that got done up in black tie and started the night with dinner at Chambord, an elegant East Side restaurant: Herb and Nora, Steve Sondheim, Mary Rodgers and various extras depending on who was dating whom. The New Year's Eve before *Wholesale* went into rehearsal, Tom and I went up to Gerry's for our ritual glass of pre-Chambord champagne. She looked unbelievably beautiful when she opened the door but said with no preface, "Oh darling, I have a lump in my breast."

"It's nothing," I said and knew I was lying. Tom said later I didn't know; I wanted it to be nothing because I loved her so much. But I did know, I felt a stab.

Gerry had recently gone into analysis. Her analyst told her women starting therapy often developed a lump and she believed him. Why not? Why not believe what you want to hear, especially an explanation so simple it must be true? And being a licensed psychoanalyst, he was an M.D. as well as a psychiatrist so wouldn't he know? But the lump didn't disappear. By the time she went to a specialist, it was time for a biopsy. The procedure was laid out for her with terrifying clarity: she would be on the table and under an anesthetic for the biopsy. If it was malignant, a mastectomy would be performed then and there. The surgeon wanted Gerry's written permission. She gave it.

Self-esteem was not Gerry's strong suit; it was too dependent on her beauty. What was her state, I asked when Tom phoned me in Boston. Scared, but not terrified, not panicky. Not stoic, either. Part of her, the part that made Gerry Gerry, was that she had always been a woman with a young girl's optimism. She doubted very much she'd lose her breast but if she had to, at worst she'd be alive and cancer free.

There were forty-eight hours to get through before she went into the hospital. I was in Boston, Tom was in New York, we were her best friends (except for a girlfriend who was panicking badly). Tom stayed with Gerry for all forty-eight hours. They talked, sat over meals and talked, walked all over the Village

For seventeen years, only Gerry knew there were still cancer cells floating in her body.

and talked, sat up late over wine and talked—not only about Gerry, about Tom: she wanted to know more about him and about us. They both talked and they both listened; they were both very good at both.

Attending to business at the Colonial Theatre during those forty-eight hours, it was difficult to keep perspective, to know what was perspective. This was not a national or natural disaster, this was my beloved friend Gerry with a possibly malignant tumor. That made the show less important but it didn't make it unimportant; my responsibility couldn't allow it to be unimportant but David Merrick ranting against Barbra Streisand and Elliott Gould was easier to slough off. At the same time, Gerry was a reminder that Barbra and Elliott were people, that their problems were important to them and that I had to concentrate so I could help them. Concentration was the solution: I worked harder and better. Concentrating on holding anxiety in check forced me to fight thinking what difference did a show make and to summon up every bit of passion for the theatre that was in me. If you can't feel that passion for whatever you do in the theatre, if you can't care perhaps even more than the show is worth, then it has little chance of being any good.

· · ·

Merrick was still complaining about Barbra but not as vehemently: he sensed something was possible there. But he balanced his unsureness about her with the conviction that Elliott had to be fired. We had tried to cure Elliott's flying sweat with a prescription from Dr. Miracle Max Jacobson in New York. The medicine stopped the sweating but dried up Elliott's vocal chords so badly he couldn't sing. That stopped medicine and reinforced Merrick's determination: Fire him now! I understood his hope for a leading man more palatable to the audience but Elliott was good; the show wouldn't work with one of the conventional juveniles being flown in and out of Boston to audition as a replacement.

My anger at what had happened unfairly to Gerry Brooks was converted into anger at David Merrick being unfair to Elliott Gould. I used his own tactics: I was not going to see one more actor, I would not fire Elliott, I would rather quit and I was not bluffing. Nora burst into tears when she heard. She liked Elliott and Barbra personally but it was the artist in her who cried.

We were all like rubber bands due to the tension and pressure of the last mile; the anxiety that produces is inhuman. At one and the same time that you know now, if ever, you cannot stop working to improve the show, you are also convinced the show is a flop, so what difference does it make whether you drive yourself or not? Gerry Brooks made the difference for me: I drove myself for her.

Gerry lost more than a breast; the mastectomy was radical. The muscles in her arm were cut out and still she wasn't clean. Her façade disappeared along with her defenses and her optimism. When she came out of the hospital, she made the belated and bitter discovery that there was a family history: her mother had had a mastectomy but had never told Gerry.

Because it was too hard for her to be alone, she moved into the guest room in our house in the Village. We felt helpful because it helped her so much. Her humor returned, some of her enjoyment, even some of her ever-cheery façade. What badly needed restoring was her sense of herself as an attractive woman. For that, she needed to be wanted by a man. The first man to take her to bed after the operation was her analyst.

Unorthodox, against the rules, even unethical maybe, but it helped. It helped a lot. And never mind judgment and analysis of what followed: she brought a man home, then another. She was not a Blanche DuBois in any sense including numbers; these were affairs, however brief. They made her begin to feel attractive which made her like herself more which made her become more and more the old Gerry. Then she brought Budd Schulberg home. He was a good deal older than she which wasn't a problem for her. But Budd was a problem for me: he had been an informer in the Hollywood Witch Hunt.

The House Un-American Committee didn't subpoena Budd Schulberg; he sent a telegram offering to testify and literally chased the Committee from one city to another before he caught up and could inform on his friends. For Elia Kazan, he had written *On the Waterfront,* an apologia for informing. The highly praised movie may be a first-rate piece of work but it glorifies informing; it was made at a time when informers like Schulberg and Kazan could make movies whenever they wanted while the friends and colleagues they informed on were thus finished in movies and out on their asses.

I told Gerry I would not have Budd in the house. She understood and moved back to her own apartment; it was time to be back on her own anyway. Then they got married—Budd Schulberg who had volunteered to testify before HUAC and Geraldine Brooks who had flown to Washington to protest HUAC's existence. Well, she loved him and love is at least a more acceptable reason than money or fame or power. Tom and I stayed close to her because we loved her—same reason. She and Budd bought a house in Quiogue, the next community to the west of us. We saw both of them together now and then but only Gerry at our house on the beach.

The summer they married, Budd borrowed a little cottage out in Montauk from Kazan and they invited us to dinner. For Gerry, we went; for Gerry, I kept quiet. Tom didn't; he was right, I was wrong. The four of us were sitting at the bar, chitchatting over drinks, successfully avoiding any contentious issue until Gerry prodded Budd: "Buddy, darling, explain to Arthur and Tom what they don't understand." Whether we didn't understand out of naïveté or ignorance or sheer stupidity, she didn't specify. Apparently, deeply in love meant deeply brainwashed but this was Gerry and I reminded myself what she had been through and what Budd had restored to her.

Budd Schulberg stuttered which made interrupting unfair; it didn't bother him because he didn't listen to anyone anyway. He lectured at great length, Gerry hanging on every word adoringly. To reduce a long polemic to a brief gist, his thesis was that the Hollywood Communists protested censorship in this country but never said a word against the imprisoning of writers in gulags and death camps in the Soviet Union. There wasn't even a silence before Tom said:

"What does that have to do with informing on your friends?"

The effect was that of a precocious child correcting his parents in the presence of company. Tom was still a young actor then. What is a young actor? What he looks like. In Tom's case, a healthy, handsome, open-faced innocent from the American West where he was born. Budd gaped, for once silenced; Gerry quickly switched to another subject and war remained undeclared. It continued to remain undeclared until a cold winter night in the Seventies, a year or so after *The Way We Were* was released.

The four of us and Trudy, a friend of Gerry's who did some secretarial work for Budd, had drinks at the beach house, then went on to dinner at a restaurant on Montauk Highway called the Trolley Barn. Almost as big as an actual barn, it seemed vast in its emptiness. Only two tables were taken: the five of us at one, and an acre away, two men and a woman at the other. All eight of us were well oiled. When we left the beach house, Budd and Trudy went ahead in his car, Gerry stayed behind to drive with us.

"He's having an affair with Trudy," she said. "I don't care. I just wish I could have one more last affair myself." That was the first indication that she wasn't clean, more of shock than the revelation about her husband and her duplicitous friend.

At the Trolley Barn, drinks were on the table when we arrived, the talk was talk until, apropos of nothing, Budd began to hector me about *The Way We Were*. It could have been a good picture if it hadn't been such a lie politically—which it was because I was under the influence of my Stalinist friend Lillian Hellman. Lillian was an acquaintance, not a friend; I would very willingly have attacked her myself, not for her idolatry of Stalin but for her admiration of Hannah Arendt. Lillian and her ilk were so enchanted intellectually by the oxymoronic phrase "the banality of evil" in the subtitle of Arendt's book on Adolf Eichmann that they swallowed whole her vile defense of her indefensible, vile subject. Both Arendt and Lillian were loudly anti-Israel—Arendt the anti-Semitic Jew, Lillian the Stalinist Budd said she was.

I might have granted him that much to calm him down but he was really getting into slamming me, *The Way We Were*, the Soviet Union, Lillian, the Hollywood Ten, all at the top of his voice. The bartender didn't even look up. I let Budd rant, Trudy muttered into her drink, Gerry began to weep and Tom ordered more drinks: it was that kind of night. Budd fired a final salvo and stormed out of the restaurant in search of a windmill. Drinks came, Gerry cried harder, I ordered food.

We were eating when Budd returned. Gerry put her hand out to him; he preferred the drink at his place. Invigorated, he launched a fresh attack on *The Way We Were* and me. Very drunk now, he pounded the table for attention he wasn't getting. Infuriated by the inattention, he stood up and hurled a chair across the room. By ill luck or good luck, depending on your viewpoint, the chair flew through the air and hit the woman at the only other occupied table. San Juan Hill! Verdun! Pearl Harbor! One of the men with the startled woman jumped up: machismo *über alles.* He and Budd met halfway, locked horns, then roared out like racing cars, presumably to the parking lot to put up their dukes. We kept eating and drinking.

Meal finished, drinks drunk, check paid, we left. No sign of Budd or his sparring partner. Down the road, the neon sign of a serious bar glowed fuzzily in the frosted night. No one, male or female, was willing to check it out but it was odds-on Budd was there, boozing and lecturing on the perfidy of Lillian Hellman, Reddest Writer of All. We left his car for him and took Gerry (and Trudy) home.

Whether Gerry's support of Budd's politics had also changed, we didn't ask. She would never leave him: he loved her and had married her knowing all about the tainted cells and the mastectomy. How much of her love for him was gratitude didn't matter: he had made her happy again. But he was an informer and always would be. She had not been very lucky in her life; I hoped it would turn and bring her that one last affair she wanted while she still had time.

Barbra and Elliott were a Jewish show business Romeo and Juliet in love with each other and ice cream. After the New York opening of *Wholesale*—the city hers now for those fifteen minutes—she rented a small penthouse apartment in the Nineties on Central Park West and Elliott moved in. It had once belonged to Larry Hart of Rodgers and Hart which gave it a musical provenance. She whirled around decorating her first home with red-and-gray herringbone tweed curtains in the living room and antiques scrounged from thrift shops. Barbra, like Nora Kaye, had to be pried away from any bargain but I cheerfully played chauffeur for her antique hunting because being with her was fun.

After *Wholesale,* I wanted her for one of the leads in *Anyone Can Whistle.* Steve Sondheim was doubtful, and while he was deciding, she was offered *Funny Girl.* The two shows were in fateful Philadelphia at the same time: she was a hit, we weren't. When I took my parents to see *Funny Girl* in New York, the composer David Shire, who was the pit pianist, said the audience should thank us for being there: it was the first full-out performance Barbra had given in a week. The theatre, a small town on the way to the big city of Hollywood, was boring her.

One Sunday during the run, Barbra and Elliott, Tom and I went to our favorite restaurant in Chinatown. We knew it as "Coca-Cola," after the only sign outside. During the meal, Barbra announced that if she ever did another show, she would only play four performances a week. Elliott went to the men's room. I pointed out the financial problems but she brushed them aside: producers and investors were the capitalist enemy. She beamed, proud of her political awareness.

At the annual Xmas tree–trimming party at our house on St. Luke's Place, in the Village, her aggressive brashness vanished at the sight of Nora dressed in an elegant dress from ballerina days. Suddenly Barbra Streisand, the New Girl of the Year, was so shy she had to be pushed into the living room and blocked from hiding in a corner behind the thickly decorated tree. This wasn't her Promised Land three thousand miles away, this was New York and a world where everyone was comfortably at home with Lena Horne and Anita Ellis, idols to Barbra, old friends to the rest of us.

When she decided to give a party for her good friends, Bring Lena, she said grandly. Lena was reclusive, fussy about friends and not mad about parties; I didn't ask her. When I arrived at Barbra's party, her good friends Ava Gardner and George C. Scott were sprawled on the floor. He was drunk and called her Mommy; she was beautiful with bruises on her legs. I left early.

Lena, a part of the annual Christmas tree–trimming party Tom and I gave.
Now the annual party is on New Year's Eve and Lena is not there.

The end of the day came not very long after. I arrived at Barbra's to find four men in dark blue suits in a row: her manager, her agent, her press agent, and her accountant. She was a certified, incorporated Star: Streisand.

"Oh damn, I forgot." I didn't say what I forgot, I didn't have to. The Four Horseman of her apocalypse couldn't have cared less and I left. They didn't notice and I doubt Barbra did whenever she emerged to call them to attention. After she moved to the Coast, we had minimal contact. She'd call from time to time if she needed help. Once, from the set of *Hello, Dolly!*

"I've got a tap dancer for a director!" she wailed. She meant Gene Kelly. "What can I do?"

"Nothing."

"Nothing??!!"

"Nothing. You shouldn't have taken the part. You're at least twenty years too young."

She had taken the part because *Dolly* was a hot property; all the possible female candidates were eager to play Dolly. Barbra should not have been considered but she was hot, which in Hollywood meant she was right for any role and the picture was a sure hit. If it wasn't because some planet wasn't in ascendancy, there was plenty of time and another picture to make before it was released and everyone ran like hell.

I didn't come back to her Central Park West apartment until Ray Stark business brought me there. It was her New York pied-à-terre now: the herringbone tweed curtains were gone, Art Deco was in residence.

She had been too busy with her movie career to be shaken as deeply as the rest of the country by the liberations of the Sixties but women's lib had made some dent. The lack of an education beyond high school bothered her; she read treatments, not books. Like too many who never got to college, she had an exaggerated respect for a degree. She asked me for a reading list; I gave her one that included *One Day in the Life of Ivan Denisovich* and *Cancer Ward*. The day Aleksandr Solzhenitsyn was awarded the Nobel Prize, she called excitedly from the Coast.

"Hey, your guy won!" As though I had won.

"Did you read it?"

". . . No."

"Did you read any of the books on the list?"

". . . No. It's like climbing a mountain. There's so much to get through before you can even get a look at the top."

Not as touching at thirty-one as it might have been at nineteen. It was the Hollywood mountain she was concentrating on anyway, climbing as fast as she could and getting a good squint at the top. To her eyes, all that stood in her way was Ray Stark.

Enthusiasm is the prime requisite for a Hollywood producer. Money can't buy enthusiasm but enthusiasm can get money no matter how inane the idea so long as the studio hasn't been burned by the producer more than four consecutive times previously. Why four is the magic number, I don't know. Really infectious enthusiasm can obtain the creative participation even of a writer in full possession of his faculties and without his back against a financial wall. Proof: Ray Stark got me.

Of all Hollywood producers, none had more infectious enthusiasm than his; it was so infectious, it even infected him. He was certifiably out of his head over his idea for the movie I was to write for Barbra: a cross-pollination of Julie Andrews conducting the singing Trapp Family in *The Sound of Music* with Anne Bancroft teaching the handicapped Helen Keller in *The Miracle Worker* would hatch Barbra Streisand teaching handicapped children to sing in Brooklyn. Brooklyn Heights, actually: more photogenic.

I can't claim being swayed by palm trees; he told me the idea in New York, not Hollywood. And sold me. It isn't even embarrassing to admit: his enthusiasm was so catching, I actually thought I could find a way to make that sappy idea work. I hauled out my old radio plotting tricks—twist Device 3, combine with Device 10, and twist both again—and came up with a plot that brought tears of admiration from Ray. The story was the sure winner he knew I'd come up with, perfect for Barbra! The infected infected the infected: we sold each other, hook, line and aptly named sinker. All I had to do was sell Barbra.

Then came dawn. As I walked up Central Park West to her apartment rehearsing the story I had invented, I couldn't make myself believe it. It wasn't just a lousy idea, it was no idea. I would say so to Barbra and run.

"I'll think of something else," I told her. "How've you been?"

How had she been? Well, she'd become a movie star. I'd lived with one and among enough of them to know that anyone who becomes a movie star must be superhuman to remain human. Superhuman, Barbra was not. There was hope: it was less than ten years since *Wholesale,* seven since *Funny Girl* on Broadway; she still had the apartment in New York along with her anger and her passion. The anger was against Ray, the passion for the kind of movies she wanted to make—*Yentl* was high on her list. But as she tummeled, she kept reminding me of someone else, a girl I had once known. Who, where, when, I couldn't place. I couldn't see her. Like Barbra, unlike Barbra; younger, another time, an earlier time, against another background. Cornell! Frizzy hair and sensible shoes, a brown skirt and blouse, a red scarf, handing out leaflets in

1937 on the Arts campus. "Stop Franco! Stop the war in Spain!" Her name—the coincidence was surely an omen—was Fanny Price.

While this journey was taking place in my head, I was talking away a mile a minute with Barbra but looking at her, I knew Fanny Price was going to be transformed into the heroine of the movie I was going to write for her. The lack of a story was momentary: with Fanny's outrage and convictions, the story would tell itself. Beginning at Cornell, it would be close to me and right for her. And if it was right for Barbra, it would be right for Ray.

CHAPTER FIVE

The Hunting Season
The Way We Were *and* *the Way They Were*

NINETEEN THIRTY-SEVEN WAS MY SENIOR YEAR AT CORNELL—
the year of campus peace strikes to end the Spanish Civil War and witch hunts
to find undergraduate Reds. It was also the year of smoothies in saddle shoes,
necking in convertibles, dancing to big bands at the senior prom—and the
only year I enjoyed. Freshman year had been miserable. At sixteen, too young,
at once too sophisticated and too naive, I overcompensated by learning to
smoke, drink, and gamble. I also wore bow ties and joined a fraternity too
quickly—a second-rate fraternity and against my father's wishes but I would
listen to no one. Because they wanted me, I insisted on joining.

My fraternity brothers believed if you were a virgin, you weren't a man. It
was their upperclassmen's responsibility to make a man of me and the other
intact pledges. Ithaca being whorehouse free, two juniors piled six of us non-
men into their cars and drove us to Elmira.

The whorehouse was a walk-up which smelled of failure. My whore's room
was shabby and bare except for a thin bed, a chair, and a rickety dresser on a
cold linoleum floor. Naked except for her shoes, she was skinny with thin,
pancakelike breasts. Embarrassed and terrified that I wouldn't be able to get it
up, I undressed as ordered, put my clothes on the chair, careful not to disturb
her kimono draped across the back. With old soapy water, she washed off my
penis. Her touch didn't help. If anything, the reverse: my homosexual prick
tried to crawl back in. She struggled to find it in order to put a condom on it
but failed. Shaking her head (she foresaw our future), she played with my gen-
itals lackadaisically. Foolish optimism.

"You a virgin?"

I nodded, not looking at her.

"Hey, I got a cherry!" she shouted.

"Me, too! Me, too!" came from other rooms. Misery didn't get company. From those other rooms soon came shouts of pleasure; not from mine.

"You have to pay anyway," she said.

I did and got dressed as fast as I could. I never looked at her, hoping she would forget my face.

In the car, I was again the fraud as I celebrated being no longer a boy or a virgin. My tale of triumph wasn't as long as those told by the newly made man next to the driver or the even bigger braggart next to me in the backseat. I got myself off the hook of describing details by claiming I was beat from all the humping; I had to go to sleep. Oh, yes, me, too, the others chimed in and the humper next to me settled in with his head in my lap and dozed off.

He was quite good-looking, big, muscular; played basketball, softball, touch football, and was unfairly smart, a science major. I didn't much like him—too sure of himself, too arrogant. He made a pillow of his hand, putting it under his cheek as he dozed. I was praying my penis wouldn't betray me again but he cupped it—of course it was hard now—then unzipped my pants

At Cornell in 1934, trying to pretend I wasn't sixteen. I learned very little in my four years.

and put it in his mouth. Another fraud. I was angry but excited and wasn't about to stop him.

For four years, Stan and I had occasional sex that under his guidance became more and more sophisticated. We did it at odd times and places, often after a double date, but never did we talk about it, not once did we even mention it. I more than liked the sex, I less than liked him. I knew I was homosexual yet was afraid of being a homosexual. Upset, scared, confused, I wanted desperately to talk about it to someone.

Senior year, I was living off-campus with a straight friend from summer camp as my roommate in an apartment on the ground floor of an old house. For sixty-five dollars, we owned a car together—not sixty-five dollars apiece, sixty-five dollars total—an old Buick we called Herman. There were holes in the floorboard and the brakes locked regularly. When they did, we poured water on them; when we didn't have water, we peed on them. But Herman got us to campus in time for class. One morning when I was later than usual, Marty was yelling "Come on, come on!" as usual but I had to pee. "Do it in the car!" he shouted as usual. "OK! OK!" I ran after him, got in the car, and peed. Marty laughed. Most of it went through the holes in the floor but he would have laughed anyway, he was very easygoing—the one person at school I thought might understand my sexual problems and be sympathetic. Half a dozen times there was an opportune moment but I was too ashamed to bring up the subject.

We shared a large bedroom whose window fronted on a covered veranda. The room had a big double bed in a dark alcove on one side and a single far across from it under the window. I was sleeping in the single on a Saturday night when there was a light tapping at the window. I knew before I looked that it was Stan. Very quietly, I raised the sash to let him in. The smell of gin explained his visit as he quietly clambered onto the bed. It was pitch dark in the room and so silent I could hear Marty was awake. There was a long minute when I didn't cooperate with Stan, then I went ahead deliberately.

I knew Marty could hear us. I knew he was unsure exactly what he was hearing but sure enough to get the general idea. I wanted him to hear, I wanted him to know: now I would be able to tell him and talk it all out.

When we finished, Stan quietly crawled out the window without a sound from him or me, or from Marty. I escaped swiftly into relieved sleep. In the morning, I awoke ice cold with fear. Desire had blinded judgment; I had made a terrible miscalculation. I wanted to burrow deep under the covers but pretended I was asleep, keeping my eyes closed as tight as Marty's surely had been while Stan and I were at it because I could hear him getting dressed with none of his customary effort to be quiet. His footsteps were loud, not careful, as he stomped into the living room on his way to the kitchen to make himself breakfast—but he didn't go to the kitchen. He stopped in the living room—I could hear keys—then went out, not shutting the door but contemptuously letting it bang. Neither of us ever took the car without asking the other but I didn't have to get out of bed to check the side table where the keys to Herman were kept. I knew they were gone.

It had never occurred to me that homosexuality was disgusting. The religious regarded it as a sin; most everyone thought it wrong; at the fraternity, fag jokes were as common as babe jokes. But Marty thought it was disgusting. I knew he went off with the car because he was repelled by what Stan and I had done. I understood and I didn't. It was disgusting that I did it with Marty in the same room, yes, but what we did, what Stan and I did, I didn't think that was disgusting.

For a week, Marty and I lived in the same apartment, drove to class in the same car without saying a word. If I needed a match to light a cigarette, rather than ask him, I turned on the gas stove and singed my eyebrows when I bent over the flame. I didn't blame him for putting me in Coventry, I deserved it. When he went home for the weekend because he had to get away—he made sure I overheard him on the phone—I called Stan with a double purpose. The first was part of our customary silent routine. The second came afterward, when we were lying in the big double bed, my arm cradling his head on my left shoulder. Since freshman year I had wanted to ask but it took Marty's disgust to give me the guts.

"Stan, have you done this with other boys?"

"Oh no," he said.

I hated him then. There were acts he had initiated, variations and nuances he had taught me that could only have been learned through experience, his experience. He was over six feet, I was well under, but I hauled off and socked him. He got up, dressed and left without a word—just like Marty. But he had a black eye that lasted. Not for four years, though.

Marty left a letter on the table next to the car keys, obviously for me to read. It was from his cousin, an egghead intern at Mount Sinai. Its subject was Marty's friend, X. X should go to a psychiatrist, X was suffering from a disease, the sooner X got help, the better X's chance of being cured.

Being reduced to X infuriated me even more than being diagnosed as diseased. "Where does he think X is going to get the money for a psychiatrist?" I asked angrily.

Practicality is a great leveler. It was Marty's turn to be embarrassed, but we had exchanged words, the subject had been mentioned however indirectly. We didn't talk it out; only my fantasy made me think we could have. It wasn't that he was so straight, so square, or even so unimaginative; he was, like most people, simply uncomfortable with the whole subject. He neither condemned nor condoned, he just didn't want to be touched by it. I apologized for what I'd done that night and vowed it would never happen again. With Stan's black eye, it hardly had a chance but a period was needed to say finis, so I renounced homosexuality; I would take the veil. I knew that would please and it did. Marty was relieved and happy, I was neither, but we were roommates again and the subject was never mentioned again.

Of course, we were both only pretending. It was there, the elephant was on the coffee table in the living room, even larger in the bedroom whenever we were there. How could it not be seen? And so we were friendly but no longer friends. It was easy for Marty not to see the elephant because he didn't want it to exist; it was hard for me because I wanted badly for someone to see it who would let me talk about it.

The penis-anguish episode with Marty happened in my senior year, yet that was my one happy year at Cornell. Campus life was familiar, I enjoyed being an editor of *The Cornell Daily Sun,* and I became involved politically which provided the outlet for all the roiling emotions I couldn't put a name to. Joining hands to do battle left me no time to be lonely.

The political ground had been prepared early by my father, most vividly the evening he came home from his office to tell us he was canceling his annual trips to Germany. It was the Depression; trips in behalf of rich clients were lucrative but not enough so for him to set foot in Germany ever again: Hitler had arrived.

Formal politicization was taken over by my cousin Marion who wasn't really a cousin but the daughter of the man my father had accused my mother of having affair with. The two couples were so close her parents were aunt and uncle and she was cousin. The irony made me, at fourteen, feel quite worldly.

A few crucial years older, Marion dragged me with her on her quest for the Answer. We tried Christian Science but couldn't take our eyes off a woman sitting and sitting and still sitting next to the pulpit in a wheelchair. Marion switched allegiance to the Communist Party. As, of course, I would have but they told her to leave the kid home.

At Cornell, my sophomore year had flamed into life in an eye-opening course in political science given by an Englishman on loan from Harvard. I couldn't wait for his class, his lectures were so exciting but the Dean found them inciting and fired him for being a Red. That made him a pariah which made him a hero to me.

My active political involvement was traceable to the last weeks of my junior year when the *Sun* held its competition for the next year's editor in chief. The outgoing senior board's selection was determined by the number of editorials printed and where they were positioned on the editorial page. From the go, mine were featured. My writing was angry and passionate on national or international issues, acerbic and funny on campus issues; a temperate middle ground on any issue didn't exist for me. I was pretty confident of being knighted until two senior board members beckoned me into their sanctum.

Simultaneously hush-hush and casual, they were very complimentary, so much so that while I heard, I didn't hear them mention en passant that a Jew, as I of course knew, could never be editor in chief: the circulation of the paper would drop. At the white houses, I thought—that was the spoken campus name for gentile fraternities at Cornell. Secretly—they knew they could trust me, however Jewish—I was assured I was a shoo-in for assistant editor. I went blank, I said nothing but at least didn't thank them as they seemed to expect. Being marked down as a pariah with such gentlemanly condescension was an unintended invitation to alter the world of the vested Wasp, a demand I tried to meet in my senior year.

The first witch hunt I got caught up in was at Cornell in 1937. It was led by the militantly pro-Franco State Senator John McNaboe. Based on rumor and a couple of anti-Franco editorials, he decided the university was a breeding ground for Communism. For some unfathomable reason known only to politicians, he also came to Cornell to root out "reefer smokers." The combination was irresistible. The *Sun*'s editorial board sponsored a mass Maryjane Smoke-in on the Art Quadrangle with free droshky transportation. The Senator was laughed off the campus and back to Albany, a city in which it was easy to disappear.

The Peace Strike belonged to us, not politicians. Its objective was to stop the civil war in Spain before Hitler and Mussolini provided enough support for Franco to defeat the elected socialist government. Fanny Price—small wonder Barbra had reminded me of her—was both the prime motivator behind the strike and the prime obstacle to the strike. While she wanted the strike to pressure FDR into negotiating an end to the war, she also wanted to crucify him for staying out of it. PEACE AT ANY PRICE BUT FANNY PRICE was the header of a Mel Shavelson humor column in the *Sun*. But Fanny couldn't be laughed off. Unlike the American Student Union, whose members were liberal socialists like me, Fanny's Young Communist League wasn't content to talk about a peace strike. She moved, she acted, she got a permit from the Dean allowing the YCL to hold a rally on campus. Any fool who asked how

Eve Merriam in front of the girls' dormitory at Cornell in 1934, our freshman year. The inevitable book is waiting patiently at her feet.

Fanny Price managed to get a permit didn't know what the Dean knew: the YCL had a total membership of eleven, including Fanny. Who would even see she was having a rally?

Timing is all. The demand for peace in Spain began to thunder on campuses all across the country, becoming so popular that the conservative Cornell Student Council roused itself to get in on the act and, droit du seigneur, take over. Fanny was not pleased; Fanny was not willing; Fanny was shrewd. She knew me from the odd YCL meeting I dropped in on now and then; she also knew I knew some of the B(ig) M(en) O(n) C(ampus) on the Council. She and I appointed me mediator, as a presumed neutral from the ASU.

I loved the power of a go-between. I loved shuttling back and forth in Founder's Hall, from the Council's large sunny room on the main floor to Fanny's dank cubicle in the basement; getting a concession from the Council—not too hard: they were fair because they had no real convictions—and a concession from Fanny—not impossible because she was practical. She assessed the size of the turnout Student Council sponsorship would guarantee and her eyes glowed in anticipation of a captive audience for her beliefs.

Two sticking points on which she would not budge were where I was of some use. I was all for her, she deserved to win both: one, that it be called a peace strike and not a peace rally as the white shoes wanted; two, that she be the first speaker. The first point I got the Council to concede as a matter of their balls, the second as a matter of their chivalry. Both Fanny's wins are in *The Way We Were.*

Fanny Price, fiery campus radical, was a colorful beginning for the character of my heroine but little more than a beginning. What did she want beyond the overthrow of capitalism? I knew nothing about Fanny after college; I certainly couldn't ask her, this being 1971 and that being 1937. What did *I* want back then? A scene instantly popped up on my screen, a painful moment I'd had myself in freshman English class but pain has no gender. The class had been taught by an instructor who affected my life as strongly as Judd Marmor would years later.

His name was Raymond E. Short. About thirty, sandy-haired, fresh-complexioned, a Cornell graduate magna cum laude, he unfortunately exemplified his surname: he was under five feet. And a humpback. Who had married the Prom Queen in his graduating class. Back then Raymond Short must have stood tall; he still did.

Our first assignment was an essay—on what, I don't remember, but I won't forget the advice from sophomores in the dorm. This wasn't high school, they warned; don't bullshit, just write plain simple declarative sentences. Piece of cake.

The day Dr. Short handed back our essays, he divided us up into groups: the largest was those who were passable but would not make any waves—I was not included; smaller, those who might make a ripple—I was not included; smaller still, those who needed a remedial writing class—I was not included; and two who were exceptional. Oh God please. I had wanted to be a writer since I was ten, I was a writer—I was not included. Dr. Short would see me after class.

After class, I was so frightened I wore a smile the whole time he gently explained that while I wasn't quite bad enough to need remedial writing, his advice would be to take the extra class if I had any spare time.

The Arts campus at Cornell was perfect for a movie: ivy-covered Gothic buildings on a hill that dropped to ivy-covered Gothic dormitories below. Background music from chimes in a nearby Gothic tower were ringing away as I came out of Dr. Short's classroom, walking fast until I reached the top of that hill. Then I let go and fell apart, crying as I plunged down the slope, running, stumbling, half-blinded by tears, the world whimpering to an end. If I couldn't be a writer, there was nothing I could do with my life.

His next assignment allowed us to write whatever we wanted. I wrote a short story, mostly in dialogue. Again, I was not included in any of his stupid groups; again, I was asked to wait and see him after class. This time, he was curious to know if I had spoken to anyone before I wrote that first essay. He didn't think it advisable that I speak to anyone before I wrote anything.

"Why not?"

"Because you're a writer," he said.

No matter what assignment he gave the class in the future, I was to write anything I wanted. He suggested trying a short play because I had a talent for dialogue.

"You're a writer." That sustained me through three unhappy years. One teacher out of I don't know how many but Dr. Raymond E. Short, I thanked you then for giving me belief in myself and I thank you now.

Character rather than plot drives the better stories. For the movie story I was developing, Fanny's passion to be a writer added a new dimension to her character. The rejection of her essay, contrasting sharply with her belligerence at the Peace Strike, followed by the scene where she's told she is a writer—all that was good, the story was slowly taking shape. Except it really wasn't. And couldn't because I couldn't believe Fanny was a writer. Passion, conviction, desire? Yes; brimming over; she had them all. Talent? No; not for one minute could I believe she had any. No reason, just instinct but I knew I was right. But recognizing what she lacked gave me something better, something basic to her character: resilience. The English instructor could destroy her only temporarily; she would never go under or give up. That rang true and that would shape her story. In the end, Fanny was indestructible, a phoenix, and her name wasn't Fanny it was Katie.

Katie because like Becky or Jenny, it was Jewish but less pointedly. She had to be a Jew; Barbra herself had arrived as one. Not flaunting, not defying, just simply declaring at Hollywood Customs: Here is a Jewish movie star. And Katie could only be a Jew because of her insistence on speaking out, her outrage at injustice, her passion, her values, and because I was a Jew. Besides, it was fresher and high time that the movies, the only industry founded by Jews, had a Jewish heroine.

But Katie who? Well, who and what were her parents? Poor, they had to be—one of Katie's jobs in college would be reading proof in the Linotype room of the *Ithaca Journal News* as I did. Not from New York City but upstate because Katie wasn't smart-assed urban. And first-generation; her parents were immigrants. Poor immigrant Jews then, whose surname had to suggest that without being a mouthful and without being an ordinary Jewish name because Katie was not ordinary. She was too passionate about too much, though not about sex or romance. Prudish and naive, she was more fighter than female. The boys would call her by her last name—Morosky. Katie Morosky. It wasn't in the phone book but whether it was an actual name or not didn't matter. "Katie Morosky" suited Barbra Streisand and sounded like a Jewish Communist who became fiercely romantic because she had to put her excess passion somewhere.

All her passion for justice for underdogs stayed, it was money in the story bank, but the passion she'd poured into writing, what was she to do with that now that she had faced she had no talent? Another cause? Just more of the same. Pour it into a person? Not intentionally. Not unless it was in spite of herself. A person who was everything she wasn't; a person who was unattainable; a fantasy; a beautiful blond goy.

A jock but not just a jock. A jock who was a writer in her English class. It was his short story that would be read aloud to the class by Dr. Short the way Dr. Drummond read one-act plays aloud in his playwriting class. The jock's story would reveal his flaw, a flaw that would allow Katie to roll up her emotional sleeves to help him. A flaw like Tony Blue Eyes had.

I met him at Arthur's, the disco much-loved Sybil Burton had opened "for us," in the mid-Sixties. "Us," Tom included, clustered in the Champagne Room in back; I defected to the main room, which had a live band, because I loved to dance. Tony Blue Eyes wasn't much of a dancer but he was a great source of dope and I loved to dope. The extraordinary color of those eyes had made and ruined his life ever since he was a little kid in grade school when his homeroom teacher sent him to another teacher with a note. That teacher read the note, looked at Tony, sighed, kissed him, and sent him on to another teacher who read the note, sighed, gave him a kiss, and sent him on to another teacher who sent him on to another and another until he opened the note and read: "Did you ever see such fantastic blue eyes?"

From then on, he became Tony Blue Eyes, relying too much on those eyes to make life easier. Which they did but easier wasn't necessarily better. For Katie's jock, I changed the eyes to a smile and entitled his short story "The All-American Smile." It began:

"In a way, he was like the country he lived in: everything came too easily to him. But at least he knew it. And if, more often than not, he took advantage of everything and everybody, he knew that too. About once a month, he felt he was a fraud. . . ."

The fraud, of course, was me; that there was some of me in him began to bring him alive. He wasn't as colorful as Katie but being less certain than she, he was more complex. His name came quickly: Hubbell Gardner. Everyone wanted a Hubbell Gardner for one thing, or if not, for another.

The "Hubbell" came from Hubbell Robinson: a wearer of elegant suspenders, as comfortable with women as with a never empty glass, the handsome head of the distinguished advertising agency Young and Rubicam. I couldn't get hired at Y&R after college—they weren't too keen on Jews—but thirty years later, Hubbell, who had married Vivienne Segal and dated her friend, Steve Sondheim's mother, persuaded me to do a special for ABC's series *Stage '67*.

Tom produced it and I wrote it, a first and last for both of us. In addition to our fees, we kept whatever money we didn't spend on the production. That included insurance on my old friend Lauren Bacall who costarred with John Forsythe. There was no need to insure John but Betty was appearing on Broadway in *Cactus Flower*. The TV shoot was one day only; if we didn't finish before her curtain time, we lost her. Insurance was very expensive so Tom decided to gamble: no insurance on Bacall.

The show was an original musical called "The Light Fantastic, or How to Tell the Past, Present, and Future through the History of Social Dancing." Television was live then which was nerve-racking enough for us without the danger of no insurance. Bacall was really petrified, scared stiff her hand would shake so hard in the first scene—when Forsythe came out of the television set into her bedroom to warn her about the stock market—that she would spill the champagne she poured for him. Simple safety net: new lines to say just that—how nervous she was, how her hand would shake. It didn't and she sailed—funny, charming and glamorous in one knockout Norell dress after another. The gowns were all her own (big money savings for us), each taken from her closet in its own cellophane bag, each as classically timeless as she was.

The "Gardner" in Hubbell Gardner wasn't quite as classy as the "Hubbell." We picked each other up on Lexington Avenue one groiny afternoon and went to his place a few doors away. We never did it again but we remained fairly friendly. That was back in the Fifties when Lexington Avenue and all the boys who strolled along it were relaxed and had no subtext.

Dancing with Betty
Bacall during a break
in the shooting of our
TV special, "The
Light Fantastic," for
ABC's *Stage '67*.

. . .

Katie and Hubbell in college were a breeze: I could pick and choose incidents from my Cornell days and transmute me into whichever one of them the situation required. Katie, after college and during the war, works on my army radio show as assistant to a director like Bill Robson. Her political protests are a pain in the ass to Washington's official censor but Morosky never lets up. Hubbell is ever the glamorous fantasy in a navy lieutenant's summer whites splashed with combat medals. He stays over in Katie's walk-up apartment in Murray Hill just as I did in Eve Merriam's. The Sutton Place apartment becomes a grander apartment on Beekman Place and he gets there through an old college-cum-navy buddy with undertones of gung-ho Hal Prince.

Details could wait; my worry was larger. I couldn't see where the story was going, I didn't know what it was about. Basically all I had was a Jewish radical and a Wasp jock writer. Katie and Hubbell. Katie and Hubbell like Jigee and Peter Viertel. Why did those names pop up? It took all of thirty seconds to figure that out.

. . .

I became intimately involved with the Viertels in Paris, where I lived after leaving this country because I'd been blacklisted during the Hollywood Witch Hunt. *Witch Hunt* was the phrase that explained Why Jigee and Peter. It pulled the ribbon and opened the gift box: they gave me the arc of my story. It was like a rainbow; the pot of gold was its climax, which would come during that shameful but exciting period with Katie and Hubbell facing what Jigee and Peter had faced.

Peter was a jock writer: an expert tennis player and skier who had written a very good first novel at nineteen. After that, he slid and became a screenwriter. He wasn't blond but he kept the razor-cropped crew cut he'd had as a Marine. He wasn't a true goy either but half-Jewish, not very Hubbell, and a flaw he tried to overlook. Unfortunately, it was his mother, Salka, who was the tainted half. His boast that he wasn't even circumcised was turned against him: we all told him he'd missed the best part of being Jewish. In mongrelized Hollywood, he was a Hubbell—to Jigee anyway.

Virginia—her actual name though never used—was a beauty with chestnut hair and the naturally red cheeks no cosmetic could duplicate. She never bothered to look beautiful, she just was. When she arrived with her sister Ann in Hollywood from the Midwest at sixteen, she tap-danced in movies, then grew up to be a story editor. An autodidact, she never finished high school but was the best-read person I knew. Authors were the center of her universe, cerebral and/or sexual. There was always a writer in the crosshair of her sights: Hemingway and Ring Lardner Jr. during her marriages to Budd Schulberg, with whom she had a daughter, and his successor Peter, with whom she had another. Soon after she and I met, she traced an X on my arm with her index finger.

"My mark," she said without explanation.

None was needed; I was hers. I adored her in Paris, in Klosters, and back in New York, even after she became an alcoholic, all the way to her dreadful end in California, a not-so-indirect result of informing. The one Jewish thing about her was her sister's husband but as she was a member of the Party, she was naturally a target of anti-Semitic cracks. She shrugged, just as she did when she was informed on by her ex-husband Budd and by her sister whose married name was Ann Frank. That wasn't funny but Ann was very funny so it seemed funny. Then the FBI came after Jigee through Peter. The husband of a Party member wasn't welcome in either the Marines or the studios. That wasn't funny at all. It was down to her beliefs, his beliefs and who loved whom and who didn't. That was what it was going to come down to with Katie and Hubbell.

Peter Viertel and Bob Parrish shirtless on the Chaplin tennis court. A year later, in the South of France, Peter made his chest hairless as well.

Jigee Viertel, somehow beautiful, not interested in the game at the Chaplins' court. In the background, Norman Lloyd and me.

Hubbell was only part Peter. He was also part Bob Parrish, who was blond and Aryan; part me; part a naval lieutenant named Dougal Wyatt who had a coterie of Yale buddies (all gay); and he would be part of whoever was going to play him. Just as Katie would be part Barbra as well as part Fanny and Jigee and me and Katrina Wallingford, the owner of that Sutton Place apartment and the girl who asked a quasi Hubbell of her own if he was leaving her because she wasn't attractive. All those component parts would finally be melded and submerged into the Katie and Hubbell I invented as I wrote. I was eager to start writing them. I didn't know how they were going to meet in New York and what was going to get them to Hollywood—that was not going to be easy but I would find a way. Most of all, I wanted to know how they were going to end up. I wasn't worried, I knew they would tell me.

Until *The Way We Were,* my screenplays were adaptations, based on someone else's work. As a screenwriter, I put on a hat different from my playwright's hat—it was only fair. The studios were paying me X dollars to reach X million people; my job was to give them their money's worth. It was as much a mistake to be superior and write down as to be unduly serious and write pretentiously. What a screenplay demanded, I offered: craft, a respectably high level of skill, and the implicit agreement to a limit on what could be said and how complex the characters could be.

But this was an original based on me, my life in college, during the war and during the Hollywood Witch Hunt. I had never seen a movie or a play set in that period in which those I knew either lived by fighting for the Ten or died by turning informer. There was no middle ground. I was blacklisted, I had my passport taken away. I believed it wasn't un-American to be a member of the Communist Party, it was un-American to be on the House Un-American Committee. I still believed that and I wanted to say it through a heroine who was a Jewish Communist. In a Hollywood movie.

Writers always fool themselves to some extent; I was no exception but I wasn't a totally idealistic idiot either. I was aware of the realities: *The Way We Were* was for a major studio; Ray Stark was an establishment producer; it was a movie. But I was going to counterbalance that with an apple from the garden: it was a love story. What's more, a love story between two people who were not meant for each other. Different beliefs, different styles; they loved each other until their principles were put on the line. What happened then, I wasn't sure but I did know it would not be a political polemic: I was too familiar with all the jokes about messages and Western Union.

One risk I wasn't as fully aware of as I should have been, considering what came later: the story was so personal, I cared about it. That was dangerous for a screenwriter. When the producers, stars, directors, when the powers want a script, they kiss your ass; when it's delivered, they throw you out on your ass. I trusted Ray Stark—a sentence guaranteed to make a lot of people laugh. However, I did. I always preferred the mistake of trusting to the larger (to me) mistake of holding back and shutting down in self-protection. Of course, lurking somewhere in me was the protective "It's only a movie." But even if that weren't there, even if I hadn't trusted Ray, I liked Katie and Hubbell—and what their story was about—so much, I wanted to write it. So I did.

Ray wanted a treatment before deciding whether the story would make a movie for Barbra and money for him. That was more than fair since he was willing to pay very well for the treatment and was willing for me to own it if he didn't like it. Give me something I can sell it with, he asked, ten or twenty pages. I gave him 125, which I later expanded into a full-length novel. He read the treatment on a plane flying back to California. The minute he landed, he grabbed a phone in the L.A. airport. He was ecstatic, he loved it. Barbra read it: she loved it. They wanted the screenplay yesterday.

My Blackwing pencils couldn't write fast enough on the long yellow legal pads to keep up with the rush of words in my head. When Katie and Hubbell got to Hollywood, I slowed down to make sure the political element didn't overpower the love story. There was a plethora of incidents from life but those that didn't center on either Katie or Hubbell were cut, sometimes later rather than sooner, but eventually, always. I was good with a red pencil for:

- A Thought Control Conference in response to the House Un-American Committee's investigation was held at the Beverly Hills Hotel the summer I arrived in Hollywood. I was one of the speakers but Hubbell wouldn't have spoken. Cut before a word was written.

- A lunch at George Cukor's in the fall, just after the Friendly Witnesses had testified for HUAC. Ronald Colman and his wife were cheering for Adolphe Menjou et al.; Kate Hepburn and I were against; George Cukor and Lion Feuchtwanger, the refugee German novelist, were neutral. Constance Collier settled the argument. "Any man who repeats what a guest says in his house is a cad," she said decisively. As we left the dining room, Feuchtwanger said with that smile political refugees wear like running shoes: "There's always another border I can cross."

I liked his line and Connie's but I couldn't imagine Katie Morosky and Hubbell Gardner at George Cukor's.

- A party at Clifford Odets's where Charlie Chaplin, doing his parlor pantomime of a matador fighting a bull, crashed into a wall and knocked one of the paintings from Clifford's magnificent collection to the floor. Dangling from the hook was a tiny microphone, a bug. Combining that with an Irene Selznick screening where machinery lowered a Matisse to reveal a movie screen behind it, I had Katie and Hubbell at his director's house when the bug ripped the painting. A little dramatic license.

One scene I tried hard to keep in the picture. When the Hollywood Ten were sentenced to prison for contempt, there was a Screen Writers Guild meeting to endorse a united stand for the Unfriendly Witnesses and against HUAC. At the request of the Motion Picture Producers Association, which had just had a conference at the Waldorf-Astoria in New York, Dore Schary and Walter Wanger appeared to explain the producers' position to the writers. Dore had stated publicly his support for the Ten and opposition to any blacklist so we were glad he was on the bill. The act he performed, however, wasn't the act we expected: it was a song and dance endorsing a blacklist. Forget the Ten and move on, he advised: protect the loyal writers among us. All friendly smiles like Louis B., he reminded us that he too was a writer—he was head of RKO at the time—so he knew what we felt, he understood his fellow artists. Music up and close-up of the flag, the American flag, lest there be any doubt, and waving in the breeze.

Schary and his fellow toads did not have an easy time leaving the meeting. In the best of times it isn't easy to walk down a rickety flight of wooden steps, however short, and hold your head up, let alone hold it high with dignity. Theirs went down on the first step and drooped lower as they proceeded down the long aisle to the exit door. The aisle became a gauntlet of row after row screenwriters: the hissing began softly, turned to booing, got louder and louder. The producers, only halfway to the door, heads ducked to their chests, began to walk-run like the rats they were. A devastating scene and a theatrical one but what would Hubbell do during it? Sit with the other writers and hiss?

When the door shut behind the producers, there was another devastating scene. The floor microphone was clutched by Marguerite Roberts, a woman who had been writing movies for a hundred years but had never before spoken at a meeting. She had a terrible stutter. One sentence was all she managed to get out: "I don't know how Mr. Schary can look at himself in the mirror every morning without vomiting." It took her a long time to say that one sentence but when she was done the room stood up and cheered what she said and what it took her to say it.

Another terrific moment, but during Marguerite's ovation, an irony struck me: along with informers, the Witch Hunt uncovered stutterers. She and Budd Schulberg each had a heavy stutter; Jigee and Ring Lardner had rather attractive stammers; Paul Draper had a whopper of a stutter that led his psychoanalyst to push him toward self-destruction.

Paul and Larry Adler could always be counted on to perform at fundraisers. Paul danced elegantly to Larry's harmonica, Larry played the *Boléro* and often made the collection speech. But Paul's analyst thought public speaking might help cure Paul's stutter, so the fund-raiser arrived where Paul wouldn't perform unless he made the collection speech. We didn't raise a dime. Paul Draper's Freudian fiasco might have shown the left wing had a sense of humor after all but would Katie holding the empty hat seem funny or cruel? I cut both stuttering scenes before they were on paper.

The Jigee-Peter scene that had given me the story took an unexpected turn for Katie and Hubbell. It didn't come at the point I had expected and its tone was very different. But it said everything I wanted in a few painful lines and led to a bittersweet ending I hadn't anticipated and thus enjoyed writing all the more.

Then the processing of the screenplay into a movie star movie began.

Sydney Pollack was my choice to direct. I got him, alas. Intelligence and imagination, never too plentiful in Hollywood, were seriously depleted by the Witch Hunt; for almost two decades, the product suffered. *They Shoot Horses, Don't They?* directed by Pollack was an exception. I admired the picture and I admired his work. One something does not a something make but I campaigned for him because of that one movie. Barbra was impressed that Sydney had studied acting with Sandy Meisner at the Neighborhood Playhouse in New York and then taught there himself. Ray was dubious but went along because he didn't want Ryan O'Neal.

Originally we had assumed O'Neal would play Hubbell but by the time the picture was ready to go into production, his affair with Barbra was over, the movie they made together (*What's Up, Doc?*) was over, their chemistry was over. Ray wanted a new blond for Barbra: Robert Redford. Sydney Pollack was the key to Redford; they were like Butch Cassidy and the Sundance Kid. Ray would take Sydney Pollack if he brought Robert Redford with him.

Redford started as a very talented young actor on the New York stage with a great flair for comedy. In the movies, concomitant with becoming a star, he was becoming cute and mannered but he was the prime candidate for Hubbell. My guess was that like Astaire and Rogers, he would give Barbra class and she would give him sex. There was one slight hitch: Robert Redford didn't want to play Hubbell Gardner.

He thought the character was too weak and Barbra's part too big, this assessment according to Sydney. Everything Redford said was according to Sydney. He never allowed me to meet Bob Redford before or during the making of the picture. He was arm-around-the-shoulder reassuring that it was really best that any idea old Bob came up with be filtered through old Syd to me and vice versa. As a result, Redford glared at me the first day I walked on the set and didn't say hello until a decade later. I had absolutely no idea why and finally thought, Oh, fuck him. My money was on Barbra anyway.

After the customary meetings, hagglings, concessions and rewrites, Redford signed. Then it was time for the last final polish of the final draft of the final screenplay. Ray decided that would be done best in the calming ambience of Sun Valley where he had a condo. Sydney and I could be billed to the picture. As could Ray himself. But he also chose Sun Valley because we had skied together in Switzerland and he knew how much I loved skiing. St. Moritz at the time when it was St. Moritz—the Shah at Suvretta House, Niarchos in a chalet with a swimming pool and a helicopter to lift him to the top of the mountain, Dietrich galas at the Palace, which was the most glamorous hotel in the western world—that was the St. Moritz where Ray and Fran and Tom and I skied together.

Corvatch was a challenging mountain a few kilometers outside town. Fran could ski and with some style, but like Hal Prince on water skis, she was afraid of turning in powder. Her malicious guide laughed each time she fell. We convinced her to take the easier of the two ways down the mountain but Ray, who really didn't ski as well as she, would not take any easier way. He was determined to stay with us if it killed him, which it almost did. The man fell all the way down a very long mountain, but each time he got up laughing and tackled the next stretch. He got to the bottom through sheer willpower—the same way he had gotten to the top in Hollywood, if there is a top for producers.

I was over forty-five when I learned to ski. That was in St. Anton, thanks to a superb teacher named Robert Falch whose English was worse than my nonexistent German. "Have you seen! Have you seen!" he would call out to the slopes when I finally made parallel turns. *"Elegante! Elegante!"* was his command to which Tom responded as though to that manner born. As a kid, he had skied in Colorado; then after a very long layoff, picked up again when I started. Hotdogging or bombing the mountain were never for us; we wanted to be *elegante,* in control with the style Robert Falch said was skiing.

It still is. Every year we take a ski holiday in Switzerland, and every year we ski better even as we get older—unbelievable but true—and love it more. To stand in the sunshine at the top of a run, breathe the air that is as pure as the snow, look up at the magnificence of the Alps, then ski the long run down the mountain, not a thought in your head except skiing, concentrating on *"Elegante! Elegante!"* and out to prove nothing, alive and bursting with joy still felt at this age—what can compare? Nothing. Definitely not the injections of sheep gland that writers like Noël Coward, Somerset Maugham, and Truman Capote went to Switzerland for. My fountain of youth is on skis in St. Moritz, the place we decided to return to.

It isn't that St. Moritz anymore, the Palace isn't that Palace anymore (not that we stay there), and the chalet life ain't what it used to be. But it's still in the Engadine Valley where there's more snow than in any other place in Switzerland, where it's always warm, and where the waiters in town at Steffani's—Maurizio and Maddelena—and on the mountain at the Huber Hutte—Mario and Frau Huber herself—give us a big welcome home. The glamour, what's left of it, goes to Gstaad if it goes to Switzerland at all. But the skiing there is second-rate, if there's any at all.

Tom and I learned parallel skiing via the Arlesberg method in St. Anton. The teacher would shout, *"Elegante! Elegante!"* Tom responded, I tried.

We've skied all Europe, even Yugoslavia while it was still Yugoslavia and Communist: the chair lift went down. We skied Zurs but not after Kurt Waldheim was elected president. We skied Aspen but not after Hollywood moved in. We skied Klosters but the first night, I dreamt Hollywood and Vine met in the center of the village. Sun Valley reminded me of Klosters.

Ray and Fran gave a dinner party for Sydney Pollack and me at their condo: catered, sexy ski teachers for the hungry wives whose husbands were back at the studio, Fran with a slightly sprained wrist in a sling of the same material as her dress. She had a slew of matching slings, Ray had revolving ski suits, and everything Sydney wore was a hand-me-down from Robert Redford. Everything, hat to skis; I don't know about underwear and boots but everything else. Redford was a first-class skier; Pollack may have thought Redford's gear would make him one. It didn't. Ray did fine on the runs at Sun Valley but Sydney fell his way down the mountain, like Ray at Corvatch but Sidney didn't get up laughing. He got up swearing and took forever. It didn't occur to him I might not be having any fun so I directed him to a lift that took him down the last stretch, allowing me to get in one run before we settled down to work on the final final draft.

In Sun Valley, like Hollywood, you were dead without a car. You couldn't get to the slopes, to Ketchum for a decent meal, to the Inn, the Lodge, Ray's condo, or the chalet he had rented for us along with a car. A charmless two-story box of imitation wood, the chalet was one of a few hundred identical ones in the Sun Valley version of Levittown. Anticipating a problem in finding which box was home, the developers had painted the doors different colors—three different colors for three or four hundred boxes. Some nights the erratic lighting was absent from the doors; some nights the blowing snow hid the doors; some nights we were loaded. But the final final had to be completed before we could escape.

"We have to set the period with the opening shot," Sydney said, seating himself at the typewriter. "What would have been playing at Radio City Music Hall during World War Two?"

I looked at him. He started to type.

"I'm a very good typist," he explained.

I looked over his shoulder as he typed away. He was good; he could touch-type while I was restricted to a thumb and two index fingers. But I could write.

At first I thought he wanted me to dictate to him; then I thought by "we" he meant he would edit me and we would sort of collaborate; finally I realized the "we" was royal or editorial, i.e.: Sydney. What he was writing was a kind of cinematic masturbation. At times I would comment and make a suggestion, which he would ponder, then accept or reject, touch-typing away with commendable speed. The procedure was senseless but I knew sooner or later he would finish or not finish, spring would come, the snow would melt, the dog turds underneath the snow would float down the streets and we would be released from Sun Valley.

The script wasn't progressing but Sydney didn't seem to care. He took a lot of breaks for food and drink during which he'd talk openly and intimately, surprisingly so, about himself and his wife. Openness is appealing and it was hardly unusual for people to talk intimately to me. Still, Sydney didn't really know me and I was getting to know more about him than I was comfortable with. At a certain point, I'd ask if he minded if I took a couple of runs. "No, go, man!" When I got back, he'd be asleep.

He also talked about a young writer friend who'd saved him on the troubled scripts for his pictures. Very talented, David was, a talent Sydney was sure would be recognized as soon as one of David's own screenplays was produced. No suspicion was aroused in me that Sydney had plans for David to save him on this one; it should have been but it wasn't.

One conversation was memorable. Work for the day was done, we were having a drink when Sydney said, "You don't know how everybody in Hollywood is amazed by you."

"Why?"

"Because you've written the best love story in years and you're a homosexual."

What do you say to a man like that? Do you attack him? Do you attempt to educate him? Or do you just say to yourself: What an asshole! I had no interest in assailing or educating Sydney Pollack, and what ensued during the making of the movie confirmed the designation.

The final final screenplay differed very little from the final screenplay, so I could go home. Everyone was or pretended to be happy with it and no longer wanted to change anything. They'd even given up on the title. Nobody, including the publishers of the novel, ever liked "The Way We Were." They considered it a temporary title until the day it passed into the language.

The really chosen people are those who work at what they want. In New York, Ray, bubbling with that infectious enthusiasm, worked overtime at the job he wanted: casting young actresses. He took me with him to a casting session at an excellent Chinese restaurant convenient to his apartment on East Fifty-seventh. The other guests were Oleg Cassini and his very pretty girl who had no interest in becoming an actress, and an even prettier girl who was an actress and extremely interested in being recognized as one. Her name was Lois Chiles. I liked her; it was a pleasure just to look at her. Although she gave the impression of being the well-spoken, fresh-faced graduate of a very good private school, she got all Ray's jokes which flew thick, fast and dirty.

The part she wanted in *The Way We Were* was a good one. The requirements for the role were simple; understanding the requirements for getting the role was also simple. Lois understood.

"In other words," she said to Ray as though she were talking to a broker who had just explained the contents of her portfolio, "I get the part if I fuck you."

"Right!" Ray winked and laughed as though he might not have meant it. No one was going to catch him.

Lois got the part. Whether or not she fucked him, I didn't know; the proximity of the Chinese restaurant to his home might have been for naught. He didn't get even close when he was far from home, as at Rosemarie Kanzler's chalet in St. Moritz when it was St. Moritz. Introduced as a famous, enormously successful American producer, he used his bubbling, enthusiastic approach on a young, beautiful Italian actress who was also a successful one.

"Oh, thank you," she said charmingly, "but I prefer to fuck a young director."

Ray and Sydney took me as their guide when they flew to Ithaca to scout locations. Swooping over Cornell in a helicopter allowed me to pretend the campus looked unfamiliar because I'd never seen it from that expensive angle. But down on the ground, walking across the quadrangle I had crossed thirty-five years earlier, I was drenched in disappointment. I couldn't find even one vista I remembered. New structures consistently obscured the view: brusque Modern cheek by jowl with old Gothic each made the other a mistake; ivy-covered walls no longer looked romantic but more as though they needed a weeding; "functional" wasn't excuse enough for the undistinguished angularity of all the recent additions. The combination of old and new was unsightly, unbalanced contemporary America.

The following week, when I drove out to Brooklyn to have a home-cooked meal with my folks, I stopped off at my other alma mater, Erasmus Hall High. When I attended, even when Barbra did, it was the miniature model of an Ivy League college campus. If anything was a permanent, indestructible classic, it had to be Erasmus. Now graffiti defaced the scarred and chipped stone walls; the green-lawned quadrangle in the midst of the Gothic buildings was half-obliterated by wooden huts for additional classrooms; the stained-glass windows of the chapel were replaced by plywood or plain glass; and a black student body spilled out of the arched entranceway, blocking the sidewalk in front. How would the minister's daughter who reported our anti-Semitic French teacher to the principal decades ago react now to the blacks? I didn't know any more than I knew why the architectural landscape had gotten uglier since the end of the Depression and the arrival of affluence.

Even the dunes of Quogue showed inroads: new houses that were too big, too unshapely, too grand for the beach. Space was disappearing. Fortunately, the living room of my house had two walls of windows from which I could look out and not see change. The south windows overlooked the beach and my swimming pool, the Atlantic Ocean. The north windows afforded a view through black pines, past the garage-with-guest-cottage, across three acres of empty wetlands and a wide expanse of Shinnecock Bay to a distant, sparsely inhabited shore. The south view was expensive because ocean frontage was nonexistent and therefore desperately desirable; the north view was the unexpected view, the sweeter. I was lost in it when the phone rang a few weeks before *The Way We Were* started shooting. Sydney Pollack was calling from California.

"I'm afraid I have some bad news." His voice had the insincerity of a director who had been an actor. "Ray's going to fire you."

"But you're the director."

"Oh, man, I tried. Believe me! But Ray's made up his mind, he won't listen. Oh, man, I'm sorry."

There was more of the same, always punctuated with an "Oh, man!" To Sydney, "man" was hip, funky, with-it, young. I always thought blacks used it as rebellion against over a century of being called "boy." "Boy" would have been accurate for Sydney.

"One piece of advice, Sydney." I managed to keep the anger out of my voice. "You're going to build up Redford's part because you're in love with him. I don't mean homosexually but he's the blond goy you wish you were. The picture is Barbra's no matter what you do because the story is hers. Be careful you don't destroy it trying to give it to him."

Half an hour later, the phone rang again. It was Ray.

"I'm afraid I've got some bad news, pal." Ray used "pal" the way Sydney used "man." "Sydney is going to fire you."

"He just told me you were firing me."

"He's full of shit."

"But you're the producer."

"Yeah, but he's got Redford. It's the two of them together and I need Redford."

I believed him.

"I'm sorry, pal."

The hurt was unexpected. It was very painful, I was surprised how painful. It was only a movie, for God's sake. But of course, it wasn't only a movie. The story was mine; it came from me, the characters came from me, there was some of me in all the people and what happened to them. It hurt and what made it hurt more was why I was fired. Robert Redford was dissatisfied with his part. That much, Sydney told me; why he was dissatisfied he never told me. Maybe he didn't know, but basically, the one thing Sydney Pollack did know was that he believed in Robert Redford. Which wasn't very good for Redford though neither of them understood that then.

Eleven writers were brought in—eleven, count 'em, eleven. As I later discovered from writers like Larry Gelbart, this was Sydney's distinguishing characteristic as a director. Among the eleven were Dalton Trumbo, Alvin Sargent and Sydney's protégé, David. Ray made his contribution: two playwrights from New York, Paddy Chayefsky and Herb Gardner, but they told him he was an asshole, the screenplay was great as it was. Whether they believed that or partially believed it and were being loyal to one of their own, they were a class act and I saluted them.

Shooting had to be delayed for the rewrites and the rewrites of the rewrites. Cornell was lost as a location: shooting at this late date would interfere with classes. Ray was affronted: this was a major Hollywood movie, a Columbia Pictures Ray Stark produced production starring Barbra Streisand and Robert Redford! He was even more affronted when lesser universities, smaller and smaller colleges turned them down. That I as a Cornell alumnus might possibly have helped them didn't occur to any of them. True, they had fired me but I doubt that would have mattered to them. Certainly not to Ray. The small college finally used didn't provide much of a photographic opportunity but that turned out to be among the least of the troubles. The phone in Quogue rang again.

"You win, pal!" Ray was eating crow with enthusiasm.

They hadn't kept track of the rewrites of the rewrites. There were holes in scenes, the story was garbled, Barbra was unhappy, Redford wasn't any happier—would I come back? They wanted me to repair the damage, cover it and make sure that what remained to be shot was kept on track.

I was past hurt and anger; I had no feeling of vindication or victory, pyrrhic or otherwise. I cared to the extent that I had pride in my work. I'd take a crack at salvaging and protecting it as much as I could but I would not let myself be hurt again. I would keep reminding myself it was only a movie and movies were not really for writers.

I asked for an exorbitant amount of money which I knew I would get: they will always pay during what they won't pay before. I told Ray I would say what I thought and would write what I wanted. If Sydney & Co. wanted something else, I would take the first plane home. Ray agreed to everything and guaranteed the others would. Which didn't mean he would agree after I got there. Happily, I knew that while "the others" meant Sydney and Redford, it did not mean Barbra. She had been a wonderful pest, dredging up a scene here, a line there from my early versions, lugging them to the set and utzing Sydney to put them back. She knew Katie Morosky better than he did and fought like her for her.

When I arrived on the set, I was nervous, not even very confident. I'd read the changes on the plane, I'd seen the footage shot earlier that day: Sydney had been shooting some other picture. Inevitably, there was going to be a confrontation somewhere down the road and I wasn't looking forward to it. He had called the night before to welcome me but his acting hadn't improved. Redford I still had never met. Barbra—ah, Barbra! We were on the phone for over an hour: old home week, old friend week, old thank you week. The first person I saw on the set, however, wasn't Barbra; it wasn't Sydney or Redford; it wasn't even Ray. It was Lois Chiles.

She raced over, threw her arms around me as though we knew each other, and burst into tears. Sydney was mean to her, Redford was glacial, Barbra invisible, Ray ignored her—could we please have dinner please? Of course. Here, take my handkerchief, call me at my hotel later to fix the time.

When she called, she asked: "Would you mind if I brought a friend? Would it be alright?"

"Sure. Who's your friend?"

"Bob Evans."

Jesus. "You don't need me, Lois. You're doing fine."

The Great Gatsby, her next picture, was produced by Bob Evans. Hollywood was full of Chinese restaurants.

When I saw Redford on the set, I decided to make a fresh start, throw the first ball, say the first hello. I walked over. He was checking proof sheets of publicity stills of him and Barbra. She had put a big red X across the shots she wouldn't approve, he Xed whatever was left. At least I wasn't in publicity. Finished, Redford looked up with a stare of ice that could sink a *Titanic* and before I could open my mouth, walked by, cutting me dead. Why? I did not have a clue.

Years earlier, a man I knew suddenly cut me dead. When I asked him why, he said: "You're an intelligent man. You should be able to figure it out: I don't want to speak to you."

I was an intelligent man; I figured out Redford didn't want to speak to me. But why? Why didn't he? That Sydney Pollack might well have been the "why" didn't occur to me.

In my original screenplay, the extent of Hubbell's jockdom was stroking the crew. As filmed, he is a decathlon man, a thirty-year-old undergraduate who rows, races, shot-puts, throws a javelin, and plays football, albeit touch football. When he rows, the students on the bank, far from cheering for their college like normal students, shout, "Gardner! Gardner!" for Robert Redford. Pollack wouldn't cut the cheering any more than he would cut the number of golden boy shots. I consoled myself with the possibility that since Hubbell in his various tracksuits is at the very opening of the college sequence, maybe the audience would think "Gardner" was the name of the college.

Forty–sixty was my split with Sydney over a big scene shot in New York in a Beekman Place apartment. A section important for Katie had been excised for no reason. I managed to get it shot in the studio—admittedly against a weirdly fake mock-up of the original background but shot nevertheless. The core of the scene, a bitter argument between Katie and Hubbell written to be played at a distance from Hubbell's friends, didn't fare as well. It was rewritten by one of the Pollack Eleven and staged by Sydney so that Katie harangued Hubbell in front of his friends. Making her a shrill, insensitive harridan while he is a strong, true gent who takes no crap. One way of building up Hubbell— the purpose, I suppose—but achieved at Katie's expense. Ray wouldn't agree to re-shooting: too expensive, even if Sydney would agree.

Zero–one hundred was my split with Sydney over a love scene between Streisand and Redford shot—what was Sydney thinking?—in front of a roaring fire in a small walk-up apartment. Katie and Hubbell have been to bed but he was drunk and she is not sure he remembers. As they start to make love in front of the accommodating fire, Hubbell says: "It'll be better this time." But he didn't; Redford wouldn't say the line. Or Sydney wouldn't let him say it. Someone was trying to say Robert Redford couldn't be better: he was always good.

One cut remained an unsolved mystery: the Tony Blue Eyes moment that occurred in Barbra and Redford's first scene together in the picture. What made

Bob and Barbra or Hubbell and Katie? Whichever, a rare spontaneous moment.

it mysterious to me was that it would have been good for Redford. But when the moment came for Katie to ask Hubbell why he always smiles, she asked instead:

"Do you smile all the time?"

And instead of telling the story of the teacher sending him around with the note, Redford repeats "No!" four times with a laugh in between each two—a trick he often uses but why here and what it meant, Sydney couldn't explain. Nor why Redford wears a white wool turtleneck in late spring. Yes, he is as gorgeous as a matinee idol and he sweateth not, but he looks unreal in a scene that already looks unreal, taking place as it does in a hastily assembled sidewalk café in a small town that obviously never had a sidewalk café until a set decorator arrived from Hollywood.

I had more success with writing inserts or moments or even scenes, whatever was needed to fill in the holes and cover the gaps left in the story by the rewrites of the Eleven. The set was an unacknowledged battlefield—Sydney and Redford on one side, me on the other, Barbra in between for more than the obvious reasons: she was infatuated with Redford. That itself was obvious to everyone on the picture, not excluding Redford who handled it well, neither encouraging her nor using her crush to his advantage.

What maddened me above all was that the scenes under way or coming up all occurred during the Witch Hunt and no one knew a damn thing about the Witch Hunt except me. Sydney depended on in-depth studio research that consisted in the main of newspaper photographs from the period; the newspapers at that time, like all the media except *The New Masses,* reflected the attitude of HUAC: Down with Commie Reds.

That actual slogan on a handmade sign was in the newspaper photograph Sydney used as the basis for a politically crude scene that never would have happened to the characters in the movie and was completely unnecessary. It exemplified everything that went wrong with *The Way We Were* and illustrated why it did.

The scene takes place at Union Station in downtown Los Angeles. Katie, her political friends—a fictionalized John Huston and other members of the Committee for the First Amendment—return from protesting the HUAC hearings in Washington to be confronted by an angry crowd of Red-baiters. Just that much alone was absurd.

In actual life, the First Amendment group of people like Huston, Bogart and Bacall and Gerry Brooks flew to Washington and flew back to Los Angeles. Trains to Washington were not for the starry: the ride was too long and the station downtown a foreign land. At the airport, they were more likely to have been greeted by fans seeking autographs than by Red-baiters waving signs. Sydney would listen to none of this; he wanted the station scene badly. Why? The answer is in what happens in it.

Katie & Co. are confronted and jeered at—she, not so incidentally, is wearing her hair in a very unattractive snood. No one in Hollywood that I ever saw wore a snood at that time nor did any coed I saw at Cornell wear a hat—but Katie Morosky does. Studio research was the source of the styles along with the slogans and signs, undoubtedly authentic. But the relationship between authenticity in files and usage in life—not only in movies but in books, museums, anywhere—is so questionable, it throws history into a dubious light. The photograph Sydney used was from a newspaper but it did not authenticate the scene he used it for.

Hubbell, who vehemently opposed Katie's going to Washington, is nevertheless there, waiting for her. Well, he's her husband and our hero. So he's on hand to escort her through a small mob of crackpots and reporters shouting insults and questions. Katie's polemical responses are so much a caricature of the left-wing position that she and the scene are banal and boring. Then it peps up: a man yells, "Shut up, you Commie bitch!" and Hubbell swings into action. One roundhouse sends the man who insulted his wife sprawling. Two policemen grab Hubbell and prevent him from protecting himself, making it his turn to get punched in the jaw and sent sprawling. The blood that instantly spurts from his mouth is David Merrick red and now we know why the scene is there: Hubbell may be a writer but he is a man of action. Robert Redford is strong.

Losing the battle over that scene out of a John Wayne Western made me determined not to lose the war over the scene in the Union Station restaurant that immediately follows. Katie and Hubbell are rushed out of more harm's way by the same two policemen who pinned Hubbell's arms and are shoved into the deserted restaurant. Why deserted during business hours and when a train has just pulled in is anybody's guess. Except this time, Pollack decided he didn't want anyone around for the misplayed argument between the two stars. Barbra's notion of a woman with strong political convictions is to fancy up her speech and shout. Hubbell is an intelligent man who doesn't have to shout to register. If only as an actor, Redford might have realized restraint would undercut Streisand and make Hubbell truly strong. But under Pollack's guidance. Hubbell shouts and Katie shouts and we don't believe either of them.

The confrontation over the last two lines in the scene was inevitable. In his penultimate speech, Hubbell tells Katie people are more important than witch hunts and causes and principles. Katie's answer is:

"Hubbell, people are their principles."

Sydney cut her line—the point of the whole scene, the political point of the whole picture. I knew why he cut it, I knew he and Redford were fed up to the teeth with me by then. But I knew I was not going to let him cut it. I dug in. And worked to get Barbra into the trenches with me. Even before I arrived, she had been constantly debating and pleading with Sydney for the restoration of pieces of scenes, of lines he cut. Not her lines necessarily, lines she felt vital to the piece. After I arrived, I took over most of the never-ending struggle.

Most but not all. Barbra wanted "people are their principles"; she knew what the line meant to Katie and the picture but it was hard for her to stand up. Beyond her infatuation with Redford, she was intimidated by his acting skill and by the mutual adoration of Redford and Pollack that allowed them to control the picture. Her own clout, her own power, she was hesitant to use. She believed the director should run the show even when she disagreed with what he was doing. I needed her power because I needed someone to stand up with me. Which would never be Ray—the only thing he stood for was to pee. So I pushed Barbra, I pushed her hard, and like Katie Morosky she stood fast: the line stayed.

But Pollack wouldn't let the scene end on Katie. He ended it with Redford shoving a table over in furious disgust. Robert Redford shoved the table over, not Hubbell Gardner. Hubbell would have gotten Katie's point. Hubbell was too much of a man to crash furniture because he'd lost an argument with his wife.

I didn't begrudge Sydney his macho moment. Katie had her line, the picture had her line, I had her line. That, if nothing else, made me glad I had come back.

There was always tension on the set. Sydney, never totally in control, consequently spent more time with the lights than with the actors. A few exhausting days later when the tension level was even higher than usual, there was another battle over another definitive line that ended another important scene. The scene itself was like a Christmas stocking for the actors, filled with one moment after another moment where they could do what they loved doing: act. Emotion, both released and repressed, was all over the page but the actors were playing blandly—text without subtext. Not one moment was really working and they knew it. The simple problem was that the man who was directing a political love story knew even less about love than he did about politics. Any doubts on that score were wiped out when they reached the last moments and Sydney took out his scissors.

By the end of that scene, Katie and Hubbell have hit bottom in their marriage. She is in tears, refusing to face what he really is and not her fantasy of what he is. In despair, he asks her what she wants.

"I want us to love each other!" she cries.

"The trouble is we do," Hubbell says sadly.

But Sydney Pollack wouldn't let him say anything: he cut the line. What Bob Redford thought about the cut, I didn't know. Sydney said Bob didn't want the line. He always said that; it may or may not have been true but if Redford had wanted the line, the odds were Sydney would have kept the line.

"The trouble is we do" summed up the relationship between Hubbell and Katie: they loved each other despite, not because. Sydney looked blank. To him, if they loved each other, they'd surmount any trouble; if trouble was continuous, they didn't love each other. The line made no sense and was sentimental anyway so cut it. How do you explain the complexities of love to a Sydney Pollack? How do you get him to comprehend? You don't because you can't, no matter how hard you may try.

To make a mantra of "It's only a movie" was as useless and foolish as feeling pain. No matter what I felt or thought, no matter what I tried to accomplish or how, Sydney Pollack would ultimately have it his way. That was what I had to face and accept. They didn't cry "Author! Author!" in the movies, they never had. Now they cried "Auteur! Auteur!"—even if the auteur fucked up the picture. "Film," they said, but I reserved "film" for the very few that warranted it. A "movie" was what Sydney was directing. It would be his movie, then Ray's, then tomorrow the world's.

Pollack came East with a rough cut of the finished picture and ran it for me. It was a mess, literally. There were good scenes, good moments, but most of it was jumpy, bumpy, lacking coherence and poorly photographed. The last scene held out hope: the ending worked. As Rose says in *Gypsy*, "If you have a good, strong finish, they'll forgive anything." What made the last scene work was what made the love story work despite all the glitches: the chemistry between Streisand and Redford. Astaire-Rogers but more because he had more sex to begin with than Astaire, she had more class to begin with than Rogers, together they made the screen swoon every time they were in the same frame.

Individually, their performances were in and out. Each was not merely a star but a superstar, and that always comes between the persona and the role. He was Bob Redford playing Redford playing Hubbell Gardner. She was Barbra Joan Streisand playing Streisand playing Katie Morosky. Every now and then, especially when they were together, there was a marvelous moment when he was Hubbell Gardner without teeth and hair getting in the way and she was Katie Morosky without grand accent and fingernails getting in the way.

That grand accent came with the fixed speech that afflicts New York actors trying to raise their social status—Pacino, depending on the role; Bacall, no matter what the role. It rings false in words like "first" and "perfect," loudest in the *a* sound in "man"—no one was born saying "man" that way. Self-conscious, self-imposed, the phony accent makes the actor phony and unreal. It damaged Barbra's performance.

Katie Morosky was an Oscar-winning role. What could have guaranteed Barbra's winning was a long, heart-breaking telephone call. Instead, I think it lost her the Oscar. Almost from the first word, there was the fixed speech; it came and went, taking reality with it. Her concentration seemed to be on producing tears, which she did. But real tears don't guarantee reality, and her discomfort was too evident in the way she kept hiding, covering her face again and again with her hand which inevitably drew the eye to those unreal fingernails.

How I wished I could have directed her in that phone call! There was no reason for her to hide her face; Barbra Streisand understood rejection. What she needed was help from someone who understood her; then the Oscar she wanted would have been hers. More important, then she would have had a real emotion to bring to the late-night scene immediately after the phone call when Hubbell comes over to her apartment. Instead, when she opened the door, she had nothing for him, Redford brought her nothing, nothing makes nothing. The acting was all artifice; the words, not the actors, got the scene to where it had to go. But those actors, Streisand and Redford, could have gone beyond the words to connect and make that connection rip the audience apart. Watching them in the screening room, my stomach told me I still cared about the misshapen movie. Foolish, but I did.

After the screening, Sydney and I went to Pearl's, a Chinese restaurant on West Forty-eighth Street, a hangout for theatre people that was a sort of home. Sydney's face defined "ashen." After a big drink, he apologized for doing a bad job: the picture was not good, it was his fault, he was responsible. He apologized again. Tears that had been brimming spilled over and dribbled down his cheeks but they were for him, not me. I wondered if he had thought the picture wasn't good before he watched it sitting next to me and saw it through my eyes.

The next day we went into that house of tricks, the editing room, to make whatever magic we possibly could with what we had. The picture was better for it—not as good as it should have been, not good enough for me, but better. There was hope.

Barbra sang two versions of the theme song over the phone long-distance: which did I prefer? Ray previewed the picture in San Francisco and his wild enthusiasm almost short-circuited the long-distance wires. The audience loved it! They loved the love story! Wild about the love story! He sounded as though he hadn't known it was a love story but now that he did know, he became a dangerous man. Nobody cared about the Witch Hunt, nobody cared about the politics, he was going to cut them the hell out of his picture. Time was short so he, Sydney and Margaret Booth, editor emeritus on loan from Metro, went for what was quick, easy, and simple: they whacked out one big chunk. If that cut more than politics, what the hell.

I cheered myself up thinking at least the detested scene at Union Station would go. Delusion; it didn't. What did go, among others, was one of Barbra's best moments: Katie watching a younger Katie on a California campus protesting the Vietnam War now, not her Spanish Civil War. But more devastating, the most devastating, they cut the climax of the entire picture. I couldn't believe it. It came in the scene between Katie and Hubbell based on the end of Jigee and Peter Viertel, the scene where the love story and the political story came together—the climax of that scene was the climax of the picture. That was precisely what that unholy trio cut.

Sydney had shot it; I had seen it; it was well done. The marriage is falling apart but Katie, who is very pregnant, still loves him. Dinner is ready when he comes home from the studio to their house on the beach in Malibu. They sit awkwardly, silently, picking at the food until Hubbell gives her his bad news: someone informed on her. To the studio, he has a subversive wife. Unless she clears herself—meaning unless she informs—he will be fired. After a long awkward pause, Katie says: "It's amazing how decisions are forced upon us willy-nilly." Her decision is to divorce him; then he won't have a subversive wife and can keep his job.

What Ray and Sydney left in the picture is Hubbell and Katie having dinner, polite but uncomfortable with one another. Then out of an awkward silence, she says "It's amazing how decisions are forced upon us willy-nilly." Cut to Hubbell who looks at her bleakly. Cut back to Katie who asks: Will he stay with her until the baby is born? He nods. The audience gets that they are divorcing and is not surprised because it's been clear from the beginning that Katie and Hubbell were not destined for one another. But why they are divorcing at this moment, the audience doesn't really know. Nor, apparently, did it care. That was what was hardest for me to take: Nobody cared. Nobody even noticed.

One possible exception: Pauline Kael may have noticed. If indeed she did, she didn't care. Kael was taken too seriously as a movie critic, at least by other critics and the movie industry, until she made the mistake of trying to get a job in the business. She was not the first critic to make that mistake although the others usually tried and failed by attempting to write a screenplay and sell it.

In her review of *The Way We Were*, Kael points out that "the decisive change in the characters' lives which the story hinges on takes place suddenly and hardly makes sense." On the nose: one for me, zero for Ray and Sydney. She further says the movie has "the sweat stains of interfering hands." Another for me, zero for Sydney—well, not quite. Concluding, she credits the picture with "some very well written (Alvin Sargent was among the uncredited writers) and well directed moments."

I wrote her, asking why she might not just as well have written: "the movie has the sweat stains of interfering hands (Alvin Sargent was among the uncredited screenwriters)." Her reply: My point was valid and why didn't we have a drink? I refused the invitation; I didn't believe in fraternizing with critics. My next and last movie, *The Turning Point,* was panned by Pauline Kael.

As for her "uncredited writers," they were claiming credit for scenes that were in the treatment I wrote. They pitched the Screen Writers Guild for screen credit. Did I contest this? the Guild asked. The *Snake Pit* shoe was on the other foot but my answer was that the writing credit should be shared with Sydney Pollack and Robert Redford. The Guild didn't agree.

Footnote: The success of the picture prompted Ray to talk sequel but none of us were interested.

Another footnote: My consolation prize was money. On a percentage basis, not in actual dollars but on a percentage basis, I made more money than either Streisand or Redford. Their percentages were based on the picture's gross; they had to sue to collect. Their lawsuit revealed each had put his or her personal secretary's salary on the picture's payroll.

I didn't have a piece of the picture as they did; I had a piece of what Ray Stark made from the picture. He, of course, had a piece of everything that wasn't, as they say, nailed down. That wasn't my acumen, that was the smarts of my agent at that time—Shirley Bernstein, Lenny's sister. Agents pontificate about making a "creative" deal; Shirley made a creative deal.

Almost a decade later, Robert Redford's story editor called to arrange a meeting at his office in Rockefeller Center. I took a book with me; like Marilyn Monroe, Redford had a reputation for being late. And he was, well over half an hour. But I complimented him on *All the President's Men* anyway and the conversation went smoothly. The ice between us melted quickly after we tracked it down to the iceman: Sydney Pollack. We didn't do him in but it was enjoyable to be open about what he had done and why, and done to so many others. Sydney was quite famous for betrayal.

What Redford—I called him Bob but didn't yet think of him as Bob—wanted from me was a love story. We discussed what that meant at length, not only in his office but a few days later at my house in the Village. If he was chronically late and he was, I didn't mind waiting where I was able to do whatever I was doing until he showed up.

What I came up with was the last thing either of us thought we wanted: a sequel to *The Way We Were*. But it had the makings of a very different kind of love story with many facets and unexpected permutations. Hubbell and their daughter (a radical like Katie), who comes on to him not knowing he is her father; Katie and Hubbell who never stopped loving one another; Katie jealous of her daughter and deeply attached to her second husband, David, who loves her and the daughter he has really been a father to. Add outtakes from the original so that, for one example, when Hubbell and Katie talk long-distance for the first time in fifteen years, what each visualizes on the other end is the other fifteen years ago. Add an ending at the chaotic 1968 Democratic National Convention in Chicago with police brutality against marching protesters who are shouting to the TV cameras: "The whole world's watching!" The possibilities were exciting.

Redford and I had gotten on well. He suggested we be together on this, keep it between the two of us and thus keep control. When I finished the screenplay, I would send it to him before sending it to Ray Stark, even before sending it to Barbra. Neither of us mentioned Sydney who didn't appear to be the foregone conclusion I would have assumed.

Writing the screenplay was stimulating. I liked a speech where Hubbell said his looks were a problem because people didn't get past them. I liked the new characters, especially the daughter and scenes where she came on to Redford, her father. When I finished, I did as he asked: sent the screenplay first to him. I didn't expect to hear back quickly from a man who was always late but it got so late, so much time passed that I wrote him a letter.

It began "Dear Arthur" and apologized for not getting back: I'd been up to my neck, but I would read the script now and get back immediately, "Best always, Bob." Amusing, no danger of offending, no accusation—and no response. I never heard back. To this day, I have never heard back, unless one uncompleted phone call counts.

In 1982, I was in Boston, directing the tryout of *La Cage Aux Folles.* From the first preview, the show was an enormous, unbelievable success. Returning from a rehearsal, I found a message at my hotel: Robert Redford had called and left a number. I returned the call: no answer. Ever.

When an explanation came—a partial explanation—it came from Sydney Pollack who arrived in New York to discuss the sequel. Who asked him? Ray, I suppose. Sydney, like Ray, was enthusiastic about the project though he did, naturally, want a few changes. Very deadpan but meaning it, I said:

"You know I don't trust you, Sydney."

"Oh, I know," he answered as pleasantly as though I had said I did.

His explanation of why I hadn't heard from Redford was that Bob hated Ray and would never do a picture with him. Oh. But Redford knew from the start that Ray owned the rights. Why did he go along with the idea of a sequel? And why didn't he tell me he wouldn't work with Ray? Sydney smiled as he gave a not-altogether-charitable explanation of Redford's behavior. The friendship between those two was beyond me. Just as telling the whole truth was apparently beyond them.

. . .

In 1996, Barbra dug up the script of the sequel. So did I: it wasn't as good as I had thought; it needed a hefty rewrite. Which suited Barbra. She was going to direct, produce, and co-star with Bob who had said he would do it with her. Redford directed by Streisand? I couldn't wait but knew I would have to—forever, probably. And what about Ray? Had Bob changed how he felt about working with him? Had Barbra changed how she felt about working with him for that matter? No; Ray had agreed to sell it to her. Really? Well, when he does, I said, let me know and I'll get to work. I was safe.

Positively last footnote: In 1997, Ray called to ask me to adapt *The Way We Were* as a musical for Broadway starring Kathie Lee Gifford.

When Katie and Hubbell came to their end, she went to New York and the Witch Hunt disappeared from the picture. Not so with me. When my professional and personal lives in Hollywood came to their end, the Witch Hunt didn't go away. It stayed very much in my picture and framed it.

My personal life ended with Farley growing up or at least trying to, first by breaking away from Goldwyn. Goldwyn sat him down for gentle, avuncular advice, then told him how he had kept Ronald Colman off the screen for a year when he wanted to break away. Farley didn't care; he wanted to be rid of Daddy. I too was a Daddy, but unlike Goldwyn, I was unsure what I wanted. My lease was up on the house in Laurel Canyon so I bought time with a short holiday in New York to be with my folks and friends I missed and to catch up on the theatre.

The blacklist had reached television but not the theatre. It never would reach the theatre, not so much because theatre folk were so liberal but because the producers were self-employed individuals, not companies, and weren't beholden to corporations or banks. The short holiday became a month; when I got back to Hollywood, I moved in with Farley who had taken a glitzy apartment in the hills above Sunset known as the Swish Alps.

Boys rang the doorbell day and night, even though Farley was working at the studio; phone numbers on little scraps of paper kept turning up like a deliberate paper trail; and he kept playing one record over and over: "The End of a Love Affair." Very Joan Crawford. In New York, unbeknownst, I'd been having a not innocuous affair with Frank Coyle, the new hot man in town. I hadn't given him my California number because it was Farley's; if Farley knew,

I couldn't play martyr. Of course, I knew when and where to call Frank even though I sometimes had to hang up in midsentence because Farley had come home early from the studio.

Oh, we were a pair all right. Each of us thought he had been dumped by the other but we didn't discover that until years later. At the moment, I didn't want him to have anyone else. I knew the romance was over but I was nostalgic for it; I wanted it and I didn't want it. I waited for an omen, a sign saying Pack Up. One finally came from an unexpected quarter: Jerry Robbins asked me to adapt *Look, Ma, I'm Dancing!* for the screen. He was going to direct it at Paramount.

I owed it to him for walking out years ago when I was supposed to be writing it for Broadway. It would be fun—he hadn't informed yet, not that I knew of anyway—and the money would be nice with Irving, no longer Swifty Lazar making the deal. But there was no deal.

"You're blacklisted, my dear boy."

"How do you know?"

"Bernie said you were too expensive before I mentioned money."

I was elated. A blacklist was illegal; we hadn't had been able to prove there was one but now we could! Bernie, the studio's man responsible for making deals with writers, was a pal and a comrade from all those meetings to raise funds for the families of the Ten.

"He'll back up Lazar and we're home!" I exulted to Lorry and Millard Kaufman. Mil was as excited as I was but calm and cool Lorry wasn't sanguine.

"Bernie?" she said, skewering him merely with her inflection. "It might cost him his job." Her implication was clear and of course she was right; she usually was.

For Bernie, there was no issue to discuss; this was a time when you kept your mouth shut and hung on until it was all over. Not everyone was certain it ever would be all over but I still felt elated, rather than angry, at being blacklisted. The reason for that feeling I acknowledged only to myself: it allowed me to take my place in the ranks of martyred victims. It also left me with no excuse for staying in Hollywood: no work, no love affair, time to go. I had gotten my sign.

I asked Judd Marmor for the name of an analyst in New York. Instead, he suggested I try to go it on my own and write him. "You may go into a tailspin," he said, "but it won't last. You'll never go down for the third time."

Lorry was having her first child any minute; I was to be godfather so I delayed departure. Waiting in Farley's apartment was very strange. We might have been English, we behaved so well. My bags sat there, packed and ready to go. We looked at them, walked past them, stepped over them, both of us sad

Lorry Kaufman, pregnant with my godchild. As eager as I was
to get out of Hollywood, I waited until she was born.

and relieved, each very considerate of the other. Lorry, being Lorry, tried hard
to have the baby on my birthday but didn't give birth until the day after.
Which was better: it gave Mary a birthday all her own.

With Mary, I knew I'd miss the Kaufmans more, even though friendship
doesn't usually flourish long-distance. I wouldn't miss Farley: he was going to
jump in bed with Jimmy Mitchell the moment I was gone. I was nostalgic for
what we'd had but nostalgia is for what's over and my California time was over.
I would never come back to live here, that was a certainty, the only one I felt
when I boarded the plane to fly East. New York might be only a stopover.

Frank Coyle persuaded me to rent a house on Fire Island for a week. Sex with
him was great, the boys trolling the beach were pretty, the whole place was
probably beautiful but you couldn't see the forest for all the pretty trees. Much
as I liked sex, a community existing solely for sex, concentrated exclusively on
that one subject made me think, What in God's name am I doing here? I

didn't have to come there to get laid but it was the only thing I could get there unless I wanted a lesson in how to camp. A big step backward to a place I'd thought I was done with; it sent me into the predicted tailspin. I left the island the third day.

In New York, I was temporary—not visiting, not living there, just momentarily occupying an apartment belonging to an absent admirer of Nora's. Summer in New York is empty and hard to get through alone. Even without being in a tailspin and no matter how many letters I wrote Judd. The day I left California, I knew what I wanted was to follow the political refugees to Europe but I delayed because I felt fraudulent. I wasn't a legitimate political refugee: I hadn't been called before a committee, I wasn't even a Communist. I was just blacklisted and that in an industry I didn't want to work in anyway. So of course a fraud.

Good friends were in Paris: Ann Selepegno and Tola; Ethel, Buddy, and Judy; Jigee and Peter. I wasn't flush but Paris was cheap and what was I staying in New York for? I booked passage. The decision invigorated me. I rushed to buy luggage and renew my passport and was shot down. The passport was confiscated. That lifted me out of the tailspin. The problem was serious and not self-induced. I wasn't being neurotic; there was a reason to yell Fire: my house was burning.

Jerry Robbins recommended a lawyer who was immediately likable, relaxing and reassuring. Some preliminaries had to be gotten out of the way—nothing important, he said, nothing to be concerned about, just a few facts to get him better acquainted before proceeding.

We went into a small room, with a secretary to take down in shorthand my answers to his questions. They were very specific and there were so many, I began feeling oddly apprehensive. The grilling continued for almost four hours: anything I had given my name or money to; which political events I had appeared at, when and where; anything conceivably political I had written; any and every meeting I had attended for the Hollywood Ten and who was there; every meeting of the Marxist study group LA and who was there. Impasse: I wouldn't give names. Not of the other fund-raisers whose names were widely known, especially not of the other members of the study group whose names were not known. Maybe it was my exhaustion or his insistence but I had begun feeling threatened; now I was feeling frightened as well and angry that I did. Who was he?

"I'm your lawyer. I need all the information—"

"I know you're my lawyer but I don't see the purpose of giving you those names."

"Let me worry about the purpose—"

I flared up. "You don't need to know and I'm not going to name any names!"

The phrase hit both of us at the same time and resonated. He switched gears. Patting my shoulder, he smiled. "Good boy. We're all pooped. Let's all go home."

That ended the grilling. For the next phase, he gave me a name and a telephone number at the State Department to call. A lawyer calling would be a presumption of guilt, he said. Alice in Wonderland, I thought, and indeed it was Down the Rabbit Hole when I called the State Department myself. The voice answering had a southern accent, it was that corny. He drawled that my name had appeared on page so-and-so of the such-and-such issue of *The Daily Worker:* did I care to explain why?

"What does it say?"

"Oh, I don't know but if you care to explain, write us a letter."

On page so-and-so was a review of *Home of the Brave.* I explained in my letter. Oh, thank you; your name also appears on page so-and-so of the such-and-such issue of *The New Masses:* if you care to explain . . .

This continued for three months. Then the lawyer suggested I write a letter explaining my political beliefs in detail: say it all, everything, hold back nothing. He would vet it and then we would send it to the State Department. So I put it all in writing and held back nothing except names. The lawyer changed nothing.

"This is going to do me in!"

"No, it's going to get you your passport," he said confidently. "Your beliefs are too idiosyncratic. They'll know you can't have been a member of anything."

I sent the letter. The Monday of the following week, the passport arrived; on Wednesday I sailed for France; on Thursday a cable arrived on the boat from MGM offering me a job. The chain of scoundrels was that blatant and that efficient. Red tape could be cut in a matter of days when the State Department, the House Un-American Committee, and the Motion Picture Industry put their minds to it.

The ship was the *Ile de France* and Lena Horne was on board—how much is hidden in that sentence! I was as unprepared as she was for an indefinable relationship that lasted fifteen years and then collapsed in a week.

Lena and Lennie were in first class, I was in tourist but spent most of the

crossing in the first-class bar with them. The French Line, unlike its English
and American counterparts, had no upstairs/downstairs passenger restrictions.
For the English, the class system was the way of life. At a large gay cocktail
party I once went to in London, the guests stood around in segregated clus-
ters: titles, theatre and money, Cockneys, Americans, and, bringing up the
rear (pun intended), Australians. On the *Queen Mary,* the gates between
tourist and first were locked to preserve the class system; on the *United States,*
they were locked to preserve the money system.

It would be somewhat true to say that once we boarded ship, Lena and I
bonded—and with Lennie: Lennie was where Lena was—because wary of
what an expatriate life would be, we clung to someone from home. Even
though we were running from a home that had rejected us: they were fleeing
America to marry and work in Europe, I was fleeing to be as free as only a
stranger in a foreign land can be free. It would be more true if less lofty, however, to say Lena and I bonded because of our mutual dislike of Gene Kelly.
We didn't rip into Gene or the pretense that animated the house on Rodeo
Drive; we laughed with the sheer delight of finding someone else among all
those kiss-asses who felt exactly the same and could say it. We also laughed at
ourselves for participating and pretending for so long—my reason was Farley,

With Lena Horne. Her then manager, Ralph Harris *(far right),*
obviously wasn't worried.

hers was Lennie. Lennie drifted in a haze of goodwill and brandy; he was fond of Gene. He adored "the girl," as he and their musicians called Lena: if it made her happy to joke about Gene, he was happy to see her happy; if it made her happy to be with me, it made him happy. He was totally at ease with homosexuals; he didn't think we could pose a threat.

By the time we disembarked at Le Havre, Lena and I lit up when we saw each other. What, if anything, was happening between us was just chalked up to liking being together, that was enough. But in Paris, as the seasons changed, something unexpected was happening. It wasn't a love affair but it wasn't not a love affair. It wasn't definable, certainly not by us, but it thrived in Paris.

Paris adored Lena. In return, she sang "Que Restes-ils?" and the city was totally hers. One more reason to feel more at home in Paris than back home was the belief Paris was color-blind. She would never have walked down Fifth Avenue as easily as we walked down the Champs-Elysées one day, looking for a drugstore that sold makeup. The base she used was much darker than her own skin and covered her sprinkle of freckles. That day, her skin against her light lavender cashmere sweater and skirt made her more beautiful than any of her lighter sisters. The laconic Parisian saleswoman in the store gaped adoringly:

"I know! You're Doris Day!"

"No, I'm Doris Night," Lena answered. She would not have made that joke back home.

But France wasn't color-blind. Neither she nor Lennie knew that beginning with the Twenties, the Bal Negre and Josephine Baker were exotics to the French. Algeria was the French South and they had their own version of back-of-the-bus. When Lena and Lennie returned to Paris from a London booking, they settled in rooms I had reserved for them at the small, elegantly louche hotel La Trémouille in the rue Boccador, just behind its wealthy cousin, the Plaza-Athénée. The manager was ecstatic—Lena Horne at the Trémouille!—until he saw her trio of musicians check in. So black? *Merde!* Why hadn't I told him? Prejudiced? He was not prejudiced, he just had to consider the prejudice of his other guests. If Mme. 'Orne were not Lena 'Orne—well, it was too late but could the black men keep out of the bar? Oh, never again, never! Was I clear? I was clear.

I never told Lena or Lennie. It would have spoiled Paris for them and in any event, they wouldn't have wanted to know.

Walking into the slobby lobby of the Hotel May Fair felt like going back to kids' camp at the beginning of summer. I was back, back in my old apartment overlooking the rooftops, back with the choice between losing a phone call or getting an omelette. My plan was to reconnoiter and sound out friends about work prospects. I was a little concerned that no money would be coming in before too much went out but I was always confident I would support myself with writing even before I could. Peter Viertel assured me I would have no trouble, thanks to Sam Spiegel, who had produced *The African Queen*. Sam apparently met all boats bringing blacklisted writers to Europe. The writers, grateful for any work, came cheap; offers came from Sam as promptly as the cabled offer had come to the boat from MGM.

And Peter was right: Spiegel was waiting—just for me. He had an offer just for me. I was perfect to adapt a story for Bergman and Brando. An odd combination, I thought, but big names meant a big budget meant big fees. I could fantasize as well as anyone but I knew the writer would not be an equal part of that financial equation. And I wasn't. Spiegel offered half the weekly fee in francs, half in dollars; no agent so no ten percent, darling wonderful boy, so no bargaining, that's the deal, take it or leave it, the new refugee writer in town going once, going twice, sold to the bighearted producer with matching belly.

That the project wasn't quite as big and grand as Spiegel claimed emerged very quickly during a lunch with Marlon Brando and Ellen Adler. Marlon had never heard of the picture I was writing for him; he hadn't even heard he was to costar with Bergman. He had heard of Sam Spiegel. Had I not been through the Hollywood mill, I might have been surprised or disappointed although I had no right to be either: I was writing for money, not movie art. It wasn't of major importance. The lunch would have been very existential-enjoying-France if I hadn't brought up an ad I'd read just before I joined Ellen and Marlon. Printed in the international edition of *The New York Times,* it was signed and paid for by Elia Kazan—apparently the same ad he had taken in the national edition.

It was sickening. Going beyond the by now familiar "I informed to save my country," Kazan proselytized for more informers, urging those who hadn't yet betrayed their friends and colleagues to come forward and do so to save the country as he had. No question that my description of the ad was biased. That it might be accurate, Marlon wouldn't consider. The adoration in his star-director relationship with Kazan left him enraged and disbelieving in certain, insulting terms.

"Get a paper and see for yourself," I told him.

He stalked off. Ellen tried to calm me down; like Stella, she was blind about Marlon. When he came back, penitence was in his eyes though not in his mouth and not at all in what he did. Shocked as he was by Kazan's ad, when he returned to the States he went to California and starred as the informer hero of *On the Waterfront,* the apologia for informing directed by

Kazan from a screenplay by Schulberg. Both writer and director knew the subject firsthand.

The real problem with writing for money occurs when the money stops. The lovely fat envelopes of French francs hadn't arrived for two weeks. With no agent involved to do the dirty work, I had to take my begging bowl to the elegant George V where Spiegel's office was in his grand apartment. In the lobby, I ran into Billy Wilder and Charles Vidor, two bon vivant directors, European-born cynics with black humor. They looked at me and laughed.

"What's the joke?"

"You're working for Spiegel?"

"Yes."

"You'll never get paid." They howled.

I laughed ha ha but had a premonition that sent me straight to the lobby phone to call Sam. M. Spiegel was busy. M. Spiegel continued to be busy. I walked around the block: busy. I came back at the end of the day: he wasn't busy, he wasn't there. He had gone to London. I called the Dorchester: he was busy.

Paris was not to be underestimated. I was so happy to be living there, Spiegel didn't upset me, he really didn't even annoy me. Somehow his shenanigans were part of the Paris adventure; life in Paris was too good. It was golden for the American expatriate, pure gold for the expatriate who was also a political refugee. We had been forced to come to Paris to have a good time and incidentally earn a living at the profession we were barred from practicing at home. When the familiar feeling of fraudulence threatened, I reminded myself I was a playwright and I was writing another play as well as a brainless movie. After three tries, I still hadn't been able to support myself from the theatre; the money from *Home of the Brave* was from the sale of the movie rights. It didn't suit me to look down on writing for movies and bite the hand that fed me; that was how I'd earned the money I was living on.

Fortunately, life in Paris was cheap as well as golden. The May Fair wasn't a hotel, it was a helter-skelter disorganized Yaddo under a manager who was thrilled when a bill was finally paid in francs because he then could pay his delinquent electric bill. The city offered a freedom I'd never known: in addition to Lena there was a hulk of an existentialist at the other end of the rainbow with whom I was having an affair, a sexual one. I was giddy with a happiness Sam Spiegel couldn't touch. Oh, I wanted to be paid all right; I knew I had to keep on his back, so I followed him to London. But Lena was there.

And he wasn't. At the Dorchester, I was told he had suddenly gone back to Paris. This wasn't like Jean Valjean and Javert, for although it was a hunt to bring Spiegel down, he could wait while I spent a day or two in London with Lena. I stayed a week. Back in Paris, I ran into Lewis Milestone in the lobby of the George V. On a hunch, I asked:

"Are you going to see Spiegel?"

"Oh, yes," Milly answered. "I'm preparing to direct *Melba* for him."

I laughed.

"What's the joke?"

"You're not going to get paid." Unlike Billy Wilder and Charlie Vidor, I didn't howl, I explained. The next morning, I had an appointment with Sam at the George V.

He ushered me from the foyer of his suite to the salon to the bedroom so swiftly, I wondered who he was hiding in the salon without realizing it was me he was hiding in the bedroom. His explanation was that he had forgotten a business appointment which he didn't want to interrupt us. He would get rid of the man and then we could go back to the salon and pick up wherever we were. Or something like that. He went too fast and I didn't listen too carefully; I knew he was in his bullshit mode and made myself remember that he had married Lynn Baguette—the Texas beauty I used as a model for the heroine of *Caught*—only because he wanted to get into the United States. Once he was in, he got rid of her fast but with charm. He always cut loose and his victims just shrugged at the inevitable and laughed at his chutzpah.

In the bedroom, I sat on a little gilt chair—one thing Sam didn't dare do. He was far too overweight so he stood in the center of the room, rocking on his expensive heels as he eased into his spiel, finally getting to some point—not the point but a point—in his unplaceable accent.

"Artur, you are very moral man. Everyone knows how moral so it is more terrible when you tell people I am a crook. You must not say that."

"But you are a crook, Sam."

"Artur, don't say that again. Say I am not a crook."

"But you are."

"Artur, once more and I will have to hit you."

I got up to meet him in the center of the carpet. We faced each other, standing as close as we possibly could which wasn't all that close because of his huge belly. "Then I'm afraid you're going to have to hit me, Sam. You are a crook."

"Retract."

"I can't."

"Then I'll have to hit you."

"Then you'll have to hit me."

"Take it back."

Fortunately we were interrupted by the door buzzer. Sam excused himself and left to open the door to the apartment. After a very few minutes, he returned to beckon me into the salon. A large pile of francs was on the ornate desk.

"Count them, please," he said.

I did.

"That is all the francs you are owed?"

I nodded. He stuffed them in a large envelope, handed it to me and ushered me out past Lewis Milestone who was sitting there and had witnessed the whole transaction staged for his benefit.

Spiegel never paid me the dollars. Contemplating suing was a waste of time: his creditors stretched all around Radio City and I was at the end of the line. I was never paid in full and the script was never finished but I wasn't finished with Spiegel.

Peter Viertel had written a book he wanted me to recommend to a friend of mine who was Doubleday's man in Paris. The book, *White Hunter, Black Heart*, was based on Peter's experience with *The African Queen*. He had worked on the screenplay, and both he and Jigee had been on location in Africa during the shooting.

My Doubleday friend, St. Clair Pugh, was a great partner for tearing around Paris with no pain. I introduced him to Lena and Lennie which really took, and to Françoise Sagan which didn't, but recommended he pick up *Bonjour Tristesse* for Doubleday, which he also didn't. How much good Saint could do Peter at Doubleday was dubious. But I dutifully read Peter's book.

"I'm really afraid John won't like it," said Peter. I thought he was joking; it was hardly a secret that Peter hero-worshipped John Huston, the director of *African Queen*. Years before, when the Viertels were living in Malibu, a group of us were sitting around the fire, listening to Willy Wyler tell of his exploits in the Air Force during the war. John, never happy out of the spotlight, was on his feet the second Willy finished describing a dangerous aerial battle. Very tall and thin, he draped himself against the fireplace and took over the room:

"I was flying high once," John said in a muted, breathy tone, "so high . . . all I could see . . . no matter where I looked all I could see . . . were clouds. Clouds. Nothing but clouds."

Jigee and I looked at each other, glassy-eyed. Peter, at John's feet, looked up with reverence. "God, John!" he exclaimed softly to his Dalai Lama.

White Hunter, Black Heart didn't go that far in its portrait of Huston but John would relish every word Peter wrote about him. Sam Spiegel, on the other hand, wouldn't. Why he wouldn't was troubling.

Peter chuckled at my objection. "Sam? What won't he like?"

"The way you've written him as a Jew."

"He is a Jew."

"Peter. You've written him as a terrible old kike."

Peter chuckled. "He is a terrible old kike."

"Oh, Peter," Jigee protested. We were sitting around the dinner table at their house.

I said: "I won't give the book to Doubleday unless you let Sam read it and he signs a release."

Peter was very agreeable. That was the other side of him: put to the test, he was fair and cheerful. We didn't have to wait long for Sam's reaction to the book. We were at our long window table at Fouquet's—Peter, Irwin Shaw, the two Bobs, Capa and Parrish, and me—when Sam walked in. He had read the book; he recognized a betrayal when he saw one.

"Not nice, Peter. Not worthy of you," he said.

Peter grinned. "The writing?"

"Me," Sam said. "What you do to me."

"What did I do to you?" Peter teased.

"You make me a terrible old kike."

Peter grinned his grin and chuckled his chuckle. I didn't believe he would say it but he did. "You are a terrible old kike."

We all cringed. It was really dreadful; Peter rejecting his own Jewishness, yes, we were accustomed to that Peter. But Peter so vicious and vulgar, no. Not one of us moved a millimeter. Neither did Sam; he just looked at Peter. That fat man, sweating in an expensive bespoke suit that couldn't hide his gross belly, suddenly acquired enormous dignity.

"That is not funny, Peter," he said. "You must apologize."

"I don't apologize," Peter said.

"Then I must ask you to step outside."

"OK," Peter said, getting up from the table. He would have. He knew he could have beaten Sam to a pulp, we all knew it. Sam knew it too but the line had been crossed and he was beyond caring. Someone grabbed Peter—Bob Parrish and Irwin, I think—and pushed him back down in his seat. Peter's grin ended almost before it began; he knew he had lost us. I don't remember whether he apologized out loud or not; it hardly mattered. Sam blotted his forehead with his silk square and left.

Peter rewrote the book, Sam gave his approval, I passed the book along to Saint, and it was published. That moment at Fouquet's was bad but it wasn't

Peter at his worst. That had been at the dinner table in their house where he had first called Sam a "terrible old kike" and Jigee had quietly protested, "Oh, Peter." He had shot her an angry look at that and set out to get his revenge, which he did. That was Peter at his worst.

The dinner had been awkward enough before we talked about the book. Jigee was eight months pregnant; the marriage was in bad trouble but she had asked him to see her through the birth of the baby. As Katie asks Hubbell in the awkward dinner scene in the Malibu beach house in *The Way We Were.*

Seemingly out of nowhere, Peter said, "My wife likes girls." A remark like that is never from nowhere.

Jigee had her head down, her eyes fixed on the *petits pois* on her plate. Her body was bloated, she was physically uncomfortable, she might not have heard. She said nothing; she never said anything after that protest of "Oh, Peter."

"Well, her husband likes boys," I said, not very Noël Coward but trying to keep it light. Peter and Irwin had removed all the body hair on their torsos with Nair, a sissy thing to do in their macho eyes for which they had paid with a bad rash that ruined the rest of their summer. I sensed my remark had made Peter think of that: he scratched his chest.

"No, I mean she really likes girls," Peter said.

Tears dripped slowly down Jigee's cheeks. She concentrated on getting the peas on to her fork.

"We all like girls," I said.

"I mean she's a dyke," Peter said.

Jigee's head dipped lower, the tears dripped onto the peas.

"I don't like that word at the dinner table," I said. A brilliant riposte, really brilliant, one for the books. I knew he had had an affair with the same girl himself; that was why he was so angry.

Shortly after that ghastly dinner, Peter went to New York for a week. On his return, he called me from the airport at Orly. "I have to see you. Can I come over?"

He came through the door to my apartment at the May Fair and with no preface said, "I was seen with Bettina in New York." Bettina was a very beautiful, very nice model we all had met through Sophie, Tola's new wife. "I have to tell Jigee before someone else tells her."

"Peter, no one is going to tell a woman eight and a half months pregnant that her husband is having an affair. You just want to atone for your guilt. Don't tell her."

"You're right," he said and went right home and told her.

In Malibu, Peter and Jigee had dreamt about riding horseback along the beach up to Zuma and Trancas. When the baby was born in Paris, Jigee said, "I guess we should have had the horse."

. . .

After the baby, they parted—the beginning of the slow downhill slide she wallowed in. Driving to Tola's house in St. Tropez with him, she was severely injured when he crashed into a tree. Not a scratch on him but she suffered a bad concussion that left her with an irremovable bubble on her brain. The doctor warned her she could never drink again. So Jigee, who had always drunk a little too much, now drank a lot too much and smoked more than ever.

After we all came back to the States, Peter went to the coast but Jigee remained in New York. Though she was a full-blown alcoholic, her still fresh-faced beauty contradicted her tongue which got sharper and more indiscreet in proportion to her increased intake of booze. She stayed with Joan and George Axelrod, old friends whom she successfully alienated by informing them with pinpoint clarity what pretentious phonies they were. Out of their house she went, only to move in with a loathsome leech she acquired as a lover who couldn't hurt her.

The last time I saw her in New York was at an apartment I had on East Fifty-ninth Street. Drunk, but that only showed in the way one crossed leg kept swinging and one hand was continually held out for a refill. Her usual casual, outdoor look was replaced by one very New York: black dress, black shoes—"black heart," she laughed. A reference to Peter I got without fully understanding.

Our conversation was mainly about *A Clearing in the Woods,* a new play I had just finished and given her to read. She was very pleased the heroine was named for her but was relentless in her objection to a line just before the final curtain: "An end to dreams is not an end to hope."

"Of course it's an end to hope," Jigee snapped. "And vice versa. They're intertwined. You can't have one without the other." She downed what was left in her glass. "One more for the road. One big one more for the very long road and then I'm off on my mission."

She had been harping on her "mission" but was elaborately secretive about it except to confirm that it concerned Peter. He was in Hollywood job hunting but it was still the Time of the Toad, as Dalton Trumbo wrote, and Peter was associated with one Virginia Viertel, a card-carrying Communist and thus an obstacle to his employment at a studio. Spreading the manure, Peter himself was in the Marine Corps Reserves, making his association with one Virginia Viertel of interest to the FBI.

In *The Way We Were,* Katie solves the problem of standing in Hubbell's way as a subversive wife by divorcing him. Jigee solved the problem by informing. I think she chose to inform to demonstrate to Peter just how far she would go for him. I also think she chose to inform to demonstrate just how awful she was.

I saw her once more, in Hollywood. I wanted Tom to meet her. She was living in Santa Monica in a pathetic bungalow with a low, crumbling wall around the unplanted front yard. Whether the lover was there or not we couldn't tell: she didn't ask us in, just stood there in a thin dressing gown, drink and cigarette in one hand, still a beauty but now with the first signs of decline and fall. She was vague, not hospitable, disconnected. All she seemed to want was to get back to the bed where she spent most of her time in the leech's care.

He would make sure her glass was full, then set about doing whatever else it was that he did. He wasn't on hand when she passed out and set fire to her filmy nightgown with a burning cigarette. The nightgown went up in flames; ninety percent of her body was covered with third-degree burns. The face somehow wasn't touched, that was something to be grateful for, but we all were more grateful for the coma she was in the few days she lasted. I don't think it was a true accident. The way she would say "Pick up your gear, men," to her daughter and Ethel's daughter when the little girls were leaving a Paris restaurant with us? I think Jigee was picking up her gear because she wanted to leave. I think leaving was her choice because she had betrayed herself by informing. To attribute her death to the Witch Hunt might be an exaggeration; on the other hand, no one on either side who was touched by the hunters escaped undamaged.

CHAPTER SIX

Informing Revisited
Jolson Sings Again *and*
Other Betrayals

TWENTY YEARS AFTER *THE WAY WE WERE*, I again wrote about the Hollywood Witch Hunt, but this time a play where I could say my say without having it distorted or omitted or ending up on a cutting room floor; a more personal play about what I had experienced myself and people I'd experienced it with, people who lived in houses like the Sol and Ethel Chaplin's house on Doheny. I'd known I was going to write it: the subject haunted and nagged and kept cropping up. Whenever I saw a Jerry Robbins or a Gadge Kazan, "informer" was not the first word that flashed on my screen or the second or even the third, but sooner rather than later, it flashed. And I wasn't atypical.

Betsy Blair, whom I knew back when she lived on Rodeo Drive married to Gene Kelly, had been living in London for a long time married to director Karel Reisz. I hadn't seen her in years, then saw her twice in one day in New York—the second time at a party where even before "Hello" she said, "I couldn't ask her. I like her too much." No translation was necessary. Earlier at lunch, I'd seen Betsy across a restaurant with a woman we'd both known in Hollywood during the Witch Hunt, a woman suspected of being an informer. It diminishes over the years but it doesn't disappear.

Much had changed when I sat down to write what became *Jolson Sings Again*. I wasn't relaxed in my big chair with a long yellow legal pad in my lap and a Blackwing pencil in my hand but upright in a sculptured-for-the-back office chair at an unfriendly, if not outright hostile computer. A big change for a writer. Halfway through the first act, however, I stopped resisting the machine; I actually developed a fondness for it because it made revisions easier and I was revising furiously. I had started so confidently, so certain I knew exactly what I thought of informing and informers. Then, as I went deeper into the characters—who were hardly total inventions—I had to face how I had behaved with Kazan and Jerry.

I had only a nodding acquaintance with Kazan, mainly from the Actors Studio, when he asked me to write the screenplay of his novel *The Arrangement.* It had been a best-seller but he assured me that didn't negate its importance as a book. Instead, it would provide a public for the Important Film it would make starring Marlon Brando and directed and produced by Kazan himself for Warner Brothers. Why, then, wasn't he writing the screenplay himself? He'd written his movie *America, America,* he had even gotten that screenplay published. Why not write this one? Ahhh. He grinned appreciatively, then his face went serious: he was very good. He wanted another eye and an observant one; he needed a writer capable of true objectivity, a writer who was a master craftsman. He was a master seducer.

This was late in the liberated Sixties, fifteen years after the HUAC hearings where Kazan was a star informer with his betrayal of his old Group Theatre buddies, destroying their movie careers but securing his. The theatre had no blacklist and Elia Kazan was the most desired director in the theatre. He could have his pick of plays and actors, even stars, name his price. He could have called all the shots but movies were what he wanted. He flourished there while people he named were forgotten, along with most of their names. Forgotten. The subject itself was largely forgotten except by those who had been damaged. I knew what Kazan had done but he had done it years ago; I hadn't forgotten but who else hadn't and how much did it matter? The money he was offering was impressive and true to writers, I thought I needed money. On the other hand I didn't like movies, I didn't even much like his movies. What I admired, enormously, was his work in the theatre. To me, Elia Kazan was the greatest theatre director of my time. I was flattered that he wanted me, so flattered that I joined the willing-to-forget-and-overlook.

When I read *The Arrangement,* I thought Kazan really did need me. The book was a pretentious potboiler. Still, a potboiler could make a good hot fudge sundae of a movie—if he could somehow be steered away from trying to make an Important Film, always his Achilles' heel, and toward whomping up a steamy melodrama which was his forte in pictures.

He gave me complete freedom to keep or lose whatever I wanted from the novel, go as far out as I wanted, even invent if I deemed it necessary. All he asked was that I send him thirty pages at a time. Which I did; each time he read them, he was extravagant with praise. Until the day I sent the last thirty pages.

We met at his office, oddly small for a director. He handed me a complete screenplay of *The Arrangement* written by Elia Kazan. Completely unembarrassed, he explained that since he was producing and directing the picture, Warner Brothers had insisted on a first-draft screenplay by a writer they approved.

Even if he had realized I was much angrier with myself than at him, it wouldn't have mattered. His concern of the moment was that I like him no matter what he had done. He *had* to be liked while we were physically together in the same room; once I was gone, he wouldn't give a rat's ass. Magnanimously, he released me from my contractual obligation to write a second draft. I was free to go to Switzerland and ski though he hoped I would find time to read his script and send him any comments. I didn't have to but he hoped I would, I was so smart and perceptive any comments would be invaluable. Didn't he think I might be a little biased? That would only make my criticism sharper and more valuable! And I was not to worry about screen credit: he would share it with me. No, no, I had to take it; it would be a very important credit. No, think it over, don't decide now. But ten minutes after I was back home, the doorbell rang: a messenger was at the door with a release for me to sign, renouncing any credit. I signed. I couldn't go to prison for contempt of Kazan.

Nor could I pretend surprise. No one becomes an informer at the moment he informs; he's always been an informer, he's just been waiting for the opportunity. And that man is a man who goes on to betray friends and coworkers in other ways. I learned that ten years earlier from Jerry Robbins; we were old friends when we began *West Side Story* but not when we finished. Which made it easier to work with him again on *Gypsy.* When it suited him, he pretended we were but again, his betrayal wasn't restricted to informing. (I'm not avoiding details, I'm holding them in abeyance.) *West Side Story* and *Gypsy* with (and without) Jerry warrant a separate chapter and will get one. I worked with him and I worked with Kazan knowing they were informers; I crossed that line knowing what it meant that they both were. In *Jolson,* the young playwright tells his director-turned-informer: "You're not evil because you informed, you informed because you're evil." I could hardly say I didn't deserve what I got from either Jerry or Kazan.

· · ·

Harsh black and white, which was what informed writing *Jolson Sings Again* until halfway through the first act, the characters made me look back. Zero Mostel. Zero was named by an informer and blacklisted but he worked with Jerome Robbins on *Fiddler on the Roof*. When Hal Prince, the producer, asked Zero how he felt about working with Jerry, "I don't have to have lunch with him, do I," Zero said.

A much quoted, much applauded remark—by me as well—until some said it was a cop-out. Was it? Zero had been unemployed and unemployable for a very long time and here was a role that comes once in a performer's lifetime. That couldn't be my defense. I hadn't liked Kazan's novel, I didn't like writing movies and I knew going in he had behaved like a shit. I knew going in Jerry had, too, and I told him he had. But it was different with Jerry. We were old, close friends. I did want to work with him; I was proud to be part of *West Side Story* and *Gypsy* and proud of my work on both, particularly on *Gypsy*. Different from Kazan but a defendable defense for crossing the line? Bizarrely, Jerry had a line he wouldn't cross. "Kazan had the nerve to ask me to dinner," he said in very high dudgeon. There was a hierarchy among informers.

And there was Sterling Hayden. In his very moving autobiography, he confessed deep disgust with himself for informing. Did his remorse make him acceptable? Did the fact that he had damaged himself lessen the damage he did to others? Brando, in his autobiography, regretted being part of *On the Waterfront*. Did his remorse make him acceptable?

It wasn't so black and white after all. There was a line not to be crossed but what was that line and who would determine it? With Jerry, the line I wouldn't cross was that I would never be his friend again. I wasn't when we did *Gypsy*, but work should be enjoyable; once rehearsals began, it hadn't been enjoyable on *Gypsy*. It never could be with Jerry—there was another line I wouldn't cross. There had to be a line the playwright in *Jolson Sings Again* would not cross—there was too much of me in him—but what was that line?

The title was a reference to Larry Parks, the actor who was made famous first by playing Al Jolson and then by being the first Friendly Witness to betray his friends publicly. He was a sweet, much-liked man until he testified. It wasn't merely informing that destroyed him and his career—Sterling Hayden chirped with impunity—but his craven attempt to have it both ways when he did inform. Sitting at the HUAC witness table, he leaned into the microphone and begged that un-American Un-American Committee not to ask him to name publicly the names he had already named in executive session.

He knew he was going to name them publicly, the whole country knew he was; whatever dignity he had went out with the garbage and the country knew that, too. On Hollywood Boulevard, the newsboys hawking their papers shouted, "Jolson Sings Again! Jolson Sings Again!" and Larry Parks was finished off with laughter.

I wanted to capture the paradoxical feelings of that crazy time when HUAC terrorized us in our middle-class Hollywood houses. In the first act, Julian, the young playwright who is more me than the other three characters but less me than people assume, describes himself as "excited" in the beginning. That *is* me: I *was* excited because, as Julian says, "suddenly, for the first time in my life, it [was] all simple, clear cut, black and white. Good guys, bad guys. People rising to the occasion and behaving magnificently, people going under and behaving like total shits." The fight against the Committee, futile though it was, brought people together in camaraderie that was immensely moving.

It was perpetual motion: running to a fund-raiser for the Hollywood Ten, hitting up people individually for contributions they were afraid to make publicly, writing speeches for stars to deliver on a broadcast for the Committee for the First Amendment, relaying the latest report on who was handed a subpoena, bolstering those who got one to stand fast. Something popped every day: a friend—the woman Betsy was lunching with when I saw her across the restaurant—rubbed her own neck while reporting that Meta Reis broke out in hives on her neck before testifying. That, too, turns up in *Jolson*.

We weren't standing up for Communism, we were standing up for the Bill of Rights. HUAC wasn't in business to root out Communist propaganda in the movies because there wasn't any and the Committee knew it. Ayn Rand could point to smiles on the faces of the peasants in *Song of Russia* as proof that Louis B. Mayer had made a Communist movie but the Committee knew she was absurd even as they thanked her. When they thanked Reis for her testimony, they complimented her on her breasts and she thanked them. That is not in *Jolson*. Politicians first and foremost, they were pounding the hearings gavel in a frenzied grab for publicity and power. They had no patience with constitutional rights. Patriotism was defined as informing on friends and coworkers; with the consent of the Supreme Court, an authorized committee of the Congress of the United States sent citizens to prison when they refused. Another government agency used its authority to scare the community into silent compliance with illegal searches and bugging and constant surveillance. And congressmen like John Rankin, viciously and openly anti-Semitic at the hearings as well as on the floor of the House of Representatives, frightened the Jewish studio heads into promulgating a blacklist to please their government.

The Communists did have one point: the real enemy was the system. Certainly the system rewarded informers; still, I doubted that it was the system that made them informers. It may well have been easier for believers in the Party to stand up to the Committee and go to prison rather than inform but I didn't believe that was basically why they didn't inform. I believed they didn't inform because they basically were decent men and women. They were the good guys: informing on their friends was the line they would not cross.

Each of the characters in *Jolson Sings Again* has to decide what is the line that will not be crossed. As I got deeper into the play and betrayal bred betrayal, it wasn't the director/informer who was a problem: I understood him, I knew why he informed and what I thought of it, and that never changed. The character who informed for a reason understandable to some wasn't a problem either. But the character who wouldn't inform and the character who would rather hurt his career than work with an informer, they were a problem. Did they hold on to their integrity or did they later cross a line they wouldn't have crossed the way Eddie Dmytryk did? The play covers a span of fifteen years to show what happened to them later. With Dmytryk, only one year was needed.

During the bad time, I sat next to him in meetings where we discussed how much money the families of the Ten, families like his own, would need while the dads were in prison. I watched him, admired him; he served his time behind bars for contempt of Congress because he had refused to name names. Then he came out of jail and named them. No one needed to ask why: because he wanted to direct movies again, that was why. But did he still have some line he would not cross? Does each person have one?

My plot springboarded from an incident involving Arthur Miller and Elia Kazan and a line Miller crossed. Very early in his career, he was fortunate to find Kazan. They worked wonderfully together, they shared beliefs, they became great friends. Every playwright hopes to find that one director: the collaborator whom he can trust, the friend he can rely on, the talent who can bring his plays to blazing life. Miller had astounding success with Kazan. Then Kazan informed, against every belief both men held. A man of Miller's rectitude could neither condone nor ignore what Kazan did and Arthur Miller didn't. He parted company with Kazan but he never had that kind of earthquaking success again. Whether the fault was with the plays or the productions depends, in part, on your opinion of the plays done with Kazan and without. *The Crucible* failed in its first Broadway production directed by Jed

Harris. Whether it is as pompous and heavy as I found it, *The Crucible* with Harris did not give Miller what he had had with Kazan. Nor did the plays that followed. That may not be why Miller came back to Kazan to direct *After the Fall,* but when he did, Kazan had not changed: he was still the informer Miller had walked away from. And Miller attacks the party members in the play as savagely as Kazan attacked them in his public statements and *New York Times* ad. Was that Kazan's influence or had Miller changed? One of his closest friends stopped speaking to him for what he considered a betrayal but ironically, Miller himself was publicly attacked for the heroine of the play, who was considered a betrayal of Marilyn Monroe, his ex-wife. *After the Fall* was not any kind of success for anyone.

In *Jolson Sings Again,* Julian breaks with Andreas, the director with whom his plays were a success, because he informed. Ten years later, he goes back to Andreas with a new play. That's all there is of Arthur Miller to be found in Julian. Except that Julian is Jewish, but then, so am I. Not that anyone ever thought Julian was based on Arthur Miller. Except for a few who thought Andreas was based on Jerry Robbins, most of the theatre community assumed he was based on Elia Kazan. Well, there's very little of Jerry in Andreas, very little; there's more of Kazan but there are big, basic differences. One of the most important is why each of them informed. Or says he informed. Kazan said he informed to save America from Communism. Andreas says, "that's bullshit rationalizing. And how does it justify becoming an informer?" He continues, ending:

"There is no political justification for informing on your friends and coworkers. But I did it. I named names. They had all been named before and couldn't be hurt by me. Still, I named them. I informed. Why. Have you never wanted something so badly you threw shame out the window? That's what I did. Making films is everything to me. It's my center, my identity, my reason for being. I don't claim that's a justification. It's my explanation. And I didn't hurt anybody."

As one of the other characters says, "Andreas is a shit but he's an honest shit."

Kazan said he, too, had only named people who had been named before. How did he know they had? Isobel Lennart said she had only named people who had been named ten times before. How did she know? Andreas is more modest: he says he only named people who had been named five times before. Later in the play, Julian repeats what another informer told him: "If you don't give them at least one new name, you don't get clearance." He says this to Robbie who also has informed. "I would say that's accurate," she says. It was.

Robbie is an agent, housewife, mother, adulteress, etc. who inspired wild guesses as to whom she is based on. Except for the tuna casserole she always makes, she isn't based on any one woman: she's pieces of a half a dozen. Characters are both amalgams and inventions but with a fictional work, especially one set in a specific place and time, the guessers go overboard. Even other writers who should know much better. Oddly, it's rarely, if ever, that someone actually recognizes himself or herself when there really is something to be recognized. Robbie's husband Sidney is based, in part, on a left-wing writer friend of mine who was an ex-Marine and overused the word *fuck*. When he read *Jolson,* his only objection was that there were too many *fucks.*

"If there are, we can cut some in rehearsal," I said.

"Right," he said. "What the fuck difference does it make?"

In the spring of 1992, when I began *Jolson Sings Again,* it had been fourteen years since I wrote a full-length play—*Scream,* a black comedy about the holocaust (sic) produced at the Alley Theatre in Houston—and I was unaware how much the fortunes for a legitimate play had changed. Those years had been eaten alive by two mammoth musicals: the first, one of the happiest of theatre experiences and a huge, unexpected hit; the second, hands down the worst theatre experience I ever had and a huge, expected flop. The correlation only appears to make sense; in the theatre, it could just as easily have been vice versa.

La Cage Aux Folles, which I directed, was the success. Collaboration with Jerry Herman and Harvey Fierstein was glitchless, even when they gave me notes at breakfast every morning in Boston; the production stage manager was invaluable Fritz Holt who was also one of the producers and the cheeriest; Theoni Aldredge designed the literally fabulous costumes, which set the tone of fantasy for a show that danced a very tricky line; the whole team was a team. Merely walking into rehearsal hall reminded me of walking in the employees' entrance at Bloomingdale's, where I worked the Xmas rush after graduating college, and seeing a big sign: BEGIN THE DAY WITH A SMILE! With Theoni and Fritz and the others, no sign was necessary. The love we had for the frog that turned into a princess imbued every company that performed the show all over the States, in London, in Sydney—Sydney! Where the stage crew was gayer than the dancers, and in *La Cage* all the dancers wore drag. I directed all the companies, too many of them but I was having a great time. Which made me myopic and helped me blunder into directing and then writing *Nick & Nora,* the flop.

Collaboration with anybody was nonexistent on that one. A coven of producers summoned me twice a week for the seven weeks we mistakenly previewed

1982. What does this motley group have in common? *La Cage Aux Folles.*
Front, left to right: Jerry Herman who wrote the score; Alan Carr, the original
producer; and the director who thought it would never happen.
Behind, left to right: Fritz Holt, the peerless production stage manager as well as
a co-producer with Barry Brown to his right. (Absent: Harvey Fierstein,
who wrote the book, and Scott Salmon, who was the choreographer.)

With Theoni Aldredge whose costumes for *La Cage* were literally fabulous.

in New York—Death Valley in Shubert Alley. The purpose of the meetings was to vent their anger at me for giving them the worst show they ever saw, individually and collectively. However, one of them surreptitiously gave me a three-thousand-dollar Cartier clock, whether to confuse me or cheer me on, I couldn't figure. Fritz had been taken by AIDS; Theoni stood by and at least had the pleasure of telling a perennially complaining producer that her skirts were too short for her age and dresses onstage were costumes, a factor beyond her ken. Was anyone surprised when the show closed in a week? I was relieved. Free of responsibility, free of three people I wouldn't want to walk into an elevator with, free to go back to being what I was: a playwright. The joy in the simple act of writing seemed new only because it had been so long since I had felt it. The change in prospects for a play, however, *were* new, scarily so. The twists and turns, the betrayals along the long, potholed road *Jolson Sings Again* traveled before it actually arrived on a stage in a theatre is a cautionary tale but one hardly unfamiliar to playwrights.

When I came into the theatre, there were thirty to forty new American plays on Broadway every season; in the Nineties, of the four or five plays on Broadway each season, two were London imports and one was a revival. Even Neil Simon, the cash cow, had shifted to Off-Broadway where new plays were competing for theatres. I knew Off-Broadway from the Sixties when *The Time of the Cuckoo* and *A Clearing in the Woods* were revived in the Village in tandem, and from the late Seventies when *The Enclave* played on West Fifty-fourth Street. From *Enclave,* which began at a small theatre in Washington, D.C., I knew another venue where new plays were now heading as never before: regional theatre.

But there was a fourth venue in New York: the institutional nonprofit theatre with subscription audiences guaranteeing a run, however limited. Very desirable but virgin territory to me. *Jolson* was deflowered by the two most important—first, the Manhattan Theatre Club.

Its artistic director, Lynne Meadow, a tall, disheveled woman always on her way to someplace else, offered a reading of the play even before it was finished. Ten years earlier, a playwright gathered a few friends in his living room and he or some actor friends read through his new play. The purpose was for the author to hear his play and some opinions he respected. In 1992, a reading was a production with a starry cast assembled by a Casting Director and a Name director. One rehearsal, then the Reading in a large, professional rehearsal room before an audience of forty or fifty including interested producers, possible investors, skeptical staff, sages, agents, spies, a few friends, a few Schadenfreuders and the author. The purpose was clear-cut: to get the play produced. Just before Christmas, I accepted Lynne's invitation and directed a reading at MTC. The reception overwhelmed me; I was unprepared for such extravagant praise, particularly after the beating I took on *Nick & Nora*. I looked eagerly at Lynne Meadow. MTC was known for presenting new plays and nurturing playwrights but she, its artistic director, walked by without seeing me. She said nothing for three weeks. Then she welcomed in 1993 with a call to say she "passed." She didn't like the ending. No explanation, no discussion, curtain.

Anticipating Lynne's rejection, I had sent the play to Bob Whitehead. A week after she passed, he enthused: he loved *Jolson;* it was an important play, the best I'd written. Two weeks later, he bowed out. Kazan was an old friend, had been going through hard personal times, wasn't in the best of health. Bob agreed the play wasn't about Gadge but felt it came down so hard on informers, Gadge would be upset. And the people Kazan had come down on like a guillotine? I didn't mention them. What for? To discomfort Bob? I knew what not to expect but I liked him.

Stockard Channing, who had done the MTC reading, took *Jolson* to André Bishop, artistic director at Lincoln Center, the preeminent nonprofit institutional theatre in New York. André, a shy, self-effacing man, liked the play and sent it to Dan Sullivan to direct. Under Dan, the Seattle Rep had become one of the most distinguished regional theatres in the country. He came to St. Luke's Place to check me out and see if my reputation was true or whether I would submit to him. Bearded, attractively saturnine, carefully casual in expensive, shapeless black, he spoke less than I'd hoped. But I wanted to get the play on so I found his few words perceptive; besides, I liked the glint in his eye. After a month, word came that Dan Sullivan would direct a reading of *Jolson Sings Again* at Lincoln Center. Immediate fantasies: Dan Sullivan was the director I had long been waiting for.

Dan had asked me not to attend the rehearsal but when I arrived for the audition—to call it by its rightful name—a very upset Stockard grabbed me: Stanley Tucci, who was playing Andreas, was doing nothing but mumble in a monotone. Speak to Dan! I spoke to Dan. Dan reassured me: Stanley Tucci was a fine actor.

Act One: Stanley Tucci just mumbled, I could barely hear him. Sweat began trickling down my back. I wanted to shout to Stanley Tucci: At least, speak up! I wanted to tell the audience they were not hearing my play; I wanted to stop the reading. But I sat. Under my jacket, my shirt was sopping wet.

I had never seen Stanley Tucci before that reading. I have seen him since in a movie he also cowrote and codirected. I liked the movie; I could see he was very good. I liked him better in a glossy, short-lived television series because he was miscast and quite bad. Self-indulgent, heedless actors who did what Stanley Tucci did at that reading commit first-degree murder: they kill the playwright and the play. They deserve capital punishment. Dan was the director but in my hero-worshipping mode, it could not be his fault as well.

Nevertheless, André Bishop agreed to do *Jolson Sings Again* at Lincoln Center but only if Dan directed. He made that very clear. Dan was on sabbatical from the Seattle Rep with a commitment to a movie that he didn't want to happen and didn't believe would happen. Still, it prevented him from giving André a definite date when he would contractually be free to do *Jolson* at Lincoln Center; André had to fill his slots; *Jolson* didn't have one. Dan was unfazed: he believed in *Jolson,* he was committed, he was ready to go elsewhere. By then, I wanted him to direct all the plays I was sure I was going to write. When he said he was ready to go elsewhere, he didn't know the elsewhere was waiting in the wings in London.

My great friends Toby and Millie Rowland—he headed the Stoll-Moss theatre empire and was more English than the Queen even though born in Libby, Montana—had introduced me to Robert Fox, the new young, smart London producer. Robert, then married to Natasha Richardson, was known for his charm and sharp quips as well as familial good looks which worked well but his attractiveness was really his stance of observer and nonparticipant. A bond between us developed quickly and Toby took advantage of it: he sent Robert *Jolson.* Robert liked the play and brought in a coproducer: Scott Rudin of Hollywood and New York. Scott was a big, bearded, affable bear in black and sneakers who had made millions producing Cineplex entertainments like *The Addams Family;* his fee for producing a picture was two million, regardless of how much producing he actually did. That, he explained, was how he could afford to produce plays like *Jolson* with his own money, not caring whether he won or lost. What he loved was theatre; what he wanted to do was produce good theatre; what he needed, despite his bicoastal busyness, was a friend. I reached out to him and he was wreathed in gratitude. He believed in the friendship for that minute just as he believed in the play but with movie stars. As did Robert. A reason Dan distrusted them but they distrusted him. I liked all of them but then, it was my play.

. . .

Robert Fox and I called Scott Rudin, his co-producer on *Jolson Sings Again,*
"the Roller" because . . .

James Woods was our best shot at a male star. He didn't remember that I had
gotten him his first movie role, in *The Way We Were,* but any leverage that
might have been leverage wasn't needed. He liked the play and wanted to do
it—for six months. Scott and Robert regarded six months as financial suicide.

The best female shot was Ellen Barkin, who began flirting in November of '93.
She and I had a long, exhausting lunch at St. Luke's Place—exhausting
because as much as I liked her, I had to remember I was making a pitch to a
woman who was first a Hollywood star, then an actress eager to prove herself,
and a forgotten last, a middle-class Jewish girl from New York. Scott went into
negotiation with her agent; we excitedly began debating whether Boston or
Washington was a better tryout town; Ellen Barkin gave me a New Year's present for '94: she passed. Not enough money. When I pointed out she could
make $750,000 for only six months in *Jolson*—by then they were willing to
take a star for six months—she quoted her business manager who said she
needed to make $2,000,000. Had she forgotten where she came from? Oh yes,
she said, we all do. She had a crooked smile I also liked. Over and out.

· · ·

. . . Scott had his minions roll his phone calls at dawn when nobody was up to take them but Scott got credit nevertheless. His reaction to the nickname is in his face.

In the spring, with *Jolson Sings Again* still starless, it was clear it couldn't get on before the end of the season which was when Dan's sabbatical from Seattle Rep ended. Ever resourceful, Scott came up with Plan B: the play would begin at the Rep with a Broadway cast and come into New York. He and Robert would put up $150,000 in enhancement: Seattle would be a cheap tryout.

Dan was happy, I was happy, Robert was not so happy: he didn't think he could pony up his $75,000. Ever reassuring, Scott told me not to worry: he would cover for Robert. What was $75,000? And a star who was a distinguished actress wanted to do the play! Fiona Shaw was flying over from London to read for us! Only the logistics of when and where had to be worked out.

In love all over again with playwriting, I had finished a second new play, *The Radical Mystique*. While waiting for Fiona Shaw, Dan directed a reading of the play at Lincoln Center. This time, all the actors performed and the audience cheered and gave me a standing ovation—at a reading! Followed by a bizarre scene with André Bishop: friends of his encircled him, shouting he had to do the play now, this season, this minute, now! Assaulted, he was enraged. In the morning, he phoned to say he passed. I thanked him for the reading and meant it. The next call was from the Manhattan Theatre Club: a representative had been at the reading and guess what? Lynne Meadow wanted to do the play.

August, not April, was the cruel month: Toby Rowland died. The lights of all the theatres in London were lowered in memory of the generous, witty Englishman from Montana. He had survived removal of his larynx and with scarcely an interval, had learned to talk because he loved to talk. His legacy to me was Robert Fox. Remembering Robert was remembering Toby.

Later in August, Fiona Shaw came to read *Jolson Sings Again* at St. Luke's Place. Her American accent was fine, she was intelligent, she was charming but there wasn't a shred of passionate Robbie, the mother, the wife, the agent,

Toby and Millie Rowland photographed in London by their good friend
Lord Snowdon for their fiftieth anniversary: April 10, 1992. My best English
friends, he was born in Libby, Montana, she in Seattle, Washington.

the mistress, the damaged, torn, self-loathing, extremely sexual woman in the play. Not one of us had a clue why she had flown over. We thanked her, she thanked us, and the producers resumed star chasing. August was not a good month.

September wasn't much better: Jule Styne died. It was easy to speak at his memorial. I not only loved Jule, I enjoyed him. On New Year's Eve at St. Luke's, we toasted Jule first because it was his birthday, then the New Year. We toasted him that year, too.

And in September, I finished another new play, *My Good Name,* which Dan directed at MTC this time. Continuing to write enabled me to remain removed from the trials and tribulations of the star-hungry non-production of *Jolson;* and again, the sheer pleasure of writing was giving me a perspective I hadn't had before. An idea for another play began to take shape.

In the fall, *Jolson* took a deceptive turn for the better: it was set for January rehearsals at the Seattle Rep; Scott was in negotiation with Patti LuPone who loved the play so much she wrote me a letter of admiration. She had her demands but Scott reassured everyone she could be handled. That was the good news; the bad news came in London where I was sopping up theatre. *Betrayal* was en route.

Robert Fox asked to meet at the Savoy where we never met; it was always the San Lorenzo, the pasta pallazo he relished. Clearly, he was bringing bad news. It came in a false syllogism: The Shuberts, who were investing in *Jolson,* pulled out because they didn't consider Patti LuPone a box office star; Robert didn't have his half of the $150,000 enhancement money; therefore, Scott and Robert would only be giving Seattle Rep $50,000 and were pulling out. They would not be bringing the play to New York.

"Scott said he would put up all the money if you couldn't put up your share."

Robert shrugged.

"Patti LuPone won't go to Seattle for eight weeks without a guarantee of coming in to Broadway. Nor will the other actors."

"No, I wouldn't think so."

"We have to go into rehearsal in January." This was December. "How can we get a first-rate cast between now and then?"

Robert shrugged.

"What did Dan say?"

"We haven't told him yet. We wanted to know first what you thought."

"I think you're shits."

"So do I," Robert said.

In the play, Andreas says, "Robbie's pissing remorse so that makes her more acceptable."

It got worse. Scott said the check was in the mail. Not on the way, "in the mail." He continued to say it was "in the mail" all the way to the end of rehearsals in Seattle in February of '95. I faxed both of them, asking whether the check was "in the mail" or was it just the old joke? They jumped on that: they were insulted; they didn't put up a cent. It *was* the old joke. Their betrayal was complete.

I was bitterly disappointed, more at Scott because he had the money and to spare, because he brayed how much he loved the theatre, because he had been so grateful for my friendship. I still liked Robert. Why? For him, just as much as for Scott, for any producer these cold days, the star, not the play, was the thing. But Robert had always said he didn't have the money, he'd admitted he was a shit, he was pissing remorse—what difference? I liked him. Months after the play's run in Seattle, I saw a movie he produced, liked it, and wrote him saying I had. Friendship repaired. Sometimes friendship is as difficult to explain as love.

During rehearsals in Seattle for *Jolson Sings Again,* a newspaper interviewer asked me: "Why do all you gay Jewish men write so many plays?"

"Edward Albee isn't Jewish," I answered. Too late, I learned the interviewers doubled as critics.

From the first day of rehearsal, it was dishearteningly obvious that the last-minute desperate pressure to find a cast had landed us one with three of the four roles completely miscast. And the absence of sexuality in what was meant to be a highly sexual play. Plus—and when or why it happened, I don't know—but suddenly, clear blatant dislike by two of the four actors for Dan. He returned the compliment.

He had worried that the penultimate scene was too similar to the last scene in the first act. I revised both. The revisions didn't make any difference, they couldn't: the actors played both scenes in exactly the same way. Dan said nothing. The impasse reminded me of Shirley Booth and Harold Clurman on *The Time of the Cuckoo.* Except that Shirley Booth was a superb actor and was determined to make the play work. These actors were not superb, they had stopped caring about the play and were just waiting for it all to be over. The play was flat and lifeless but confrontation was not Dan's style.

With Dan Sullivan backstage at the Seattle Rep in happier days.

Why was I as tolerant of Dan as I had been intolerant of Harold? Dan was the director I had been looking for, I thought; he was going to direct all my plays. We had become good friends; I treasured the friendship; I didn't want to walk on any eggs and break them. But I wasn't seeing the play I wrote.

"These characters are very passionate," I said carefully. "They're juicy, they bleed, but when the actors casually—"

"I don't like a lot of yelling," Dan said.

I retreated. Perhaps he was right; perhaps there was too much passion, too much confrontation. That was the way I wrote but perhaps it was old-fashioned. I was a mass of uncertainty.

Paradoxically, the loss of enhancement money resulted in a play that was over-produced. What I had envisioned was minimal scenery; what was onstage were large, characterless, clunky rooms that spun lethargically on and off, occasionally bumping into each other. The lack of specificity as to period wasn't overcome by old movie posters stuck up on the walls. It was Theoni, in Seattle for me, who established place and period through minimal costumes and her own money. That was Theoni. She denied that it was her own money; that was also Theoni. She was silent about what she saw up there on the stage which increased my fear of what was going to happen with what I saw up there.

. . .

The reviews were mixed and too easy to dismiss: the most important never even mentioned there was a woman in the four-character play. Dan dismissed them; he had warned me the Seattle press was always unkind to him. His tiny, feisty, adorable wife, Shelley Plimpton, had more than enough fury at the reviewers for both of them.

Frank Rich flew out to see a matinee and interview me afterward on the stage of the Seattle Rep. He had written, inquiring about a crusade I had embarked on with Steve Sondheim to save Broadway for the new American play. No longer drama critic for *The New York Times,* he was now writing an op-ed column that I much admired. I didn't even know what he looked like but I had my own idea based on his lethal reputation. I was totally wrong. He was instantly likable: a ready laugh, a good listener and a provocative questioner. I had no qualms asking what he thought of *Jolson* and he had none about answering that the play revolved around a sexual triangle but nobody on the stage had any sexuality.

Frank Rich interviewing me in 1995 for *The New York Times*
on the stage of the Seattle Repertory Theatre after a matinee
of *Jolson Sings Again.* Unintentionally, he outed me.

We both enjoyed ourselves during the interview, thereby giving the audience of several hundred people a good time. His questions took it for granted that my sexual orientation was public knowledge; then, back in New York, in a column about my theatre crusade, he referred to me as a "gay liberal." What he didn't know was that he had outed me: the stage of the Seattle Rep and the op-ed page of *The New York Times* were the first public acknowledgments that I was gay. The subject had never come up in a public forum. I wasn't bothered; I'd always assumed everyone knew. Frank, however, was appalled and embarrassed until I introduced him at a charity luncheon as the man who had outed me as a "liberal."

We became fast friends—the only positive that came out of Seattle. The play, the reason I'd gone there, had failed. I had made all the cuts and revisions Dan asked for but the play failed anyway. And I knew why. Not because of the cast or the production or the director but because it wasn't good enough. If it had been, it would have come through. That was the unpleasant reality I had to face and accept. At least, that was what I decided.

A week later, I put all of it out of my mind. Our annual ski holiday had been delayed because of *Jolson*, but Tom and I were back in St. Moritz. Once again it made no sense but we skied better than ever and we were not getting any younger. Emptying the mind on the slopes paid off after we came home. In the winter isolation and peace of Quogue, I revised the play to please me. Some cuts I restored and replaced with a few of my own, and I made a significant revision in those two scenes Dan always felt were too similar. Very often a scene is criticized for one reason when another is really the fault. I threw out the too subtle character element on which the scenes pivoted, replacing it with a vivid plot element that now drove them. The change improved the play; I liked it again. But I had liked it before and it had failed; my liking it didn't mean it was good. Then *Jolson* was given its third reading at a nonprofit theatre, the most prestigious of all, the Royal National Theatre in London.

There wasn't an open slot in the National's schedule but its director Richard Eyre said he would direct a reading if I wanted one. Wanted? I grabbed. English actors in a very American play but they had all the passion and all the sexuality—yes, the English had all the sexuality the Americans in Seattle hadn't. They knew more about the Witch Hunt in America, those actors in London, than the American actors in Seattle did. And they had good American accents to boot.

I was immensely grateful for that reading. It restored my belief and the reaction justified it. Robert Fox was there, surprised to discover he had misread the play, that beyond the politics was an unconventional love story. Maybe the revisions had made more of a difference than I thought, but basically it was still *Jolson Sings Again,* and *Jolson Sings Again* was a good play. Whatever happened or didn't happen to it wasn't as important as believing that.

The reading at the National in London was held on January 16, 1996. The first reading had been held at the Manhattan Theatre Club in New York on November 22, 1992: over three years since the first audience to hear *Jolson Sings Again* had overwhelmed me with its reception. Three years of what? Disappointments and betrayals? The disappointments along the way to the production at the Seattle Rep were minor, regrettable par for the course of a new play in this country: without stars, expect trouble. The disappointment in the Seattle Rep production was major; the effect on me, devastating. But in London, I got back the belief I'd lost in Seattle. It took another three years before that belief was vindicated in a place and to an extent beyond self-indulgent daydreams. On the rainy night of March 3, 1999, *Jolson Sings Again* opened at the George Street Playhouse in New Brunswick, New Jersey.

In the theatre, there is a superstition that rain brings luck. The production wasn't luck; it was the collaboration of exceptional talents guided by David Saint, artistic director at George Street. The luck—another word for serendipitous timing—was the reemergence of Elia Kazan as an informer of note.

In the weeks before rehearsal, informing and betrayal were on the national mind thanks to the determination of the Republicans in Congress to impeach the President of the United States for trying to conceal his juvenile affair with the fellatial Monica Lewinsky. "Sexual McCarthyism" entered the language; Linda Tripp raised disgust with informers to an all-time high by delivering to the obsessed "Independent" Counsel, Ken Starr, the tapes she secretly recorded of conversations with her girlfriend Monica. *Jolson* was always relevant beyond its specific period; now its relevance became obvious, bringing unexpected and most welcome attention to the play. But there was a line the real Al Jolson made famous: "You ain't seen nuthin' yet!" We hadn't. Then the Academy of Motion Picture Arts and Sciences decided to award Elia Kazan an honorary Oscar for his contribution to the film industry.

Protest was immediate and angry; too many people were still alive, too many people had not forgotten. Honor that despicable man? they asked rhetorically. His contribution to the film industry was the destruction of careers! Actors he had worked with came to his defense: he had named only eight people; he hadn't damaged any of them because they had all been named before. The blacklisted countered: How do we know he named only eight? How did he know they had all been named before? Didn't all informers claim that? Someone must have named someone first! Arthur Schlesinger Jr. countered: Kazan was a patriot! He hadn't informed for a movie contract but to save his country from Communism! The families of the blacklisted jeered: Save it how? Tell us exactly how! By betraying his old friends, actors and writers he had worked with, that's how!

The controversy that had begun modestly picked up speed, took off and hit the media with a bang, not merely in L.A. and New York but all over the country, all over the world. In London, *The Daily Telegraph,* a conservative if not right-wing paper, ran the headline HOLLYWOOD PARIAH TO GET OSCAR. Kazan was a famous director but not that famous. He was, however, *getting an Oscar*! What event gets a bigger TV audience? With the ceremony less than a month away, that honorary Oscar made Elia Kazan a world-class informer. It also made *Jolson Sings Again,* in rehearsal at the George Street Playhouse across the river in New Brunswick, New Jersey, the most talked-about play in New York.

There was a certain symmetry: Frank Rich was interviewing me for *The New York Times* once again. This time, however, he hadn't seen the play (he had read the revised version), the interview wasn't for his op-ed column, and we weren't on the stage of a theatre. We were in his office at the *Times,* happily gabbing away into a tape recorder set up by Andrea Stevens, the drama editor of the Sunday "Arts & Leisure" section. Andrea loves the theatre like a woman who knows everything about her faithless lover but loves him anyway. The interview was her idea, Frank generously agreed, and she sat there, encouraging, appreciating, gently guiding us back on track whenever we went laughingly rambling down irrelevant roads.

We started with the extraordinary timing of *Jolson's* production and the Kazan controversy; continued on to my revised feelings about informers (not Kazan and Jerry—I still thought what they did was unnecessary and thus despicable and said so); discussed whether working with a tainted artist—T. S. Eliot or Jerry Robbins—was betraying oneself; examined how, in ordinary ways less grand and dramatic than witch hunts and congressional hearings, each of us faces or commits betrayal almost daily. He played devil's advocate about the honorary Oscar, finally forcing the admission that I couldn't take any Oscar seriously. Or any prize or award, for that matter.

Transcribed, the interview came to over eight thousand words, which Andrea somehow cut to under three thousand that flowed seamlessly. And very effectively, judging from the response, not only in New York and New Jersey and Hollywood but all over the country. Unexpected and gratifying. Frank got some vicious hate mail which he was used to—if you can ever get used to that—from his op-ed readers; I got off easy with a few mild disagreements in letters to the *Times*. But the praise we both got was eloquent and widespread. Mine was not so much for what I said but for speaking out. Usually I got clobbered for that, but not this time. The admiration made me realize how reluctant people are to speak out on anything, even an honorary Oscar.

The best calls of all weren't about what I said, nor were most of them to me. They were calls from New York producers and theatre owners to my agent or to the George Street Playhouse: they wanted to reserve tickets for the play.

It took seven roller-coaster years for me to see the play I wrote called *Jolson Sings Again*. A few who had seen it in Seattle four years earlier came to George

David Saint and I going over the script of *Jolson* during rehearsals
at the George Street Playhouse in New Brunswick in February 1999.
Thanks to David, everyone who had seen the play at the Seattle Rep
couldn't believe they were seeing what was basically the same play.

Street; they too felt they were seeing it for the first time. Frank Rich and André Bishop generously credited the big difference to the work I had done, but David Saint was equally responsible.

David's strength is his ability to find emotional subtext most directors aren't aware is in a scene, and to tap the emotional core of the actor and free him to use it in the scene. He kept a firm hand on the political, keeping the story line clear but preventing it from becoming preachy by always going for the passion. Instead of a play about informing and political betrayal, *Jolson* was the play it was meant to be, a play about the damage all betrayal inflicts—betrayal of partners, lovers, friends, betrayal of ideals and goals in work, betrayal of oneself. At the very end, the damage was epitomized by a visual coup de théâtre that startled the audience.

On that lovely rainy opening night, the actors were tingling with impatience to show the audience how good the play was and how good they were in it. In the first few lines, there was a laugh that had been expected but had never come in the three previews. A laugh, a small thing, but to the actors a sign they were home, the audience was theirs. It was theirs and the performance they gave was tremendous.

In the early scenes, laughter was frequent and strong; late in the play there was an audible reaction to a revelation. Both sounds were welcome but neither was the sound that I was waiting for, the most marvelous of all sounds to be heard in the theatre during a play, the sound of silence—a silence so rapt, so intense that the audience seems to have stopped breathing for fear that a word might be lost. No sound in the theatre is as thrilling and gratifying as that silence and it dominated the evening. The audience sat enthralled—you could feel it—then at the end kept applauding and applauding even after the house lights came up until the actors came back to bow again and again and once more.

Tom and I stayed in our seats.

"There's your play," he said.

I nodded; there was a lump in my throat. I turned to look up at David—the George Street Playhouse is an amphitheater, David likes to sit in the last row. We nodded in wonderment; he got up to accept compliments from his Board of Directors. I didn't want to move; I didn't need to hear praise; what would happen to the play was secondary. I had seen *Jolson Sings Again* and I felt fulfilled.

. . .

A postscript: at this writing, *Jolson Sings Again* is scheduled to be produced Off-Broadway. One of the producers is Scott Rudin, once again my friend but this time, even if the production should be derailed, the odds are we will remain friends. We've talked; we differ, of course, about a detail or two, but we agree on the main point: we missed each other's company.

CHAPTER SEVEN

The Moon Comes Out

West Side Story, Gypsy, *and* Tom

ON A MUGGY NIGHT IN 1957, I was inducted into one of the more barbaric rituals of modern American theatre: the audition to raise money for a musical. The musical was *West Side Story,* the audition was in the apartment of a wealthy lady who nonetheless lacked air-conditioning. All the windows in her large drawing room overlooking the East River were open to the soggy night air and the farts of passing tugboats.

The audition had been set up by Cheryl Crawford, coproducer of the show with Roger Stevens. Cheryl got away with persona murder. She had the appearance and manner of the stereotypical butch lesbian: short and stocky, mannish garb and hair, dry and humorless, an alert eye for a pretty, available girl. As a former director of the Group Theatre along with Harold Clurman and Lee Strasberg, she was guilty by association with productions stamped by socialist philosophy as much as by Method acting. Neither her politics nor her sexuality was ever mentioned by the theatre community; she was far too respected as a moral Christian New Englander to be either a socialist or a lesbian. Off the record, the theatre community was wrong all the way, with one exception: Cheryl was not a socialist.

The community also misjudged Roger Stevens, who had the stoop of an extremely tall man and friendly blue eyes that turned into frozen agate when he became foe. In the theatre, he had the aura of money. Since he had come to Broadway via a fortune made in real estate, it was assumed Roger was all and only about money. He wasn't; he felt blessed to be in the theatre: money was the blessing that allowed him to coproduce what he believed in—coproduce because he knew his limitations. The artistic and theatrical aspects of production were not in Roger's province although he had opinions that he would offer shyly if asked.

When he coproduced *A Clearing in the Woods* with Oliver Smith, he took it for granted that Oliver would be artistic producer as well as scenic designer. It pleased him that Oliver, who was truly an artist, was fond of him and respected him; it didn't displease him that he was wanted because he could and would raise the money. That was his role, he was clear-eyed about it. The odds against *Clearing* making money were heavy and Roger knew it, but he believed in the play and he adored its star, Kim Stanley. He was there for both and he stayed. Similarly with *West Side Story,* he was there from the first and he stayed. If he hadn't, the show might never have happened.

Roger lurked in the back of the clammy drawing room during that audition. Musicals and auditions were new to him; he had to learn the rules of the ritual just as I did. There were none, however, relating to the quality or quantity of the audience at an audition.

At one audition for *Anyone Can Whistle,* Steve Sondheim and I performed before an audience of exactly two: the head of a movie studio and a former Miss America. Fifteen minutes into Act One, the money fell asleep but the beauty kept smiling. *Whistle* was in three acts. I would have walked out but for Steve, singing and playing the whole show as though he enjoyed it. Despite a cast including Lee Remick, Angela Lansbury, and Harry Guardino, it took thirty-two auditions to get the money for *Whistle.* Steve did most of them alone.

At that *West Side Story* audition, there were between thirty and forty putative investors, all well heeled, well dressed, well behaved—you couldn't tell the players without a scorecard: homogeneous, that was the problem. Theatre party audiences, notoriously the worst to play to, are always homogeneous; it's not a coincidence.

Few in that East River apartment were there to listen; it was a social event. Perhaps half a dozen brought a checkbook that might conceivably be opened, perhaps another half dozen might take a flyer for a thousand bucks. All that and more, I learned later from Sylvia Mazzola, a lovely young woman who tilled the money fields for Roger. At the audition, I was an enthusiastic newcomer full of optimism. My collaborators may not have been audition virgins but were just as optimistic. We all believed in *West Side Story* and in one another: Mickey and Judy on the Upper East Side.

The hostess opened the rites by welcoming her guests with the charm that must have gotten them there in the first place. That gain was lost when she introduced Cheryl who introduced the four of us sounding like a veteran drill sergeant roll calling new recruits. Faces brightened when she connected Leonard Bernstein and Jerome Robbins with shows like *On the Town* and *Wonderful Town;* Arthur Laurents got an "Oh, yes, Shirley Booth" for *The Time of the Cuckoo;* and Stephen Sondheim as composer-lyricist of an unproduced musical drew a blank until Cheryl threw in the credit that its book was by the authors of *Casablanca.* Then she passed me the baton, which I twirled, foolishly eager, confident that investors would be throwing money at us. I condensed the story, limiting myself to setting the scene for each song Lenny and Steve played and sang, augmented by three singers and the farting tugboats.

The opening number, performed with great gusto, went well; the next number less well; the ones that followed less and still less. The gusto became terminal. There was no way to make a romp of the end of the first act with two dead bodies littering the stage; the response was nil unless boredom qualifies as a response. I mentally ducked: I had flashed back to the night at Leon and Eddie's when the patrons flicked butter pats at us with their knives. No butter flew on the Upper East Side but one last dead body in our socko musical and we were finished, literally. The audition didn't raise a dime.

Unprepared for fiasco, we were less prepared for facing that we had demeaned ourselves not by begging for money—why else were we there?—but by continuing to beg after the audience had stopped listening and closed its checkbooks. That was done in the first ten minutes; they didn't have an inkling of what we were trying to do and couldn't have cared less. Which was their right. Unfortunately, audition ritual required them to keep sitting and us to keep performing. One thing we all had in common: a desperate desire to get out and home to a drink.

Roger took me aside before saying his good nights. He was leaving for London the next day but suspected Cheryl might have gone a little cold on the show and wanted to reassure me he was with us as strongly as ever. He gave me his number in London in case of an emergency. It didn't take psychic powers to know there was going to be one.

That was a Thursday night. Friday, after Roger was out of the country, Cheryl summoned us to a Monday meeting in her office. Rehearsals were scheduled to start in six weeks; they had to start then if only because of Lenny's fall conducting commitments. We all had commitments, though; we shared everything: good, bad, blame, disaster, whatever—it only brought us closer.

The failure of the audition combined with Cheryl's recent run of flops understandably influenced her opinion but she had been venting her dissatisfaction with the show in memos. A long one, a memo in form only but really a treatise, faulted the book for not tracing the socioeconomic history of the neighborhood where the play took place, then advocated Cheryl's solution: delineating how middle-class Wasp had given way to immigrant Jews to poor Negroes to motley mix. Set that to music. A memo-length memo to Jerry blistered me for being recalcitrant, one to me blistered him for being an inept director. Why did the woman put this on paper where we could pass it around? Worse than foolish, it was ignorant: ignorant of what we meant to one another, ignorant to assume we wouldn't show her memos to each other, and to Lenny and Steve as well. Or did she figure each of us would enjoy the other's being trashed by a perceptive producer? Could it be that this good, this moral Christian New Englander was not above being devious?

At the meeting in Cheryl's office, Sylvia Mazzola huddled in a corner as Cheryl—she didn't smoke a cigar but I always saw one in her hand—got right to her point: as the audition proved, it would be folly to proceed because the book was no good. Since what we had auditioned was the still unfinished score, her reasoning was slightly difficult to follow. I didn't bother, I simply asked one question: Did Roger agree with her?

"Oh, absolutely," Cheryl said.

In her corner, Sylvia Mazzola eye-signaled desperately. On loan to Cheryl from Roger, she couldn't say anything but I could. And did. It mattered less that she was pulling out than that she lied about Roger. I called her on it by repeating what he had told me, and then said:

"Cheryl, you're an immoral woman."

That hurt as I meant it to. I stood up and left with the other Musketeers right behind me. A few doors up the street was the Algonquin where we went for a drink and to decide the next move. It was not my day: the Algonquin wouldn't serve me because I wasn't wearing a tie.

So on that warm, sunny day of rejection, Lenny Bernstein, Steve Sondheim, Jerry Robbins, and I stood on the corner of Forty-fourth Street and Sixth Avenue contemplating no future for *West Side Story*. Every producer in New York had turned it down as too depressing, too operatic. Too uncommercial was what every comment translated into except Clinton Wilder's: his turndown was singular.

Clinton coproduced all of Edward Albee with Richard Barr. He was a friend of mine, a rich friend who couldn't understand why anyone with money paid taxes. Before Cheryl joined Roger, I brought *West Side* to him without much hope but we were scraping the barrel. Clinton was very pleased, flattered in fact but regrettably, he had already booked his compartment on the train to Palm Beach for the season.

. . .

On the sunny street corner, we considered City Center where shows were slapped on for a two-week run. For a desperate moment, we debated the option without even knowing whether it was available to us. Then Steve suggested I call Roger in London, which I did from a phone booth on the street. Roger was calming: not to worry, he'd be back in a few days and would work out something. That boosted our morale, but it wasn't a something we needed, it was a producer.

Eight years earlier, Jerry had approached Lenny and me about writing a musical based on a contemporary version of *Romeo and Juliet*. Romeo and the Montagues would be Catholic, Juliet and the Capulets Jewish; the action would occur on the Lower East Side during Easter-Passover.

I had long wanted to write a musical. For me, nothing said Theatre more than walking down the aisle as the overture to a musical began and colored lights hit the front curtain. If the music for the show was going to be like the electrifying theatre music Lenny wrote for *On the Town,* I wanted to be part of that show, I wanted to write the book.

At the first meeting at Jerry's, all three of us overlapped one another, blathering excitedly, bubbling with ideas, stumbling only momentarily over the obstacle Lenny always put in the way: he wanted to write "an American opera." When he talked about that meeting, and Lenny always talked, he so often quoted me as saying I was "not going to write the libretto for a fucking opera" that it became another Bernstein legend. Proxy attribution was not atypical of Lenny. A journalist interviewing me for an article about him asked: "It was you who first called Mr. Bernstein a Renaissance man, wasn't it, Mr. Laurents?"

"Who told you that?"

"Mr. Bernstein."

No, it was Mr. Bernstein who first called himself a Renaissance man just as it was Mr. Bernstein who said I didn't want to write a "fucking opera." I didn't protest either attribution. It was obvious why Lenny said the former, less so why the latter. I think it was to justify what he considered his capitulation, because *West Side* wasn't an opera.

Neither Jerry nor I wanted to do an opera any more than we wanted to do a musical comedy. What we did want, what all three of us agreed we wanted, was impossible to categorize because we couldn't define it. "Musical theatre" would have been fine with me but Lenny was conducting the Philharmonic and Jerry had begun working at Balanchine's New York City Ballet; their aspirations were higher, grander. We settled for "Lyric Theatre." It sounded good. What it meant, the work would say.

That was in January of 1949. I was still living in Hollywood with Farley, being analyzed, playing tennis, fighting the Witch Hunt. Collaboration with Lenny was long-distance, which wasn't ideal. I took a crack at an outline for what I entitled "East Side Story," but the Catholic-Jewish Romeo and Juliet concept seemed curiously familiar. For good reason. A hundred years ago in the Twenties, there was a long-running hit play called *Abie's Irish Rose*. "East Side Story" was *Abie's Irish Rose* set to music. I bowed out.

Thankfully, Jerry didn't hit the ceiling as he had when I pulled out of *Look Ma, I'm Dancing!* because Lenny, deciding long-distance collaboration was impossible, also bowed out. "East Side Story" was put in storage, we went about our individual lives, Jerry called me "baby" and we remained happy friends. When Farley and I came back East on our way to our first trip to Paris, Jerry invited us to his house in Sneden Landing. We only went for lunch, a ballet lunch for acolytes.

The acolytes, the duo pianists Robert Fizdale and Arthur Gold, were two of Jerry's best friends; most of his friends were acolytes. They cooked up a splendid lunch and their regal conversation was very funny until they considered, pondered and ruled that ballet was the highest art form of all. Jerry agreed, Farley rolled his eyes, I went to the john.

The boys, as Jerry called them, were also acolytes of Balanchine. Whether he or Jerry was the greatest choreographer of the century depended, I supposed, on which was in earshot. That's the way of acolytes. Lenny's anointed him the great conductor of his time, and not merely of Mahler. Steve's, later on, crowned his musicals as not merely the best of our time but the only musicals of our time. Acolytes are harmful and I think can be damaging. What an artist needs is a judicious naysayer; what he gets from an acolyte is an indiscriminate ass-kisser.

Happily, Jerry didn't bring up "East Side Story," he was too involved in his ballets. After lunch, he played a recording of the short Stravinsky piece he was using for a new ballet to be called *The Cage*. It was about Amazons and a neophyte who, after sex with a male, castrated him. As he described the movements in graphic detail, Jerry couldn't stop himself from chuckling, then guffawing, then going off into gales of hysterical laughter when he got to the castration. The ballet was to be for Nora.

She would have nothing to do with Amazons. "If you don't want to get stoned," she said, "you better change them to bugs." He did, casting the ballet in a totally new and fascinating light. But Nora continued to be trouble. My "friend"—always a bad sign—was the way Jerry referred to her when he invited me to a rehearsal. I was bowled over by the ballet. It was startling, even shocking and Nora was astounding but Jerry was furious with her.

"Look what she's doing!" he complained angrily.

I had no idea what he meant. "If it's not what you want, tell her," I said.

"I can't, that's the problem," he grumped. "Technically, she doesn't give me anything to criticize but she knows, she knows!"

That she did know, I could tell when I took her out afterward. She wouldn't say what it was, but opening night, she carried her rebellion a step farther, too far for Jerry. He wanted the women—bugs or Amazons, they were female—he wanted those females to be ice, inhuman. Nora didn't and added choreography. After the first vivid castration gesture, she clutched her belly in a piercing image of remorse. Jerry was ready to kill her, he ordered her to omit it. She didn't and after the reviews, he didn't press the point. *The Cage* was hailed as a brilliant ballet: that brief image of remorse made it human, identifiable, and a success for Jerry. And, of course, for Nora. She always weathered her disputes with Jerry; sometimes they could be mirror images of one another.

Then Jerry informed. Nora knew before I did because he had come to her for her advice.

"You told him not to, I hope."

"No. What for? He was going to do it anyway, so I said the sooner the better and save yourself the agony."

Pragmatist or cynic, she was never surprised by Jerry the way I was. I dreaded his telling me he'd informed. I remembered when he'd joined the Party and dated an actress who always had five toothbrushes in her pocketbook but he felt accepted as a man.

I remembered a party he'd given in his apartment down on Tenth Street in the Village for his family. The director Mary Hunter and I were the only outsiders; we had a lot of fun with Jerry's aunts and uncles, who were ex-vaudevillians. His sister Sonya, who had recruited him, called him Nellie; when I resisted kissing her good night she asked me if I was a Nellie, too. Leaving, I thanked Jerry for a good evening which, except for that poisoned dart from Sonya, it had been. Not for him, though, he was bitter: he had given the party only because his analyst told him to.

I also remembered that Jerry had wanted me, not Comden and Green, to write *On the Town,* just as he wanted me and not them or anyone else to write

"Romeo." I didn't want to hear that he had betrayed friends, people he'd worked with, his agent's secretary, none of it. But he told me, nervous and upset as he did, but he wanted to tell me and I listened.

He had gotten the subpoena in Boston, while choreographing *The King and I* for Rodgers and Hammerstein. They didn't care that he'd been a Communist. He could be whatever he wanted; their interest was in his work. But Jerry wanted to work in movies as well where the employers did care that he'd carried that card. Simple solution: inform. Not that he said that was his reason. He gave several, dancing from one to another—he'd been duped into joining the Party, he was scared, the Communists were a threat, Russia was anti-Semitic—but even Nora believed movies were the real reason.

Ironically, Hollywood had no use for him. He was fired from the movie version of *West Side Story* early on because he took too much time and spent too much money; he accepted two Oscars anyway. Not that I had anything to say about it but I thought they got rid of him too fast. Except for "Cool," reconceived cinematically by Jerry, *West Side* wasn't adapted from the theatre, where all is illusion, for the screen, where all is either literal or surreal. In the movie, gangs became boys with dyed hair doing ballet steps down city streets and clothes became costumes. Even the deaths were overblown in rotating color as was the acting. Only the vitality of the music survived.

When Jerry informed, he assumed Hollywood would be his just as Broadway was his, and therefore his talent would excuse any behavior, including informing. "I suppose I won't know for years whether I did the right thing," he said.

"Oh, I can tell you right now," I answered. "You were a shit."

He cried. It was the first time I had ever seen Jerry Robbins cry; it got to me. He knew how I felt about informers—God knows he had heard it enough. But we were friends, he expected the loyalty from me that he himself hadn't given friends; I realized all that but we had a past, our friendship was special. What I didn't realize but came to learn was that no one is special to an informer except his own special self.

Neither Nora nor I approved or condoned but we both worked with Jerry anyway. I, of course, wrote what had originally been "East Side Story" but before that, in 1952, Nora danced for him in a revue starring Bette Davis, *Two's Company,* in trouble the night it opened in Detroit. The next morning, I was called in New York to come help and I came: for Nora, for Jerry, for a dancer I was having a minor affair with—and who wouldn't fly to Detroit to help Bette Davis in a musical? Even Edward Albee had the musical bug: he took over

Breakfast at Tiffany's from Abe Burrows. His memorable contribution to musical theatre: Mary Tyler Moore, America's Mary, pushed a prison matron away, calling her a "dyke." In 1966.

Bette Davis had thought she would be doing a small intimate revue along the lines of those she had seen in London. *Two's Company* was huge, lavish, endless, produced by, among others, Ralph Alswang who had designed *Home of the Brave*. His scenery for this one was mainly purple. Nora walked off with the show. When I told her that in her dressing room afterward, her reaction was one that few if any performers have.

"She's the star," Nora said. "I don't want to steal it. If it's not her show, the show doesn't work."

This, even though she knew the star wasn't fond of her. Bette loathed Jerry who choreographed Nora's numbers; he had no patience with Bette who necessitated that the four boys who danced with her also walk like bears, yet informed him, "If there's one thing I've got, it's rhythm." And added, "This whole show is routined so Miss Nora Kaye can change her costumes."

My task was clear to me: it was of paramount importance that Bette Davis, the Movie Star, kid herself as soon as possible after the curtain went up. I wrote a sketch for her which did that. It was funny, generous, she liked it, and then chickened out at the last minute, demanding it be rewritten so that it was Tallulah Bankhead whom she played and kidded. Hollywood in Detroit.

In all fairness, she was terrified and the producers were terrified of her. She wanted to quit but she wasn't a quitter. Help arrived: subzero weather in Detroit. Each night, she washed her hair, stuck her wet head out the window and screamed. Alas, she was Bette Davis, she didn't even get a cold.

To help her and the show, the producers brought in John Murray Anderson, her old acting teacher who had gone on to great fame as a specialist in musical revues. Making more than the most out of a cough, she turned to him and asked:

"What can I do with my throat?"

"Why don't you try putting a knife to it?" he answered.

When the show opened in New York, Walter Kerr wrote: "Bette Davis in 'Two's Company' is like hearing the Fifth Symphony played on a comb." Such a line can make a critic famous but nobody had to tell the lady what she hadn't achieved. She still wouldn't quit. She was Bette Davis: lost, in over her head, but with a built-in spotlight that encouraged her to behave in the theatre as she did in the studio. Before each performance, the conductor came to her dressing room: How many numbers will Miss Davis do in the first act? How many in the second?

For the actors' benefit, which is always given at the hundredth performance, Nora asked me to bring my car to the theatre to help her take her belongings home: the chorus gypsies had told her this was going to be the star's last performance. The theatre parties were finished, Herself wasn't about to play to small houses.

The gypsies always know. *Two's Company* closed that night. Artistically, Bette Davis shouldn't have done the show; neither should Nora or Jerry.

At least *West Side Story* was worth doing. In 1955, three years after the Bette Davis revue, it finally got under way, although only after yet another detour: *Serenade* by James M. Cain, which Martin Gabel was going to produce. The same Martin Gabel who had told me during the war that if I didn't stay home from parties, I would never write a play. I stayed home and wrote *Home of the Brave;* now Martin wanted me to write my first musical about an opera singer who discovers his homosexuality. I liked the idea, enlisted Lenny, and we both went after Jerry. Jerry brushed us aside: if we were all going to do a musical, why not "Romeo"? Lenny agreed and quit *Serenade.* But "Romeo" was still *Abie's Irish Rose* to me and I had a commitment to Marty Gabel. Marty brought in a young composer-lyricist to audition for me. His name was Stephen Sondheim.

Unprepossessing, an indoor complexion, droopy clothes, he sat at the piano to play what Martin and his friend George Oppenheimer touted as a remarkable score. It was for a soon-to-be-produced original musical called *Saturday Night.* I didn't much care for the music but I was enormously impressed by the lyrics. Which I told the composer-lyricist. He wasn't much impressed by my opinion and that was that. *Serenade,* like "East Side Story," was put on the shelf. I took off for Hollywood and movie money because I had spent everything I'd made from *The Time of the Cuckoo* building a house on a dune in Quogue overlooking the Atlantic Ocean.

Brooklyn born and bred, I had always wanted to live on the ocean. The desire didn't seem strange to me even though I hadn't been wild about Brighton Beach where we went swimming when I was a kid. The lakes at summer camps were more inviting but I had no desire to live on a lake. Fire Island was mad and fun when I went during and just after the War; physiologically it qualified, but its monomaniacal behavior disqualified it. I wanted air and space, the expanse of sand, sea, and sky, a house on a dune. Not a summer house, I told the architect, but a house in which I could live year-round for $2,500, excluding food.

The summer after *Cuckoo,* I rented a beach house in Westhampton to reconnoiter. Object: the best dunes closest to New York on a lot I could afford.

Quogue, next door, was quiet and costly but there was one lot that might be affordable since it was nonconforming. No house on either side for a quarter of a mile, no vegetation except dune grass, not pretty to many but beautiful to me. The widow who owned the lot rarely came to Quogue anymore and wasn't much interested in selling anyway, according to the real estate agent. But by a stroke of luck, she happened to be in town. That didn't mean she would sell, he said, but I knew she would: Quogue was going to be home.

The widow and I stood on her dune, looking out at the ocean. She was a breezy woman, yet sad about the property: she had wanted to build but her husband died. She wanted to be sure I was going to build, then warned the lot had cost her $22,000 in the Twenties, a price that was never coming back; beach property had had it. Of course, her ocean frontage, which determined price, wasn't as wide as most, but her dune was thick and strong and the lot ran from the high water mark on the beach, across Dune Road, across the wetlands on the other side to Shinnecock Bay. Five acres in all. A farewell sigh: she would let me have it for $5,000 cash.

Never mind what the land is worth today: my house is on it. Never mind what it's worth: I love my house qua house, I work happiest at my house.

The beach house in Quogue in 1954 before neighbors and landscapers moved in and the living was even easier.

There are other houses now, absurdly large, absurdly expensive, absurdly designed all up and down the beach, but the zoning is good so none are close. There's been a lot of planting: rosa rugosa and black pines, Montauk daisies and even bamboo. I've survived hurricanes and nor'easters that sliced my dune but it's back and built up better than before. Guest quarters were added onto the garage below some years back; the house is unchanged except for new shingles and a new bay window. To afford to build the house on the Quogue dunes, I had to go back to Hollywood. Which turned out to be worth more than the money I went there for.

The assignment Swifty Lazar came up with was for a new version of *The Painted Veil,* with Ava Gardner in Garbo's role. With any deal, there was always something Lazar failed to mention, something that might get in the way of his commission—in this case, that I had to sign a paper saying I was "not now nor had ever been . . ."

The Witch Hunt was over but not over. I argued angrily with Swifty, whose glasses were now huge and as round as his As. On the phone with various famous clients—an agent ploy: there may well have been no one on the other end—he said it didn't matter what I signed as long as I signed something, I could make it up myself. I could? OK. I typed out a sentence my conscience could live with:

"I have not now nor have ever been a member of the Shoe Shine Boys Union."

Signed and dated. If I were ever called on it, there was no one I could inform on. But no one could have read it because I was never asked for anything more. Admittedly a small point but small victories were what we were still reduced to.

The Chateau Marmont was the hotel for New Yorkers in Hollywood before they made it on the screen. Around the backyard pool were Paul Newman, Joanne Woodward—in Hollywood, she claimed, because she did the best Kim Stanley west of the Rockies—and Anthony Perkins, all of them on their way up, and Dylan Thomas on his boozed way down. I wasn't going either up or down; I was there because it was inexpensive.

Outside my window overlooking Sunset Boulevard was a twenty-foot-high showgirl mainly in cowboy boots and a ten-gallon hat. Poised on one foot, the other seductively touching her knee, she beckoned with the hat held high in one hand; the other caressed her hip as she revolved 360 degrees all day and

This cowgirl was spinning outside the window of my room at the Chateau Marmont in 1955. She's still spinning today, still waving gamblers on to Vegas.

night, always smiling knowingly. I took endless snapshots of her, in clean air and smog.

Lenny was in town, conducting at the Hollywood Bowl and staying at the Beverly Hills Hotel. We sat at the edge of the pool there, just talking, but it was that conversation that began *West Side Story.* Lenny had been thinking about *Serenade* as an opera. No response from me but he wasn't to be blamed for trying. Then he brought up "Romeo." One on one, Lenny was at his best, as endearing as a child, a listener as well as a talker. It was when an audience— even a third person was an audience—was added that he could become outrageous. His ache to compose something for the theatre was so exposed, I wanted to please him. I also wanted to work with him.

Legs dangling in the pool of the Beverly Hills Hotel across from the moguls and the beauties in their cabanas, we discussed the recent phenomenon: juvenile delinquent gangs. They were in the headlines of the morning's Los Angeles papers: MORE MAYHEM FROM CHICANO GANGS. Lenny began chattering away in half-Spanish (he dropped foreign phrases like names), but no comic strip lightbulb went off, no *"Olé!"* in a little cloud over his head.

"We could set it out here," Lenny mused, hearing Latin music. I loved Latin music, I loved to dance the mambo and the meringue, but any Chicanos

I wrote would be movie Chicanos. The actual were as foreign to me as downtown Los Angeles beyond Olvera Street. But New York and Harlem I knew firsthand, and Puerto Ricans and Negroes and immigrants who had become Americans. And however it turned out, the show wouldn't be *Abie's Irish Rose*. It would have Latin passion, immigrant anger, shared resentment. The potential was there, this could well be a "Romeo" to excite all of us. We called Jerry.

Lenny was jumping with excitement—if Lenny was excited, Lenny jumped. We had the concept, we were convinced the writing would pour out, any problem would be minor. True, there was a schedule problem but there always would be a schedule problem. He was leaving soon but Jerry was coming out to do the dances for *The King and I* at Fox; Jerry and I could talk until all three of us were in New York again at the same time with enough time to produce a work of Lyric Theatre. Lenny could ignore reality better than anyone; he could also be more depressed by it than anyone.

Instinct told me the juvenile delinquent gang concept was right. The racial mixture was a plus that made the project even more attractive; nevertheless, it didn't mean as much to me as *A Clearing in the Woods*. I had finished the play just before coming to the Coast; I knew its unconventionality would make it harder than ever to get a production; I also knew that between us, Harold Freedman and I would find a way to get it on. While meeting with Jerry about "Romeo," I had to keep in mind what I was doing in California: making money by writing a movie for MGM. I was going to need even more than I had thought. I never counted on *Clearing* to fatten the bank account; I didn't count on our foray into Lyric Theatre to do it, either.

My first day at MGM, I was greeted by Gore Vidal from his office down the hall from mine.

"One must admit at least the hustlers out here are good," he said. "All clean-cut young athletes. Straight, of course, but the boys will do whatever you want for twenty-five dollars an hour."

Returning to the Chateau Marmont at the end of the day, I ran into neat and natty Miles White, the costume designer. "The hustlers out here are marvelous," he said with the slight stutter that escaped from under his trim moustache. "Very pretty and all straight but they'll do whatever you want for fifty dollars an hour."

"Gore said it was twenty-five dollars."

"Oh, that's because he has them before six o'clock."

Gore kept pressing me to try one of the all-straight but all-willing stable. When I kept refusing, he shook his head in mock pity.

"Typically homosexual," he said. "A romantic seeking an affair. I have the perfect mate for you. A would-be actor. His name is Tom Hatcher. You can find him at William B. Riley."

I first met Gore in the early Fifties; the next day, he gave me two of his novels inscribed so floridly it suggested an intimacy that didn't exist. I never figured that one out unless it was a way of increasing his fan club. Unfortunately, I had read *The City and the Pillar* and thought it a shop girl novel. Gore the essayist was what I enjoyed reading: as witty and trenchant as everyone said except on the subject of sexuality, particularly his own.

He quickly invited me to his country house on the Hudson for the weekend. We drove up: Gore, John Latouche, Ken Elmslie—another lyricist, and as erudite as Gore and Touche. Twenty Questions was the game of Gore's choice as we drove. The depth of their knowledge of historical figures, esoteric and arcane, impressed and intimidated me as intended. Satisfied, Gore switched to general conversation, also as intended. Every hour of the whole weekend was filled as intended: it wasn't so much a weekend in the country as a guided tour of the mental landscape of the host.

The conversation in the car centered on his rich neighbors and a few literary ones—Names I hadn't met and didn't know, some I didn't even know of. Gore and Touche worked well as a team: they were very funny about these people, even witty, but they reminded me of Sybil Burton's remark about a mutual friend: "She's very funny, I just don't want her to be funny about me." Listening to their chatter about the Names, I realized I wouldn't recognize these people if I ever met them. Their portraits were too superficial; what these people felt, what concerns they had, how they behaved, who they were besides Names—Gore didn't seem to know or care.

His house on the Hudson looked like a spindly Tara. It had a good many sparse rooms but no maid, nobody to take care of them or anything else; housework and house arrangements were left to Gore's boyfriend, Howard Austen. They called him Tinkerbell or Tink; he responded to either. Reddish-haired, freckle-faced, a friendly lad—I would never have thought I'd call anyone a "lad" but the invisible lace handkerchief up Gore's sleeve made it natural—the lad, then, carried bags, fetched drinks, cooked meals, cleaned rooms, sprayed bugs, and worshipped the master.

Our first order of the day was to swim. So: put on trunks, race across the bumpy lawn, dive into the river, and land in mud. Wisely, the host had not joined us. After the invigorating swim, we had drinks on the veranda and listened to him tell anecdotes with perfect timing. His timing had to be perfect because right behind the house were the tracks of the New York Central Railroad. When a train roared by, and trains were not infrequent, the sound was deafening, the house shook like the house in *A Letter to Three Wives*. Competing conversationally with Gore, even a dialogue with him, was futile: he knew the train schedule by heart. His punch lines were delivered just before the shriek of the train whistle and the ensuing shake, rattle and roll. Timing made his jokes doubly funny; his whole performance was a marvel to behold.

Sleep was another matter; ignorance of the train schedule made the night a nightmare. Special torture came from the railroad siding directly behind the house. There, trains from opposite directions met, discussed plans, argued, settled, rested. Quiet—until one train slowly inched backward onto the siding, allowing the other to advance. Quiet, a brief respite, then wheels began to turn, pick up speed, a shriek and they were off with a roar. Quiet, brief rest, then the whole procedure anew with the second train. I lost count of how many times I was on the verge of sleep, finally slipping into peace only to have it shattered by the New York Central Railroad.

I took a sleeping pill, I took another sleeping pill; the sheets were wrinkled with railroad tracks. At last, just before dawn, I was finally sound asleep when Tinkerbell came into the room and jumped in bed.

"I'm exhausted!" I groaned. "Get out and let me sleep!"

"Sweet dreams," he said and left.

The next day, Gore took me for a stroll around the estate while we conversed. Four main topics: Harold Lang, Truman Capote, money and sex. His relentless efforts to pump me about my relationship with Harold made him sound like Lorenz Hart's unrequited bore.

About Truman he was brief: Truman was a liar and older than Gore.

About money: "We men of letters must have an outside income to rely on." He pointed out a bread tray factory he owned. That impressed me. I wasn't sure what a bread tray looked like and I'd never heard of a factory that manufactured them. I wondered how many such factories there were and how much money his made. Not much was my guess: it was the notion of owning a bread tray factory that he liked.

About sex: Sex is what it comes down to if I haven't made that clear before, and sex is what it did come down to. "I'm homoerotic, you're homosexual," Gore informed me. Homosexual being obviously inferior, I was his inferior.

The thin semantic line he drew explained his reputation for being a belly rubber. Unwittingly, a great deal more became clear with his pronouncements over the years and his summation in 1995 with the publication of *Palimpsest,* his memoir.

By the time he was twenty-five, Gore writes, he'd had "more than a thousand sexual encounters" with young men (they had to be younger than he) but he never "sucked cock or got fucked." This deprivation is presumably what made him homoerotic rather than homosexual. Like too many queers—"gay" is a political term for me and I doubt Gore would allow many others to be homoerotics—so, like too many queers, Gore thinks role playing is all important, i.e., it's the position in the sexual act, what the male does and does not do, that makes him more masculine and less queer. Not generational, this juvenile attitude. Even after the Sixties and Stonewall, too many young men struggle with it until some, at least, grow up and realize it isn't the act that determines whether a male is homosexual, it's the sex of the person he consistently chooses to do it with. Over a thousand young men before the age of twenty-five seems a fairly consistent indication of homosexuality.

Homosexual men aren't alone in confusing role playing with masculinity and masculinity with sexual behavior: heterosexuals can be equally juvenile. What is the denial, what is the fear that has turned old, good words like *fuck* and *suck* into pejoratives? "Fuck him!"—why angry? "He sucks!"—why disgusted? "Oh my boy," I would have said to Gore in Harold Clurman's words, "enjoy, enjoy it all!"

The underlying explanation is Vidal's: he writes that he "wanted nothing more than orgasm with as many attractive partners as possible" and wasn't "interested in giving pleasure to his partner." He adds his friend Jack Kennedy's endorsement of that view presumably because a presidential endorsement endows glamour. It does but doesn't make it special. Scores of American males behave that way, that's why they remain boys all the way to the end. Boys don't realize they have cheated themselves as well as their partners. Making sure to pleasure a partner is making sure to increase your own pleasure. Gore's partners, of course, were anonymous quickies; he didn't care about them or believe he should or could, for that matter: he was homoerotic. Never mind; whatever he did or didn't believe, his homoerotic bias led me to Tom Hatcher.

William B. Riley was the best men's shop in Beverly Hills. Much of its pricey merchandise was made exclusively for the store, some of it designed by Riley himself. Tom went there to model for the new catalogue and stayed on as the new manager.

Shortly after he arrived, the employees got into a battle royal over nothing and they all quit. Riley had just met Tom but he asked him to take over. Part of the explanation for this was Riley: an hysteric, an alcoholic, a young married homosexual, and a fellow Oklahoman. The other part was Tom: great looks, great smile, great tan; blond hair made blonder by the sun, green eyes, full, ripe mouth; intelligence apparent in two minutes; and kind and generous to a fault literally, as the takeover illustrated.

To remove any suspicion that I was just a queen who'd dropped in to cruise him—I was sure they were legion—I explained myself by saying, "You're a friend of Gore Vidal's."

"That man of letters," he grinned. We both laughed and were on our way.

It was lust, not love, at first sight: for me, his mouth; for him, my forearms. He had no idea I was a playwright, I had no idea he was an actor. The air was sparking but he had a date that night. It was his birthday; Riley and his wife were taking him where I had invited him: to the Greek Theatre to see Ethel Merman in *Girl Crazy*. His birthday, the same theatre, Ethel Merman—an omen it wasn't all lust?

After a meal the next night, we went back to his apartment for a drink. It was hard to sit across from him and sit still but he would proceed at his pace only. Mentally, I gave him a time limit past which I was either going to pounce or leave. We exchanged vital statistics while he unpacked and stowed away birthday presents a girlfriend had given him: china, pots, kitchen gadgets including an egg cooker that lives on the kitchen counter in Quogue to this day.

He was born in Ada, Oklahoma; brought up in Tulsa, an Eastern city in the West; and graduated OU. His mother was from Kansas but his father, a geologist, was born in what had been Indian Territory before it became Oklahoma. He knew California and movie stars from when he was sixteen and summered in Los Angeles as Oklahoma kids did, took out Norma Shearer's daughter, ran around with David O. Selznick's sons, was unimpressed and remained so. Tulsa, after all, was then the oil capital of the world; the parents of the kids Tom ran around with at home had real money. As for movies, they didn't interest him until after the Second World War when foreign films came to Tulsa.

Presents were left unpacked before we got to the pouncing-or-leaving limit and went to bed. Despite all the sex I'd had and all I'd thought was terrific, I didn't know what terrific sex was until this. This was marvelous, this was why people changed their lives, this was sex.

Afterward, I started to get dressed but he stopped me: he took it for granted I was spending the night. No, sir; he didn't know me. I had never spent the night in someone else's bed and I wasn't about to start; it had some meaning I didn't want to think about. Furthermore, he had twin beds and he was insisting we sleep together. Impossible. I would never be able to sleep. I would be exhausted and irritable in the morning, I was not going to stay. I stayed. In a twin bed with him. And slept. And when I awoke, it was without aches or cramped muscles, we were in each other's arms, it was a glorious morning and I wished we didn't have to go to work.

The producer of *The Painted Veil* was a mild, pleasant man who dreaded week-days because he was certain every morning he drove through the studio gates was the day someone would discover he was gay. Our relationship was fine because it was silent and impersonal until we met at dinner at the Kaufmans'; they had also invited his boyfriend. Then the producer became afraid of me, so much so it took him a week to tell me Ava Gardner was lost in the wilds of Spain and Eleanor Parker was replacing her in *The Painted Veil.* Eleanor Parker in a Garbo role rewritten for Ava Gardner? That called for a rewrite of a rewrite I would not do and since my contract had just about run out and I didn't have to extend, I wasn't about to do. It was time to go home except— Tom. And Tom again. Jerry Robbins resolved the conflict.

He had arrived with secretary to take over a moderately grand house in one of the canyons of Beverly Hills with swimming pool and a guest room for her and another he offered me: I would be available for discussions about "Romeo" when he wasn't at the studio preparing *The King and I.* There was still enough of the romantic in Jerry he couldn't squelch: he liked looking at Tom and me together. We liked being together and were every night, usually driving down to a little restaurant-bar in Santa Monica, always ending up in bed at Jerry's, trying not to make too much noise. His bedroom was at the other end of the house but his secretary's was down the hall. We would emerge cautiously in the mornings but she always greeted us with a benevolent smile; either she didn't hear us during the night or she got a vicarious kick out of it. Or maybe, like Jerry, she enjoyed seeing us together.

Tom took acting class with the distinguished Batami Schneider, mentor to him as well as teacher. Batami counseled caution: I knew who I was, she said, but he was twenty-five, he didn't know yet who he was. She was wrong, I think. She mistook his not being sure what he wanted to be with not knowing who he was. Tom always knew who he was. I always knew what I wanted to be; I had to discover who I was. He was younger only in years.

Tom in 1960, as happy as when he had come to Quogue
five years earlier. So was I.

When he took me to dinner at Christopher Isherwood and Don Bachardy's house in Santa Monica Canyon, I realized I was there on approval. Their fondness for him, their protectiveness placed them as foster parents judging their child's suitor. Very original parents to be sure and each of them a delight. Christopher, a confirmed Vedantist, rattled away enthusiastically over the screenplay he was writing about the life of Buddha for Russ Tamblyn, a freckle-faced redhead who turned up later in the movie of *West Side Story*, where he didn't belong, either. But Christopher was mad for Rusty Tamblyn.

Summer, 1955. Tom holding up Jerry Robbins in the pool of Jerry's rented house in Beverly Hills. It made Jerry very happy to see us together.

Don's portraits were skilled line drawings. Younger than Tom and as American, Don spoke exactly like Christopher who was more than twice his age and English, and had the same, highly individual barking laugh. The mimicry was uncanny but never commented on by anyone, just as Christopher's penchant for teenage boys was never commented on by anyone. Even in that open household, there were unmentionables.

Then it was my turn: I took Tom to the Kaufmans' for mutual approval (theirs was limited; they were nostalgic for Farley); I took him to meet Jigee Viertel, not for anyone's approval, just to meet an extraordinary woman. There were very few friends left in Hollywood, the Witch Hunt had chased most of them out. George Cukor was still there, he would have been very hospitable but his world wasn't for Tom or me. We didn't want to be with other people anyway; our time together was limited.

And then time was up; the half-nude cowgirl outside my window at the Chateau Marmont would be revolving on her pedestal without me. Jerry was shooting his movie, Lenny was in New York waiting to talk about "Romeo," *A*

Clearing in the Woods was waiting for a production. It was always difficult for me to sit and do nothing. It was time to go back to New York. Leaving Hollywood was easy, leaving Tom wasn't. We talked around it rather than about it; neither of us was certain what the other wanted to hear so neither of us knew quite what to say—at least, I thought neither of us knew until one of the very last nights.

We were driving to the little restaurant-bar in Santa Monica with the top down because of the heat. As we descended into Santa Monica Canyon, I heard him say that he loved me and that I loved him. He didn't ask if I loved him, he told me I loved him. The ragged ending of the affair with Farley had left me leery of admitting love; admission meant losing control of what followed. But Tom knew me so well, he removed choice. And he pushed. I couldn't deny I loved him so I supposed I did. Then admitted I did; then let go, let it all go and took my chances on the high wire: I asked him to come to New York and live with me. What followed would follow.

Waiting for him back in New York, I went to an opening night that had a salutary effect on *West Side Story.* The play, *Isle of Goats* by Ugo Betti, had one unforgettable moment: Uta Hagen, flat on her back as far downstage as she could get, knees up and spread wide, writhed and moaned for a goatherd. An evening of high art. At the party at the apartment of Ruth Ford and Zachary Scott, Steve Sondheim emerged from the congregation of disciples to come over and say hello. He knew *Serenade* was history; he even knew Marty Gabel had me pay to be released from the project. He knew more theatre gossip than anyone and had since he was sixteen and a quasi Hammerstein. He knew "East Side Story" was now *West Side Story* because the locale had been moved from the Lower East Side with its religious mix to the Upper West Side with its racial mix. The only thing he didn't know was who was doing the lyrics and that he didn't know because Lenny, Jerry and I didn't know.

Lenny had planned to do the lyrics himself but there was going to be so much music for him to compose, he would need help with the lyrics. He and Jerry asked Betty Comden and Adolph Green; happily, they chose to do a movie instead. "Happily" was my characterization. Fond as I was of both of them, I thought their strength was light satire, not exactly suitable for a musical tragedy.

Steve relished telling how he had never seen anyone actually smite his forehead until he asked me, "Who's doing the lyrics?" and I smote mine, saying, "Why didn't I think of you?!" Because he was ideal. I was sure Lenny would love him; I would call the maestro in the morning. Not asking Steve, mind you, but assuming he would be pleased, probably flattered. He wasn't. He wasn't even at all sure he wanted the job.

What he did want was a score all his own on Broadway before he reached the terminal age of thirty. "Score" meant both music and lyrics; this wouldn't even be writing all the lyrics: he'd be collaborating with Lenny. Lenny as in Lenny Bernstein but it took Oscar as in Steve's adored mentor Oscar Hammerstein to convince him he might learn, perhaps even benefit from working with Lenny and Jerry, and me.

They met and immediately Lenny's enthusiasm, like any Lenny emotion, was extravagant: he adored Steve. They were both wild about words—double acrostics, anagrams, scrabble, any word game old, new or self-invented. Then Steve met Jerry, who also impressed and who also loved games. Not word games, though. Words were his enemy; he often mispronounced them and he wasn't articulate. It was Steve's gift of language that impressed him.

The happy result of the collaboration on *West Side Story* owed as much to the nature of the collaboration as to the talents it comprised. We enjoyed being together as well as working together: we liked each other, we played bridge together—Steve, Jerry, and I, not Lenny. Lenny played double piano with Felicia, his wife. We admired, we challenged each other, we respected each other's opinion as well as each other's work. No one was odd man out. Then the acclaim began and the quartet became a trio and one self-proclaimed soloist.

With the applause came inflated claims that we had made history, influenced the course of musical theatre, changed the history of the American musical theatre by being courageously innovative. Jerry lapped it up. Lenny had proclaimed it himself even before we began writing but said it louder during and louder after. He also kept a journal in which he jotted down the progress of the work long after the events occurred. But that was Lenny: outrageous talk, grandiose claims, but the composer of the most electrifying theatre music ever heard on Broadway. And no one was a better or more generous collaborator.

As for those inflated claims, if *West Side Story* influenced the musical theatre, it was in content, not form. Serious subjects—bigotry, race, rape, murder, death—were dealt with for the first time in a musical and as seriously as they would be in a play. That was innovative; style and technique were not. They had all been used piecemeal in one way or another before. *West Side Story* had more and better dancing but the innovative use of dance to further story was begun by Balanchine with "Slaughter on Tenth Avenue" in *On Your*

Toes in the Thirties, and then developed and expanded by Agnes de Mille in *Oklahoma* and *Carousel* in the Forties. Similarly, the music in *West Side,* though more demanding of the singers, is not used in any basically new way; the Quintet, while extraordinary, is straight out of dreaded opera. The music for the dances is extraordinarily exciting; that music and the basic story are the lasting strengths of the show. The difference between the music of *West Side Story* and other shows, however, is in quality, not in purpose.

The book is the shortest on record, yet the last third of the play doesn't have one musical number, neither song nor dance. That was new for a musical but it was an accident. The last scene culminates in a monologue in which Maria threatens everyone with a gun. The monologue was intended to be an aria sung by Maria; the speech I wrote for her was a dummy lyric. But Lenny never found music that satisfied him and so to this day, *West Side Story* innovatively ends with a speech that is a dummy lyric.

What we really did stylistically with *West Side Story* was take every musical theatre technique as far as it could be taken. Scene, song and dance were integrated seamlessly; we did it all better than anyone ever had before. We were not the innovators we were called but what we did achieve was more than enough to be proud of.

Every musical, like every play, begins with the word—no matter how much music it is set to or muffled by. We began with an outline I put on the table, giving us more to discuss than theory. I divided the play into two acts, detailing in each scene the characters, action, and musical elements. The story line followed Shakespeare's fairly closely, although I eliminated and changed to suit contemporary time and place, and to allow song and/or dance tell as much of the story as one or the other or both could.

The first change I made was early, in the opening scene, in fact: I threw out Rosalind. Heresy, but I think Shakespeare should have. His Prologue establishes Romeo as lovesick for Rosalind but two minutes later, one look at Juliet and he is lovesick again. Making him callow and explaining why Juliet is so much the better role. Love at first sight for her is her first love; I made it his as well. Jerry's suggestion that each have a short, introductory scene before they meet added to the effectiveness of both roles but his staging of the meeting did more than any words could. It was theatre magic, a literally breathtaking example of why he was without peer in staging a musical. No one else could have or would have taken a murderous knife fight and an attempted gang rape and choreographed them so vividly and theatrically that the impact was emotionally devastating.

The parents of both lovers I also eliminated because the play no longer centered on a family feud but on a tribal feud: ethnic warfare between juvenile gangs. The impartial, civilized Duke who ruled the territory became the police who ruled the streets. Bigoted and brutal themselves, they encouraged and promoted bigotry and brutality among the kids they controlled. Shakespeare's Prologue sets up lovers and love, *West Side Story's* Prologue sets up a world of violence and prejudice in which the lovers try to survive.

My first play and my first musical center on prejudice. Possibly a coincidence, probably not, but no matter: a decade after the play, I still had more than enough anger at prejudice to fuel and fire the musical.

I made other changes: no potion for Maria (Juliet) to fake death with— Jerry's suggestion she take a sleeping pill garnered three blank looks—and no suicide for her, either; this girl was too strong to kill herself for love. The change I was most proud of was the reason that prevents Tony (Romeo) from getting the message that Maria is alive. In Shakespeare, it's a convenient plague; in *West Side,* it's prejudice—the factor basic to the story and the theme. In England, that change was regarded as an improvement on Shakespeare. Hardly a reviewer failed to praise it; in this country, to my knowledge, not one reviewer noticed it.

Language was a tricky problem. Four-letter words were rarely used in the theatre in the Fifties but would have jarred Lyric Theatre anyway. Current idiomatic slang was useless because most of it would be dead by the time the show got on—Cheryl was deeply disappointed that I resisted her constant nagging to use "That's how the cookie crumbles," a perfect candidate for extinction. My object was to raise the level of language and heighten it, without letting it slip into purple prose, so that what was spoken could move seamlessly into what was sung.

What I did or tried to do was invent street talk that sounded like real street talk but wasn't. That meant inventing words and phrases—"cut the frabbajabba," for example, meant "cut the bullshit"—and trendy words I thought would last but giving them a new meaning—"cool," for example. There was no rule for this, I simply depended on my ear. "Cool" was given a new meaning in *West Side Story,* doesn't mean today what it did then, and will, according to my ear, be around tomorrow with yet another meaning. It's a word that will always sound contemporary.

Linguistically, I tried to be as evenhanded with the two gangs as in every other way. "Daddy-o" was invented for the self-proclaimed "American" Jets, "kiddando" for the Puerto Rican Sharks. For Lenny, who dropped musical terms in Italian like names, I inserted the stage direction: "Braggadocio and Divertimento cross hand in hand with Brio."

· · ·

Using only the outline, Lenny wrote bits of lyrics as well as sketches of music without waiting for the first scene to be written. Not Steve. I always wrote ahead and he waited because before Steve Sondheim wrote a lyric, he had to know the characters, their diction, the situation. That known, he wrote lyrics that could be sung only by the characters they were written for at that moment—one of the many reasons he is unsurpassed as a lyricist.

The totality of the collaboration left both Lenny and Steve free to do what Steve called "raiding the dialogue." When it was realized just before the first run-through for an audience that Tony needed a song, they took a long speech from his first scene in which he said "something's coming, around the corner, down the river," and turned the lines into a lyric. The finished song gave the character an impact stronger than any speech could in a musical.

For the second act, there was the "Officer Krupke" dispute. I'd had to talk them and Jerry into the Krupke scene. There was a need, I thought, for comedy relief which, by lessening tension, would increase the impact of the tragedy that followed. After getting nowhere with dramaturgical arguments, I invoked Shakespeare's use of clown, his porter scenes, etc. Pretentiousness, however shameful, can be useful: it worked. The song did everything it was supposed to and more. In the movie, the song was shifted to the first act where, since there was no tension to relieve, it contributed to the depiction of the gang as lightweight chorus boys.

The music always came first for me. My task, as I saw it, was to drive as eloquently and economically as possible to the musical moment, be it song, dance, or both. Although *West Side* was my first musical, I think my love for the form enabled me to adapt to it quickly: swift, brief lead-ins to songs came easily. In the second act, I needed only two short lines to slam into a highly dramatic duet for Anita and Maria.

Anita bursts into Maria's bedroom and yanks back the bedcover, exposing the rumpled sheets on which Maria and Tony have made love.

"All right: now you know!" Maria says.

"And you still don't know! Tony is one of them!" Anita says, and sings: "A boy like that, who'd kill your brother," her next line in the scene. I doubt any lyricist other than Steve Sondheim would have seized that line and known how to expand it into a lyric that works both dramatically and as a song. Matched by music I doubt any composer other than Lenny could have written. However, when Maria entered the duet, he lost his operatic head and gave her a musical phrase reminiscent of the mad scene from Lucia: "Oh, no,

Anita, no!" rested on notes to pierce the ears of dogs. For opening night, Steve gave me a gold disc engraved with those musical notes as a reminder of our escape from the jaws of opera.

Whatever disagreements we had about the songs were minor. There was a tough, crackling version of the "Jet Song" that I preferred to the version eventually used but Jerry didn't. I thought "America," witty as it was, had too many words that came too fast but I was alone on that. Love lyrics are always difficult—it's very hard to avoid the platitudinous—but *West Side*'s were a mismatch not made in heaven: Lenny, a master of extravagance, went overboard, feet first; Steve was still, at that time, influenced by his mentor, Oscar Hammerstein, a master of candy-colored trompe l'oeil in both book and lyrics.

I objected to "One Hand, One Heart" for the balcony scene as being too pristine for hot, passionate young lovers. Lenny and Steve liked it because it was pristine until Oscar came to a rehearsal and disagreed with them. "Tonight" was then written and "One Hand, One Heart" was shifted to the bridal shop wedding scene. (Recently, Disney proposed an animated *West Side Story* with a cast of cats. "One Paw, One Heart"?) Out of town, whenever the first slow notes of "One Hand" were played, three doors in the auditorium opened and three of the collaborators walked out for the "cigarette song." Poor Lenny, heaviest smoker of all, stayed inside, gasping for a cigarette but moved. Music makes some composers weep. Especially their own.

"I Feel Pretty" was prototypical Hammerstein and a puzzle. Hardly what a Puerto Rican girl would sing, out of the style of the show, but the audience loved it. They still do and it still doesn't belong. Another song, "Kid Stuff," which might have been similarly successful with the audience, was written in Washington immediately after we opened there. Steve and Lenny played it for Jerry, me and the producers, we all agreed it was terrific and it was. Then, regretfully, I pointed out it would tip the show over into musical comedy. No discussion, no dissent, no protest: the song was out before it went in. It was the last time the show came first for each of the four of us.

That was in August 1957 in Washington, D.C. Earlier, in the fall of 1956 in New York, *West Side Story*, lacking some music, was ready to go but the participants weren't—we were busy elsewhere. Jerry was the first, in November, with *Bells Are Ringing*, the Comden and Green musical starring Judy Holliday. Jerry's ambition was still a house divided: *Bells* was designed for commercial success and that's what it was. But that's all it was.

Lenny came next, in December, with *Candide*, directed by Tyrone Guthrie, with a book by Lillian Hellman and lyrics by Richard Wilbur et al.

Extremely ambitious artistically, it was the failure it had to be. Lillian took the beating but they were all culpable. They should never have chosen Voltaire: *Candide* is basically undramatic. Every scene was essentially the same scene played over. Musically, however, it was glorious—even if only for the overture and Barbara Cook's "Glitter and Be Gay."

I was last, in January 1957, with *A Clearing in the Woods,* also artistically ambitious and also a failure, despite the glorious Kim Stanley who humbly said to me:

"I know the humor in the first scene is essential for the audience to go with the character and I will get it, darling. Just be patient with me."

Patience isn't necessarily a virtue in the theatre. The night Kim asked for mine was the night before we opened in New York. It was a lesson: If you haven't seen it before opening night, you're not going to see it then. I knew the play was going to fail and accepted it, astonishing Steve. He, not Tom, came to the opening night with me because Tom was in the play. The week after we opened, Hollywood tapped him for a screen test that he didn't want to take— he was in New York to live with me—but I insisted he go. His understudy went on, he flew out for the test and didn't get the part, making both of us relieved, happy, and guiltless.

Steve and I had become friends while writing *West Side.* He was guarded; intimacy was slow in coming. His mother, a dynamic, jazzy dress designer, he regarded as a gorgon of mythic proportions. I couldn't imagine a mother called Foxy by her son and everyone in the theatre. Nor would I have brought my mother to theatre parties. Steve brought his to one Tom and I gave, and when I introduced her to Edward Albee, Foxy, closing in on Edward seductively, asked:

"How is your mother?"

Edward, never the charmer, snarled: "Oh, you know how mothers are."

Foxy laughed, Steve shuddered. He was fond of his genial, rather weak father and of his gracious stepmother. When he was a boy, his father had carefully explained that he and not Foxy was responsible for their divorce.

"Yes, he explained it so well that you hate your mother," I pointed out.

Steve understood, but it didn't really register. It was curious what did and didn't register with him, what was hidden consciously and unconsciously. At our first dinner, he was rattling off anecdote after anecdote about his adored friend Burt Shevelove, later the co-author with Larry Gelbart of the book for *A Funny Thing Happened on the Way to the Forum.*

"One thing about your friend—" I began when he quickly interrupted, "I know what you're going to say: he's homosexual. Well, he's not."

I hadn't been about to say anything of the kind. I didn't know Burt Shevelove but at that moment I knew he was homosexual and the subject was distasteful to Steve. Tom had asked whether Steve was gay and I had answered:

"I don't think he's anything."

"Nobody does nothing," Tom said.

But I was so taken in by Steve's carefully constructed façade I, the resident expert, blithely assured Steve he had no need for therapy. Perversely, that was all he needed to show me I was wrong by dropping a bombshell. He was elaborately casual but I knew I had to take his confession very seriously and yet balance it with a joke. Get thee to an analyst, I said, and he got. Confiding something that personal was opening his door, I happily walked in and there we were: friends as though we always had been.

Being his friend wasn't easy because he could catch you unaware by what offended him. He couldn't wait for me to meet Mary Rodgers; he knew we would love each other because he loved each of us. He introduced us, we did love each other, Steve got mad.

"I'm jealous and possessive," he admitted but he still was. Mary and I walked carefully for a time.

Many years after I suggested an analyst, he was still going to the woman he had chosen but without much visible progress, not to me at any rate. Unwilling to chance offending him, I said nothing until he and Tony Perkins staged an elaborate treasure hunt. Limousines were provided to drive teams, voluntary and shanghaied, from clue to clue, each more arcane than the last. One led us to the vestibule of a house in the East Sixties where the next clue, the number 245, was to be found in the Sinatra standard "One for My Baby (and One More for the Road)" ("It's quarter to three, there's no one in the place," etc.). A recording was played just inside the door on a portable phonograph that had to be wound over and over until all the hunters heard the song. Who was crouching on the other side of the door, winding the machine? Steve's analyst. Time to switch to a new one, I thought, and said so. Offense charged and convicted: I was on his shit list.

I gave *West Side Story* three months if it ever did get on, but standing on the corner of Forty-fourth Street and Sixth Avenue after calling Roger Stevens in London, chance of any production seemed nil. None of us, not even Lenny, the only believer among us, believed in miracles. However, since every producer in New York had turned us down, a miracle obviously was what we needed. As it happened, what turned our corner was even older than miracles: the perverseness of human nature.

That night—the night of Cheryl's defection—Steve, bottoming out in

New York, was on the phone with Hal Prince, bottoming out in Boston. If Alexander Graham Bell hadn't invented the telephone, Stephen Sondheim would have had to: it was his lifeline. He and Hal were one-upping each other as to which of them was facing the bigger disaster.

They were the closest of friends, the theatre was life to each. Neither could ever accept failure as another part of life which, according to Hal, was "swell." What wasn't swell professionally, buried him; what wasn't swell personally, he buried. Life according to Steve was imminent disaster. In the theatre, when one of his shows was out of town or in previews, he would be lurking as the audience came up the aisle after the curtain, eavesdropping hopefully for negative comments, the worse the better. Outside the theatre, he hid in games: the walls of his apartment were decorated with antique games, the rooms were for playing all sorts of games, parlor and personal, formal and informal, acknowledged or unacknowledged. As with Hal, the love of Steve's life was the theatre which each was determined to take over and make over in his own way.

Like Steve, Hal had a mentor bring him up in the theatre: George Abbott, who taught him well and whom he revered. He stage-managed for Mr. Abbott, as everyone called the director-playwright-actor. When Hal became a producer, his partner was another, older Abbott stage manager, Bobby Griffith—sweet, calm and calming. They had quick success with two Abbott musicals, *The Pajama Game* and *Damn Yankees,* but the night he and Steve were complaining long-distance, Hal was in Boston having difficulty facing that George Abbott was not God.

He had expected *New Girl in Town,* the new Abbott musical he and Bobby were producing, to be at least a candidate for a Pulitzer Prize but the theatre has a habit of resenting and punishing expectations: *New Girl,* at war with itself, was floundering badly. Nevertheless, it was on a stage in a theatre and *West Side Story* was nowhere: Steve's disaster was worse than Hal's. And so Hal asked that the book of *West Side Story* be sent up to Boston.

When Hal and Bobby had first read it, they'd given it to Mr. Abbott who advised them to turn it down, which they did. Everything they produced was with Mr. Abbott's participation, anything they considered needed his approval and blessing. The book had been slightly revised but this time when he thumbs-downed it, he was not Mr. Abbott, he was George in trouble: wrong about *New Girl in Town,* ergo wrong about *West Side Story.* Hal and Bobby liked the book, flew down to New York to hear the score, and decided to produce the show.

Abbott still had influence. While we were in rehearsal, he ruled that "West Side Story" as a title was worse than just uncommercial, it would keep people out. Something livelier, jazzier was needed. As a joke, I suggested "Gangway!"

They took it seriously, so much so it was stenciled on the back of the scenery as permanent identification when we opened in Washington. Reason somehow prevailed and it was never used.

Immediately after *New Girl* opened, Hal and Bobby went to work on *West Side*—cutting royalties, cutting the budget, raising money, full steam ahead until Jerry Robbins brought everything to a horrified halt: he didn't want to choreograph the show. What? Correct: someone else could do the dances; Jerry liked the book so much, he only wanted to direct. Authors and producers were never so unified as we were in that moment of astonished horror. I was flattered but frightened. A Picasso who only wanted to make picture frames? Bless Hal Prince and genuflect to a real producer.

First, he flattered Jerry with the truth: he wanted him on the show because he was hands down the best choreographer on Broadway. Then, he confessed that that had been a big factor in his decision to produce *West Side*. In fact, if Jerry wasn't going to choreograph, Hal wasn't sure he was going to do the show. Check and checkmate. Jerry's response was rage and a series of demands. Four weeks was the normal rehearsal period; he demanded eight. Reasonable, said Hal. And a co-choreographer. Absolutely, said Hal. Four rehearsal pianists. Three, said Hal.

In the end, the eight weeks of rehearsal were well worth it. We went out of town in such good shape that there were almost none of the usual changes and changes of changes—with the exception of Jerry's second-act ballet. And the long rehearsal period wasn't all that expensive. The cast was paid next to nothing; the money budgeted to cover the expected half-empty houses (we had no advance) was never spent. In Washington, where we opened, we sold out; in Philadelphia, the next stop, crowds at the box office were kept in line by mounted policemen. This was not Cossacks at a pogrom, this was a gorgeous sight. Only once did we see it and the show was never that big a hit anyplace ever again but we did have that once to remember. With even more pleasure because we were at the unwanted Erlanger Theatre; the desirable houses in Philly wouldn't book us.

Roger Stevens, pushed to the back of the bus, was allowed up front because we had a housing problem in New York as well. Roger was waiting to be needed; he liked being needed because he liked coming through. We needed a theatre, he could get us one. The most desirable were occupied or booked, but on West Fifty-second Street there was the ANTA Playhouse (now the Virginia), with a good-size stage, a profitable seating capacity, and controlled, fortunately, by Roger's former real estate partner, Bob Dowling. Both Roger and Dowling considered Dowling a man of the theatre but it was Bob Dowling who called *West Side Story* a "fucking opera," as in "I wouldn't give any theatre of mine to that fucking opera."

With theatre lovers like Dowling, it was easy to make history. Until that moment, the respected theatres on Broadway were movie palaces. A legitimate theatre situated on Broadway was a white elephant; only the unwanted or the desperate took one. We were both so we took the Winter Garden. The rest is Shubert history.

Late the night before *West Side Story* went into rehearsal, Lillian Hellman called me. We were acquainted but not well enough to justify her donation of venom. Possibly she was boozed up, it wouldn't have been unusual; more likely she was still seething over the failure of *Candide*.

"This is Lillian." No Lillian Who; certainly no Hello, how are you. "You are in for the worst experience of your life. Leonard Bernstein is a meglomani-acal monster. He will destroy every word you write. Good night." Click.

Lucky Voltaire: he was dead.

Before beginning his dance rehearsals, Jerry came to me for help. No one had to tell him what the Prologue had to establish, he knew it was the warfare between the two gangs but what were they dancing about? A scenario was what he wanted so I wrote a one-act play with a beginning, middle and end: a line of action, incidents revealing character and ending not with a Big Finish, Lights up, Hand but a seamless transition into dialogue.

Very few connected to the production were political so very few noticed the point made in that first dialogue scene that there was a "difference between bein' a stool pigeon and cooperatin' with the law." Jerry never commented but neither did he ever explain the line to his dancers-trying-to-be-actors. He made sure it was spoken clearly and went back to cleaning up the Prologue. When it was put together, finished though not polished, he had the dancers run through it for me. It was stunning the way his best work was, but it was unexpectedly moving: I had tears.

"Not for what I did," Jerry said. "It's the first time you're seeing what you did brought to life."

There was that side to him, too.

Peter Gennaro, the co-choreographer he chose, was a compact little imp with a big grin, sparkling black eyes and fantastically fast feet. Jerry choreo-graphed the Jets and gave Peter the Sharks. Peter must have done dozens of variations of the quick, tricky steps he choreographed for Chita Rivera in other shows but he surpassed himself for her in "America," which, as Anita, she danced with the Shark girls. And in the competitive dance at the gym, his mambo for the Sharks won over Jerry's for the Jets.

All Peter's work in *West Side Story* sparkled but it was Jerry who pulled it into the style of the show and made it dazzle. A little change here, a small addition there; an attitude made specific where it had been general; the structuring of a number like a play. What made Jerry's touch individual and so brilliant were his humor and his use of dance to express emotion. He would not choreograph a dance as a dance, he had to know what the dancing was about.

Like Hal, Jerry had been a George Abbott disciple. For *West Side Story*, he switched to Stanislavsky: he was going to direct the first Method musical. Everybody read Stanislavsky, but how to use his Method, how to put theory into practice was influenced by how the Group Theatre did it. The Group itself wasn't of one mind. Understanding of the Method varied from guru to guru, from Harold Clurman to Lee Strasberg to Sandy Meisner to Bobby Lewis until Stella Adler went to Paris and actually studied with Stanislavsky. On her return, she passed to the Group what she herself had gotten from the great Russian in one sentence:

"We got it all wrong!"

Havoc, dissension, factions to this day. For Strasbergians, use your neurosis: play yourself as the character. For Adlerians, use your imagination: play the character. Stella's classes had students like Marlon Brando and Jerry Robbins. What Jerry learned from Stella he adapted to directing dancers in his ballets. To a choreographer, dancers are bodies, flesh constructions to be moved at will and told precisely what to register while moving that finger—no, that finger—that leg, that head. Directing actors is totally different. Actors have questions and their own ideas, very difficult for choreographers who demand strict obedience to "five, six, seven, eight." Especially difficult for choreographers who have trouble with words is directing dancers speaking words for the first time. As in *West Side Story*.

The bulletin board backstage at the Broadway Theatre where we rehearsed overflowed with newspaper clippings about juvenile delinquents, Puerto Ricans, gang warfare, rent evictions, anything Jerry thought related to the play. The dancers brought in clippings, so many that the corridors backstage were wallpapered with newsprint. The two gangs, Jets and Sharks and their girls, were ordered not to eat together, sit together or talk together in or out of the theatre. The dancers were thrilled. They had never been treated like this before; they weren't just bodies, they were actors! For the first time, the Method was being used in musical theatre! Some of the use was peculiar, though.

Returning from lunch one day, I found Gerald Freedman, Jerry's assistant director, standing on a chair outside one of the dressing rooms. The door was closed but the transom was open so he could overhear Larry Kert and Carol Lawrence as Tony and Maria rehearse the balcony scene with the privacy the scene demanded. When they got onstage, they were so private, they couldn't be heard.

Rehearsing the rumble, Jerry could get what he wanted choreographically but he wanted more and didn't know how to articulate what it was. The frustration that produced was, I think, part of the reason for his cruelty to Larry Kert. It humiliated Larry and embarrassed the company which loved him.

"Faggot!" Jerry shouted at him over and over. "Do you have to walk like a faggot? Can't you move like a man, you faggot!" Larry was a natural gymnast. "Jesus Christ, just stand straight, faggot!"

Larry was almost family to me. He was Anita's kid brother. (I had written the role of Anita for her but she couldn't dance and Chita Rivera could.) I knew him from musical nights at the Chaplins' on Dohney Drive; Tom knew him longer, from acting class at Batami Schneider's. He was a California extrovert, laughing, bubbling, really funny, and openly gay. He was auditioned a hundred times for Riff, chosen to play Tony, would have been happy just to be in the show. He said nothing. Jerry rubbed salt in the wound by appropriating Larry's boyfriend, who was also in the show. That stung. Larry's jokes dried up, his lips got thinner but he kept trying to please Jerry. Everyone always did because everyone had so much respect for his talent.

Larry survived but the episode left a sour aftertaste. Two of the straight dancers struggling to play little tough hoodlums onstage became little tough hoodlums offstage. Pets of Jerry's, they took "faggot" as a message from their leader to be emulated. "Faggot" and "fag" echoed around the theatre but when one of them was busted for smoking pot, he called me in the middle of the night. Why me, I didn't know. I kept him out of jail, he stopped using "faggot," at least when I was in earshot, but I never liked him. And he was Jewish.

Everyone had been very impressed by the newspaper headlines plastered all over the walls and in awe of Jerry's division of the cast offstage to intensify the enmity onstage. But connecting this with the play itself was a step the cast didn't quite know how to take and Jerry didn't quite know how to help them take it. Puerto Rican immigrants versus Polish Americans wasn't something they could identify with so he divided them into Jews and Nazis in a concentration camp. Some of them were uncertain what a concentration camp was, some sat backstage knitting when they weren't needed. A run-through of the first few scenes was heavy with labored acting.

I thought Jerry was in over his head and said so to Hal and Bobby. Hal asked if I would repeat this in front of Jerry, which I did. Unlike most directors, Jerry Robbins took help anyplace he could get it. He had me sit by him during rehearsals, playing ventriloquist. Sometimes he would have me take small scenes in the rest room lounge. Our mutual objective was to head the actors in the right direction. Jerry would never be good with actors but far better that he go on his own instinct than as a Hoboken drama major lost in the Method wilderness. In time, by trial and error and feet to the fire, he would get the performance he and all of us wanted.

The long rehearsal period helped; his determination to succeed no matter what helped; the company's respect for him, their desire to please him, to do what he wanted hit or miss but somehow do it and get it, helped. His intensity and belief were contagious. And always, there was the music. Its rhythms gave the performers tempo and pace, its drive drove them, its pulse was the pulse of the show.

Washington, D.C., was a steam bath in August—which wasn't good for the tension during technical rehearsals. Once or twice, there was a relieving serendipitous moment as when the curtain of colored streamers caught on a pipe and came in late, swirling down unexpectedly in crossing beams of light—"Keep it in! Keep it in!" everyone shouted from all over the theatre. But black moments were more prevalent. Jerry decided to cut several bars in a dance and cut them, without asking Lenny. Lenny started out of his seat, then sat down and kept silent.

In 1990, at the Memorial Tribute to Lenny that I organized at the Majestic Theatre, I introduced each performer or speaker with an anecdote or two but for Jerry, one sentence was enough:

"There were only two things Lenny Bernstein feared: God and Jerome Robbins."

Lenny was far from alone in his fear of Jerry; most people were afraid of him. I never was—one reason I think Jerry respected me—nor was Bobby Griffith. When the orchestra rehearsal was about to go into golden hours of overtime in Washington because Jerry wanted them to continue after midnight, Bobby walked calmly down the aisle to Jerry, who was standing at the edge of the orchestra pit. Putting a fatherly arm around him, he said: "Come on, kid, I'll buy you a drink." And to the orchestra: "That's it for tonight, boys." Like Hal, Bobby was a rare producer.

. . .

A real brouhaha broke out over Oliver Smith's scenery for a real reason: it was polarized between stunning and scabby. His designs for the dances, particularly his painted drop for the rumble under the highway, were breathtaking: Oliver was a painter. His sets for the book scenes were little matchbox pieces that shuddered on and off with no tone, no feeling of place and in one instance, lacking an element vital to the plot.

Oliver's sketches were so beautifully drawn, they deceived. Once, Steve the neophyte had the chutzpah to question; the snob in Oliver bit Steve's head off and spit it out with contempt. He was easier with me on another because we were friends and he knew I admired him from the day he told me how, when still an architecture student at the University of Pennsylvania, he had hidden in a box in the old Metropolitan Opera House on Seventh Avenue after a performance of Ballet Theatre. When the house was cleared out, he sat up at the front of the box and decided one day, he would be artistic director of Ballet Theatre. Not your ordinary dream and Oliver made it come true.

He lived in a big old house in Brooklyn Heights with a tiny Truman Capote in the basement and a very tall and very drunk Tyrone Guthrie and his equally tall and drunk wife on the top floor. Dinner at Oliver's was fascinating, funny and wet.

Friendship hadn't prevented me from pointing out his mistake in the rickety little set for Maria's bedroom. "There's no place for Chino to find the gun," I said.

"What gun?"

"The gun he kills Tony with."

"Oh, that gun." Oliver giggled.

When the set appeared in Washington, it had a phony little cabinet attached to a sliver of a wall. But there was worse: the set for the drugstore, used for two big scenes but also for a big dance number, "Cool," was clunky and a nauseous green. Looking at it, you could barely wait for whatever was going on in front of it to end. Jerry hated it as much as I did and took after Oliver who exacerbated matters by blaming me:

"The book's no good. It didn't inspire good work."

Irene Sharaff came up on the stage to make peace. She was a Russian Jew whose lover, the aristocratic daughter of a Chinese ambassador to the United States before China went Communist, taught this most brilliant of costume designers how to dress offstage. The result was a rather homely woman transformed by eyes heavily outlined with kohl, black hair pulled tight in a bun, and a red-slashed mouth into a bizarre, striking exotic.

Irene had been sitting out front, quietly sipping from a paper cup of what

With Jerry Robbins and stage manager Ruth Mitchell, right, during the tryout of
West Side Story. It was August and hot as only Washington, D.C., can be.

we thought was water but was straight vodka. Haughtily and dismissively, she
told all of us to cease behaving like children: shut up, go home to bed and
meet in the morning. We all shut up and left.

Oliver called first thing in the morning. To apologize? Oliver? "Cookie,
you and I are the only ones with any brains around here. Meet me downstairs
in the coffee shop and let's figure out how to fix that pissy set. I must have
been drunk when I did it."

A new set was really the only answer but Hal and Bobby were hardly about
to spring for one. The solution we came up with helped some but not enough.
By that time, there were other scenery problems. The penultimate scene in the
play took place in the cellar under the green drugstore. Oliver's drop was a
Rube Goldbergian collage of twisted pipes, suitable for a Feydeau farce. I'd
had it by then.

"If that isn't thrown out into the alley now, I'm going to come up there and
pee on it," I said.

Nora Kaye had come down to Washington for the fun. She was sitting out
front with Tom when I made my threat, which succeeded: the drop was
thrown out then and there. But not in Nora's version which became a minor

legend and still persists. As told by Nora, I walked up on the stage and peed on the drop. The more I protested the tale, the more she enjoyed my discomfort. But a better story, a more dramatic story, was one neither she nor anyone else ever told, probably because it was about Jerry and Jerry was feared:

The basic set Oliver designed for *West Side Story* was a dark blue box that made his fire engine red fire escapes stand out dramatically, hanging in midair. For his second-act ballet, Jerry wanted the entire stage cleared, losing the claustrophobic threat of the city, bringing air, space and light for the first time. But the ballet was led into by Tony and Maria singing on a bed and the bed couldn't be cleared. Why not? Jerry asked angrily. Because there was no open-ing in the wall of the blue box. Make one, he demanded. The crew carpenter said he couldn't. But Jerry could.

"Get me a saw," he said.

They got him a saw, he sawed through Oliver's set with Oliver standing there. The carpenter finished the job and however inelegant, there was an opening to push the goddamned bed through and offstage in time for the bal-let. That story, Nora didn't tell. Peeing was better than sawing. She and Jerry had been in the tap-dancing chorus of *Stars in Your Eyes* together when they were beginners. They were still together.

The night of the first performance before a paying audience, all the grum-bling about the scenery, about the still-missing final aria for Maria, about the pasted-together pieces called an overture instead of a written overture (there never was one), about this actor, that line, all of it was silenced by fear: What was going to happen when the curtain went up? Neither we nor the audience had any idea. We had hopes but they must have, too. Because they were ready, they wanted it to be good and at some point in the first act, I don't remember when, Jerry, who was sitting behind me, began pounding me on the back, cry-ing: "They like it! They like it!"

They didn't like it, they loved it. The reviews were ecstatic and that was beginning of the end of what had been a marvelously harmonious collabora-tion.

Steve wasn't mentioned in the reviews. He was unknown and was listed on the program as co-lyricist with Lenny, who, because he was Lenny Bernstein, got all the credit for the lyrics. We—Jerry, Lenny, and me, without Steve—were given the keys to the city on television because of what *West Side Story* did for juvenile delinquency. "This was your conception, Mr. Robbins," the presenter said, and Jerry agreed. Lenny and I looked at each other but said nothing: we were on television.

West Side's witty lyrics, the ones quoted—"Officer Krupke," "America"—

were written by Steve; most of the florid lyrics were written by Lenny. Both Lenny and Jerry had gargantuan egos; in an ego contest, Lenny even had a slight edge. But Lenny was fair and Lenny was generous: he went out of his way to praise me for the economy of the book and for its contribution to the lyrics raided from its dialogue. Of infinitely more importance, his ego didn't get in the way of the most magnanimous act I ever heard of in the theatre before or since: he removed his name as co-author of the lyrics because Steve was just beginning his career, the credit was important for him.

Steve didn't get down on his knees, the offer didn't make the heavens crack open for him. In all seriousness, he asked me whether he should accept it. I suspected his hesitation was caused by his doubt whether to take credit for lyrics he thought were over the top and beneath him. My advice was to say yes fast and be grateful.

Jerry was not Lenny; Lenny would never have been an informer. I continue to bring that up because I believe informing is more than a political matter, it defines character. It wasn't that Jerry behaved like an informer but that informers behave like Jerry.

When the contracts for *West Side* were ready to be signed, Harold Freedman phoned—ninety percent of his agenting was done on the telephone—to report that "Mr. Robbins wants a rather presumptuous credit: 'Conceived By.' " The notion of a contemporary Romeo and Juliet was Jerry's; I thought the credit fair and agreed to it. On that television show, I realized that "Conceived By" meant something very different to the world.

Lenny and Steve were new friends, only since they began working together. Jerry and I had been friends for over a decade. After Lenny's generosity to Steve, I asked Jerry to remove "Conceived By" for me. He didn't ask for an explanation; he knew why and said he would think about it. The next day he said he had thought it over: I was right but the credit was too important for him. He would not give it up.

The decision seemed to dissolve all modesty and restraint. From then on, he took over the show, riding roughshod over everyone. His concentration was almost entirely on his second-act ballet—and it was his ballet—rehearsing one version after another after another, ordering new backdrops (until Hal put his foot down), doing what he pleased with Lenny's music until in Philadelphia, he achieved by accident what he had been after all along: the second-act ballet stopped the show.

We had agreed at the outset that the show would never stop for a hand. The ballet ended with the lights going out on everyone except for a spotlight on Tony and Maria as he picked her up and brought her back to the bed where they finished their song. The applause that came covered their embrace as the bed slowly slid off into darkness and the fence drop came in for "Krupke."

One performance in Philadelphia, the lights went out at the end of the ballet as usual but accidentally, no spot picked up Tony and Maria. Instead, there was a complete blackout, telling the audience the ballet was over. The applause was thunderous. It continued after the spot for Tony and Maria finally came back on and drowned out their singing. It ended just as they ended, leaving them sitting there, looking as though they were waiting for a hand that never came. And they sat waiting in embarrassed silence until the bed at very long last shuddered off and the lights finally faded out to total silence and a stage wait until the fence drop could come in.

Jerry kept the blackout; he was happy and thrilled. His disregard for the actors, the song, the moment, the show, for anything except the satisfaction of his ambition for *his* ballet appalled the three of us. But since Lenny and Steve were afraid of Jerry, I was delegated to ask him diplomatically to behave. He didn't argue; he understood, shrugged and agreed to eliminate the blackout and restore the lighting as it had been. I checked this with his lighting designer, Jean Rosenthal, because I didn't trust her.

Jean was a marvel at lighting ballets but lighting an empty stage for dancers is very different from lighting actors on sets. George Abbott, who knew comedy needs light, wouldn't have hired her. There wasn't much comedy in *West Side,* and what comedy there was in the scene before "America" was killed by a stage in artistic shadows. Jean denied this, claiming the stage was as bright as it could be; I pointed out the lights bumping up for the dance: she denied they did. I stood her next to me, made her watch with me; the lights bumped up, she said they didn't. But the next night, they were brighter for the scene—not as bright as I would have liked but with Jean Rosenthal I took what I could get.

Opening night in New York, she sent me a telegram saying Shakespeare's clowns could get laughs in the dark, and the scene before "America" was once again played on a stage in shadows. She and Jerry were a good team. That opening night, they shared another triumph: the accidental blackout in Philly was restored for the New York critics. As the applause hit in the wrong place for the show but the right place for Jerome Robbins, Lenny came running up the aisle saying, "I'll kill the son of a bitch!"

The audience that opening night was glamorous but the reception they gave the show was not spectacular. They entered the theatre cautiously, quietly, as though they were novitiates filing into a Temple of Art. Not until "America" did they relax and enjoy the show for whatever it was. But even had they been the best audience in the world for the best show in the world, there would still have been a sour taste for us.

The four of us had started the show together, created it together, had a wonderful time being together. It was opening night, work done, the time to rejoice together, all four of us together, but three of us weren't talking to Jerry. There was no pleasure in that; if anything, there was an additional load of resentment because he had caused the estrangement, he was why "together" had lost its meaning.

He knew what he was. At the party where we couldn't get as smashed as we would have liked, he came up to me and asked: "Do you still think I was wrong to keep the billing?"

"Yes."

He turned to Tom who was standing with me and asked him the same question. He knew Tom, he knew what we were to each other. Did he expect him to answer no?

"Yes," Tom answered, and Jerry never spoke to him again.

In Quogue, four decades later, I told Jerry how I felt about him. He had driven over from his house in Water Mill because he needed something from me. Fame as the best American choreographer of ballet in the country wasn't enough for him: the ballet world was too small, modern dance had long been encroaching and now Merce Cunningham, Paul Taylor, and Mark Morris were getting more attention than he. He had fooled around with a musical without any words, sung or spoken; it got nowhere. He had tried his autobiography in dance and abandoned it in mid-life. All his energy and concentration were on what he was readying for rehearsal, an event to display what he had done for the American musical, what his place was in the history of musical, how important Jerome Robbins was. The show, called *Jerome Robbins' Broadway* at his insistence, was a revue composed of material from all the musicals he had choreographed and directed. The hitch was that he didn't own the material.

The producers of this nine-million-dollar production, their lawyers and the lawyers and agents for all the authors involved, had backed and forthed before finally coming up with a royalty agreement whereby each author's percentage would be based on how much stage time his material got as well as on what percentage his original royalty was on the particular show being used. The agreement made sense but had one factor that led to what seemed a hokey plot contrivance. The author with the highest royalty and who therefore would establish the base royalty from which all the other authors' royalties would be calculated, was Arthur Laurents. I didn't really understand how the royalty was calculated or the complicated domino effect that had on the other authors or very much of anything. I did understand I had to accept a set roy-

"You can always put this in the cigar box—but keep the FRAME!
With <u>love</u> and gratitude—Jerry"

The silver frame Jerry referred to in the inscription was real, the love wasn't.

alty without any guarantee how much of my material Jerry would or would not use. If I didn't accept the terms, the others couldn't and his canonization was out the window. The terms were cloudy but the point was clear: Jerry needed my consent.

When he came to Quogue, we didn't talk about that. He told me his ideas for his show, we discussed how to encapsulate all of *West Side Story* in twenty-odd minutes—which led us back to the original and me to 1957 and his behavior back then. It was so far back and I had changed so much that what I said was said without anger and with very little residual rancor. Jerry didn't refute any of it, didn't deny, didn't even comment. Instead he launched full-throttle into a bitter attack for what I had said about his direction of *Gypsy.*

I don't know which surprised me more: the intensity of his attack or its content. I had certainly made my share of derogatory cracks about his direction of *Gypsy.* But the remarks he attributed to me were fantasy. The spin was familiar enough for me to finger the source—a bow-tied playwright with a gift for networking and the knife—and I was aware my reputation for being too outspoken set me up for such attribution. As wisecracks were attributed to the

Elaines, May or Stritch, to ensure a laugh, so acid remarks were attributed to me to ensure credibility.

My being right about his informant but admitting what I really had said calmed Jerry. He looked around the room for the first time since he had walked in and asked whether he was still in the cigar box. I had forgotten that one wall of my study upstairs used to be covered with photographs of friends that I'd taken myself. When a friend fell out of favor, the picture came down and was put in a cigar box.

"I haven't had the cigar box in years," I laughed. "Or any pictures on the walls, either."

That made chatting easier for the moment. Then his eyes started to dart, he got up, he sat down; he was returning to his normal state: nervous and suspicious. I wanted him to go home.

"Listen, Jerry," I said, "there's only one way to deal with this royalty contract stuff. I'm going to have to trust you."

He looked at me and cried. Second time. Jerry Robbins never trusted anyone; it was therefore incomprehensible that anyone, no less me, would trust him. He invited me to rehearsals of his show. When I showed up, he asked my opinion and took my advice. He invited me to a preview. The *West Side Story* segment of *Jerome Robbins' Broadway* was such a huge success, he classed it up as *West Side Story Suite* for the New York City Ballet. He invited Steve to a run-through and to the opening. He didn't invite me to either. Why? I didn't know; I didn't know whether Jerry knew. What had happened in between? Nothing.

A few years before Nora Kaye died, Jerry gave her a birthday party. "Do I have to ask Arthur?" he asked her.

"Not if you don't want to."

"Do I have to feel guilty if I don't?"

"There's no reason to."

"Then I'm not asking him!"

Nora herself reported the conversation to me with a little smile. No guilt, but with that smile, lots of subtext and a little pleasure.

I didn't care that I wasn't invited or that Nora went out of her way to tell me. I think I meant more to both of them than I should have. I can't say they meant less to me than they should have because neither of them was any longer the person I had cared about. Certainly not Nora whom I had loved but who, in Beverly Hills, had become a very different woman. I had really cared about Jerry, paradoxically most in Beverly Hills when he was so good to Tom, and to me and Tom. But he had done an about-face about Tom; so had Nora, for that matter. If a deciding factor was needed to stop caring about either of them, that was it. Truthfully, I didn't need one.

. . .

The New York reviews of *West Side Story* were good to Steve but trust him to find one that sent him up the wall: Harold Clurman's notice in *The Nation*. Because I was so fond of Ellen Adler, his adoring stepdaughter, I had blanked anything adverse about Harold from my mind and concentrated on the pleasures of his conversation. The review blew it. It was presumptuous; insulting if you believed his reputation was deserved, as Steve and Lenny did. I, having been there twice, did not. He said the show was phony, that we were guilty of intellectual slumming and that we had done it simply to make money.

A musical with two dead bodies onstage at the end of the first act and the hero dead onstage at the end of the second was written to be commercial? The same musical that, according to Bob Dowling refusing to give us a theatre, was uncommercial because it was a "fucking opera"? Which of these influential men of the theatre was more damaging to the theatre? The real estate mogul who booked his theatres with mindless entertainment, star vehicles or imports from London because they were critically approved? Or the guru whose artistic theories failed in practice but whose influence continued because he lectured eloquently to disciples and wrote fervently for academics?

Producers also cause damage to the theatre with their misjudgments but Hal and Bobby made one that was damaging only to them and their investors. Much as they admired the music, they didn't think it was commercial; consequently they handed their music rights over to the authors. That was a blessing to me because I had a percentage of cast albums, the first librettist to get one. Lyricists and composer always had a percentage of the published play, admittedly worth about two cents, but book writers got nothing from the score until I did. Beyond the money, which I do not and did not dismiss, the percentage for the librettist was an admission that the book was the source of the score. One of my peers who subsequently profited complained that I hadn't included a percentage of the income from individual songs—"the really big money," he said. Granted, but all these years later, I still don't see anyone picking up the baton.

Hal and Bobby's estimate of Lenny's music was on the money or, rather, on the no money because the sales of the *West Side Story* cast album were minimal and almost nobody picked up the songs. Then the movie was released; we hit a jackpot nobody knew was there to be hit. Songs previously dismissed as tuneless or fucking opera became pop hits: the whole country sang "Maria"; the whole world sang "Tonight." The sound track album was a huge best-seller and continued to be year after year. I cleaned up and I didn't even like the movie.

Arriving early to a meeting at Lenny's to discuss another project after *West Side Story*, I found him with the reviews of his concert the night before spread all over the floor. They were depressing the hell out of him. More surprising than how much they mattered was his explanation of how he tried to inure himself to them.

He had ended the program with a piano concerto he had both played and conducted. "If they say I'm not the greatest conductor, I can say I'm a pianist. If they say I'm not the greatest pianist, I can say I'm a composer of classical music. If they say I'm not the greatest composer of classical music, I can say I'm the greatest composer on Broadway."

He lit another cigarette and grinned as though to say he was exaggerating but he meant it. Just as two minutes later, he meant it when he said the subject for our next musical had to be "important." All his sophistication, his learning, his intelligence were no match for his defeating desire for importance and greatness.

That desire was as destructive to his creative work as his attitude that music composed for Broadway was inferior to anything composed for the opera or concert stage. Even if the latter was second-rate, it was superior. So the critics and essayists said, so the culture said, so he said to himself. And believing it, too often allowed it to stop him writing musical theatre even though *West Side Story* is some of the best music he composed. I wish there'd been more.

When we met to find a subject for a follow-up to *West Side*, my suggestion of race evoked shrugs from Steve and Jerry, but Lenny would have gone along. At the next meeting, Jerry suggested *The Dybbuk*. Despite my atheism (then) and antipathy toward organized religion (still), I would have gone along with a *Dybbuk* centered on mysticism. Oddly enough, that was fine with Lenny, the Seder Jew, but not with Jerry, the secular Jew. "It's about Judaism or we forget it," he said angrily. We forgot it and didn't meet on another project again until 1968.

Jerry, aiming high and ironically to the left, wanted to conceive a musical based on a Brecht play, *The Exception and the Rule*. John Guare was to write the book and Jerry had inveigled Lenny and Steve to write the score—Steve despite his dislike of Brecht and his determination to compose his own music for his lyrics. Zero Mostel was set to star, Stuart Ostrow to produce ($35,000 already put up for a reading and a workshop); the crystal ball for the production had a golden glow.

In Quogue, I nursed a Walter Mitty fantasy that they would get in trouble and call me. I was reading in the sun—no ozone layer worries back then— when the call came. Jerry was sending the script and inviting me to a reading. I read the script and was startled by its anti-Semitism. Aware of my sensitivity on that subject, I gave the script to the secretary I had then, an Irish Catholic theatre aficionado; she, too, was startled. At the reading, Zero Mostel exacerbated the problem. Afterward, I met with the conceiver, the authors and the producer at Jerry's house.

They were prepared for criticism but not for the opinion that the piece was anti-Semitic, exacerbated by Zero. That shocked them. They had been so busy experimenting with form, transforming Brecht into a play within a play in a television studio with television screens multiplying the action, that the viciousness of the content had escaped them. But they examined and agreed.

In five minutes, Jerry made them cheerful. All could be fixed: I would be consultant for a nice fee, John could clean out the Goebbels touch speedily. And he had a revised version almost overnight; it was still anti-Semitic, however. At that meeting, I was confessing my doubt that the piece could ever work when an odd thing occurred. Stuart was developing $35,000 worth of unhappiness with me, Lenny was foreseeing that he had embarked on yet another abortive project, Steve was anticipating getting out of a project he wasn't happy with anyway, John was examining his unconscious when suddenly every one of them was no longer in the room and I was alone with Jerry. How he had presto chango abracadabra whisked them out was a mystery but they were gone and he and I were facing each other after a very long time.

"There's one way the show could work," he said.

"What's that?"

"If you wrote it."

"Why didn't you ask me from the beginning?"

"Because I knew you wouldn't have done it."

He was right. *West Side Story,* where Jerry's brilliance balanced his betrayal, was worth it; *Gypsy,* where Jerry was controlled, not controlling, was more than worth it; but the combination of a Brecht play I didn't like and another Jerome Robbins conception could not be worth it. I bowed out. They plowed on for a couple of weeks until without explanation or warning, Jerry walked out on everybody, Brecht included, and went to Europe.

. . .

A few years later, Lenny asked me to direct a new musical he was writing with another icon: Alan Jay Lerner. "Two rich old Jews" was how they described themselves with typically Jewish, deprecating so-called humor. They were alike and unalike: Alan's lifestyle was chauffeur-and-yacht, Lenny's was kisses-and-cape—"the Kissing Bandit," Aaron Copland captioned him. Alan had innumerable wives, Lenny had innumerable boyfriends; Lenny was ten-gallon hats, tumblers of scotch and joyful exuberance; Alan was bespoke suits and ties, daily shots of amphetamines from Dr. Miracle Max Jacobson and white cotton gloves to stop him from biting his nails which he chewed through the gloves. Both were clever and funny, both were seriously concerned about Nixon's mark of Cain on a country they loved passionately, both thought they were writing about the power of the presidency. I thought they were writing about blacks.

The subject and importance of the piece were proclaimed by the title: *1600 Pennsylvania Avenue*. It was to be a musical history of the first hundred years of that house and thus the country told through its occupants. Even though Lincoln was missing as an occupant, the viewpoint was largely that of the black servants backstairs. It was also a play within a play where the actors debated the political content of their roles. It was, in sum, an unstructured, ambitious mess.

Pondering the bland revival of *West Side Story*
with Jerry Robbins and Lenny Bernstein.

I had been so flattered and excited by the invitation to direct a musical written by Leonard Bernstein and Alan Jay Lerner that I suspended disbelief at our first meeting. At our second, trying to be positive and constructive, I suggested they develop and concentrate on the story of the blacks backstairs which could be the strongest and the most relevant. Lenny and Alan waved that away; the blacks were important but not that important in what they had already written. No, the actor playing all the presidents was to be the star, it was about the presidents, not the blacks. They granted the script had bumps but in rehearsal the bumps would be smoothed out, the structure would work itself out. Or if not in rehearsal, then out of town in Philadelphia. Philadelphia! I didn't really need that red flag but it helped me decide to withdraw.

That night Lenny called me at home. "As my friend, please tell me honestly what you think I should do."

I knew how much of himself and his time he had invested in the show; I knew how badly he wanted and needed a hit; I knew what he wanted to hear but instead I said:

"As your friend, I think you should drop the show."

"You're not my friend," he said.

Three years later, he and I were writing an original musical based on a four-page outline of mine that stimulated him. It was a picaresque tale, a quest to discover what it really means to be free, set in a time and place where "Exit, pursued by a bear" would make perfect sense. *Alarums and Excursions* was the title and both of us would be doing the lyrics together—my idea and not a good one.

Lenny immediately began casting, a favorite pastime and stall. He hired a director, Tom O'Horgan. He wanted a short holiday; Tom and I went with him, his sister Shirley, and a small entourage to Round Hill in Jamaica. The natives were very restless: our posh hotel was patrolled day and night by guards with machine guns. To swim, we had to trudge five hundred yards through a mushy sea until the water was deep enough; the food was crummy and the toilets didn't work. We talked a lot about the show but wrote nothing. Back to New York we went but didn't get much done there either.

Then it was ski time. Off to Aspen with Tom and me, and a piano and a boyfriend for Lenny in his condo on the slopes. The whole town was wild about him and his cowboy boots and hat. He skied like Ray Stark: careening down the mountain, hair flying, legs spread as though he were on a horse, falling hard with frightening frequency but always getting up, back on his skis, tearing down the mountain even faster, reaching the bottom and celebrating with a barrel of whiskey and a horde of admirers. We did no work but we had a wonderfully crazy time.

At his apartment in New York, we finally got down to a schedule. We would work in the afternoon until four o'clock when his secretary or whatever he was arrived with a tumbler of scotch and a Benzedrine. Lenny would always offer me a drink, which I didn't want, but not a benny, which I did because I'd never had one and always wanted to try. Not with Lenny: he was very protective of me and he adored Tom.

When I arrived to work, I would run up the stairs to his floor in the Dakota—it was only the second—but as we got farther along, I would leave with very heavy shoes. He was determined to turn the piece into an opera and I wasn't a very good lyricist. We gave up on the play but not on each other. We stayed close, not always easy with Lenny if you spent public time with him. As Aaron Copland also said, Lenny wasn't housebroken.

In Miami for the tryout of a misconceived revival of *West Side Story,* he wanted to learn scuba diving. The equipment was to be used first in shallow water; Lenny and a young friend marched into the hotel swimming pool with fins and masks and with oxygen tanks on their backs, the full regalia. The lifeguard was used to obedience, not to being dismissed with an "I am Leonard Bernstein. Get the manager!" The manager went by the rules: no foreign objects in the pool. Sorry, Mr. Bernstein—out. Lenny was bewildered; he was unaccustomed to dealing with refusal.

Coming up the aisle at the intermission of a play, Tom and I heard our names called too loudly: Lenny, arm around sister Shirley, both smoking away like Czar and Czarina. A scene similar to that at the Miami swimming pool ensued, this time with an old usher instead of a young lifeguard. Then the manager appeared, trying to keep his theatre smoke free while Tom and I tried simultaneously to pretend we barely knew Lenny and Shirley and to lead them out to the sidewalk. Still smoking, Lenny demanded to see the Shuberts but they were long dead.

At a party in a restaurant, he had his arm around Bobby, his Aspen boyfriend, while he proposed marriage to the writer Shana Alexander. Shana laughed affectionately: she didn't appear embarrassed—though who knows?—and she knew him too well to take him seriously. But he was serious for that moment.

Tom and I went up to Tanglewood for Lenny's seventy-fifth birthday, a celebration of special music and songs written and performed by his friends and his children. We knew what the first night would be so we arrived the following day: calmer and less glittering but the concert, which was encored, was both fun and moving.

The last night, the glamour long gone home, we went to the house where Lenny was staying to say good-bye. He sat at one end of a long table, autographing a large stack of books. It was very hot; a cowboy hat was pushed back from his wet, matted hair and his distended, naked belly was hanging over a pair of shorts. He looked tired, worn out, very alone, too glad to see us. The response to him and his concert had been extraordinary, the love for him was extraordinary.

"But what do I do with it?" he asked, autographing books for people he didn't know.

The last time I saw him was two months before his death. We had an early dinner alone at the Dakota; his friend Matt Taylor was arriving later. I could see the pain hit him; it was unbearable, I wanted to duck. He would gasp—freeze frame, pause, take a breath—not a deep breath because a deep breath started coughing—pause again; then a rueful shake of his head and off he would go, picking up the conversation at full clip. Not necessarily where it had left off, more likely where he thought it had been or where he hoped it was going.

"You'll lick it," I said. "You've always been lucky."

He gave me a look. "Not this time."

That was the most uncharacteristic remark I ever heard Lenny make. I wanted to hold him to keep him there or to run out the door. It was hard to keep sitting there, watching the pain hit and run, his attempt to do more than just make talk, and then—pure Lenny, master of the unexpected and the outrageous—his eyes became mischievous and sparkled.

"I've always wanted to know," he said. "What do you do in bed?"

What kind of a dying man was this? Maybe he did want to know. If he did, an answer would have had him pressing for details; a simple answer to anything was not for Lenny, he was far too curious. And keeping a confidence was anything but his forte. But whether he wanted to know or not, what he was saying was, Don't give up on me so quickly, don't write me off so fast; I am not a dying man to be humored.

I want to leave him there, alive, mischievous, and curious as he waits for my reply, determined to get it—very Lenny, a lovely way to remember him—and switch. Not to another subject (hardly!) but a variation on the subject in another place at a much earlier time. Replace the image of Lenny and me at his dining table in his apartment at the Dakota with a roomful of young gays and lesbians in my beach house in Quogue, drinking, smoking, laughing, challenging one another in the game of Most Interesting Firsts when Liz Smith's very funny new friend, Selma Lynch, said her first lover had been Gypsy Rose Lee's mother.

Gypsy had two producers: David Merrick and Leland Hayward. Merrick, a St. Louis lawyer before he became Broadway's arguably most successful and avowedly most colorful producer, wore a cheesy, lopsided toupee despite his success. He owned the rights to Gypsy Rose Lee's imaginative autobiography; Hayward was an agent turned producer who owned the rights to Jerry Robbins. Both he and Merrick wanted Jerry to choreograph and direct but Jerry wouldn't do either unless I wrote the book.

As a ten percenter, Leland Hayward had been an anomaly: tall, charming, good looking, an elegant WASP with the right tailor and a WASP crew cut. He handled classy clients only: gents like Henry Fonda, dames (his word) like Katharine Hepburn whom he romanced and Margaret Sullavan whom he married and then divorced to marry Slim Hawks—sleek, smart, sharp tongued—who divorced Howard Hawks to marry Leland. While she and Hawks were together, they created Lauren Bacall of Bogie and Baby fame out of Betty Bacall, model and usherette.

Leland loved 'em and left 'em: Slim was on the way out after he met Pamela Churchill whom I met at about the same time at a party Irene Selznick gave at her apartment in the Pierre Hotel. The auburn-haired Mrs. Churchill had that incredible pink-and-milk-white English skin; a femme fatale to men attracted to milkmaids they could pretend were virgins. Assurance that Pamela Churchill's reputation was more than well deserved came from Micheline Lerner, Alan's fourth or sixth but undeniably French wife. Micheline, who had known Pamela in Paris, was no slouch herself: beautiful, chic, funny, attractive to women as well as to men—French, remember—and incongruously, a respected lawyer.

"The price of lunch in Paris with Pamela was a diamond bracelet," she reported. And as Irene would say, that was only for openers. What puzzled me as Micheline progressed to more lurid details was what Pamela Churchill was doing at Irene Selznick's. Irene was a prude and a puritan; Mrs. Churchill was what sounds better in French: a courtesan. Micheline laughingly explained what was A-B-C, not a contradiction to her.

"You Americans worship success. Pamela Churchill was the most successful courtesan in Paris."

. . .

In the worthy cause of *Gypsy* and Jerry, Leland gave me lunch at the Colony to woo and impress. More agent than producer, names were his priority. If you had a name, you were talented; vice versa sometimes but not often. He himself had glamour. He drank like a Fitzgerald fan, behaved as though to the manner born and his objective was fun and to make things fun for those around him.

Jerry revered Leland and adored Slim. More than just friends, they were the gentile parents he wished he had but he never let them meet his lover, Buzz Miller. They would have liked Buzz. Eventually, Buzz refused to remain hidden and left Jerry.

Gypsy Rose Lee's book was a jazzy read but the story of a woman who became the striptease queen of America didn't interest me. Leland persisted; he was used to eventually charming anyone into doing his bidding.

"You'll come up with something," he kept saying, not at the Colony because once there was enough. Lunch was sandwich and soup to me and I didn't want to be beholden to Leland Hayward. But there is persistence that irritates and persistence that flatters and insinuates. Leland's was the latter; his constant purring over the phone kept Gypsy in the back of my mind until she was moved front and center at that party at my house in Quogue with Selma Lynch's winning remark about Gypsy Rose Lee's mother.

There had always been speculation that Gypsy was a lesbian, but her *mother*? Not just anybody's mother, Gypsy Rose Lee's mother. Gypsy Rose Lee didn't seem to be a woman who even would have had a mother. But she did and her killer mother was Selma Lynch's first lover. Bells chimed, lights flashed, I ushered Selma out to the deck. The night was warm, the moonlight was speckling the ocean, the drinks were fresh. Tell, Selma, tell all!

June Havoc, in one of her books, wrote about the lesbian cocktail parties Gypsy and her mother gave for their friends, who had to pay an admission charge. Selma knew details: how tight Rose was, how she finagled and seduced, how tough she was on her girlfriends—Selma was no exception— and how deceptive was her appearance. A pretty blonde with curves; the possessor of unbelievable charm that enabled her to get away with murder—literally. Rose, Selma reminisced, once pushed a hotel manager out the window; he'd threatened eviction because she had five boys sleeping in a room rented to one daughter. (In the musical, I tamed that down: she gets rid of the manager by yelling "Rape!")

In Gypsy's mystery novel *Mother Finds a Body*, Rose finds the body of a dead girl buried on the farm Gypsy bought for her. Selma's report: Rose shot the girl, buried her, then had a couple of the pretty young girls who did all the chores on the farm for their keep but no wages dig up the body which Rose then promptly found.

Other incidents were less lethal. In one, Rose, driving a carload of her pretties to a Chinese restaurant, smashed into another car and blackmailed the driver into paying for what he had done to her car. The girls were her witnesses and they were all mad about her. The guy didn't have a chance.

True or not, a character was taking shape, intriguing me. *Gypsy* could be a musical after all, not about the striptease queen of America but about her mother. A larger-than-life mother, a mythic mesmerizing mother, a monster of a mother sweetly named Rose.

Jerry liked the notion, the producers liked the notion, everyone liked the notion of a musical about Rose because Ethel Merman wanted to play Rose. When I'd finished the script, I let Lena Horne read it. As I walked into her dressing room at the Imperial after a matinee of *Jamaica,* she looked up from the script and said:

"This is going to make Ethel Merman a star."

My mother was proud I was going to be the author of a musical starring Ethel Merman; my father liked her singing but questioned whether she could act. I didn't even know Merman. A meeting was arranged at an almost empty Sardi's late one afternoon. She was subdued and dressed quietly for her; her

Chattanooga, 1989. The first performance of the revival of *Gypsy* with
Tyne Daly. During technical rehearsals, Tom photographed Tyne, Jonathan
Hadary (Herbie), Christa Moore (Louise) and me (director) doing "Together."

hair seemed smaller. She ordered a Horse's Neck (ginger ale with a twist). I'd never seen anyone actually drink a Horse's Neck but I caught the significance: an actress was meeting her playwright.

"Rose is a monster," I told her. "How far are you willing to go?"

"I'll do anything you want me to," she said.

She did her best and was hailed for being her best but Ethel Merman was a voice, a presence, and a strut, not an actress. "A talking dog," was Steve Sondheim's description of her "Rose's Turn," which was performed to counts. Repeating that even years later was to risk dismemberment. In 1989, when I directed Tyne Daly in a revival of *Gypsy*, Tom was walking home in the Village when a queen screamed at him from across the street: "Shame! Outrage! Tell him!" In the Village, they knew who was with whom; the outraged fan wanted Tom to pass the word to me that I had desecrated Ethel by comparing her acting unfavorably to Tyne's.

Acting hadn't made Ethel Merman Ethel Merman but she had personal qualities that made her right for Rose: not very bright but shrewd, common but charismatic, able to defeat you before you could get a swipe at her and, pure Rose, a walking, exuberant advertisement for Self-ignorance is bliss. To help the acting, I wrote stage directions for her speeches: "slower," "softer," "louder," "faster," "starting flat, then building." An actress would have broken pencils furiously crossing them out; Ethel quoted them if any of her line readings were questioned.

Two lines, however, no actress could have delivered more chillingly than she did. One was her command to her daughter: "You are going to be a star!" When Ethel Merman said that, you knew how she became a star; her determination was naked, frightening and gallant.

The other line was motherly advice Rose gives Louise about to face her first audience of men: "Make 'em beg for more and then don't give it to them!" Merman lashed into that and followed with a gleeful laugh that was scarily revealing. She must have had odd sexual problems. Four-letter words were as at home in her mouth as saliva but when it came to any word for female genitalia, she would say "down there," pointing to the cursed place.

In the *Gypsy* company, she was famous for a sexual joke she didn't get. When she asked Jack Klugman, her leading man, whether Tab Hunter was gay, Jack replied, "Is the Pope Catholic?"

"Yes," said Ethel, still waiting for the answer.

Not bright, no, but endearing and despite a life spent in saloons, childlike.

Gypsy Rose Lee was not childlike and was untroubled by her sexuality, whatever it was. She was amusing, she was bright, she was also allergic to the truth—of any fact of any importance, that is. Oh, there were a host of small, true details in her book—she was born with a caul, she was mad about animals, she was a good seamstress—which provided color. But facts of importance? Facts that I needed? That might be helpful? The one fact she insisted on was the show would be called *Gypsy:* that was in her contract, everything else was up for my grabs. Typical was her reaction to the character of Herbie I dreamt up to be her mother's lover. "I wish I'd thought of him for my autobiography," she said.

She liked the character I gave her. She couldn't wait to turn the page and find out what she was going to do next; she even found herself quite moving at times. She did question whether she wasn't a little too harsh in her fight with Rose in the scene before "Rose's Turn" but if I thought that was what the scene needed, I knew best. I was free to explore, expand, and invent a character who, despite the title, was not really Gypsy Rose Lee.

Great gaps in her story of her life sent me to her ramshackle house in the East Sixties. It meandered around an interior courtyard that was a homemade jungle. On one side were rooms she rented to tenants on condition their doors were left open. Closed doors meant she was running a multiple dwelling which meant permits and taxes, which meant money. Like mother, like daughter—a useful thought for the play.

She was more than willing to talk about her life, not her past life, her current life. All right, her secretary Erica—was her son named for her? Her answer to any question was always amusing but no answer explained anything or filled in those gaps. Did the fifteen-year-old "Hollywood Blondes" her mother booked into a burlesque house appear in the nude? "Oh, wasn't Mother something!" What got her into stripping? "Wasn't that the phone?" Where did she get her name? "Oh, darling, I've given so many versions, why don't you make up your own?"

But it had to be called *Gypsy.*

Even with Merman as a lure, Irving Berlin wasn't interested in writing the score. He knew it wasn't going to be the story of the striptease queen of America which didn't interest him, either, but he couldn't see where her mother came in. Leland then went after Cole Porter who needed a new show to lift him out of terrible depression: his legs, badly broken in a horseback riding accident, had finally been amputated. Much as Porter loved Merman, he didn't want to work ever again; he didn't want to anything ever again.

I brought up Steve. I knew no one could write lyrics as brilliant as his, particularly for what I had in mind. Doubts about his music were outweighed by my eagerness to work with him; I knew we'd have a great time. Jerry was hesitant until convinced by some songs Steve had written for what was to be *A Funny Thing Happened on the Way to the Forum*. Merman's agent, however, put the kibosh on Steve. Ethel wanted a composer with a reputation, he said. I suspected it was he, not Ethel, who said it but Steve, ever in love with injustice, was sure it was Ethel. She disliked him anyway, he was sure of that, too. Neither Leland nor Merrick was eager for an unknown composer; they'd take Steve as lyricist—but who was going to write the music? Jerry's candidate was Jule Styne.

I balked. Jule wrote big, fat pop hits, great tunes, but *Gypsy* was not going to be a razzmatazz Ethel Merman bounce; it was going to be a tough musical play with a dramatic range the music had to match. Jule Styne music? I doubted it.

Jerry brought Jule in to audition for me. The whole notion embarrassed me but not Jule, nothing embarrassed Jule. He rang the bell at my house in the Village frantically one night and when I opened the door, slammed it shut behind him and scuttled down the hall as though he was on the lam. He *was* on the lam—from gangsters out to break his legs because he hadn't paid his gambling debts. But he wasn't embarrassed. Now that he was safe with the door locked, he wasn't scared, either; he just laughed at the fix he was in.

An audition wasn't embarrassing or demeaning. Jule wanted the job, Jule went after it. That natty, dapper little man peacocked into Jerry's living room and told jokes, truly funny jokes: they even broke him up. His audience warmed up, he seated himself at the piano like a concert pianist, which he had been, and did what he loved: played music on the piano, his own music, a surprising variety of music. It was love—at first sight for him, at first hearing for his music. I adored him then and there and for the rest of his days.

Jule agreed Steve would be the perfect lyricist. Even Ethel, after a little persuading, agreed. The lyricist himself didn't. Once again, Steve was less than thrilled; once again, he went to Oscar Hammerstein; once again, thanks to Oscar, Steve did the lyrics which were remarkable, every one of them, and still are. No one is his equal.

Work went fast: four months for a book and score that were pretty close to what we finally opened with in New York. The speed may have been one of the reasons *Gypsy* turned out as well as it did or the collaboration may have been one of the reasons for the speed and the success. Chicken or the egg, *Gypsy* was a pride and joy.

Steve and I were on the phone almost daily, talking in shorthand that got shorter and handier as collaborating on the show brought us closer in our very different lives. Jule never allowed his greater experience and success to diminish one bit of the respect and admiration he had for Steve. And Steve, despite his disappointment at being only the lyricist again, despite whatever he felt about Jule as a composer, worked better with Jule than he had with Lenny and pushed him to write an historic score. More than pushed, helped, Jule said; without Steve, the music would not have been that good. Another generous composer but Jule was generous in all ways to everybody.

He and Steve were mutually protective when they played a song for me. Jule would waltz in and toss the lead sheet on the nearest surface with a blithe "May I say: another classic." If I disagreed, he didn't take offense but he wanted to know specifically what I didn't like and why. Only once was there a real disagreement—over "You'll Never Get Away from Me." Both Jule and Steve thought it would be a hit; that Steve thought so made me think twice. And one line in the lyric, a pure Stephen Sondheim line—"How you're gonna not at all get away from me"—almost made the song worth keeping. Almost, but the tune was undistinguished and the lyric didn't go much of anyplace. By the time I directed the revival with Tyne Daly, I had learned how to make a song get someplace in spite of itself.

Turning what was largely a solo into a duet with a very sexual subtext resulted in a duologue encapsulating the basic nature of the relationship between Rose and Herbie. With Tyne and Jonathan Hadary, it was easy: not only were they excellent actors but with them the sexual element in the relationship could be played for the first time. With Ethel and Jack Klugman it would have been impossible. As good an actor as Jack was, Ethel was always somebody's buddy; he could never be more than her pal.

"You'll Never Get Away from Me" stayed in the show. I didn't think it would be a hit and it wasn't, but it wasn't as fresh as Steve had thought it was either. Two days after the cast album was recorded, he raced up to my apartment on East Fifty-ninth Street with a copy he had managed to sneak. How? So fast? From where? He babbled his answers until the record blasted the first chords of the overture. Not the familiar chords from *Gypsy* but chords heralding the familiar "You'll Never Get Away from Me." From what? From *Ruggles of Red Gap,* a musical for television written by Jule Styne.

On that cast album, it wasn't called "You'll Never Get Away from Me"; it was called "I'm in Pursuit of Happiness." Jule had sneaked one out of his vast trunk right under the nose of Steve who knew every tune and could parse every lyric anyone had ever written for any musical. The culprit was Jule but what could you do? Laugh as hard as he did.

· · ·

Writing *Gypsy* began once again with an outline that had to wait until I solved
the ending. I began with the ending. I knew we had to see Louise gradually
transformed into Gypsy Rose Lee in a strip that became more and more successful until she was indeed the Striptease Queen of America. Rose had to top
that, not because Rose was going to be played by Ethel Merman but because
the show was about Rose, not Gypsy. But how do you top a strip? Especially a
strip that would be a series of strips, a journey begun by a scared, awkward,
pretty girl who would end up a confident, sophisticated, beautiful young
woman. What could Rose top that with, even a Rose with Ethel Merman's
voice? A sung strip of her own. OK: where? What theatre would have a middle-
aged mother strip? All right, where else could she strip? In her imagination, in
her head: she would perform a mental as well as a physical strip. But why?
What would prompt it? Her need for recognition.

For me, that was what *Gypsy* was about: the need for recognition. Rose
needed it in lights; Louise needed it from her mother. Parents who live their
children's lives, children who grow up to become their parents—these are the
stories of Rose and Louise in *Gypsy,* these are themes in *Gypsy.* But the theme
that drives all the characters and the whole show is that need for recognition, a
need everyone has in one way or another.

Fortunately, Jerry Robbins was busy rehearsing the London company of
West Side Story and wasn't around while we were writing *Gypsy,* because he
envisioned a totally different show: a "panorama of vaudeville." The first time
he heard a song from the score was in Manchester, England, where *West Side
Story* was getting tuned up for London. Steve and I had just come over; we
couldn't wait for Jerry to hear something from the score. At a piano in the
hotel, Steve played and sang "Everything's Coming up Roses." We beamed at
Jerry expectantly. He scowled.

"But that's her name," he objected. "Everything's coming up Rose's what?"

All of Manchester was permeated with a soupy fog, which seeped into the
theatre where *West Side Story* was opening. Anyone sitting in the saturated
auditorium during long rehearsals might well have had his brain marinated.

The ending of *Gypsy* in place with the idea of Rose's strip, I went back to the
beginning: her entrance. Again, having her bellow "Sing out, Louise!" from
the back of the theatre as she charged down the aisle was not to provide a spectacular entrance for Ethel Merman—which it did—but an action that would
establish Rose swiftly and theatrically as a gorgon; to demonstrate how she
favored Baby June at Louise's expense; to show how she worked the world by

bulldozing anyone who got in her way. Seemingly a tall order but the setup was in place: the two girls were in a kiddie show that was being rehearsed. The missing ingredient was the way to get Rose in as Rose. Easy if you knew Rose. Kicking all the mothers out, thereby highlighting the one mother who would find a way to get back in. How? From the front of the house. Once in, once down the aisle, where else would she do battle? On the ground she wanted as her own: the stage. Once she was there, I sat back and let her take over the show.

I loved the theatricality of that entrance. I looked for other places to use it in *Gypsy*—not that I believe in theatricality for its own sake any more than I believed in style for style's sake. Content determines form, theatricality highlights a purpose. Louise is never seen in anything but pants until the moment she puts on a dress to become Gypsy Rose Lee. That's a theatrical moment but the reason she has only been in pants until then is that, until then, she hasn't existed as a daughter Rose can use.

Another theatrical moment. Baby June and Louise have to grow up to become Dainty June and a Louise big enough to become Gypsy Rose Lee. The easier way would have been to have it happen offstage but that would have been untheatrical and a cheat: the audience had to see it happen. We were using dif-

With Fritz Holt at Thanksgiving dinner at the St. Luke's Place house during the Angela Lansbury *Gypsy* in 1974. I'm glad we were sitting: he was six feet four.

ferent musical versions of "Let Me Entertain You" to chart the development of the girls and the act. Simple, then: have them get older with fast-flickering lights and the music quickening from a Baby June version to a Dainty June version. Jerry took that notion one step higher and better by adding June as the Statue of Liberty, Louise as Uncle Sam and just to make sure, John Philip Sousa and the American flag. Thrillingly theatrical, mission accomplished: when the lights came up, the switch had been made—the girls had grown up.

One of the most theatrical moments in *Gypsy* wasn't in the original production. Louise, in her first dress, a long evening gown, walks upstage to the curtain behind which is the stage of the burlesque house she is going do her first strip on. Rose waits at the curtain, ready to hold it open and push her frightened daughter through. A drumroll and the announcement: "Miss Gypsy Rose Lee!" The curtains part, Louise steps through, the lights go out except for a huge spotlight that blinds the audience. At the same time, little footlights come up on the edge of a platform stage that is rolling forward over the real stage, riding down front, over the orchestra pit to bring Louise into the lap of the audience. That was what it said in my script. It didn't happen in that first production.

Jo Mielziner, the brilliant scenic designer, said it couldn't be done. Jerry and his production stage manager, Ruth Mitchell, said it couldn't be done. David Merrick said nobody in the balcony would be able to see Louise. I really didn't understand because I could visualize it, could see it. But they were the experts. I dropped it until 1973 when I was directing the first London production of *Gypsy* with Angela Lansbury.

Fritz Holt—it's not easy to write about him because of all the people I knew who died of AIDS, I loved him most—Fritz was one of the producers along with his lover, Barry Brown, and Edgar Lansbury, Angela's brother. Fritz was also the production stage manager, trained by Ruth Mitchell but more imaginative and gutsier. When I mentioned the platform overstage for the strip to him, he asked, "Do you want it?"

"I would like it."

"But do you want it?"

"I want it."

"Then you got it."

It was spectacular. It worked every performance in London; it worked every performance in Toronto where we opened the American tour, every performance across the country, every performance at the previews in New York at the Winter Garden (Home Sweet Home) until opening night. Then it jammed.

There is a pass-through door at the end of the aisle audience right in the Winter Garden from the auditorium to backstage. The aisle is short and I ran, but when I got backstage, Fritz was already there even though he had bolted out the front doors of the theatre on Broadway and run around the block to the stage door on Seventh Avenue because Ruth Mitchell was sitting on that right aisle and Fritz didn't want her to see him running backstage panic-stricken.

On the stage behind the closed show curtain, every plug that could be plugged and unplugged had been plugged and unplugged by electricians, stagehands, stage managers and Fritz: union rules ignored, gone to hell, but the platform would not budge. On the apron of the stage in front of the curtain, Zan Charisse, who was playing Gypsy, kept singing.

"Fuck!" Fritz yelled and kicked the platform as hard as he could. It moved. Softly, swiftly, sweetly, the platform moved downstage. Zan heard it coming and stepped up on it.

"Curtains open!" Fritz called.

I was out front in time to see the curtains open, the platform roll right over the orchestra pit with Zan standing on it as though this was exactly what she had done opening night in London. Fritz had said if I really wanted it, I could get it. He got it for me.

Although Jerry had read the script and heard the score, he still envisioned the show as a "panorama of vaudeville," consequently casting jugglers, acrobats and a slew of burlesque comics. The jugglers and acrobats were used in a big dance number he staged in a corridor outside the hotel room where Rose had just sung "Mr. Goldstone." For the first time, Jerry did a number whose only purpose was to be a big dance number in a show that didn't have one. It had nothing to do with anything and necessitated the cutting of "Little Lamb." He didn't bother to ask Jule's permission.

Jule revered Jerry more than Lenny did but unlike Lenny, he wasn't afraid of Jerry. Or God; only of the bookies and their leg breakers. At rehearsal the following day, he walked onstage, neat and dapper in coat and hat, carrying an executive attaché case. He came to the edge of the pit and looked out front. He was blind, couldn't see a foot in front of him and wasn't wearing his glasses but he knew Jerry was out there.

"Mr. Robbins," he said quietly with impressive dignity, "I have informed the Dramatists Guild and my lawyers. Unless 'Little Lamb' is back in the show tonight, I am withdrawing my entire score." He half bowed and walked off. "Little Lamb" was back that night and the producers had to pay the acrobats and jugglers two weeks' salary to be rid of them.

. . .

For the comics, Jerry wanted me to write a twenty-minute burlesque show that would climax in Gypsy's last, triumphant strip. There was no need for a burlesque show, we already had a great burlesque song, "You Gotta Have a Gimmick," courtesy of my high school history teacher at Erasmus Hall, William Dane, the uncle of another teacher—as a kid, he had lived on my block—named Goldstone, the "Mr. Goldstone" of the song "Have an Egg Roll, Mr. Goldstone." Dick called while we were holding Gypsy auditions:

"My cousin Faith wants to audition."

"We're only looking for mothers and strippers."

"Faithie knows that."

Faithie came out onstage in a big black pinwheel hat, a demure black linen dress (it was summer), white gloves (Daddy was a teacher) and high-heeled shoes.

"Arthur? It's Faithie."

No explanation was needed for my collaborators. Inherited legacies are part of audition life. "Hello, Faithie. The stage manager will show you where to change."

She returned dressed like a gladiator turned stripper and went right into her number, one of two numbers she was performing nightly in a joint on Fifty-second Street. In the other, dressed like Pocahontas turned stripper, she carried a smoking peace pipe she passed around the audience: there was real hashish in it. As gladiator for the Gypsy audition, she carried a trumpet; at the climax, she bent over and blew it out her ass and that's how "Gimmick" was born.

Three blowsy strippers sang "You Gotta Have a Gimmick" to Louise; it was a hilarious showstopper and all we needed. A twenty-minute burlesque show without either Rose or Louise onstage wouldn't hold for two minutes. Jerry brushed aside any argument. He wanted a place for what he did.

So I wrote the dirtiest burlesque show I thought we could get away with. Christmas was the theme: a lecherous Santa came down a chimney with presents for a lonely little girl—the classic comic Mort Marshall in Shirley Temple drag.

"For me, Santa?"

"For you, little girl. Now come right over here and sit on Santa's face."

Even Rose wouldn't have let her daughter appear in that burlesque show but Jerry insisted. We opened in Philly with a show forty-five minutes too long.

"Steve told me you have twenty minutes of cuts marked in the book," Jerry said.

"That's right."

"When are you going to take them?"

"When you cut twenty minutes out of the burlesque show and the kiddie numbers."

Brief pause. "Right after lunch. Come on, baby, let's eat."

The burlesque show was a bomb but would have been anyway in prudish Philadelphia. An uncle of mine living there used to sneak regularly over to New York to see burlesque. The kiddie numbers were a smash, though, the only part of the show that was. Philadelphia liked Ethel Merman but loathed Rose. Steve was in seventh heaven at the head of the aisle, collecting disgust for *Gypsy.* Jerry was regretting his billing.

The day before we were to go into rehearsal, David Merrick phoned: "Jerry wants his name in a box or he won't put the show in rehearsal."

"His name in a box? Everybody knows who he is."

"He says his dentist doesn't."

Three stipulations were signed and sealed in my contract. One called for the same billing for all of us: same size, same color, same whatever but the same.

"Then we won't go into rehearsal," I told Merrick.

The next day, Merrick called, chuckling. We still had not gone into rehearsal. "Well, he's a tough one. He's got to get his box. You lose."

"Why me? Why not him?"

"Because you want the show to go ahead."

"So does Jerry."

"Yeah, but you're practical."

"David, you're the producer. If you let him get away with this, he'll walk all over you and Leland. He'll do whatever he wants—order new scenery, new costumes. You signed a contract."

"How much do you want?"

I was practical, I did want the show to move ahead. I also thought the producers should pay for malfunctioning so I asked for a piece of the producers' share. David gave it to me with a chuckle and without objection—because it wasn't going to cost him a penny. It was going to come out of Leland's share and Leland was always rather condescending to David. In their contract, Leland guaranteed the delivery of Ethel Merman and Jerome Robbins; he hadn't delivered Jerry. It had cost him much of his producer's share to get Merman and Jerry, the bigger chunk to the lady; now what he had to give up to me left Leland with next to nothing. David had the laughable toupee but he also had the last laugh and I had an inside joke for the script.

When Rose and Louise find they have been booked into a burlesque house, Louise says: "One good thing: I'll bet we got top billing." To which Herbie answers: "Well—actually, they kind of had us lost in the middle. I thought last was better. . . . And I'm making them put a box around it."

Leland dug deep into his well of charm but it was David who found the way to fulfill my second stipulation: a release from June Havoc. Attention had not been paid to her. Harold Freedman worried that she was in a position to make trouble if she didn't like the way she was depicted—an icy chip off her mother's block. We couldn't call the show "June" but we might have called it "Havoc."

The producers hadn't paid attention to June because of Bill Fitelson, Merrick's lawyer. Also the lawyer for Merman, Jerry, Gypsy Rose Lee, Jule Styne and down at the bottom, so far down Fitelson had forgotten to look, June Havoc. But June Havoc was not to be at the bottom of anyone's list.

Leland and I drove up to Stratford, where she was appearing as Titania in *A Midsummer Night's Dream*. She was still in full makeup, sprinkled with glitter dust, when Leland and I limousined her back to her house.

"You were late," she purred. "I could see you slinking into your seats. But of course, you didn't come to see me act, you came to get my name on a piece of paper."

All true, and she wouldn't let up. She dismissed Leland in mid-gallantry to vent the full force of her fury on me. "You're supposed to be a playwright. How could you lend yourself to adapt my sister's book? It's vulgar! She's vulgar!"

"I found her funny and rather touching."

"Touching?! Touching??!! I'm touching! She's so cheap, she eats out of tin cans!"

We left without the signed release but attention was being paid in full; we didn't want trouble and she kept us dangling. On the advice of counsel, she broke off relations with her sister who sighed elaborate sighs as she prepared a collage of June's reviews in a play she had just opened in. All June's reviews were excellent but one; that review, Gypsy pasted carefully under the rave on top, so carefully that the eye went right to it. Mothers, daughters, and now sisters.

Contractual love-hate but sisters first and last. Walking down Gypsy's street after another maddening, futile effort at finding where she got her name, I saw a too heavily veiled woman in black tiptoeing elaborately along the other side of the street, a patisserie box swinging daintily from her hand. She lifted the veil to see where she was: Ah, just where she wanted to be.

Delicately, she crossed the street, her gloved hand ready to ring the bell, but before she could, the door opened. Gypsy was not in black.

Every word I wrote involving Baby June or Dainty June had to be vetted by Grown June. There were objections, usually minor. Rather than cause a fuss, I made changes. Until she demanded it be stated she was thirteen years old when she ran off and eloped. A mother who would let a thirteen-year-old run away with a boy and not follow her would make Rose more of a monster than an audience could accept. Besides, it wasn't true. In one of June's books about herself, she starts at fourteen and seven years later she's still fourteen. Like sister, like sister. I had been just as carefully vague about age in *Gypsy* as Gypsy herself had been; I hadn't said how old June was when she eloped and I refused to do so now.

There was a crisis meeting in Leland's office on the usual subject: art (loosely defined) vs. commerce (the producers' money). Fitelson, cold and disdainful, told David it would be suicidal to sign my contract unless I submitted to June Havoc's demand. If I didn't, as her lawyer, he claimed she could sue for libel for which David and Leland would be liable. Harold Freedman, quiet and firm, spoke of the artistic principle and of the risk of Ethel's alienating the audience. Gypsy, meek in a wing chair next to Leland's grand desk, charmingly sympathetic to me as one author to another but desirous of her little sister's happiness, was anxious above all that *Gypsy*—It was still called *Gypsy?* Yes, Fitelson assured her, it was—that *Gypsy* forge ahead and open in Philadelphia and New York on schedule. She looked at me with pleading eyes.

They all looked at me more or less like that; I looked at the line that always turns up: to cross or not to cross. Fitelson's second in command, Ben Aslan, was even nastier than his Rommel, making it easy for me not to cross. I wasn't even tempted; I just sat there, curious how the impasse was going to be resolved. Not through Leland's charming reassurance: Oh, sure I could write that June was thirteen or whatever she wanted with grace and humor—humor, that was the way to do it, my humor was swell, Ethel could charm the pants off any audience, wasn't this too much ado about very little, who wants a drink?

David, scrunched in a straight chair by the wall, relished opposing Leland. "I'm signing his contract," he said. "I'm a lawyer and I know about libel. I also know there was a third sister named Beth. We'll change June's name and that ends that."

There might have been a third sister; there might have been another husband; there might have been different fathers, different names; there might have been anything with Gypsy and June but there was nothing that could actually be proven and pinned down. I changed June to Claire immediately before we opened in Philly; the unsettled company called her Baby Clune, Dainty Jaire, sometimes Claire but by the time June Havoc came to Philly to see the show, never June. June Havoc signed the release and it was never stated how old she was when she ran away to elope.

The third and last of my contractual stipulations was a demand for twice the percentage the book writer normally got: four percent instead of two. Merrick gave me four without argument but after we opened he said: "Three percent was fair. You're worth it. But what was the extra percent for?"

"The agony of having to work with Jerry Robbins."

Merrick laughed. "You should have asked for more."

It wasn't agony, it was joyless, the opposite of the collaboration with Steve and Jule. Rehearsals with Jerry were listless. With *West Side Story,* Jerry, however despotic, was fired up, passionately involved, working at the top of his form. With *Gypsy,* he set off no sparks. Probably tired, even drained after doing *West Side* both in New York and London; more probably put off by directing a *Gypsy* that wasn't the *Gypsy* he had conceived.

Even his name in a box couldn't make *Gypsy* "A Jerome Robbins Production." It wasn't the panorama of vaudeville he envisioned and it couldn't be a dance musical: the book and score didn't leave room, they were too strong on their own. Nevertheless, disgruntled as he was, he created one number that is among the best he ever did for a musical. If anything trumpets the virtue of less is more, it's "All I Need Is the Girl," though Jerry approached it as a chore to be done with.

The result is a gem: a little one-act musical play. Simple story; a cast of two, and one, the girl, can't dance; no dazzling steps or combinations and an absence of pyrotechnics. Yet anyone who can watch it without being exhilarated and unexpectedly moved belongs in the cemetery, not the theatre.

The whole number was spun out in less than an evening. Rehearsals were on the roof of the New Amsterdam, once a theatre for smaller Ziegfeld *Follies.* The company had gone home; a tired, unenthusiastic Jerry decided to tackle the damn number and get it out of the way. One of his assistants for tap combinations was on hand. Waiting at the piano was Betty Wahlberg—patrician loveliness, owed as much to a perfectly shaped face and prematurely white hair as to her carriage and manner, belied the intensity of the music her hands coaxed out of a piano. Her dance arrangements were more than in tune with the choreographer she was working with, they urged him on to do better. "The Cookie Chase," Herb Ross's matchless ballet for *Anyone Can Whistle,* was greatly aided by Betty's invention. As was "All I Need Is the Girl."

Jerry paced, pondered—I could almost see his ideas in the movements of his body so I was ready when he turned to me and said: "You be the girl because you can't dance." He placed me on a stool which scenically became a garbage can in a theatre alley, mimed doing this, mimed doing that, asked for some lines to get him into the song. I tossed out a few, he fit them into the miming, blocked the song, asked for lines to get him into the dance. I gave him some, threw him others as he blocked the dance with an occasional break for a tap combination from his assistant. Betty's piano began to push the action and Jerry drew me into what amounted to an improvisation. He knew where he was going, so that by the time the number was shaped, its form solidified, and he went into a step I could do, I did it. He gestured to do it next to him; we did it together, Betty played us to a big climax and "All I Need Is the Girl" was finished. Not complete, not polished but characters and relationship dramatized, story told through music and movement—a wonder! Only Jerry Robbins.

Yet the same man, when it came to the strip that was vital to the show, that you would have thought he'd do something original and spectacular with, the same man came up short because he'd turned on the actress playing Gypsy.

The final choices for a role extremely difficult to cast were Sandra Church and Suzanne Pleshette. Suzanne was perfect for the second act because she could play a strong, sexual, fearless woman. But the first act called for an asexual, yearning, timid girl: that was Sandra. She had a beautiful body, which doesn't automatically mean sexual, but she was also a member of the Actors Studio. That clinched the role for her with Jerry.

Jerry was happy with her in the first act. She was lovely, quietly touching, a frightened doe at the curtain. The second act, alas, begins with the first signs that Louise can be as tough as her mother. Sandra shrank; her Method training was of no help. Although she introduced her own mother with the words "Meet the real Rose," she was unable to use that in her acting. Jerry lost patience and asked me to rehearse Sandra's scenes in the ladies' lounge. The ladies' was always roomier than the men's: in Philly during technical rehearsals, Steve and I played bridge there with Betty Wahlberg and John Kander, who wrote the underscoring and kept his aspirations to himself.

Very little of whatever progress Sandra made in the ladies' lounge remained the moment she went back to rehearse onstage with Jerry. Her terror blocked her and in turn, when they got to the strip, blocked him from inventing. He had to work it out on her but a trembling body, however shapely, was less than inspirational. The strip was still unfinished at the first run-through for an invited audience.

It took place at the Winter Garden on a Sunday afternoon that became famous. Steve and I sat in the first row of the mezzanine; he—very Steve—had his long yellow legal pad ready for voluminous note taking. Five minutes into the show, I felt the electricity in the theatre and took the pad away from him.

"Just sit back and enjoy," I said. He did and for Steve that was not easy.

Invited audiences at musical run-throughs are enthusiastic, but that audience went sky-high and higher, roaring, applauding, cheering its delirious head off. The run-through became legendary. Even the unfinished strip— Jerry came out onstage and stopped it with a graceful apology—couldn't diminish the enthusiasm. But when we got to Philadelphia where the show was overlong and the audience didn't much like any of it anyway, the strip became a problem because it didn't work theatrically and its failure denied the story.

Gypsy Rose Lee hadn't had a good body but she was smart enough not to expose it. She seduced the audience with her wit; her gimmick had been fresh and original: talking. Sandra said only "Hello, everybody, my name is Gypsy Rose Lee. What's yours?" but I sensed response from the audience. Why not let her talk more? The strip wasn't working, why not try? But Jerry had turned against Sandra and when Jerry Robbins turned, he was the rock and the hard place. A quick-change costume device Jule remembered from his days of playing pit piano in burlesque added theatricality to the strip, but more than that was needed.

After Sandra left the show, Julianne Marie, who replaced her, added lines on her own. They worked but by that time Ethel's performance had gotten mechanical—not intentionally, she truly didn't know the difference—and I lost interest in improving the show. When I directed the London production with Angela Lansbury, however, I sat down and wrote a strip. It worked a good deal better but the girl playing Gypsy wasn't quite up to the task: she appeared virginal even though she was going through the orchestra like a dose of salts. It wasn't until the New York revival with Tyne Daly that the strip really got the care it deserved and achieved for the show what it should have achieved from the beginning.

Gypsy was played by Crista Moore; good as her first act was, her second topped it. I revised the strip for her, rewrote it while we were on the road, then before we came into New York, went into a studio with her and revised, restaged, refined until we got it. It only took thirty years.

.   .   .

"Rose's Turn" took only fourteen years to get right. When Jerry first began work on it, he was still looking for ways to make *Gypsy* "A Jerome Robbins Production," so the characters from Rose's past crossed upstage, not dancing, not walking, not floating and not for long, either. He moved on to concentrate on Ethel's performance of an artful, striking musical collage, arguably the best soliloquy in modern theatre. Perfectly constructed, its vernacular, never merely clever, is the vernacular of the show heightened to the level of poetry; if there is an influence, it's Auden, not Hammerstein. "Rose's Turn" epitomizes Steve Sondheim's extraordinary power as a lyricist and Jule Styne's unexpected power as a composer.

Jerry and Ethel had a good rapport; they liked one another and she trusted him. She had a natural flair for lusty comedy but when "Rose's Turn" became dramatic, they were both in trouble. Jerry worked hard and pulled as much out of her as anyone could. Basically, however, she was not an actress and he was unable to help her shift gears when the number reached the stuttering "M-M-M-Momma."

Granted that the stuttering was a problem for anyone who did "Rose's Turn" and wanted to satisfy Steve. It was his conceit that Rose's inability to say Momma referred back to the preceding scene in which Gypsy says: "Momma, you have got to let go of me!" Thus she stutters in the song because she can't bring herself to admit "Momma's gotta let go!" But everyone, singer and audience, took the stuttering M-M-M-Momma to be a cry from Rose for her Momma. A puzzle to Steve: a writer's puzzle. I sympathize: it's always been a puzzle to me why Rose is referred to as Momma Rose when she's only called Madame Rose in the play. People, as I said, hear what they want.

People, particularly writers, often hear what isn't said because it's what they want to be said. In Philadelphia, we learned that in two songs, Rose didn't say what every one of us was sure she did. The subject was the same in both and essential for the play: Rose's avowal that everything she did was for her kids, not for herself.

"Rose's Turn" was the more crucial of the two and provoked a clash with Merman. There had been an earlier problem with "Some People" that had been solved without fuss. It was Rose's opening song but as Harold Freedman pointed out, instead of establishing Rose's viewpoint the song unwittingly contradicted it, leaving the audience confused. In the lyric, Rose says that some people may be content to sit home and do nothing with their lives but not Rose: she's going to get out and live. An interlude about her dream to create a vaudeville act for Baby June unintentionally gave the impression that Rose was using June so she could get out. What we *thought* we heard was that Rose was working to get her kids out. Inserting two lines of dialogue in which Rose said just that put "Some People" back on the rails. "Rose's Turn" was much tougher to fix.

The intention underlying the number was to bring Rose to the point where she finally acknowledges she did everything for herself. Acknowledgment doesn't mean change, however; Rose wouldn't change and she doesn't: she goes right back to doing it all for herself all over again.

We thought she had made the acknowledgment but she hadn't, the past was left unacknowledged, leaving the audience unsatisfied without knowing why. Once again, we resorted to dialogue for the fix. I added some lines to the brief final scene but this time Merman balked. She didn't care that she had said she would do anything I wanted. She refused to say "I guess I did it for me"; it would make her Rose awful, a monster. What she thought she had been playing only she knew. Jerry tried telling her she admitted in the song that she did it for herself but she corrected him quickly and firmly:

" '*This* time,' I say, '*this* time,' I'm doing it for me."

She may not have been the smartest but Ethel Merman knew what she sang and what she didn't sing. Singing was her security. She used it to counterbalance her numerous insecurities, beginning with the fear someone might think she was Jewish. One nonrehearsal day in Philadelphia, Steve and I ran into Ethel wandering around the city. We asked what she had been up to.

"Praying for the show," she said, hastening to add, "in church!"

About a week later, it was Passover-Easter and Jule decided to give a Seder for the principals in the company. Ethel panicked: "What'll he serve? What can I eat?"

Not a Christian baby, I wanted to say but "capon" was what I did say. "Capon. That's chicken, Ethel."

She arrived at the Seder, fresh from the hairdresser, sedately turned out in a reverent little black dress, carrying a small black purse. Jule beamed with pride as he led her to the seat of honor in the center of the long table. She sat down, opened her chic bag and took out a ham sandwich which she put on her plate.

At rehearsals, Ethel always had a turkey sandwich with Russian dressing. Jule went livid. She was his star but it was his Seder; her ham sandwich fouling his plate could not be ignored. He picked it up, threw it on the floor and said:

"Ethel, you're insulting the waiters!"

Then, behind her back where she couldn't see him, he broke up. That was Jule. But Ethel was Ethel: always a great sense of her audience. When the music Jule had arranged for began after the Seder, she unobtrusively—and it was next to impossible for Ethel Merman to be unobtrusive—made her way over to the piano and began to sing: songs from her shows, requests, old favorites. She kept singing for almost an hour. When she finished, she had won back everyone she had lost. Like Noël Coward years before in the Kellys' living room in Hollywood. If you got it, use it.

Ethel eventually gave in on the new lines for the scene after "Rose's Turn," but we gave in to an ending for the number by Oscar Hammerstein. Until Oscar, there was no big orchestration at the end and applause from the audience was intentionally prevented by the entrance of Gypsy applauding "Rose's Turn." Oscar argued that the audience was so eager to applaud Merman, who deserved her bow, that they didn't listen to the last scene which was what the whole play was about. He prevailed and as a result, the orchestra went out of character and blasted away, Ethel stepped out of character and bowed away and the audience, it seemed to me, listened to the last scene less than it had before because the prolonged bows cued a curtain that didn't come down but should have. Until fourteen years later when those bows produced exactly the opposite effect.

That was when London first saw *Gypsy,* a different *Gypsy* with Angela Lansbury. We had worked together before in *Anyone Can Whistle* and we not only survived a failure but became fast friends. Understandably, she worried about comparisons with Merman, but *Mame* had strengthened Angie's voice, which had the power and range for *Gypsy.* Because she was also a marvelous actress, I wanted to direct this *Gypsy:* with Angie, it would be a very different play with very different values, one much closer to the play I had written. And because of Angie's unique talent, I found justification for the bows at the end of "Rose's Turn."

I went back to my original premise: The number takes place in an empty theatre, the applause is only in Rose's head; at the end, she is bowing to no one. It is the first time that Angie has taken a bow onstage during the entire show so the audience goes wild: applauding, cheering, screaming. Rose, not Angie, keeps bowing, an odd, demented look in her eyes. The audience keeps applauding. Rose moves to a corner of the stage, lights begin to go out, but she bows again and once again, staring at something that isn't there. The applause begins to die down. More lights go out. Rose still bows. Then all the lights go except for a pale glow on Rose and Gypsy who walks on applauding. The

Jule, Angie, me and Steve, opening night of *Gypsy* in London in 1973.
Angie had brought the three of us up on the stage to share the incredible ovation.

audience stops applauding. But Rose bows again and the moment is hair-raising because the shocked audience realizes that the whole episode was in Rose's head: it has seen a woman momentarily gone mad.

Angela Lansbury is a smart woman. She knew there was a big risk the audience might think she was milking the hand. She also has guts. She agreed to try it, we worked on it very carefully. From the first performance, she was home. And for the first time, the audience really listened to that last scene. It was a chilling, moving ending, a different ending to a different *Gypsy*. Originally, Rose was back to conning Gypsy and they walked off laughing, arm in arm: Rose was undefeated. Curtain. This time, Gypsy is wise to Rose and uncaring. As they start off together, she continues on when Rose stops and turns back to stare at the platform stage, the stage where Gypsy triumphed, where Rose wants to triumph. I added one final touch of theatricality: the little lights that glowed all along the edge of the platform start to come up, brighter and brighter, beckoning Rose. She starts forward, eager to take her rightful place at last—and the lights go out in her face. Rose is finished, over, out. Curtain as she exits.

· · ·

The original production of *Gypsy* came into New York facing death. David Merrick almost gleefully reported the advance was so small that unless the reviews were great, the show would close in three weeks. In Philadelphia, his constant bad-mouthing of Jerry and how he had ruined the show irritated me so much I said, "If you really believe that, sell your share to Leland and leave."

"Willingly!" said David.

"Deal!" said Leland. But Merrick, waiting for the reviews, never signed anything.

There was one preview before we opened, with two horrendous occurrences, one before, one during, both with Jerry: the first between Jule and Jerry, the second between me and Jerry.

The pit at the Broadway Theatre was so deep it muffled the sound of the orchestra. Jerry had promised Jule a platform would be built to raise the orchestra but concentrated on rehearsing the musical numbers, he had forgotten his promise. Jule went amok, a truly amazing sight. Like a bull charging into the ring, he roared onto the stage, grabbed Jerry and began to throttle him, pushing him back, back toward the orchestra pit. The onlookers watched, mesmerized, as the *West Side Story* company had been two years before during a rehearsal. While brutally telling everyone off, Jerry had been backing closer and closer to the edge of the orchestra pit. The temptation to let him fall into the pit had been resisted, though only at the last minute. With Jule and Jerry, the onlookers didn't wait that long before intervening: nobody wanted Jule to fall into the pit.

He took care of the orchestra himself by going out and buying high stools for every player. Opening night, the audience burst into applause during the overture. Jule, standing near the back against a side wall with Steve and me, cried: "They're applauding my music! They're applauding my music!"

"They're applauding the trumpet player," Steve said.

My encounter with Jerry was worse, a tempest that began with a teapot. In the Chinese restaurant scene, Lane Bradbury, who played June, had to move a teapot to clear space on the table for a piece of business Ethel had. Lane kept forgetting; the more she forgot, the angrier Jerry got; the angrier he got, the more she forgot. Since she was a Strasberg Method actress, I suggested Jerry give her some cockamamie Method motivation for moving the teapot.

"I told her to move the teapot, that's her motivation," he snapped.

At the preview the night before we opened, the only New York preview,

Lane Bradbury forgot to move the teapot. Jerry jumped up from his seat and hurried backstage.

The dance number that follows the Chinese restaurant is the one big number in the first act and features June. For the big finish, she plucks a pair of batons from the platform of a mock railway car and twirls them madly as she goes into a split. At the preview, when Lane went for the batons, they weren't there. They had been removed from the set. The girl went into her split, twirling her fingers as though they held batons, a frightened fake smile on her face as she fought off tears before a confused audience.

Heading backstage at the intermission, Steve and I saw Leland, chortling over Jerry's funny, clever revenge for the forgotten teapot. Steve launched into a tirade he had long been waiting to deliver, I raced on backstage. Ruth Mitchell's voice was coming over the loudspeaker: "Lane Bradbury report to the stage manager's desk!" as I took the stairs two at a time up to Lane's dressing room. The girl was literally hysterical. I slapped her, then held her in my arms and said:

"Go downstairs, listen to everything that man says, and don't say a word. You have my permission to skip the bows and go home"—she wasn't in the second act—"and take a sleeping pill."

After Jerry had finished shredding her, I asked him to step into a small room offstage that the stage managers used. It's curious how often there is a comic leveler to big moments; for this one, an assistant stage manager was in the room, cowering in a corner but neither Jerry nor I saw him. We were too angry as I laid into him for what he had done to Lane by removing the batons.

"What do you care?" he asked. "It wasn't in one of your scenes."

A Jerome Robbins Production. "It isn't my scenes, Jerry. It isn't Jule's music, Steve's lyrics, your numbers—it's our show. When are you going to learn that?"

He glowered. "It's your show," he said. Not jealously, not with admiration or generosity, but with angry resentment of what he regarded as unpleasant fact. For Jerry, a musical was not a collaborative work but his by divine right.

Six months later, while Lane Bradbury was in the hospital with a damaged hamstring, Jerry and Ethel had her fired. That night, Ethel presented Lane's understudy with a bouquet of flowers onstage.

In theatre paradise, every opening night would be like the New York opening night of *Gypsy*. From overture to curtain calls, the audience was madly in love—with every word, every note, every player, every moment. They roared their love: they laughed, they applauded, they got to their feet and cheered. At the end of Gypsy's strip, Walter and Jean Kerr came up the aisle, clearly on their way out because there was no place to stand in back.

Everyone feared Walter Kerr; even Jule had begged me to cut a joke about the Vatican because Kerr was a Catholic. I wouldn't, and I wouldn't let him out of the theatre until he had seen the whole show. I blocked the Kerrs at the head of the aisle:

"Go back to your seats," I ordered. "It isn't over."

Startled, they dutifully turned around and trotted back to their seats. Jule was sure I had blown Kerr's review then and there. I wondered how perceptive a critic Walter Kerr really was if he could think a play starring Ethel Merman as Rose would end with Gypsy Rose Lee stripping.

In those days, the major critics came on opening night; the parties were in Sardi's where everyone waited nervously for the reviews. Merrick came over to my table and handed me Kerr's review:

"This is for you," he said.

It was a rave, with the famous quote: "The best damn musical I've seen in years." It went on: "To get to the astonishing news first, the book is a clean knockout."

I took that to mean Walter Kerr thought it was astonishing that Arthur Laurents could write anything that good. Paranoia? Total, but at least I recognized that it was. That was how I came to terms with myself about critics.

If reviews are to be read, they are best read for their effect on the box office which is largely in the hands of *The New York Times* whoever the critic. The *Times* denies this, points to exceptions which there are, but methinks the Old Gray Lady doth protest too much: the *Times* loves the power it knows it has.

The hurt inflicted by bad reviews lingers long after the show is gone but what is even more upsetting is not what the critics don't like, it's what they do like. No work is without flaw, so dislike, however arguable, is at least understandable—even if it's your work and thus hurts. But praise for the second-rate, for the pretentious, for the style of the month, that praise bewilders, infuriates, maddens; worst of all, it disheartens. It is that praise rather than the pans that has driven writers out of the theatre.

Jimmy Gelb's moon, which didn't come out opening night to guarantee critical success for *Home of the Brave* in 1946, came out opening night of *West Side Story* in 1957 and again on *Gypsy's* in 1959. Forty-odd years later, they're both considered classics, so it must still be out. And a sliver, a crescent has even come out for *Home of the Brave*.

The sky was empty, however, when the Tonys were awarded. *West Side Story* didn't win the Tony for best musical, best score, or best book. *The Music Man* won all that year. *Gypsy* didn't win for best musical, best book, best score,

With Tom on the spiral staircase on the beach house in Quogue in 1955. The curved brass rail had finally arrived just before he did; now the house was complete.

either; even Ethel Merman didn't win. *The Sound of Music* and Mary Martin cleaned up. All the losing was salutary; it gave me perspective early on. The Tony has little if any value aesthetically. Winners, more often than not, are winners faute de mieux; that's how *Hallelujah, Baby!* won. The real value of a Tony, and very real it is, comes at the box office, not merely in New York or around this country. The business generated by the phrase "Tony Winner" in Tokyo, Sydney, Buenos Aires, Bucharest, London and soon, no doubt, Beijing keeps the American theatre alive and well at home and abroad. It helps keep a playwright's plays produced and seen.

No award or prize that I know of, not even the Nobel, isn't tainted by some of its winners. It's nice to win, nicer than to lose, but it isn't a very meaningful moon that comes out for the success of one play or another unless success is the barometer of your life. When it does have meaning, it arrives unexpectedly; you're unaware it is shining on you because it has come out for a small moment, so small you don't recognize it as an event that will change the path of your life. It was that moon that came out the day I met Tom Hatcher.

When Tom arrived in New York to live with me, Bill Inge said, "How does Arthur get them?" He rented a house down the beach from us in Quogue,

Bill Inge didn't like the sand or the sun but rented a house down the beach to be near Tom and me.

hoping, I suppose, there were more where Tom came from but there weren't. Not in Oklahoma for 4-Hness, not in California for good looks, not in any state for anything in the individual combination that was Tom Hatcher. But Bill thought if I could, he could.

He had latched on to me when I came back to New York because he was gay and so was I, he was a playwright and so was I, and he was starting psychoanalysis which he knew I had been through and been helped by. He certainly needed help. His work made him seem a very sensitive man, which he was—to himself. He didn't understand what it was to be a friend and his sex life was limited to hustlers whom he hired to tell him fantasies. Once he accepted that Tom was a person as well as a face and a body, he decided our love affair was mature; he would have a counterpart.

At this point, William Inge was an extremely successful playwright with a string of hits like *Picnic* and *Bus Stop* and shelves of prizes. He designated as his lover my boyhood friend, Richard "Have an Egg Roll" Goldstone, now an assistant professor of drama at NYU. They knew and liked one another but neither had the slightest sexual interest in the other. Which Goldstone knew but which didn't occur to Inge. He didn't propose to Dick, he didn't ask, he didn't even suggest they be lovers; he told him they were going to be lovers. The professor, who loved to flatter and cock-tease famous writers—he was very much the coquette with Thornton Wilder—didn't have too much trouble wriggling out of the arms of the playwright and managing to keep his friendship. Bill didn't really want him, either.

A week later, Bill had switched gears but not goals: he dropped by the beach house to announce he was going to marry Barbara Baxley, the actress.

"Does she know?" I asked.

"I bought her a wedding dress," Bill said, and moaned: "This is killing me." He took off his sports shirt and loosened the corset he was wearing underneath as though there was nothing unusual about wearing a corset. Maybe there wasn't in Kansas; I didn't even look away tactfully.

"Has Barbara seen the dress?"

"No."

"Have you asked her to marry you?"

"I guess I should have made sure she liked the dress. I can return it. I bought it on approval."

He had so many sadnesses: the sadness of the alcoholic who doesn't drink but isn't sober, the sadness of the outsider in the wrong city, the sadness of the loner yearning for affection he himself is incapable of giving. And so many phobias: a fear of heights which stuck him with an undesirable apartment on the first floor of an expensive building; a fear of crowds which sat him in the last row for his own plays or put him in standing room when he came to Philly to see *Gypsy;* even a fear that he was always dressed wrong which led him to buy very expensive clothes, though he wore black tie when the other men were in suits and a sports jacket when they were in black tie.

Tom and I were not good for Bill to be around. We made him lonelier; when he was lonely, he got nasty. His hits were his life; when they stopped, when his moon didn't come out twice in succession, he was bewildered and got nastier. Unprepared for failure, he became embittered and let it destroy him.

He fled to California where he had had *Splendor in the Grass* but the movies didn't want him. He had a slip. Television didn't want him: the network rejected a play he wrote, accepting in its place a far better play written by Pucky Violett, an old friend of his and mine, one of the true and very few he hadn't alienated. He slipped, permanently this time, and the booze made him really nasty. He wrote the network a vicious letter, castigating it for its selection of a meretricious, second-rate piece of crap written by one Ellen (Pucky) Violett in preference to his own valuable work. Perhaps because she was in AA, Pucky understood and forgave. Bill didn't. He stopped looking for the moon and asphyxiated himself in his garage.

Life for Bill ended when he went back to California; for me, it began again there because of Tom. Perhaps I made that connection because "How does

Arthur get them?" stuck in my craw. I didn't get Tom, we got each other—sexually, in the beginning. When problems came, they weren't caused by sexuality, however. Tom was too wise for that, wiser than I was.

Twelve years younger with much less sexual experience, he nevertheless was clear on what would and wouldn't work for two men: no attempt at emulating a heterosexual couple, married or not; no role playing; no blinders to prevent facing that men, straight or gay, were not monogamous. But total confidence that what we really wanted was each other: Tom had it, mine was shaky. I was possessive and jealous. If I were to be unfaithful, it wouldn't mean anything but quick sex. If Tom were, the roof would come down; it would mean he was really attracted to someone else. It took time for me to get sane but he was patient and I did.

We experimented; we tried threesomes; we were never really promiscuous and never, then or later, went to the baths or back rooms. In the Fifties, why anyone on the prowl did was a mystery. There was no need. Anonymous sex, if that was what was wanted, was everywhere on the Upper East Side between the Forties and the Seventies. Cruising on Third Avenue and Lexington Avenue was available day as well as night. And there were the bars. We rarely went; if we did, it was usually for the music.

There was also a thriving gay social life: cocktail parties and dinner parties with attractive, personable young men, few in the theatre. Most were available, which might have seemed a threat to lovers but wasn't. The gay ghetto wasn't what caused trouble for us. That overflowed with camaraderie; it was good times and good friends who liked and looked to us as a couple. In the Fifties, trouble came when we stepped outside the ghetto. Even now in the Nineties, much of the straight world is still not hospitable to gay lovers.

Not too long ago, Larry Kramer paid me what he meant as a great compliment: I had lived openly with another man at a time when nobody in my locus did. If living openly meant defiantly or to make a statement, I didn't live openly. I lived as I had since I grew up with Judd Marmor: the way that was right for me. I didn't flaunt it, I was neither proud nor not proud, although I can't say I was entirely without excess sensitivity. In Sardi's one night, Arthur Penn's wife stopped me as I passed their table to tell me how much she admired my courage.

"For what?"

"Living openly the way you want."

"Don't patronize me," I said, the Jewish chip on my shoulder having been replaced by the gay chip.

Living with Tom was living the way I knew I had to live. Just as he knew, when he realized he was gay, that he had to get out of Oklahoma if he wanted to live happily. Tom wasn't mentioned in Larry's compliment. Unintentionally, he did what the straight world did—he ignored Tom. That was what made trouble for us. In the gay world, our sexuality wasn't trouble; in the straight world, it was.

It was assumed that being gay didn't matter in the theatre. That may have been true when there were chorus boys in musicals, but they were pansy, not gay. In 1961 when I directed my play *Invitation to a March,* gay was best hidden. Shelley Winters, the star, complained to Lawrence Langner, who produced the play for the Theatre Guild, that her leading man was gay. This was the same Shelley who messengered little boys to Farley when he and I were living together but she wasn't good in the play and she knew it. Langner was marvelously of his day and not.

"Miss Winters," he said, "Mr. Laurents wanted you for this play, I did not. I said he could have you on one condition: that I never have to talk to you. Good day."

He tipped his hat and never spoke to her again.

Tom and I had neither intention nor desire to live exclusively in the gay world; we also lived in the theatre world where we both worked and had friends. However, who I was and who he wasn't didn't make it easy for him; it was comparable to being the husband of a star or the wife of a producer: Would you mind getting me a drink? Worse than comparable because when the gay returned with the drink, the person who asked for it was often gone. An echo of Kate Hepburn's "I can never remember those little boys' names." Merely being supporting cast was bad; being gay was worse; being the gay lover was insupportable.

In straight rooms, an effeminate gay man was acceptable. A masculine gay, especially an attractive one, was a danger: women were hopeful and sexually insecure men—their number increasing daily thanks to all the libs—were either threatened or attracted. But two attractive, masculine gay men who were lovers were undesirable and unwanted. The room looked at them, imagined them undressed, visualized what they did in bed and got nervous: Get him out! Him, not them; him being the lesser known, being Tom. Whom they paid no attention to and ignored anyway—even good friends of mine.

Gypsy and *West Side Story* following so quickly upon each other made me too well known for my taste. Unwanted celebrity was epitomized at one extreme by a telegram from Sonja Henie inviting me to a black-tie dinner, at the other, by a map of the United States on the cover of the Sunday *Times Magazine* with my face and forty-nine other faces captioned the In People of the country.

There was the comfort of knowing I would be Out by the following Sunday. Celebrity is a trap I have worked to avoid. It has undoubted advantages: a name can help get a play on and, God knows, that's hard and gets harder every year. But watching what it does to those who court it, I feel lucky to have never wanted it.

Unfortunately for Tom and me, he was an unsuccessful actor at the time I became a half-assed celebrity. People behaved badly to him, even gays. For a time, out of guilt perhaps, I was impatient, accusing him of exaggerating, of being hypersensitive, even of asking for it. But how often did I have to be invited without him by friends I had thought were good friends? I got testy with them, they got testy with me, I got testy with me, then I got testy with Tom—vicious circles getting more vicious and more destructive. What I should have done, of course, was to drop out of those circles, but I didn't until later. Too much later: Tom and I had parted.

We had been together seven years. What is it about seven years? Why do so many separate after seven years? Why seven? Is there some ancient, mystic, Oriental explanation waiting to be deciphered? But seven years it was when, without discussion, he went back to California to seek work and I went off to Switzerland to ski.

Skiing was no fun without him. I was lonely except for two days when Anita Ellis and her husband Mort Shapiro arrived in his new Porsche. My hotel seemed grander to Mort so he moved out of theirs and into mine, disregarding a Swiss law that says a reserved room must be paid in full for three days. Mort, a prominent neurosurgeon who went on expensive safari in Africa every year—"At least he hasn't killed any people yet," Anita would say—went to court rather than pay his bill. The trial was largely in German. Mort described the room he had reserved as disgustingly shmutzic. Misunderstanding the judge's response, he heaped it on, adding *Wantzen*—cockroaches—to the shmutz. The judge ceased to be Swiss. He went into a frenzy. There had never been *ein Wantze* in the entire history of the Engadine Valley! Anita choked back giggles but as Mort blustered and backtracked, she laughed so much she literally cried. Infuriated by her on top of being humiliated by the judge, Mort paid his fine, threw her in the Porsche and drove off to St. Anton in Austria, leaving me lonely in Switzerland again.

An affair is a not unusual antidote to loneliness. In London, I embarked on one with David Bennett, a young gentleman farmer with an upper-class accent even though he was from Norfolk. He had very good manners and knew wines but even though he glowed with typical English coloring, Nora Kaye, the First Anglophile of the Western World, didn't like him. She didn't like him because unlike every other Englishman she doted on, straight or gay, David wasn't a camp. She much preferred another friend I introduced her to, Nicky Haslam: Nicky was a camp. He was even more English-looking, had an even mushier upper-class accent and knew everybody, including most of the royals in the Palace and the Ballet.

"Why don't you fuck Nicky?" asked Nora.

She was in London because Herb, switching media under her management, was working on a Cliff Richards movie. They were living in a small mews house off the Brompton Road, close to Harrods. Harrods interested her more than the movie: it was convenient for shopping. She even shopped there for another Yorkie. I almost persuaded her to buy a bat, which Harrods also sold. I knew she wanted me to oust David—was that why she was pushing me to fuck Nicky?

"It's so he'll take us in his car to see the Palladian houses," she said.

The car was a 1929 De Lage, an elegant convertible with wide, sweeping running boards, the sister car, Nicky claimed, to the De Lage Clark Gable gave Carole Lombard.

"He'll take us anyway," I said, "and be delighted to."

He did and was the most splendid of guides, pointing out Christopher Wren doorways en route to the Palladian houses. Nora and her yapping Yorkie were in English antique heaven over the furniture and china in a Palladian house. I stretched out on the English grass speculating on the common denominator in Johnny Goodwin's asking me in Madrid to fuck someone who had a car to take us to see Toledo and Nora's asking me in London to fuck Nicky Haslam who had a car to take us to see Palladian houses. Resentment, that was the common factor. Johnny's was personal, restricted to me; Nora's was general, the resentment buried in women attracted to gay men until a sexual affair flushes it out of hiding.

Nora and I gave Herb a birthday party with cold roast beef, also from Harrods, that had so much gristle our only recourse was to get the guests drunk before they got through the doorway. Which we did with enthusiasm and success, except for Michael Redgrave who was drunk before he got to the doorway. We went to the theatre which I could never see enough of in London. Nicky Haslam with his Sloane Ranger Girls was fun and a guide to more than Palladian houses. The affair with David was nice enough but he wasn't Tom, Nora wasn't Tom, nobody was Tom and nothing with anybody kept me from missing Tom. Letting him go had been a bad mistake; I had to do what came anything but naturally to me: put pride in cold storage and go to California to get him back.

Nora and her Yorkies with Nicky Haslam. It was love at first sight. He drove her (and me) in his 1929 De Lage convertible on a tour of the Palladian houses around London. They gossiped nonstop while the dogs yapped.

He looked wonderful, he was from Oklahoma again, he had *independent* written large all over him. His friends were a group of attractive, genial young men his age with no theatrical aspirations, except for one assisted blond who worked successfully as a contractor. I suspected he and Tom had had or might still be having an affair but I never asked—progress!

The group went regularly to Capistrano to surf and I went with them. Tom and I shared a room with his younger brother, David, an architect who was very Oklahoma. We made sure he didn't know we had been (were?) lovers or even that we were gay. He knew anyway; what we didn't know was that he was, too. Now we are a small, not nuclear but very happy family in Quogue.

My first try at surfing, I stood up and rode the board all the way in to the beach as though I had been born in Hawaii. I never did it again but I didn't care; I hadn't been so happy for a long time. Nothing much was said; nothing much needed to be said once Tom realized that I had come to California for one reason: because I loved him. He was cautious but he wasn't game-playing; he never did. I think he wanted me to be sure and not romanticize.

It wasn't all violins when he came back to New York, everything didn't always come up roses. There were dicey times when we seemed in need of quick repairs but it, meaning "we," continued to work because we had become incomplete without each other.

Tom and my business manager didn't get on. The business manager was a smothering, motherly, poodle-carrying queen, good at handling the finances of theatre folk who didn't get the large checks I was now getting from *West Side Story* and *Gypsy*. Despite the checks' size, at year's end I had very little money.

"You don't have enough deductions," he said.

"Such as?"

"Well, you could pay me more."

Very creative. I decided to buy a house as a test. If I found at the end of the year that I had enough money to pay for it, I would fire the business manager. I found a house where I had dreamed of living when I got out of college: in Greenwich Village. The street was St. Luke's Place, one of the prettiest in the city. It was lined with ginkgo trees planted by the owners of the Italianate 1852 brownstones that faced a playground with a bocci court; in the rear were double gardens. The house went up for sale on Wednesday; I had to commit by Friday or lose it. I committed, bought it, and fired the business-manager-with-poodle.

One tenant—the mistress of the late Jimmy Walker—had to be paid to leave, but it cost less to get her out than to hoist out a huge safe on the second floor: the house had belonged to lower-echelon Mafia. At the closing, one of the echelon, with his lawyer pinned to the wall in a choke hold, paused to say to me:

"I can play anything from a peasant to a king."

The four-story house had been turned into floor-through apartments; we wanted to restore it to what it had been: gingerbread moldings, etched-glass sliding doors, stained-glass skylight, the works. The contractor we hired was hired because his bid was the lowest, he was gay, and we knew him. Not well enough: when the money ran out, so did he. Never very patient and easily exasperated, I immediately wanted to dump the house. Tom told me to calm down in Quogue while he took over. Because he couldn't be as good an actor as he wanted to be, he had been looking for a new career. He didn't know it but he had found one: contractor.

With Bill Scott, a black his age who had been renovating an apartment on Jane Street for Herb and Nora, he formed a small company that did well in the city. But it was Quogue Tom had his eye on, Quogue real estate.

Land values are always crazy, but in the early Sixties they were crazily low: six acres with a fifty-room house and barn were for sale for $38,500—in the best

Back in Hollywood in 1962, not to write a movie but to rectify
a bad mistake. As this picture shows, my life was restored.

part of the village, the part Clinton Wilder called "the golden crescent." The
house was furnished, the barn was really a stable where John O'Hara had done
a lot of writing during the Thirties. Tom bought the whole parcel. He split the
big house in half where the ballroom had been and moved the servants' half
onto its own two-acre lot, put in a gunite swimming pool and converted an
old laundry house into a pool house. A swimming pool for the barn/stable,
another for the still big main house which had enough furniture for all three
houses, each on its own two-acre now landscaped lot and all three for rent.
Rental included pool service, a gardener and a caretaker—all one and the same
kid. Then, wouldn't you know, came the real estate boom. Rents went up,
property values went up: we were in deep, golden clover.

I never had champagne tastes. Living too high on the hog to the delight of a watching and waiting IRS was not for me, not with my father. My mother gambled on the stock market, not he. I wasn't good with money, Tom was and took charge. We both knew what lifestyle we wanted, we knew what was enough for us. Enough is living well, not for revenge but for comfort. Enough is never having to worry about money. Tom put me in that position.

"In real estate" was his new life, but it didn't prevent him from being politically active in the gay movement. I wasn't: the Witch Hunt had affected me more than I realized; I had become cautious, too wary. I didn't like myself for being chicken. Tom took me to a meeting of GAA, the Gay Activists Alliance, at the old Firehouse on Wooster Street in what is now ohso fashionable SoHo. The minute I walked into the room, I was home again with the lefties. Parliamentary rules reigned: the women shouting "Point of order!" louder than the men; the men butch with left-wing beards; all sexes trendily scruffy in blue jeans except Marcia, a transvestite in a slim tunic and heavy climbing boots who outshouted the whole room without a microphone:

"What about equal rights for us fucking transvestites? Freedom for everybody but drag queens, you cunt holes! We fucking embarrass you!" And so forth, most of it true. The gay movement has never known what to do about screaming drag queens; it still doesn't. With gay hate high on the country's agenda and rising, how could it? But it was screaming drag queens who were responsible for Stonewall and the beginning of gay liberation.

We had serious arguments about the meaning of liberation with Tom's gay partners in another real estate venture: a restaurant-cabaret on West Broadway they called the Ballroom. All the partners were GAA members but except for Tom, they all believed gay lib meant the freedom to have sex in trucks under the West Side Highway as well as in the baths and back rooms. Even during the War, as promiscuous as I had been, I wouldn't have done that. That promiscuity, I argued, was justified by my age and that it had taken place in wartime. The behavior itself was nevertheless juvenile, adolescent, and compulsive whether upheld as liberated in the Sixties or as advanced in the Nineties. Today's advocates seem to find possible suicide in the back rooms— and it is suicide until an AIDS vaccine is discovered—as exciting as anonymity and numbers.

The Seventies were the Age of No Anxiety, thanks to drugs. Tom's abusive substance of choice was alcohol; he dipped into drugs. Not me: I dunked, I wallowed, I used everything but heroin, had my favorites but loved them all for dancing and sex, especially sex. And deceived myself. When I'd had enough of whatever I was on, I would simply stop, say good night, and go to bed. Like an idiot, I assumed that was what everyone did. Then a friend OD'd on the kitchen floor in Quogue—and surprise! Everyone didn't have the governor I did. The tracks between the toes of my friend on the floor showed me how observant I wasn't.

Still, I kept on drugging while Tom kept on drinking. He saw and didn't like what I was doing but I didn't even see what he was doing. I would have kept on trucking down the road to destruction if Tom hadn't been concerned about his brother's drinking. He went to an alcoholism counselor for help. The counselor helped: Tom wound up in AA himself. It was the best thing that could have happened to both of us.

In my play *2 Lives,* the playwright's lover is in AA, but so are thousands of other lovers and the one in the play doesn't have a brother. Tom stopped drinking in February of 1982. It took David another year, but living with Tom cut my drinking in half, then in half of that half. I also became aware so many people I knew were alcoholics and didn't know it. Until I told them; I was always one for sharing knowledge.

At a dinner party, I was seated at a small table with Gloria Jones, Jim Jones's widow, and Steve and Jean Kennedy Smith. I began with Gloria because she was an unrepentant homophobe: always affable, she invariably told me how wonderfully I wrote women. Wasted point: it's men that homosexual men can have trouble writing.

"Why do you say I'm an alcoholic?" she asked.

"Because I've never seen you sober. You're drunk right now."

"So are we, sweetie," Steve said to Jean. He was one of the funniest, most engaging men I've ever met, blessed with the quality of making you feel he'd been marking time until you turned up. "Double addicted," he laughed, taking out a cigarette for each of them.

I had smoked two packs a day since I started as a teenager but in February of 1983, exactly a year after Tom quit drinking, I tried to quit smoking which paragon he had done shortly after he quit drinking. We were skiing in Killington, I was hacking away from bronchitis, I cried uncle: I would give up cigarettes for a week.

"Why not altogether?" Tom asked.

"Because I can't and I love it." I'd tried everything: Smokenders, hypnosis, acupuncture, a staple stapled in my earlobe by a brisk, brusque Chinese lady. She instructed me to rub the staple when the desire to smoke hit. I did, it hurt, I smoked.

"Try the AA steps," Tom suggested.

The first step was to admit I had a problem I couldn't handle. God knows that was true, but then what? Turn the problem over. Sarcastically: to God, I suppose. No, to your Higher Power. Continuing the sarcasm: which is God. Well, God as you see it. What I saw was bullshit.

Even in high school, I was a confirmed, untroubled atheist. The idea of admitting there was something I couldn't control had visceral appeal; actual admission brought relief and empathy for junkies. I stopped smoking for the week. There were outside inducements: pleasing Tom, skiing, fear that one drag on a cigarette would result in a fit of coughing. But amazingly, I didn't reach for a cigarette with my end-of-the-day martini. A Higher Power helping? None that I knew.

Two weeks later I went into rehearsal directing *La Cage Aux Folles*. Most of the company puffed like portable chimneys; I didn't smoke. The producers were too many and too nervous: *La Cage,* about a drag queen who wanted to be accepted as a mother, was a multimillion-dollar Broadway musical, not a gay little Off-Broadway adventure. Furthermore, AIDS had arrived under the acronym of GRID (gay-related immune disorder). Still I didn't smoke. One of the two stars would have been fired but a replacement couldn't be found; somehow, I had to get a performance out of him. Still I didn't smoke. In Boston, the first preview had to be canceled because the scenery didn't work; we had very little advance and money was tight. Still I didn't smoke. Most of the company, onstage and off, was coked to the gills half the time and the news was leaking out. I didn't snort, I didn't smoke, and there was no temptation to do either. I had stopped smoking without thinking about it. Snorting? Well, opening night.

I had agreed to direct *La Cage Aux Folles* because Fritz Holt asked me to but I never thought it would get off the ground. It did; it was a smash from the first preview, the biggest hit I'd ever been associated with. Not the best, the gayest; and the biggest in the number of years it ran, the number of companies it spawned, the numbers on the royalty checks that kept coming.

The original *West Side Story* company had a fierce love for the show. The original *La Cage* company had a more personal, deeper love for the show; every *La Cage* company all over the world had that same love. They said it emanated from me. The influence of my Higher Power? Jesus imbuing his flocks? I thought not. In *2 Lives,* the playwright is in touch with his spirituality. In life, this playwright was too rational for spirituality a.k.a. Higher Power until Tom created his park in Quogue.

He had bought twelve acres for comparatively little because they were north of the highway. In Quogue, north meant black which tacitly meant undesirable even though the oldest family in Quogue, the Arches, dated from the seventeenth century and were freed slaves. Most of the blacks in Quogue were middle-class and resident as long as if not longer than their neighbors south of the highway. North or south, as real estate became the place to park money or show you had it, land values went up and locals who were land poor and getting on began to sell. North of the highway blended into south of the highway and Tom's acreage became really valuable because of what he had done with it.

Four houses—three brand-new, one a renovation, all with pools and gardens, one with a tennis court—formed a compound. The architect, who lived in another house south of the highway renovated for Tom's parents who were living in Quogue as were mine, was his brother David—also in AA but still smoking. The compound was bounded by private roads—Laurents Way on the north, Hatcher Road on the south—and in the center was a great jungle of pine trees, scrub oak and cedars throttled by bittersweet and bramble. What is the source of an idea for a play? What was the source of Tom's vision of a park that could be created out of a jungle?

He bulldozed, landscaped and planted, not in one go but each year adding and shifting, rather like editing and rewriting: fruit trees, Japanese maples, sycamores; weeping blue spruce and weeping dogwood ringed by daylilies and burning azaleas; rose of Sharon, crepe myrtle, forsythia; hydrangeas and beds of Dutch iris and rhododendrons—slowly, the park appeared. He created allées and placed wooden benches from which we could look down the allées and across the changing vistas. He created a private park for us, a haven whose existence was (and still is) almost unknown in the village. The configuration of the land and the density of the surrounding trees kept it completely hidden.

Sitting on one of those benches, we could sometimes see deer loping through the park on their way into the woods at the edge. Late one afternoon, I mistook them in the sun for girls riding on bicycles. Occasionally, a tenant brought his dog to run in the park, but usually there was no one, just the view. Accompanied by an indefinable feeling that something was waiting. Then one day, as I sat on one of those benches just taking in the view, the feeling became definable, recognizable: I had experienced it once before—in Burma, in the spring of 1990, just before the military coup.

Burma was Tom's idea, I didn't want to go at all. Since we were going to Thailand and China, why not complete the golden triangle and see Burma? Because I had read up on Burma, that was why. Unless you were with a tour group, reservations were worthless; travel, meals, lodging, nothing could be guaranteed except that the hotels were paradigms of discomfort and the food was uniformly revolting. I had never traveled as a part of a group and I was too old to start. Moreover I wanted my hot bath and my vodka before dinner (I had given up martinis years before and couldn't even remember gin).

Our travel agent ended any argument: we couldn't get into Burma. Only five hundred foreigners were allowed in for one week at any one time and the quota was filled for the period we (i.e., Tom) wanted to go.

In Hong Kong en route to China, Tom came back to the hotel with a very pretty girl he had met at an AA meeting. Whatever part of the world we traveled, upon arrival in a new city while I unpacked, he went to an AA meeting and met all the ex-swingers with the information that was never in guidebooks. Many of the alkies he brought back to the hotel were remarkably pretty young women. Far from being disappointed that we were gay, they were delighted. It was usually men who had driven them to drink; they didn't want a man, they wanted to get sober.

The Hong Kong beauty was a travel agent who thought there might be a cancellation in a group going to Burma at the right time. If so, she'd fax us in Beijing. She faxed us in Beijing. I was less than thrilled.

At the Rangoon airport, they wouldn't let us in the country. The plane that flew us in couldn't leave because its return trip was overbooked. Four passengers were needed to stay in Burma and wait for the next plane out. Otherwise, no one could leave the country and we couldn't enter. It made no sense. Even to the Burmese officials. They laughed endearingly. Nobody got angry. Burma was crazy.

We waited in an oversized, overcrowded, un-air-conditioned Quonset hut, sweat trickling slowly down our backs while the loudspeaker called for volunteers. The next plane out was on Monday, this was Saturday. Traveling foreigners lived on a schedule; no volunteers. The loudspeaker offered a free hotel; then a free hotel and free meals; then a free hotel, free meals, and a chauffeured car to Pagan (accent on the second syllable). Eight volunteers! The officials beamed: This way please!

I sat smiling the whole time, not bothered by the heat, mildly interested, mildly curious about Pagan. Tom marveled at my uncharacteristic calm: What had happened to me? What had happened to me? Burma, that's what.

In the lobby of the best hotel in Rangoon—lizards on the bedroom walls and racks of congealed fried eggs for breakfast—a wedding party was being photographed with a camcorder while "Jingle Bells" came over a loudspeaker. The groom and his ushers were small and pretty in cutaways; the bridesmaids were small, not as pretty, in Day-Glo ruffles. The bride looked like a wedding cake figurine in tiers of rhinestoned white tulle. Like her bridesmaids, she had five o'clock shadow. If the hotel staff had any interest, it was in the camcorder.

That evening, we asked the taxi driver who exchanged our money (he said we were crazy to pay the official rate and proved it) how common such weddings were.

"They must have been rich Chinese," he said.

Barter was the way of Burma life. The guidebooks said to bring T-shirts, ballpoint pens, and American cigarettes. They also said the night markets of Rangoon were a must. The night markets sold T-shirts, ballpoint pens, and American cigarettes. So did the day markets.

The commercial airline flying us to Mandalay had three planes: one was being repaired and one had just crashed but the company was very pleased—one was still up and flying.

The windows of the rooms in the best hotel in Mandalay—no flying fishes—opened on the only corridor. Water buffalo pulled logs and barges along the river. A movie set in any year of the century could be shot with one or two minor adjustments: move the Model A tin lizzie parked in front of a great Buddha; remove the neon rainbow garlanding that Buddha.

Only men can approach Buddha; women have to stand back. One sixty-foot Buddha frowned at the men at his feet and smiled at the women several feet behind them. Nonspiritual explanation: Cut into the walls surrounding the great statue were apertures through which bars of sunlight struck his face. But both smile and frown were wondrous to behold.

All the Buddhas had a mesmerizing aura except a huge, enormously elongated one lying on his side. He was more an amusement park Buddha, smiling away like the monks—pretty young men in saffron robes, lying on their sides on the grass along the dusty back streets dishing. At mealtime, they picked up their bowls and chose a house to grace by allowing the inhabitants to fill the bowls with food. Then they returned to the grass to gossip and dish.

The Mandalay airport was a meadow. The arrival of a plane was predicted by a very old man in diapers whacking a stick against a rusty iron triangle. The moment it landed, our tour group raced frantically across the meadow to be sure of getting seats. They knew the plane was for us, that we were the only passengers, but Burma's craziness was contagious.

Four to a pirogue, we were rowed across Lake Inle shortly after dawn by a boatman, with a long pole in the crook of his knee. The air was hushed, the water lightly steaming as we passed small, lush, man-made islets that were vegetable gardens. Inle had its own aura, one that made me wish we would never get anywhere.

But we did get somewhere: a large, grassy island of toilets and souvenir shops. Man cannot live on Buddha alone. The aura had taken a break.

Tom and I wandered contentedly away from the group, along grassy paths until we turned a corner and encountered two beautiful little children. Tiny, begging hands outstretched, they sang:

"*Ditez-moi, pourquoi la vie est belle,*" from *South Pacific.*

Then we came to Pagan.

It was once a city of two thousand palaces and pagodas; most were destroyed by wars or the climate. The three hundred that remained were spread at random across a quiet, verdant landscape. Many of those made of brick were crumbling but the still-intact white pagodas of stone had an unearthly beauty.

Young boys hawking uncut rubies and emeralds swarmed around us like flies. They were as ubiquitous in the Burma we were allowed to see as the tourists we tried not to see but we had gotten accustomed to both; neither could impinge on the awesome presence of the pagoda before us. Not even the boy who approached a parody English couple in our group and, holding up a sample of his wares, asked:

"Ruby?"

"No, Trevor," said the husband.

We explored the pagoda on our own. I lost Tom when I turned into a doorway and started up an interior stairway in darkness. It was very quiet, getting eerily quieter. The dark got blacker the higher I climbed. Agatha Christie, not Buddha, was in my head. I climbed faster, gratefully reaching the top and stepping out into sunlight that was bright only in contrast. It was actually late afternoon, the warm sun setting lazily. Standing on the parapet of the pagoda, looking out over a vista of every imaginable green, I saw both a weeping willow and a cactus. A narrow footpath disappeared in the lush grass. Not a road was visible; nothing moved.

The little ring of a bicycle bell drew my eye to a boy riding slowly through the trees toward the horizon where the sun blinked on the Irrawaddy River. Two passing gem sellers came out on the parapet, stopped to size me up, decided I was not a prospect and continued past. When I looked back the boy and his bicycle were vanishing on the horizon. The Irrawaddy shimmered, the air was quiet and still. At that moment, for the first time in my life, I knew the feeling of serenity. Nothing happened. It was like the aura around a Buddha: it was just there, warming me like the sun.

How long I stood on the parapet of the pagoda without moving I didn't know; time didn't matter. There was no reason to move, there was nothing I wanted. I knew Tom would find me, so I was content. It was enough just to look at the view.

A year and a half later, serenity was as far off as Burma. A Christmas present in 1991 was that biggest and most public flop of my career, *Nick & Nora*. The story was original but the title characters were based on the Nick and Nora Charles that Dashiell Hammett had created for *The Thin Man*. Whatever was right or wrong with the show, one crucial flaw could not be remedied: the enormous popularity of the Thin Man movies had ended the existence of Nick and Nora Charles as characters; they had become flesh-and-blood William Powell and Myrna Loy. Without Powell and Loy, you couldn't have *Nick & Nora*. I didn't realize this until we were in previews; the critics never did.

In the rehearsal room with the cast of the 1998 London revival of *West Side Story*, which Jerry Robbins had asked me to re-direct. Every single member was a joy to work with.

The show and I were dead in the water before it opened, killed off during all those weeks of previews by gossip columnists unhindered by *The New York Times*'s three rules of journalism: "Verify, verify, verify." One of the killers was even on the *Times*. As writer-director I was therefore guilty of every crime including the score; the critics lynched me, crucified me, and just to make sure, burned me at the stake. What they largely reviewed was the gossip; the *Times* review began: "It's not as bad you heard." That kind of review doesn't hurt; it might anger but my anger had been spent on my colleagues who had betrayed me (and thus their own show!) with the items they had secretly fed like dead fish to the newsroom sharks. Instead I felt relief that the nightmare was over. Three months later, I was sitting on the bench in Tom's park and there it was again—that feeling of serenity I had felt in Burma.

Obviously the moon did not come out the opening night of *Nick & Nora*. It did make an appearance, however, at what by all the rules should have been the lowest point for me.

Tom had been after me to quit the show long before it even went into rehearsal. At its demise, he was not only relieved I was done with it but, always certain that nothing happened without a reason, he was now certain something good was going to come out of the failure. I didn't jump up and down when he said that; I wasn't manic, I just nodded. But I meant it, and something good did come out of that mess: I went back to writing plays. Each year for four years, I wrote a new play for the sheer joy of writing. And with the acknowledgment that what happened to them afterward was beyond my control. At last, I knew that and accepted it.

This was no sudden epiphany; change came slowly over the years since Killington, when I gave up cigarettes and jeered at the concept of a Higher Power. To anyone who thought he or she knew me, myself included, the notion that I could stop trying to control everything was absurd. The notion that I might be spiritual was farther fetched: I was too tough, too acerbic, too rational, too questioning. But I hadn't been impervious to the beneficent effect of the Higher Power concept on Tom. Actually, a little jealous, rather, so I went to some open AA meetings with him and skepticism began to diminish. What continually balked me was my need for proof; then I was given it with the disaster called *Nick & Nora*. Not only had I not been destroyed, I had been revived. I was back doing what I loved most; I was content in a way I had never been with myself and my life; I was sitting on a bench in Tom's park, just looking at the view.

I wasn't suffering from any delusion that I had undergone some great religious conversion but I was in touch with some part of me that was spiritual, believe it or not and I believed it whether anyone else did or not. That was not beatification, it was fact; a fact I could put on my passport along with "writer" and my date of birth.

Almost invariably, when I sat on that bench in the park and took in the view, there was that feeling of contentment. I didn't want to spend my life in the park any more than I wanted to walk around serene all day every day. Excitement, passion, even anger—I wanted them all and I had them all. The intensity was lessened but that made life easier.

The other day, when I was writing this last section, Jerry Robbins died of a stroke. His death was not unanticipated; he'd been in bad health, one ailment after another for some time. My last contact with him was a message, two months earlier, that he was deeply grateful I had agreed to go to London, because he was too ill, to re-direct an English company of *West Side Story* for its opening in the West End. Ironically, it would undoubtedly be the last Jerome Robbins Production of *West Side Story.*

His death, for me, was the death of a famous choreographer, not a person. I had long since stopped disliking him. Sadly, I simply didn't care about him one way or the other. Monsters erode your feelings until you no longer care. He was a brilliant choreographer, he was better at staging a musical than any-one: the ballet would miss him, the theatre would miss him, I wouldn't.

Yet his death left me with a peculiar feeling: vague anxiety, vague depres-sion. I recognized anxiety but I'm rarely if ever depressed. Why now? What was it? Then it came clear: intimations of mortality. I'm eighty-one but I never had intimations of mortality before. I'm healthy, I'm never sick, I'm more pro-ductive than ever; I'm still sexual, still skiing, still crusading. Why had Jerry's death awakened that fear that accompanies intimations of mortality? Why hadn't that happened with the deaths of others whom I cared deeply about, whom I really mourned: Fritz Holt, Jimmy Kirkwood, Stella Adler, Nick Eden, Gerry Brooks, Jule Styne, Lenny Bernstein—the list was longer but I stopped with Lenny because with Lenny, I discovered the answer. It went back more than half a century.

Why Jerry? Because he was the next to last.

Harold Lang was the first; then Nora; then Lenny; then Oliver; and now Jerry. I had met all of them at the same moment during the war and begun all my lives with them. There are others of my generation for whom I care very much and with whom I have a very long history. But they don't go back that far; I didn't begin with them. I began with Nora and Harold, with Jerry, with

Lenny, with Oliver. They're all dead, all gone; only I am left. I'm the last but very much alive and flourishing. I have begun a new play, of course, and I am still with the man I met that day the moon came out.

From Tom's pool, you can see into the heart of the park. In summer, we swim laps every day. Often, we walk through the park, then sit on that bench, looking at the view. Yesterday, we sat there a little longer than usual, just looking at the changing light, not saying anything. But Tom reads my mind.

"You're going to live twenty more years," he assured me.

Maybe even more. As long as he lives, I will.

Index